S0-COM-543

BRIDGES FOR DEVELOPMENT

Policies and Institutions
for Trade and Integration

Robert Devlin

Antoni Estevadeordal

Editors

Published by the Inter-American Development Bank

Distributed by The Johns Hopkins University Press

Washington, D.C.

2003

© 2003   **Inter-American Development Bank**
1300 New York Avenue, N.W.
Washington, D.C. 20577

Produced by the IDB Public Information and Publications Section.

To order this book, contact:
IDB Bookstore
Tel: 1-877-PUBS IDB/(202) 623-1753
Fax: (202) 623-1709
E-mail: idb-books@iadb.org
www.iadb.org/pub

The views and opinions expressed in this publication are those of the authors and do not necessarily reflect the official position of the Inter-American Development Bank.

Cover: Image © 2003 PhotoDisc, Inc.

Cataloging-in-Publication data provided by the
Inter-American Development Bank
Felipe Herrera Library

Bridges for development : policies and institutions for trade and integration / Robert Devlin, Antoni Estevadeordal, editors.

   p. cm.   Includes bibliographical references.

1. Latin America—Economic integration.   2. Globalization.   3. Latin America—Economic policy   I. Devlin, Robert. II. Estevadeordal, Antoni. III. Inter-American Development Bank.

ISBN: 1931003300   LCCN: 2003107050

382.911 B597—dc21

Contents

Preface

Latin America has been pursuing intense structural reforms since the mid-1980s. The reforms have been a primary instrument for achieving the development goals of stable and higher rates of economic growth, more social equity, and a solid democratic setting. The reforms have covered a broad range of actions of both an economic and political nature. Trade has been one of the central pillars of the structural reform process and a bridge to capturing the dynamic development forces of an increasingly globalized world economy.

Latin American countries have reduced protection in order to open their economies, gain access to a better and wider variety of inputs for production and consumption, and reduce anti-export bias. Trade liberalization has been pursued unilaterally as well as multilaterally in the GATT/WTO. However, it is often overlooked that since the 1990s regional integration and reciprocal elimination of trade barriers among like-minded partners have become a primary tool of liberalization. Moreover, regional integration increasingly has been of the second-generation type, that is, it has penetrated beyond border barriers to include obligations that impinge on domestic policy variables as well as provide stimulus for production of regional public goods in nontrade areas.

The advance on all three fronts has been quite notable. But much more needs to be done. The multilateral negotiations in the Doha Development Round are contingent on the complex dynamics of worldwide consensus. Latin American countries have a greater degree of latitude in determining the direction of unilateral policy and regional initiatives. However, it might be said that the "easy" stages of unilateral trade and regional integration are over; the next steps toward consolidation will require countries to redouble their political will to confront difficult challenges as well as to refine policies, build stronger institutional structures to support them, and work better with civil society.

The Inter-American Development Bank has supported Latin American trade and integration since its founding. The wave of market opening and regionalism in the 1990s has provided new opportunities in these areas. The Integration and Regional Programs Department of the Bank is the focal point for providing this support through both financial and nonfinancial products. This volume, edited by Robert Devlin (Deputy Manager, Integration and Regional Programs Department) and Antoni Estevadeordal (Principal Trade Economist, Integration, Trade, and Hemispheric Issues Division), is an example of the latter and is dedicated to exploring options to strengthen policies and institutions for deepening structural reforms through trade and integration. The approach is multidisciplinary in order to capture the fuller range of issues that typically confront government officials as they make policy and build institutions. I trust that this volume will be a helpful contribution to both policymakers and academics who believe that more trade and deeper regional integration are indeed bridges to development.

Nohra Rey de Marulanda, Manager
Integration and Regional Programs Department

Contributors

Alícia Adserà, University of Illinois at Chicago
Carles Boix, University of Chicago
Marise Cremona, University of London
Robert Devlin, Inter-American Development Bank
Antoni Estevadeordal, Inter-American Development Bank
Simon J. Evenett, World Trade Institute
Jacint Jordana, Universitat Pompeu Fabra
Sam Laird, United Nations Conference for Trade and Development
Walter Mattli, Columbia University
Patrick A. Messerlin, Institut de Sciences Politiques de Paris
Rajneesh Narula, University of Copenhagen
Carles Ramió, Universitat Pompeu Fabra
Alan M. Taylor, University of California at Davis
Ramon Torrent, University of Barcelona
Anthony J. Venables, London School of Economics

Acknowledgments

This volume contains edited versions of papers presented at a conference organized by the Inter-American Development Bank, which was held at the Brookings Institution in Washington, D.C. on May 31 and June 1, 2001. We are indebted to the discussants for their detailed comments on all the papers. In particular, we would like to thank Roberto Bouzas (Facultad Latinoamericana de Ciencias Sociales, Argentina), Susan Collins (International Monetary Fund, Brookings Institution, and Georgetown University), I.M. Destler (Institute for International Economics and University of Maryland), Gary Horlick (O'Melveny & Myers), Gary Hufbauer (Institute for International Economics), William Kovacic (George Washington Law School), Pravin Krishna (Brown University), Mauricio Mesquita Moreira (Inter-American Development Bank), Ted Moran (Georgetown University), and Jay Smith (George Washington University). Special thanks go to Simon Evenett, who helped to organize the conference, and Carolyn Robert, who contributed to the project in its early stages. Maria de la Paz Covarrubias and Martha Skinner provided superb administrative assistance. The financial support of the European Union Trust Fund and the Swiss Trust Fund at the Inter-American Development Bank is gratefully acknowledged.

PART I
INTRODUCTION

Chapter 1

Regional Integration, Trade and Development Strategies

Robert Devlin and Antoni Estevadeordal

Latin America and the Caribbean experienced a dramatic change in development paradigm, moving from import substitution industrialization (ISI) strategies during the 1960s and 1970s to market-based economic reforms starting in the late 1980s. In both episodes, trade policy and regional integration strategies played a central role. The goal of this volume is to explore from an interdisciplinary perspective how trade and integration policies can be effective tools for promoting a long-term development agenda in the region.

The chapters in this book examine the importance of complementarities among different economic policies, the political economy constraints under which policymakers must design trade and integration policies, the instruments that are necessary to engineer specific policy outcomes, the complexities of designing the right institutional frameworks in which policy can be effectively formulated and implemented, and the creation of a credible and transparent environment for effective public-private partnerships in promoting trade and investment. Given the broad scope and depth of the coverage of the chapters, it is useful to draw out in this introductory chapter some of the messages that we feel are most relevant for Latin America. We begin with a summary of the context that motivates the volume.

MOTIVATION

The development policy framework inherited from the Great Depression reflected pessimism about private markets. The possibility of generating growth based on international trade in the region's international comparative advantage (commodity exports) also was viewed with skepticism. This was because of an unstable (or declining) trend in the terms of trade and international protectionism, particularly in some natural resource-based products of importance to the region. The policy response to the perceived limited growth opportunities of international trade was ISI.

The goal of ISI was to drive the substitution of imports of manufactured goods by local production through the means of high external tariffs and nontariff barriers. There was extensive state economic planning and public intervention in markets. Foreign direct investment (FDI) was of the resource seeking or tariff jumping kind and often had a contentious relationship with a region suspicious of rent seeking and dependency. ISI was relatively successful from the standpoint of growth. However, the process began to lose momentum in the 1950s because the relatively small size of domestic markets limited the scope for economies of scale and efficiencies, especially in capital goods. Ambitious intra-Latin American (South-South) regional integration initiatives emerged in the 1960s as the panacea for this problem.

Regionalism was meant to create a large protected regional market that could provide the economies of scale that were unavailable to national markets. The three major initiatives of the early postwar period involved construction of a free trade area (FTA) among South American countries and Mexico and two common market projects—one in Central America and the other in the Andean Group (which broke out of the aforementioned FTA). However, for many reasons, the regional initiatives designed to rescue ISI had only short-lived success and came to an end with the protracted debt crisis of the 1980s (Devlin and Estevadeordal 2001).

The debt crisis induced a shift in the region's development paradigm to the structural reform process, which centered on promotion of economic openness through trade liberalization.[1] For example, the pursuit of unilateral opening in the region caused external tariffs to decline from an average of more than 40 percent in 1985 to about 12 percent in 1995. The opening was reinforced by active participation in the multilateral Uruguay Round. Partly due to this opening to the world, in the 1990s Latin American trade grew faster than world trade and gross domestic product (figures 1–1 and 1–2). Nevertheless, the region remained one of the more closed in the world and trade growth is less impressive when Mexico is excluded from the picture.

Along with unilateral and multilateral opening, a third tier of trade liberalization emerged in the form of a revival of regional integration. International trade policy and regional integration were complements as opposed to substitutes. In effect, regional preferential and reciprocal opening in the 1990s was a political economy instrument designed to ease the way to and lock in lower average levels of external protection, increased competition in domestic markets, and institutional modernization.

This new wave of regional integration has had a dynamic strategic goal: preparation for globalization through the special incentives that a regional preferential market could potentially offer for economic transformation and improved international competitiveness. The incentives arise from the creation of secure market access for exports—both manufactures with higher value added and knowledge content as well as traditional exports stymied by international protectionism. Moreover, a larger regional market and economies of scale are expected to induce rationalization of industries and new investment, particularly through the attraction of FDI with its technology, best practices, and international export networks.

Although they are meant to complement international opening, the goals of regional integration agreements (RIAs) often go beyond trade and investment as such. Indeed, in their more ambitious incarnations, RIAs are more appropriately interpreted as a political project where the commercial goals of regionalism are instruments for achieving a larger package of objectives. This includes cooperation that will advance geopolitical interests (such as enhanced international political and economic bargaining power, neighborhood security, peace, and democracy) and the production of regional public goods to address diverse socioeconomic externalities arising among liberalizing neighbors.

The intimate link between RIAs and support for structural reform has caused some to coin the current episode the *new regionalism* in order to distinguish it and its effects from the earlier inward-looking processes (Ethier 1998; Devlin and Estevadeordal 2001). Moreover, the new regionalism has been prolific in the number of agreements signed throughout the

---

[1] For a complete analysis of the overall reforms, see IDB (1996).

Figure 1-1

Growth in Trade by Country Group, 1990–99
(Percent)

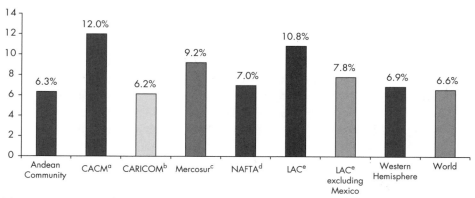

a Central American Common Market.
b Caribbean Community.
c Argentina, Brazil, Paraguay, and Uruguay.
d North American Free Trade Agreement.
e Latin America and the Caribbean.
Note: Values are average annual growth rates based on extraregional trade calculated in U.S. dollars.
Source: IDB data.

Figure 1-2

Openness Coefficient by Region, 1980, 1990, and 1999
(Percent)

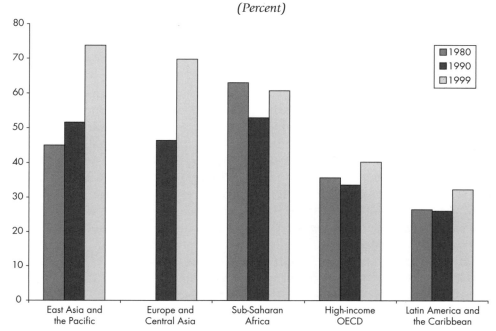

Note: The openness coefficient is trade as a percentage of gross domestic product.
Source: World Bank (2001).

region, about 30 since 1990 (table 1–1). It also has been diverse in its objectives: from simple traditional FTAs in goods to second-generation FTAs that go beyond goods to incorporate services, investment, and intellectual property, to customs unions and common market projects.

Another new dimension of regionalism has been the growing interest in North-South integration. Initially, the new regionalism emerged with common market projects in the traditional subregions of Central America, the Andean area, the Southern Cone, and the Caribbean. However, Mexico's incorporation into the North American Free Trade Agreement (NAFTA) in 1994 set off a growing wave of North-South FTAs that have paralleled intra-Latin American initiatives (South-South). These linkups include bilateral second-generation agreements with Canada, the United States, and the European Union, as well as regional initiatives, such as the Free Trade Area of the Americas (FTAA). [2] In addition to practicing the new regionalism, countries are pursuing multilateral opening in the new Doha Development Round. And unilateral trade policy, while not as active as it was in the late 1980s, continues to undergo adjustments in the face of the reform process and intense international competition.

This complex constellation of regional integration and trade initiatives places great burdens on policy design and institutions. Policy issues go beyond tariffs to a wide array of new trade issues, which impinge more on domestic policy and demand more institutional reforms. Within this context, governments must choose whether to liberalize, what to liberalize, how to liberalize (the instruments), and with whom. Consensus must be developed within governments, between them and their constituencies, and also among governments when collective initiatives are pursued. Moreover, national trade institutions meet a challenge in administering the processes at home, while regional institutions must be created when countries become part of collective initiatives.

This volume explores issues related to policy, instruments, institutions, and public-private sector interaction for international trade and regional integration as well as some of the politics that underpin decisionmaking in these areas. Countries must get the mix of these components right and sequence them effectively in the three main planes of action—unilateral, multilateral, and regional—to realize the full potential of the reform process. Latin America has made important advances in this strategic package, but much more needs to be done. Indeed, the processes are clearly only in midstream and in some cases have stalled at one or more levels due to a number of difficulties.

Part II of the book includes three chapters that examine trade policy and regional integration from broad perspectives, bringing together the most up-to-date literature on the subject. Alan M. Taylor (chapter 2) takes a long-term view of the process of globalization; Anthony J. Venables (chapter 3) presents a synthetic account of the main economic arguments on the role of economic integration for development; and Alícia Adserà and Carles Boix (chapter 4) survey the recent political economy literature on trade and integration. In part III, Sam Laird and Patrick A. Messerlin (chapter 5), Ramon Torrent (chapter 6), Marise Cremona (chapter 7), Walter Mattli (chapter 8), and Jacint Jordana and Carles Ramió (chapter 9) analyze the main policy and institutional regimes in the areas of trade and integration. The authors discuss the key policy instruments and institutional and legal frameworks available to countries in the pursuit of those policies. In part IV, Rajneesh Narula (chapter 10) and Simon J. Evenett (chapter 11) emphasize the importance of public and private partnerships in the design of policies that would encourage investment and private sector development.

---

[2] For more on the FTAA, see, IDB (2002).

Table 1-1

Latin American Integration Agreements

Agreement	Date of signature
Free trade and customs union agreements within Latin America	
Central American Common Market (CACM)	1960[a]
Andean Community	1969[a]
Caribbean Community (CARICOM)	1973[a]
Southern Cone Common Market (Mercosur)	1991
Chile-Venezuela	1993
Colombia-Chile	1994
Costa Rica-Mexico	1994
Group of Three (G-3)	1994
Bolivia-Mexico	1994
Chile-Mercosur	1996
Bolivia-Mercosur	1996
Mexico-Nicaragua	1997
CACM-Dominican Republic	1998[b]
Chile-Peru	1998
Chile-CACM	1999
Chile-Mexico	1999
Mexico-Northern Triangle of Central America	2000
CARICOM-Dominican Republic	2000
Costa Rica-Trinidad and Tobago	2002[b]
El Salvador-Panama	2002[b]
North-South agreements	
Mexico: North American Free Trade Agreement (NAFTA)	1992
Chile-Canada	1996
Mexico-European Union	1999
Mexico-EFTA	2000
Mexico-Israel	2000
Costa Rica-Canada	2001[b]
Chile-European Union	2002
Chile-South Korea	2002
Chile-United States	2002
Chile-EFTA	2003
Negotiations in progress for free trade agreements in Latin America	
Mercosur-Andean Community	
Costa Rica-Panama	
Mexico-Panama	
Mexico-Peru	
Mexico-Ecuador	
Mexico-Trinidad and Tobago	
Negotiations in progress for North-South agreements	
Free Trade Area of the Americas (FTAA)	
Mercosur-European Union	
Chile-EFTA	
CARICOM-European Union (post-Cotonou reciprocal arrangements)	
Central America 4-Canada	
CACM-United States	
Mexico-Japan	
Other negotiations in progress	
Brazil-China	
Brazil-Russia	

[a] Relaunched in the 1990s.
[b] Awaiting ratification.
Source: IDB data.

HISTORY, THEORY AND POLITICS

The change in Latin America's trade and integration paradigm has taken place in less than 15 years, a small period when viewed in a long historical perspective. The results, successes, and failures of the change can be measured only several decades from now, as is to be expected when major policy shifts embrace a whole region. This change of policy was partially driven in response to an intensification of the process of globalization in the latter part of the 20th century. However, the history of globalization goes back as far as two centuries in time. To understand how Latin America has managed and will be able to manage these international forces of globalization, it is useful to look back in history.

In his analysis of the historical sweep of globalization, Taylor (chapter 2) argues that the history of globalization can be cast as the interplay between two kinds of forces: economic and technological factors, what he calls "physical elements," and political and institutional forces, or the "spirit" of globalization. In the contemporary scene, where many of Taylor's physical changes are underway in the world economy, more attention to the spirit of globalization at home in Latin America is crucial to improving the region's trade performance and growth. This message permeates the book, that is, the importance of finding and consolidating the political and institutional basis to accompany the economic and technological transformations of globalization.

In the case of Latin America, regional integration has been an additional tool to manage this process, and the chapters by Venables (chapter 3) and Adserà and Boix (chapter 4) expand on some of Taylor's themes. Venables explores how the strategy of regional integration can play a role in the overall agenda of development; Adserà and Boix examine the key political economy questions underlying the formation of public policy in the areas of trade and integration.

Latin America has a long tradition in pursuing regional integration, first with Southern partners (South-South integration) and, only recently under the new regionalism, with some Northern partners. This sequence has political economy explanations. Trade among Latin American countries was relatively small, and the composition of factor endowments as well as levels of competitiveness were much more similar among countries in the region than with the rest of the world. In addition, there is an affinity and awareness among Latin American countries due to language, culture, consumption patterns, and history. As Adserà and Boix point out, some argue that these are factors conducive to getting together in RIAs. Another explanatory factor is that some formal remnants of the old postwar integration kept alive active links among subgroups of countries. Finally, all the countries shared a common objective of embarking on a comprehensive structural reform process; moreover, they started out under similar economic circumstances and with emerging democracies. All these factors allowed governments to use regional integration to signal their commitment to opening, reducing average levels of protection, and increasing competition with manageable adjustments and hence relatively broad domestic support.

Peppered throughout this volume, however, is the message that North-South integration can be a superior vehicle for the economic transformation of developing countries. This is most extensively developed by Venables, who shows that the advantage of North-South integration over its South-South counterpart is that it better allows all member countries to capture the benefits of the full spectrum of international comparative advantage. By contrast, in South-South integration, the partner with extreme international comparative advantage (the lesser developed member) faces the risks and costs of trade diversion. This is because it will increase imports from the more developed partner in products where that partner has a comparative advantage in the regional market, but not necessarily with the rest of the world. The more developed partner experiences welfare gains in static terms, but could pay a price in dynamic terms as production and export patterns become distorted away from international comparative advantage. Venables finds that a North-South agreement is more clearly a win-win proposition for both partners due to the greater exposure to international comparative advantage.

But we also want to point out that subregional agreements in Latin America have deep strategic objectives that go beyond what can be achieved in the FTAs that Northern countries have typically offered the region. Most subregional agreements include in their stated objectives the establishment of a common market, which is a deeper form of economic integration. Moreover, they aim to improve international bargaining power and terms of trade vis-à-vis rich countries, and to manage neighborhood issues, such as security, migration, peace, preservation of democracy, and development of regional public goods such as infrastructure. The agreements also serve as an outlet for goods trade (for example, agriculture), which faces international protection in richer markets that is difficult to totally dismantle, even in North-South FTAs. New export experience, coupled with the economies of scale and agglomeration of a regional market, can help expand sectors that may not initially have international comparative advantage, but that with time and the edge of a preference could achieve it. Meanwhile, combining regionalism with unilateral opening minimizes the risks of trade diversion, which is at the heart of Venables' concern.

North-South agreements are not a substitute for economically and politically relevant South-South integration. Nevertheless, South-South agreements clearly would benefit from linking with Northern partners because this would test the economic relevancy of the agreement and further reduce risks of trade diversion. Venables points to other advantages of North-South integration, such as greater potential for development of vertical production networks (especially with FDI) due to the larger presence of factor price differentials. Technological transfers take on more importance. The lock-in of reforms also could be tighter as North-South agreements generally are less permissive about a reversal of commitments.

Unilateral opening also can reduce unwanted distortionary effects of regional integration, whether of the South-South or North-South variety. Indeed, the parallel unilateral opening of Latin America probably helps to explain why empirical studies available to date have generally not captured worrisome trade diversion effects in the region's new regionalism. Unfortunately, countries seem to have stalled regarding further unilateral opening after making progress in 1985–95. This could be a bargaining tactic in the face of the FTAA and multilateral trade liberalization negotiations. However, not withstanding these negotiations, Chile has continued to open up unilaterally (most recently with a program to gradually reduce tariffs from 11 to 6 percent).

Finally, unilateral economic opening in Latin America is theoretically expected to raise the wage-rental ratio (improve income distribution). Since North-South agreements mimic a unilateral opening, they could theoretically produce similar results. However, as Venables shows, although South-South agreements could be expected to improve the wage-rental ratio in the less developed partner, they may have the opposite effect on the member that is more labor endowed compared with the rest of the world but relatively more capital intensive in the regional group setting.

There has been much debate about the effects of external opening on income distribution. Taylor (chapter 2) reviews some empirical studies that suggest that in the historical sweep of globalization, there is at the world level evidence of intercountry deterioration of income distribution, but not so regarding intracountry distribution. In other words, global convergence has lagged but the overall in-country effects do not point to systematic deterioration.

Nevertheless, given the reallocation of resources arising from the opening of trade regimes and interaction with other factors, Taylor expects ambiguous results at the level of specific nations, with improvement in some cases and deterioration in others. This certainly has been the case in Latin America during its recent episode of economic opening (IDB 2002). There is less ambiguity on the issue of regional disparities. Adserà and Boix point out that, when left to market forces, increasing returns and agglomeration lead opening to concentrate its effects in certain locations.

Compensatory mechanisms to deal with losers arising from Pareto optimal trade and integration policies have much bearing on social equity grounds. But Taylor in a historical perspective and Adserà and Boix in a theoretical one both point out an important political economy dimension, which, if left unattended, could create obstacles for further trade liberalization and integration. In effect, even if trade opening and regional integration were welfare enhancing on a net basis, policies that pursue these goals would be blocked by demands for protection from potential losers. Adserà and Boix review the literature and suggest that the more specific the assets of the losers and the less the costs of collective action, the stronger the protectionist lobby will be. Meanwhile, winners in society are typically dispersed and less able to organize their interests. Hence, compensatory mechanisms for losing groups and regions—such as training and education, unemployment insurance, social safety networks, local development, and competitiveness programs—may be a fundamental requirement for gaining consensus for opening to neighbors and the world. In the United States, the recent approval of trade promotion authority legislation hinged on the approval of a compensatory mechanism. The general inability of free traders to accept and actively promote compensatory mechanisms may be the Achilles' heel of globalization and regionalism.

POLICIES AND INSTITUTIONS

The most basic policy interface with the rest of the world is the design and implementation of a specific trade regime, that is, a set of policies and instruments to regulate the cross-border trade of goods and services. Today's trade regimes go beyond traditional border instruments, such as tariffs and nontariff measures, and enter the realm of domestic policies, such as competition policy (Evenett, chapter 11). However, traditional tariff-related policy is still an important component in defining the degree of openness of a country with respect to its partners worldwide and the decisions by the private sector with regard to exports and investment. Laird and Messerlin (chapter 5) conduct a comparative analysis of different trade policy regimes around the world, exploiting information on the use of these traditional instruments. Their analysis suggests that, notwithstanding important progress, Latin American trade policy has moved more slowly than elsewhere with respect to openness. Hence, the authors argue that another round of trade policy reforms is overdue. To make this assessment, they consider a worldwide sample of countries, including countries in Latin America, and develop several indexes to measure the degree of simplicity, irreversibility, and openness of different trade policy regimes.

On a comparative basis, Latin America does well in agriculture, an area where it has a strong international comparative advantage. However, with some exceptions—most notably Chile—it fares poorly in industrial products. If services were part of the exercise, Latin America would fare even worse. Laird and Messerlin think that the forums for making progress on those issues are the World Trade Organization (for openness and irreversibility) and unilateral policies (for simplicity).

The studies by Laird and Messerlin and Taylor also offer insights on other important issues of trade performance, in particular, the need to package trade policy in a consistent manner with other basic policies. Looking through the broad sweep of history and globalization, Taylor points to the importance of sound public finance, credible central banking, stable currencies, and development of domestic credit and equity markets. Of course, all these elements underpin the basic need for macroeconomic stability. Meanwhile, Taylor shows that historically there is no clear evidence that tariffs on final goods were inimical to growth. However, when placed on capital goods, tariffs raise the cost of capital and must be compensated by exchange rate depreciation if the bias against investment and exports is to be eliminated. Taylor observes that this is a lesson learned by resource-based economies, like Australia, and it could be a lesson for Latin America, where tariffs on capital goods can be high, especially in the larger countries.

Laird and Messerlin echo much of Taylor's insights and add a few. While stable currencies have historically been good for trade and investment, overvaluation of the nominal currency is a source of underperforming exports, bulging current account deficits, and protectionism. Overvaluation was a problem in Latin America in the 1990s, when many countries excessively leveraged nominal exchange rates in order to obtain anchors for domestic price stability in the absence of sufficiently aggressive fiscal reforms. The extreme case was Argentina. This approach, coupled with permissive policies on capital flows, particularly of the short-term variety, and irregular financial regulation made countries vulnerable to overvaluation, unsustainable current account deficits, and balance of payments crises. What is surprising is that many of these episodes of crisis repeated the same mistakes that led to the region's balance of payments collapse in the 1980s (Devlin 1989; ECLAC 1995). Laird and Messerlin warn that regional integration can be an aid to better trade performance, but it is not a substitute for continued reforms of global trade policy at the unilateral and multilateral levels.

Any analysis of the overall trade regime would be incomplete without bringing into the picture the policies and instruments to pursue further regional trade and economic integration. This is especially relevant for Latin America, where regional integration constitutes a basic pillar of an international trade policy. Torrent (chapter 6) has a useful way of approaching some of the key dimensions that must be effectively tackled in regional integration. They are certainly relevant for Latin American processes, especially those that have deep objectives. In particular, the chapter establishes a typology of the engineering that is needed to move integration processes forward, distinguishing between instruments, implementation frameworks, and supporting institutions. The analysis of the European model provides a benchmark against which other agreements can be evaluated.

Torrent argues that since the legal framework (rules) form the core of an RIA, a deep integration process must aim at broadening the width of its rules (coverage). In this respect, Latin America has been rather successful. However, rules must have an effective content, which means going beyond existing multilateral obligations. In Latin America, integration protocols sometimes are a duplication of already existing obligations, adding another layer of administration without real value added.

Although institutions are key in providing a supporting architecture for the legal framework or rules, there is no substitute for an inherent respect for the rule of law with a disposition for voluntary compliance. This behavior is underpinned by the intensity of the political commitment of the partners to the collective project. Torrent highlights how the European

Community relied heavily on voluntary compliance before having strong institutions for enforcement and sanctions.

Cremona (chapter 7) provides an in-depth examination of the importance of the rule of law as an intrinsic principle of the functioning of any RIA. She distinguishes between negative and positive rules. Negative rules require, for example, eliminating barriers to trade and investment. This involves liberalization and market access rules as well as those on treatment (for example, most favored nation and national treatment). Positive rules involve uniform or harmonized regional rules and standards in the domain of the domestic markets. Regional initiatives start out at their core with negative market access rules focusing on liberalization of international transactions.

Torrent points out that deeper integration requires going beyond this level of liberalization. In theory, harmonized rules would be superior to obligations on treatment due to the benefits of uniformity, but they are potentially more intrusive with respect to national legislation and require difficult consensus building for their approval. Thus, the treatment approach would seem to be more appropriate for Latin America at this particular stage of integration. However, the complexity of practice is demonstrated by analyzing the thorny issue of technical standards. The European Union has used the method of mutual recognition in its efforts to overcome indirect barriers from standards and avoid slow progress in achieving harmonized rules through consensus. However, Torrent argues that mutual recognition of national standards in the European Union is a myth because as the European Union process has deepened, the alternatives applied in practice are no standards, harmonized standards, or conflicting standards.

Unfortunately, unilateral behavior and opportunistic defection all too often corrode the credibility and effectiveness of Latin American regional rules. This in turn probably reflects a tradition of weak national governance and unsteady political commitments in the face of frequent and sudden shifts in the priorities of public leadership and in the performance of national economies. But as Cremona points out, it also can result from a too rapid wholesale adoption of new norms. Gradual and experimental development of rules that are effectively absorbed and applied at the national level may be better than a comprehensive scheme with impressive width and depth but only selective compliance. In Latin America, subregional integration projects typically have been launched with ambitious rules for a customs union, but implemented with imperfect common external tariffs, little or no common customs arrangements, and far from perfect internal free trade. If these circumstances persist, the credibility of rules is easily eroded. It might be better to consider the simpler demands of a more perfect FTA if the complexities of a common external tariff and customs union cannot be effectively managed.

The basic pillar of any integration initiative is the existence of an initial agreement that provides the foundation for the systematic development of rules. There are two basic prototypes. The first is a static treaty based on a contract among parties that is consistent with national constitutional requirements. In this context, there is no capacity to autonomously create new rules without a procedure that revises the treaty and goes through national ratification. The other prototype is a more dynamic agreement with a treaty that has built-in mechanisms for creating new rules. As Cremona points out, this is a more constitutional formula for the rule of law in which regional rules have primacy over national legislation. NAFTA is an example of the static prototype, while the European Union is an example of the dynamic prototype.

Both Cremona and Torrent agree that either approach can be equally effective in supporting a rules-based system. A dynamic treaty facilitates evolution and adaptability. But Cremona points out that it can be onerous and overwhelm countries that do not have a high degree of domestic political and legal consolidation. Indeed, this has been a problem for many decades in the Andean agreement, the only one in Latin America with a built-in mechanism for creating regional legislation. Although the Andean experience showed some improvement in the 1990s, the static approach is, and probably will continue to be for the foreseeable future, the basic reference in Latin American integration.

Typically, specific institutional arrangements are required to support the process of rulemaking under dynamic treaties or implementation in dynamic and static treaties. A traditional classification divides the institutional models of regional integration between intergovernmental and supranational arrangements. In intergovernmental arrangements, institutions are, in the words of Mattli (chapter 8), playing a technical-servant role for governments and decisions are by consensus. The risk is that the deepening process can be stymied by the least common denominator. In supranational arrangements, the primary players are above and below the nation-state and majority voting is more feasible. However, the risk here is loss of legitimacy as processes move faster than the pace that nations can absorb them. Dynamic treaties lean toward the latter institutional arrangement and static treaties lean toward the former. The European Union model is generally associated with the supranational approach.[3] Latin American (and indeed most) treaties are dominated by intergovernmental arrangements, although the Andean Community has supranational mechanisms.

The debate in Latin America concerning institutions is alive and well. Overall, there is broad support for the view that institutions are too weak given the objectives of subregional integration. Discussions often focus on whether institutions should be supranational or intergovernmental in nature. Presumably both modes can be effective if form follows substance. Moreover, Torrent makes the point that it really is not an either/or proposition because even in the European Union, some aspects of the treaty operate under supranational institutions while other aspects are the domain of intergovernmental decisionmaking. Meanwhile, we would add that the technical-servant role of intergovernmental arrangements is relative because credible, respected institutions could be influential in government decisionmaking and facilitate coordination.

Cremona observes that in Latin America, the issue of intergovernmental versus supranational arrangements is secondary to the need to effectively develop dispute settlement procedures and regularly use them. The region's tradition has been dominated by a negotiation-diplomacy approach when disputes among members arise, reflecting a past era of strong state intervention in the economy and limited private sector involvement. But relying on backroom diplomacy undermines transparency and the credibility of a rules-based system that is at the heart of the new regionalism and its ability to attract investment. Moreover, effective dispute settlement mechanisms are important in balancing the economic and political power between small and large partners.

In designing dispute settlement mechanisms, there should be accommodation for discussion and bargaining in resolving disputes. However, if the agreement is to be credible, the underlying character of the mechanism must be the rule of regional law. Moreover, as mentioned by Cremona, if flexibility is needed, perhaps this should be achieved through an integral and transparent provision of special or differentiated treatment in the regional rules. The best outcome of any dispute settlement is the effective resolution of the problem rather than the imposition of a trade sanction, which usually favors the larger markets. In the absence of a resolution, fines may be a better means of compensation and an incentive for good behavior.

---

[3] Nevertheless, some of the current debate on the future of Europe is precisely about this balance between the powers of regional institutions vis-à-vis the role of national governments as the driving forces of future integration.

While an effective dispute settlement mechanism is of paramount importance for Latin American regional integration, there are other areas that demand attention. Technical secretariats need to be strengthened. Borrowing from Jordana and Ramió (chapter 9), secretariats should be leanly designed around strategic areas to meet well-defined objectives. They must meet the requirements of professionalism (as opposed to clientelism) and generate civil service career paths that incorporate a firm commitment to the collective ideal. Torrent also warns against overlooking the importance of an adequate and predictable budget for the regional institution. Unfortunately, Latin American institutions all too often face underfunding, arrears from members, and dependence on budget support from outside donors. The level of professionalism in the institutions and the budgetary commitments are usually linked.

Although forming a customs union is a challenge, it is well worth the effort. First, efficiencies emerge from the elimination of rules of origin and the common collection and distribution of customs proceeds. Second, deepening integration enhances the economic benefits of being together and a customs union is a necessary step on the way to a common market. Third, both Cremona and Torrent point to the catalytic effect of introducing an external dimension to a regional integration agreement. In an FTA, most of the focus is on policy restraints. A customs union and the increased international bargaining power it affords to partners increase the focus on policy building. A full customs union also discourages development of the ad hoc bilateral forays that aggravate the so-called spaghetti bowl of regional agreements in the hemisphere.

Mattli makes an important observation concerning the responsibility for leadership in regional processes. In effect, successful regional integration needs a lead country (or countries) with a vision and persistent commitment that rises above short-term national politics and mercantilist interests. This is the regional paymaster that Germany (and to a lesser extent France) played in European integration. Casual observation suggests that the dynamism of Latin American integration has risen and fallen with the degree of political attention and benevolence of the lead market player in each of the subregions (Colombia in the Andean area, Brazil in Mercosur, and Costa Rica in Central America).

Finally, Cremona and Mattli's chapters highlight the fact that institutional needs are not solely a regional phenomenon. Effective national counterpart laws, institutions, and civil service personnel are critical, as is interaction between the private and public sectors. This point is illustrated in the case of the European Court of Justice, which was strengthened by its collaboration with national courts regarding implementation issues and the ability of the private sector to challenge national legislation that was out of line with community law. Mattli also explains how Europe has been able to advance standard setting by decentralizing part of the process to the private sector and national subgroups.

Good domestic institutions are a necessary ingredient for good trade policy and good regional integration. Jordana and Ramió's analysis suggests a need for serious reform in most Latin American countries. The authors analyze four basic models for ministerial organization in the design and implementation of trade policy. All four can be found in the region. No single one is in principle clearly superior to the other; ultimately, a model must be consistent with the political, cultural, and administrative realities of a country. Moreover, in developing countries, effective institutional arrangements should provide consistent links between trade policy and overall development strategies, as well as facilitate intergovernmental coordination and integrated policymaking. Jordana and Ramió seem to lean toward an integrated ministry (which includes economic sectors, typically called a ministry of the economy, and trade functions), which can more easily link trade to a development strategy. An integrated ministry minimizes the need for interministerial coordination, the risks of substitution, and the need for conflict resolution; reduces fragmentation of policymaking; and facilitates monitoring of trade processes.

However, the authors also point to the risk of radical change of the institutional arrangements in a developing country. Time-path dependency arising from political fragility and the complexity of issues often leads to an incomplete reform and fragmentation. This is especially relevant in Latin America, where major reforms involving creation of a new trade ministry or the merger of a trade ministry with another ministry has left the national trade apparatus effectively divided in interministerial bureaucratic conflict to the detriment of coherent trade policymaking. Hence, the better approach may be incremental modernization of an existing ministry (or ministries) and intergovernmental relationships. This is what Chile has done quite successfully with its ministry of foreign affairs.

Institutions are only as good as the people that are part of them. Jordana and Ramió explain that a deficient civil service model—lacking professionalism, stable career paths, skill capacity, client culture, public values, and proper economic incentives—is the norm throughout the region. The lack of a coherent civil service structure also undermines accumulated skill development (training or on-the-job learning) by defection to the private sector. There is an urgent need to strengthen the civil service culture in trade. Professional management principles should overtake classic bureaucratic approaches. However, care should be taken that ad hoc arrangements designed to facilitate more autonomy in management and overcome existing bureaucratic arrangements—such as the use of external consultants and special remuneration—do not contribute to de-institutionalization of the national trade apparatus.

Jordana and Ramió provide insights on government decisionmaking processes. Intergovernmental coordination is an essential ingredient in effective policymaking, as is a disciplined and transparent channel of communication with civil society. However, in Latin America, coordinating mechanisms are often weak and can lead to conflict aggravated by the typically passive stance on trade issues of the executive branch, which could mediate conflict. Meanwhile, formal channels of communication with the private sector, members of congress, and civil society more generally are scarcely developed, leading to potentially welfare-reducing strategies and greater risk of public authorities being captured by special interests.[4] Finally, we would add that another central component is formulation of a coherent trade strategy that is mainstreamed in government policymaking.[5]

THE PUBLIC-PRIVATE SECTOR NEXUS

The new regionalism, in contrast with the regionalism of the 1960s and 1970s, has been mostly driven by the need to provide a stable environment for private sector development and FDI in order to enhance the potential dynamic effects of integration on economic transformation, productivity, and growth. In the past, trade policy in general and regional integration in particular were pieces of a larger state planning policy for economic development based on ISI strategies. FDI was viewed with a degree of suspicion. However, this view changed radically with the reform process. In effect, FDI is now seen as contributing to institutional modernization and enhancing international competitiveness. Pursuing and deepening reforms, including the new regionalism, are seen as a way of competing in the world economy and attracting FDI.

---

[4] For an analysis of the consultation process in seven Latin American countries, see IDB (2001).
[5] Lack of mainstreaming explains why many trade-related ministries are "orphans" in government budget priorities.

The volume ends with two chapters that examine these issues in some depth. Narula (chapter 10) looks at regional integration policies through the lens of international companies and their strategic positioning. Evenett (chapter 11) looks through the lens of government policy at one of the pioneering areas of trade and integration policy that goes beyond existing multilateral trade rules. He refers to the role of competition policy, which, at the same time, is one of the best examples of the complex interaction between domestic policy and international regulations.

Narula follows Ethier (1998) in pointing out that the new regionalism can serve to attract FDI. However, the direction of FDI can vary. In a regional agreement, the creation of economies of scale will attract market-seeking investment. But the new investment may concentrate in one market and induce closure of subsidiaries in neighboring member markets. The higher the level of competence, the more likely the new investment will take place in the market with greater domestic capacity. Another possibility is that with the lowering of external tariffs, the new investment will take place in third markets rather than the regional market. Narula also points to some superior qualities of North-South integration. Northern developed countries are the major source of FDI and integrating with them will attract their investment. Moreover, the technological gap between countries in North-South integration is larger than the South-South gap, and hence the spillover possibilities are greater. The investment is also more likely to be efficiency seeking, which implies a higher degree of competence and more integration into the multinational corporation network. And the order of magnitude of the effects should be larger than can be expected in South-South integration.

Narula's analysis leads to the conclusion that not all FDI is equal from the standpoint of development. Its benefits in terms of delivering capital, technology, best practices, and exports depend on the generation of significant spillovers and a domestic sector that can absorb those spillovers, which in turn is related to the degree to which domestic industry and FDI complement each other. In this context, there is a strong degree of interaction between domestic capacity (human skills, market size, location, openness, infrastructure, and political and economic stability) and the competence of the affiliate/subsidiary of a multinational firm.

Evenett's chapter closes the volume by offering a good example of a policy that brings together some of the themes analyzed throughout this book: the interaction between different levels of policymaking (national, regional, and multilateral), conflicts between domestic policies and international regulations, policy complementarities, and the role of local institutions and legal traditions in policy design and implementation. The chapter focuses on the increasing number of corporate changes that international firms have adopted in recent years in response to trade liberalization and integration policies throughout the developing world. Evenett argues that those structural changes at the firm level could well undermine some of the benefits of trade and investment liberalization pursued by developing countries, and therefore countervailing policies may be warranted. However, a question arises with respect to the level at which those policies should be applied (national, regional, or international). The chapter goes through some standard economic arguments, but emphasizes the need to consider institutional aspects, legal traditions, and historical experiences in order to select the best policy package for an individual country. Due to the potential for spillovers from corporate decisions as well as from national enforcement policies across borders, Evenett argues that one could make the case for some regional mechanisms. However, the approach should be incremental and accompanied by substantial efforts in capacity building.

REFERENCES

Devlin, R. 1989. *Debt and Crisis in Latin America: The Supply Side of the Story*. Princeton, NJ: Princeton University Press.

Devlin, R., and A. Estevadeordal. 2001. "What's New in the New Regionalism in the Americas." In Victor Bulmer-Thomas (ed.), *Regional Integration in Latin America and the Caribbean*, London: Institute of Latin American Studies.

Economic Commission for Latin America and the Caribbean (ECLAC). 1995. *Latin America and the Caribbean: Policies to Improve Linkages with the Global Economy*. Santiago, Chile: ECLAC.

Ethier, W. 1998. The New Regionalism. *The Economic Journal* (July).

Inter-American Development Bank (IDB). 1996. Trade Liberalization. In *Economic and Social Progress in Latin America: 1996 Report*. Washington, D.C.: IDB.

———. 2001. The Trade Policy Making Process Level One of the Two Level Game: Country Studies in the Western Hemisphere. INTAL/ITD/STA Occasional Paper 13, March, Buenos Aires.

———. 2002. *Beyond Borders: The New Regionalism in Latin America: Economic and Social Progress in Latin America: 2002 Report*. Washington, D.C.: IDB.

World Bank. 2001. *World Development Indicators*. Washington, D.C.: World Bank.

PART II
HISTORY, THEORY AND POLITICS

Chapter 2

Globalization, Trade and Development: Some Lessons from History

Alan M. Taylor

GLOBALIZATION AND THE LONG VIEW

On the eve of the 16th century, with little fanfare and a perilously small fleet, a man from Genoa by way of Portugal and Spain, displaying reckless ignorance of the course ahead, embarked on a voyage of chance that presaged a global future of political and economic turbulence, with all the conquest and cooperation, prosperity and inequality that have defined the modern world. As the 21st century dawned, accompanied by considerably more fanfare and a great flotilla including an oceangoing liner, the world's leaders sailed into Genoa from all corners of the globe—but, with accusations of reckless ignorance traded on both sides, they were greeted by an equally cosmopolitan mass of protesters, occasioning some of the most violent, and the first fatal, anti-global demonstrations to date.

Not without irony, not for the first time, although rarely before with such instantly communicated mass impact, the 2001 G-8 summit raised the question of how to understand and cope with the forces of globalization set in motion five centuries ago. Although proud of Columbus, their favorite son, the Genoese were probably amazed or baffled by his quest, and certainly unaware of the ultimate global impact of his endeavor. Amazed or baffled again as the global consequences swirled around them on the same waterfront 500 years later, they were surely reaping far more than they had sown, and probably felt, like many of the discontents and doubters, that they were just an unwilling bit part caught up in a larger drama of powerful force.

Economic history is embellished by such anecdotes and reflections, but at the business end, in its art and its science, the search for causal connections, documentary evidence, and persuasive argument often proves more elusive than finding the storytelling hooks. Only when the theory, evidence, and story fit is the work complete, and an analytic narrative established. To try to succeed in all three areas is equal parts courageous and foolish. Compounding the risk, the aim of this chapter is to survey the history of globalization from 1500 to the present and so illuminate the key economic characteristics of the modern world. In this essay, I try to step back from a focus on the immediate present and ask what the longer sweep of history tells about globalization, with special reference to issues of trade and development.

The author thanks Susan Collins, Robert Devlin, Antoni Estevadeordal, and conference participants for their helpful comments.

Current economic challenges have not arisen out of nowhere and they have plentiful antecedents. Is economic divergence inevitable in a globalized economy? Will trade promote inequality? Will migration pressures increase? Are open capital markets destined to lurch from crisis to crisis? If states cannot stop this process, can they even hope to contain it? Should they? At a deeper, less tractable, but more fundamental level, can nations adjust not just economically but also socially, culturally, and ideologically to the challenges posed by the wider world perched on their economic doorstep? The economic historian contends that these questions cannot be fully answered by pure introspection, recourse to abstract theory, or analysis and debate of present-day events. Towns, cities, regions, states, and nations faced all these challenges in the past. Responses varied. Sometimes the outcomes were positive, sometimes not. Such variation is of inestimable value to the social scientist: it is the only empirical evidence of globalization, and variation represents the closest thing to an experiment, controlled or otherwise, in the global economic laboratory.

The Modern World: Globalization and Its Discontents

Globalization is nothing new. One might be forgiven for thinking otherwise, since so much recent popular writing declares in sensational tones that a revolution is afoot. The time frame of many popular studies and some academic and policy studies tends to be a few years at most. Conclusions and policy recommendations assume that recent globalization trends have ushered in a brave new world. The only battleground seems to be the question of whether this is a good or bad thing.

According to the early alarmism of anti-globalists, like William Greider (*One World, Ready or Not*, 1997) or John Gray (*False Dawn*, 1998), the subjects of globalization only dimly perceive the economic juggernaut that is rolling over them—and they are hopelessly ill-equipped for the devastating transformation it is wreaking because they have seen nothing like it before. In the view of Naomi Klein (*No Logo*, 1999) or George Monbiot (*The Captive State*, 2000), globalization threatens some combination of state weakness and corporate power that will weaken democracy and unleash greater inequality, and even authors apparently sympathetic to capitalist organization, like Noreena Hertz (*The Silent Takeover*, 2001), wonder if there should be another way. Meanwhile, a few ardent neoliberal supporters, like *Economist* correspondents John Micklethwait and Adrian Wooldridge (*A Future Perfect*, 2000), have trenchantly defended and cheered globalization, garnering an endorsement from Tom Peters that hails globalization as the "most powerful—and life-enhancing—force on earth."

It is open to question whether the experience of the past decade or two fully equips us to answer all the questions raised by globalization and its discontents. The rapidly growing new field of comparative economic history is only now starting to grapple with these issues, but already we can survey some important findings in the recent literature. With this background, I will attempt to address some key concerns about trade and globalization, especially in developing countries, as follows:

- *Economic fundamentals.* When and how did the constraints of scarcity and the desire to trade take hold? Are such forces as powerful now as they were in the past?
- *Institutional bases.* Trade never existed in an institutional vacuum. Important developments in legal, contractual, and financial systems made a difference. What do those events say about the limits on participation in trade today?

- *Technological shocks.* Revolutions in transport and communications spurred trade. Do serious transportation cost constraints still inhibit development?
- *Patterns of exchange.* Exchange occurs not only in goods, but in factor markets and technology. How have these interacted in history? What does that say about the possible substitutability of trade and other forms of integration today?
- *Human welfare.* What have been the impacts of past globalization trends on prices, risk, living standards, and income distribution? What does that say about the costs and benefits of globalization today?
- *Political economy.* Globalization suffers the constraints of, and imposes constraints on, national economic policies. How has that tension been addressed in the past? How does that speak to the future?

It bears observing that the recent trend toward convergence in global markets will not necessarily yield an inevitable "End of History," as Francis Fukuyama (1992) called the even broader process of global convergence in many spheres—economic, social, political, and cultural. Indeed, recent events seem closer to Samuel Huntington's (1996) brush with futurism, "Clash of Civilizations." But even when first proposed, the "End of History" idea had a distinctly ahistorical feel. The idea first emerged at the end of the 19th century, as the last great wave of globalization reached its peak. The view was soon discredited after 1913, as globalization receded in the 20th century turmoil of wars, depressions, and the erratic course of economic policies and political philosophies (Angell 1910).

As is now widely recognized, and as is largely taken for granted in this chapter, only in the past few years has the world made progress toward and arguably beyond the degree of globalization seen a century ago. Can this trend continue, or will it face diminishing returns or even a much talked about backlash? And what does history have to say about how we got here? To set the stage, consider two benchmarks for the degree of international market integration "then" versus "now" in two markets, goods and capital.[1] Figure 2–1 shows the ratio of world trade to world gross domestic product (GDP) since 1800 at key benchmark dates. The conclusion is clear: after a continuous rise during the 19th century, trade as a fraction of world economic activity peaked in 1913, slumped during most of the middle 20th century, and has revived recently. Figure 2–2 shows the ratio of world stocks of foreign investment to GDP over roughly the period since 1870 (data back to 1800 are incomplete, but most likely the ratio was about 0.1 at that point). A similar message emerges: after peaking around 1913, the global capital market was almost quiescent for the next 60 or 70 years, before renewed activity in the 1980s and 1990s.[2]

The Rise and Fall of Globalization: Physical Elements Versus Spirit

Various ingredients have developed over past centuries, and the present and past structures of economic globalization represent a particular and time-specific alignment of these forces. At the risk of oversimplification, figure 2–3 represents an overview of this evolution of the world

[1] Labor markets are now much more restricted than they were a century ago because migration is tightly controlled. However, despite such controls, the incentives to migrate in today's world of massive international income gaps lead to large population movement, legal or otherwise (Chiswick and Hatton 2002).
[2] In each case, the data are for selected countries for which data are available. See the discussion in Estevadeordal, Frantz, and Taylor (2003) and Obstfeld and Taylor (2002).

Figure 2–1

Ratio of International Trade to GDP, 1800–1992

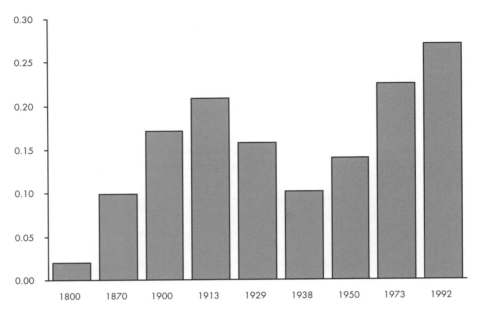

Note: Values are exports plus imports divided by output.
Source: Estevadeordal, Frantz, and Taylor (2003).

Figure 2–2

Ratio of International Investment to GDP, 1870–2000

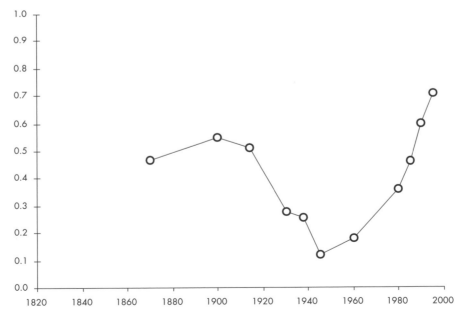

Source: Obstfeld and Taylor (2002).

Figure 2–3

All of Globalization and History on One Diagram

		Spirit *Political and institutional basis for globalization*	
		Weak	Strong
Flesh *Economic and technological basis for globalization*	Weak	Classical to medieval era (15th century and before)	Early modern era (16th to 18th century)
	Strong	Most of the 20th century (ca. 1914–1990s)	19th century (ca. 1815–1914)

economy. The story is cast as an interplay between two kinds of forces: economic and techno-logical forces versus political and institutional forces.

Economic and technological forces may promote economic globalization via market integration, including the ability to transport goods or communicate information across dis-tances at higher speed and lower cost. These are the flesh—tangible and physical elements. They include new shipping or power technologies, such as steam engines used in ships and trains, as well as new and better communication devices, such as the telegraph, telephone, or Internet.

Figure 2–3 characterizes as weak or strong the political and institutional forces that may inhibit or reinforce said globalization. I call these the "spirit" of globalization, referring to the intangible quality of the underlying thinking in which the tangible market mechanisms are embedded. At the simplest level, these qualities include trade policies, capital controls, and immigration restrictions affecting markets for goods and factors. This dimension also includes a broader array of legal and customary devices that provide public goods, such as the security of property rights, contract enforcement, stable and predictable monetary and fiscal policies, and freedom from bribery, corruption, or the diversion of resources through rent-seeking. According to this schema, and in agreement with the view that the 20th century has been on the whole an aberrant period of deglobalization, the depiction in the figure claims that the history of the world economy has been far from linear and, if anything, somewhat circular. But it is necessary to set aside any temptation to get Hegelian: the history of globalization has not come full circle and is not likely to do so.

In figure 2–3, the world begins in the upper left cell in the distant past, with both types of forces operating only weakly to promote globalization. The technologies for integrating mar-kets were rudimentary, and the political and institutional umbrellas covering trade were flimsy; as a result, it simply cost too much (or risked too much) to move goods or factors between distant locations. By the 16th and 17th centuries, some of these forces had begun to shift, but I choose to emphasize the institutional and political changes over the technological at this juncture: a movement from the top left to the top right cell in the figure. Transport and navigational technologies had improved very little, with dogged persistence rather than innovation permitting the fledgling opening of trade between the continents. But the institutional basis for trade did change.

The experience of this initial period, which might be called an era of proto-globalization, was by no means uniform; significant developments in the relationship between states and markets conditioned the evolution of commerce and economic growth in different locations. The big story, which scholars have explored in detail, is obviously the rise of European trading nations and the increasing geographical scope of their activities, usually under state protection. In the Americas, these adventures encountered no incumbents, and in the waters and ports of Asia, they increasingly crowded out local merchants and vessels. There was a marked penetration of Chinese long-distance trade on certain routes, an incursion that some have traced back to the failure of the Chinese to develop their merchant ambitions after the remarkable feats of the treasure fleet (Findlay and O'Rourke 2002).

Since the economic distances between markets remained large, there was only a slow increase in the level of trade, and prices in different locations were highly dispersed. But this trade flourished under different auspices than the early trade, with an increasing role for the state, especially powerful European states that embarked on imperial adventures with trading companies in tow. As trade followed the flag, it did so with the benefit of an increasingly pro-economic state structure of legal protection, financial and macroeconomic stability, and limited government predation.

This might bring to mind primarily the state-supported trading companies, like the British and Dutch East India companies, each an exemplar of the new involvement of the state in protecting commerce. Beyond these near-monopolies, however, the general extension of states' economic interests beyond their own borders became an increasingly important element of government objectives, diplomacy, and legal innovation. In addition to the military—principally naval—strength to make this endeavor feasible, the whole exercise rested on a significant change in state orientation.

By the 18th century, Britain had eventually overtaken its continental rivals as the key entrepôt in Europe, and the country eventually built up a huge flow of invisible earnings from shipping and merchant services. In the 18th century, the physical force of early industrialization would soon feed into this mercantile structure to propel greater specialization and a boom in trade. But even before that, the reforms of 1688 propelled institutional changes in the spirit of the economy that undergirded the expansion of external commerce.

First, the revolution in the British fiscal state steadied the macroeconomy and laid the foundations of a modern financial sector: since merchants relied on financial techniques to conduct trade over long distances with credit, they gained. Second, a new and broader franchise in Parliament kept the state's legal and regulatory incursions on business in check, with contracts and banking activities free to develop, even after episodic financial crises and downturns. Third, although the fiscal state required stronger tax tools, these were not deployed as heavy tariffs in such a way as to crush trade; fiscal power did not equate exactly with unbridled mercantilism in this sense. Tariffs could be kept low if mercantilism was pursued by military means, by taking trade market share from rivals by force—so as to expand the tax base rather than raising the tax rate. Fourth, another centerpiece of mercantilism, the state-chartered trading companies were increasingly exposed to competition as their patents expired. Over time, the government was less inclined to view the concentration of trade in the hands of one privileged company as a desirable arrangement, and in due course, a large array of commercial ventures took shape, increasing competition, hence the quantity of trade, and, again fortuitously, the government's tax base.[3]

Thus, in my depiction of the early modern period, increasingly pro-commercial regimes supported international and interregional trade, as shown in figure 2–3. This was a fundamental change in the political economy of the era, in the philosophical spirit of the age. There were limits to this change, with only a gradual dissolution of the large, state-sanctioned monopoly ventures and the gradual rise of private commerce through smaller-scale enterprises. In addition, even at this more competitive level, trade remained largely canalized and often traveled under a given flag according to whichever navy controlled the shipping lanes. Accordingly, trade expanded—faster than population and faster than output—but it still remained small in the world as a whole. Whereas the spirit was now somewhat willing, the physical elements were still quite weak—shipping technology was such that the benefits of trade, for most commodities, did not outweigh the costs. The world trade routes were mere skeletons compared with their current form.

These developments set the springboard for globalization, but the big jump was yet to come. The dawn of the long 19th century brought an end to this particular configuration of globalization. After the European powers reached a peace treaty in 1815, the seas were open again to trade, backed by strong economic and technological impulses. The Industrial Revolution implied specialization wherever it spread—and equally, where it did not—as countries traded among themselves, exchanging manufactures for primary products and vice versa. This was a fundamental international division of labor that had not been seen before on such a scale, and it heralded the Great Divergence of incomes and productivity in the last two centuries.

The economic forces, the physical elements in figure 2–3, were aligned with the spirit, promoting a boom in global economic interaction. Besides impelling countries to abandon notions of self-sufficiency and embrace specialization via trade, the modern era also brought with it technologies, such as steam power and the telegraph, that were bound to reduce the time and cost of linking markets. Jointly, these fundamentals encouraged the amplification of international linkages by an order of magnitude over what had been seen before, whether measured by convergence of prices or the surge in trade volumes.

The 20th century, since 1914 at least, was a time when globalization went into reverse and, depending on the location and markets in question, some (if not all) of the gains of the 19th century were lost. Clearly, this was not because governments forgot the important technological innovations that spurred trade; nor was it for want of any new such innovations, since there were many, including internal combustion engines, jet air transport, and advanced electronic communications.

All of the retreat in globalization can, of course, be attributed to the political and institutional dimension in figure 2–3: a choice to stop the integration of markets given the existing technological capacity to make them flourish—a weakening in the spirit of globalization, so to speak. Some see these limits on trade as a backlash, although their origins in two world wars can also be seen as the collateral damage of global international conflicts in an era of total war. Either way, the historical process of globalization has not been one of ever-closer union among countries, at least on this timescale.

Looking ahead and beyond the 20th-century experience, the choice will again be whether to embrace or restrain globalization. Economic globalization, in one form or another, is here

---

[3] This paragraph draws extensively on O'Brien's (1998) excellent survey.

to stay. But how people manage it, for better or for worse, remains a crucial and ongoing problem, a challenge that can be faced with greater confidence by remembering and learning from the centuries of experience with these issues.

THE IMPULSE TO TRADE: GLOBALIZATION PAST AND PRESENT

The division of history implied by figure 2–3 raises two overarching questions. First, what fundamental economic forces have led the world toward globalization? And second, when did such forces begin to operate on a scale large enough to make a difference? These questions matter not simply because they focus on historical episodes that are globalized enough to be relevant for contemporary comparison. Paying attention to historical eras in which globalization *did not* exist reveals key characteristics that restrain market integration and mute its impact. This in turn might help explain the situation of some developing countries today that globalization seems to have passed by.

At a fundamental level, economic historians are concerned with the deep human impulse to trade in all its forms: the desire to exchange goods, imitate technology, lend and borrow, and migrate. Archeological evidence reveals the commonly observed, age-old proclivity of humans to truck and barter—Adam Smith's felicitous phrase. This offers a flavor of the persistence of markets across vast expanses of time, but without more detailed evidence on the extent of those markets across space, the analyst remains ill equipped to decide whether globalization has been a force for decades, centuries, or millennia.

When Did Globalization Begin?

It might seem surprising that the debate over when globalization began is ongoing in the historical literature. However, for the most part, the debate might be reasonably whittled down to a battle among three camps or, equally, three rival dates for the onset of a global economy.[4]

Various scholars in the world history school posit an early start date for globalization, circa 1000. According to this view, overland and Mediterranean trade flourished in this period, with caravans and coastal shipping linking Asian and European markets, and this is enough to prove the existence of a world economy. A more conservative wing of the world history school would lean toward circa 1500 (maybe even 1492, to be precise) as the key date. This might seem more reasonable according to the view that a solution to the economic disconnect between the Americas and the rest of the world is a sine qua non for a global economy. Only following the voyages of discovery and the first circumnavigation expeditions, which had at least a partial economic motive, could world trade finally span the Old and New Worlds.

Yet, just because such trading links existed does not imply that they mattered fundamentally for economic outcomes. Indeed, early trade between these locations was minuscule compared with the size of these economies and compared with the commerce on shorter routes, such as the coastal European routes among the Atlantic, Mediterranean, and Baltic entrepôts. High transport costs, inadequate finance and insurance, risks of predation by pirates or potentates, and a fear of natural peril discouraged traders from transoceanic arbitrage. Only a few fearless, foolish, or well-equipped private merchants could flourish in such a setting. Of course,

---

[4] This section draws on O'Rourke and Williamson (2002a, 2002b, 2002c) and Findlay and O'Rourke (2002).

the newly emerging, state-sponsored, multinational trading companies enjoyed smoother sailing under imperial protection. That such trade existed at all, despite such risks and costs, speaks to the impulse to trade: the divergence in the relative scarcity of goods in different locations. Thus, pepper, spices, cotton, tea, coffee, and other luxury commodities were shipped out of Asia. Europe sold silver and manufactures. Sugar and tobacco were the principal exports of the Americas.

Importantly, all this trade carried high markups between export and import markets, a gap in autarky prices that created a profit sufficient to offset the costs and risks of transport. But the vast majority of goods had such a low profit that they were never traded. A global economy could not be said to exist, say, on the basis of a few luxury goods changing hands. These goods were a small fraction of the output of the Eastern economies, and in consumption they mattered only to the rich elite in Europe. In both places, the vast majority of individuals lived near subsistence, and produced and consumed food, clothing, and shelter that moved in a tightly delimited local orbit, and certainly did not move at the global scale. Even as late as 1820, as measured in value terms, about 99 percent of the goods produced in the world never entered trade (Maddison 1995). Accordingly, here I follow the recent scholarship in dating the widespread impact of economic globalization—defined as economic interaction beyond trade in a few goods and a small range of locations—as occurring sometime after 1800.

The Industrial Revolution brought about great change, although the direction of causation is far from clear. After about 1800, countries specialized in manufactures or primary products, and used imports to meet consumption needs. The process began with Britain, which became a net food importer early in the 19th century, and spread to other industrial countries. By contrast, another group of countries pursued comparative advantage in primary products and supplied the industrial countries with food and raw materials. This division of the world was radically new and predicated on exchange. It is a division whose legacy continues: the division of the world into nations that are producers and exporters of different types of goods, core and periphery, and rich and poor.

The Evidence

The evolution of world trade volumes speaks of this change in regime. Over the 19th century, the ratio of world trade to output increased from less than 2 percent to around 16 percent (see figure 2–1, where the trade ratio is measured as exports plus imports divided by output). Globally, the growth rate in world trade volume increased from about 1 percent a year in the 16th through 18th centuries to around 3 percent in the 19th and 20th centuries. Since the growth rate of world output in the 19th century was that much slower than in the 20th century, it was during the 19th century that the growth rate of trade-to-output ratios in the world reached its all-time peak. By this measure, the broad phenomenon of globalization arrived in the 19th century.[5]

Before 1800, just as the trade volumes were small, the large gaps in prices between exporting and importing markets also attest to the limited integration of world markets in this earlier era. International commodity markets for Asian exports—such as coffee, cloves, and

---

[5] The increase was more pronounced in those regions that were the earliest and most enthusiastic in embracing the trading and specialization opportunities. British trade rose from 8 to 16 percent of GDP during the 18th century (Crafts 1985), and Western Europe as a whole experienced an increase from 10 to 16 percent in the 19th century (Maddison 1995).

Figure 2–4

Spice and Coffee Markups: Sales Price in Amsterdam Compared with Purchase Price in Southeast Asia, 1580s–1900s

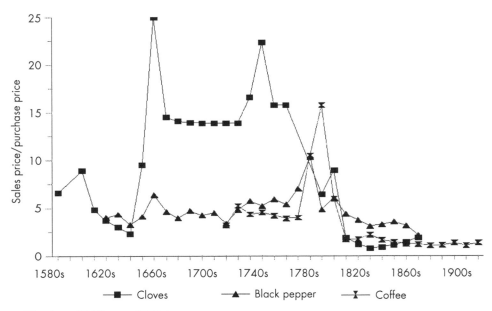

Source: O'Rourke and Williamson (2002c).

pepper—showed consistent 5-fold to 20-fold differences between the high European and low Asian prices from the 1580s to the 1820s. Only thereafter did prices begin systematically to converge, bringing gaps into the 3:1 or 2:1 range. By 1900, gaps of less than 100 percent and tending to 0 were the norm (figure 2–4).

In this respect, the exotic high-value commodities joined in the same marked price convergence during the late 19th century that was common to a much wider range of primary products and manufactures (such as cotton, see figure 2–5). Widespread commodity price convergence is one definition of globalization, and this was one correlate of the vast expansion in the range and volume of goods traded and the international division according to comparative advantage that is a hallmark of the modern world economy.

In the 19th century, a 20-fold expansion in world trade volumes and a similar decline in typical commodity price gaps marked a break from the past. More formal quantitative analysis is needed on this regime change, but recent work confirms that the 19th-century world economy was radically different from what went before in its internal equilibrium allocation and price mechanisms.[6]

Increasingly, Britain and other industrial nations could "import" land—land embodied in food imports—leaving the local economy free to pursue a logical specialization in activities better suited to a land-scarce region. The typical quantitative equilibrium characteristic of a closed economy thus began to be replaced with standard features found in an open economy.

---

[6] For example, econometric evidence shows that in a country such as Britain, internal factor prices became de-linked from local factor supplies, in particular the supposed land constraint that frightened Malthusians (O'Rourke and Williamson 2002c).

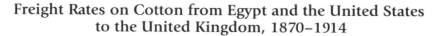

Freight Rates on Cotton from Egypt and the United States to the United Kingdom, 1870–1914

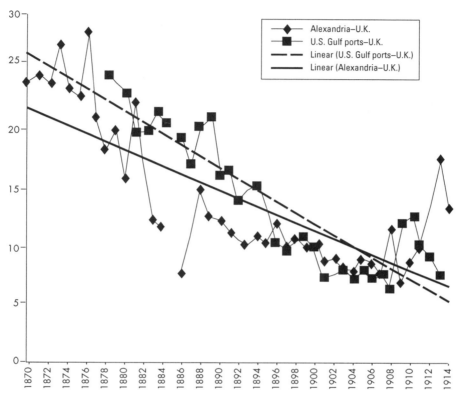

Source: O'Rourke and Williamson (2002b).

Local factor prices were soon heavily influenced by world goods market conditions (O'Rourke, Taylor, and Williamson 1996).

The evidence points to the post-1800 period in world history as the era when the forces of globalization were truly unleashed. This is also the era that coincides with the rapid acceleration in living standards associated with "modern economic growth" following the Industrial Revolution. The coincidence of these two events warrants further discussion below; the same problems of interpretation affect both phenomena.

Scholars studying the Industrial Revolution have argued incessantly about how it happened, even whether it happened and, especially, why it happened when and where it did. The "revolutionary" and "evolutionary" views of the Industrial Revolution argue not only about the size of the break from the past, but also the nature of causation. Was there a unique confluence of events found in Britain circa 1760 that made industrialization happen? Or were centuries of economic, political, legal, social, and institutional changes responsible in a drawn-out chain of cumulative causation?[7]

---

[7] The cumulative view favors a study of diverse preindustrial developments, such as the Magna Carta, the Glorious Revolution, the patent system, the enclosure movement, and the stock and bond markets—events and features that spread over time but eventually came together as a complete foundation for growth.

These same issues should lead to consideration of a broad sweep of time in identifying the foundations of today's international integration. In studying the history of globalization, even recognizing the importance of dates like 1492 and 1815, allowance for cumulative causation requires seeking out important interstitial developments between the benchmark dates. This reveals evidence on the full set of ingredients that, in periods and places when they were properly assembled, have allowed globalization to flourish so rapidly at certain times in the past two centuries.

An obvious lesson from the last millennium for today's policymakers in developing countries is that progress can be slow. Single cases of reform or isolated institutional changes do not seem to have made for a dramatic switch for or against globalization in past eras. Instead, the slow accrual of various fundamentals laid the basis for an expansion of trade and the benefits that could derive from it. History is relevant here in that a number of these same fundamentals seem to be still lacking in many developing countries even today.

INSTITUTIONAL HURDLES: MAKING THE WORLD SAFE FOR TRADE

Cutting a Deal and the Risks of Trade

An economic impulse to trade is not enough to get globalization started. With few local exceptions, trade does not occur in a vacuum. This is especially clear today in many developing countries, and it was true in the past in all premodern economies. Of course, the form and extent of institutional development will strongly influence the level of trade, if any, that can be supported.

For example, starting an import-export business calls for more than just a profitable arbitrage opportunity between two locations. Along the way, in each place, it might require legally incorporating the business, completing paperwork, satisfying regulations, employing the legal or customary currencies in use, and paying taxes and tariffs. Trade is thus embedded in a variety of institutional structures: legal, social, and political. Some examples help to introduce the issues and motivate a look back at history.

Consider first the problem of contract-based exchange. Many developing countries today have poor legal and contractual bases for economic exchange, such that it is extremely difficult to trade anonymously, with new counter parties, at a distance, or when payment is delayed. Medieval traders in the Mediterranean were the precursors to this problem. There, traders often had to work across spatially and institutionally separate entities, such as the major city-states and ports of Italy, like Genoa, Naples, and Venice. Even within a city, legal shortcomings might mean that trade was not protected as well as it is under modern systems of commercial law. But between political units, the extent of supranational standards and enforcement was practically nonexistent. Given such obstacles, how could the beginnings of a world economy be traced to this period?

Recent research emphasizes that in this era, important private-sector institutional developments could support *some* trade in equilibrium, although not necessarily the optimal level of trade (Greif 1993, forthcoming; Greif, Milgrom, and Weingast 1994). This strand of new institutional history uses game theory to focus on the emergence of self-enforcing and incentive-compatible relationships between actors that can allow some of the gains from trade to materialize. With sufficient gains at stake, trade may be supported subject to the existence of adequate and credible punishments of defectors (for example, in the event of deviations like default). Even in dispersed commercial networks, such as the Maghribi traders studied by Greif, the value of reputation and the presence of reliable enough communications could allow traders to sanction those guilty of malfeasance and enforce contractual honesty to some degree.

On the one hand, this is an optimistic lesson from history for present-day scenarios in which the fear, at least for the pro-global school of thought, is that many poor nations today might miss out on the benefits of globalization, through political malfunction or geographic isolation or infrastructural malaise. If trade simply passes them by, they will not connect to the world economy and gain the presumed benefits of trade. Despite such obstacles, history suggests they may still gain some of the benefits: some trade can occur even when institutions are weak. On the other hand, an equally distinguished branch of institutional history warns that although such trade may exist, it is likely to be far from optimal in the absence of a strong state that can offer better institutional foundations for exchange. In a paradox, despite the need for such strength on the part of the state, the state must be assumed not to prey upon trade, but rather to support it.[8]

Economic historians and political scientists focus on this issue because of the shifting locus of power in medieval and early modern states. It is of interest here because changes in the political center of gravity have often accompanied changes in legal, regulatory, or ownership patterns that affect important economic units engaged in trade. Scholars have noted, for example, the important limits placed on the crown as being instrumental in promoting private economic activity. We include here the willingness of a less mercantilist state to permit freer trade without high tariffs or tight customs control, to exercise fiscal rectitude and limit erratic economic policies, or to support a banking and financial system and develop financial markets.

The history of the developments in trade and finance can be traced back many centuries. And while the process illustrates again the rapid changes in some of the costs associated with trade, the institutional changes along the way could not have taken place without a change in the political economy of these countries' economic systems. I align this change in the spirit of the process with the realization by some states, at least the successful ones, that a mutually beneficial relationship with merchant trade and finance was an essential component in the domestic and, even more, the international success of the polity. Ferguson (2001) documents that the financial acumen of the political leaders, as much as the technological prowess of the industrialists, helped put the British state in an imperial leadership role in the 19th century.

Most historical literature focuses on the domestic impact of such institutional change. If such changes mattered domestically, they also breathed life into international commerce. For example, capital market activity linking London and Amsterdam grew shortly after the Glorious Revolution with the founding of the modern stock exchanges. These institutions laid important foundations for the commercial supremacy of the Dutch and British empires, and they underscore the point that the crown's ambition may have been served in the larger sense through important self-restraint with respect to the abuse of some key economic entities (North and Weingast 1989; O'Brien 1998; Dickson 1967; Neal 1990).

---

[8] Various theorists have studied the nature of such state formation, and under what conditions a beneficent or predatory state may emerge from anarchy or banditry (Olson 2000; Moselle and Polak 2001). Depending on the relative power of different interest groups within the polity, such a state may take on different institutional forms, for example with respect to legal structure (Glaeser and Shleifer 2000).

Trade Follows Finance? The Problems of Payments and Currencies

Many premodern economies lacked institutional innovation, such as the self-restraint of the state, a situation that continues today in some of the world's poorest countries. It is hard to know how much trade can be supported without such control. Yet, even when the state provides this public good, it is still a long leap to put in place all of the other public and private institutional innovations that, say, built up the foundations for trade in the 17th and 18th centuries.

In those eras, many of today's industrial countries grappled with key macroeconomic problems of monetary and fiscal stability and the operation of capital markets, and confronted these challenges only through some painful experiences. These issues may have once seemed only indirectly related to trade, but they are now considered fundamental. For developing countries today, stabilization and credit rehabilitation are the short-term goals in any crisis management scenario, and without such a platform to enable basic economic functions to be served, talk of a trade strategy seems premature.

What are the essential components of a good financial system that not only supports domestic economic activity, but exploits international gains from trade? Rousseau and Sylla (2002) identify five key ingredients:

- Sound public finance, an end in itself, but also historically one of the precursors to a broad-based financial system—an active and reputable government bond market tending to predate the development of commercial debt and securities markets
- A stable currency, since the retardation of financial systems often results from a volatile and unreliable currency, as nominal contracting becomes ever riskier
- The development of banks and banking, which soundly expand the narrow money base into a broader credit supply by their well-chosen use of leverage in the transformation of assets
- The establishment of a sound central bank, which regulates the money supply, monitors the banking sector, and also creates payment-clearing functions
- The evolution of securities markets, in which specialized institutions such as investment banks intermediate in equity and debt markets.

Such a combination of factors is indeed rare, limited to only a few industrial economies today. As late as 1914, it could be argued that only six economies had succeeded in all these dimensions: France, Germany, Great Britain, Japan, the Netherlands, and the United States. But while observers usually point to these factors as evidence of the finance-growth nexus, the combination also supports the idea that finance can promote trade. The six countries mentioned were significant players in world trade in the late 19th century, and narrative histories that recount how they arrived at that position emphasize the ties between commercial and financial activity that placed a high probability on such an outcome.

Looking back to the early Renaissance, deposit banks arose in Florence, and merchants first used paper as a substitute for gold coin. Once these instruments became negotiable, like primitive checks, they vastly simplified trade by removing the need to carry inconvenient metals that were an invitation to theft. Bills of exchange reached the wider market for trade in Europe and the world via the spread of this innovation to the banks of Amsterdam and London, the ports and financial centers that handled a large share of world trade at that time.

As the British economy became dominant in the 18th and 19th centuries, and as London emerged as the principal world financial center, the sterling bill rose to prominence as the world standard for international payments in trade. At the same time, financial complexity grew with the development of larger banks (such as the Wisselbank in Amsterdam or the Bank of England in London), bond markets (an innovation of a British government desperate for war finance), stock exchanges (Amsterdam and London circa 1680), and complicated financial derivative products (options were created less than a decade after the London stock exchange opened in the 1680s).

In the political economy of this symbiotic relationship between trade and finance, the market endorses the state as much as vice versa. The currency market remains as perhaps the most transparent and debated mechanism for financial markets to "discipline" governments. An old tradition in the economic history literature points to the role of a commitment to stable money, usually taken to mean the gold standard in the 19th century, as a way for governments to earn reputation benefits. Bordo and Rockoff (1996) demonstrate that the effect of joining gold was usually to lower country risk, thus boosting investment from overseas and promoting growth. Although gold no longer exists as a currency standard, the same macroeconomic stability criteria still guide bond spreads in today's capital market, so that exchange-rate floaters need to pay attention to essentially the same monetary and fiscal policy fundamentals.[9]

There may be other beneficial results of choices that condition macroeconomic policy in an open economy environment. Just as a currency standard might have capital market spillovers, it might promote trade. Recent work by Rose (2000) and others shows that common currencies appear to be highly significant in explaining higher trade volumes in contemporary data, boosting trade by a factor of three or more, ceteris paribus, in a gravity-model setting. Can such a large impact be believed? Historical data supply helpful corroboration here. Studies of trade and the gold standard explore this currency-trade relationship for the significant core and periphery economies of the globalized late-19th-century economy.[10] The results indicate large common-currency effects on trade. Joining the gold standard from 1870 to 1914 might have boosted trade by 30 to 50 percent, ceteris paribus, and by a similar amount even in the 1920s, which is arguably a much more reasonable magnitude than Rose's (2000) factor of 200 percent.[11]

This brief tour of history highlights a few points of economic significance. Public finance, and its intersection with monetary and fiscal policy, sets the institutional stage for international as well as domestic market transactions. Institutional change that buttresses these areas can promote growth and trade. Such institutional change might be self-strengthening, self-sacrificial, or self-disciplining, as in the case of adherence to new policy rules. A most attractive hand-tying exercise in the late 19th century relied on such a sacrifice to be rewarded by network externality property of the global payments system. As with a software standard, once many agents are using a particular currency, everyone else will want to use the same currency to lower their transaction costs and boost trade.

---

[9] Obstfeld and Taylor (2002) expand the Bordo-Rockoff methodology to a broader sample of countries and time periods, including the interwar period. They find that reputations were hard to build in the sense that country risk was highly persistent. However, the persistence dropped greatly after 1914, suggesting that reputation was then frittered away; the interwar gold standard was, as many have suspected, a different animal than its pre-war cousin, with considerably less confidence in the system shown by markets (and, history shows, rightly so).

[10] A serious objection to contemporary studies notes their reliance on a small and obscure subset of common currency areas in current data to generate the result (for example, countries in the CFA franc zone in West Africa). The inference based on historical data is likely to be much more robust concerning the effects on large economies, and cleaner given that trade was less distorted by tariff and nontariff barriers.

[11] See Eichengreen and Irwin (1995); Estevadeordal, Frantz, and Taylor (2003); and López-Córdova and Meissner (2001).

Empirical evidence suggests that trade and macroeconomic policies deeply intersect on this issue, and trends in recent regional and global initiatives show that the compatibility of trade and macro-finance policies is starting to be taken seriously. Fixed exchange rates are not a panacea, but narrative evidence on the importance of currency standards, like the sterling bill in early modern trade, and econometric evidence on the classical gold standard and contemporary common currencies suggests that currencies do matter. Such imperatives guided the economic case for the European Monetary Union, and developing countries will likely explore similar options.

INPUT TRADE STRATEGIES: DO-IT-YOURSELF COMPARATIVE ADVANTAGE?

This section turns to developments in the modern era and those extensions of globalization and trade that, from the historical point of view, might have mattered most for long-run economic outcomes. I take an unusual line in that I do not focus on trade in final goods.

In the past decade, a vast literature has explored the growth-promoting effects of goods trade, with little agreement about the result.[12] From another vantage point, it also proves to be very difficult to find any strong consensus in the historical literature concerning the impact of trade barriers on growth, absent a few recent noteworthy contributions. And even there, the effects often seem to run counter to conventional wisdom.[13]

Given that the jury is still out on the question of whether protection of final goods was bad for growth, I emphasize two areas where history seems to tell powerful stories about the constraints the immobility not of goods, but of factors, imposed on growth. According to conventional theories of trade and growth, the availability of intermediate inputs matters for allocation, specialization, and accumulation. These issues, in one form or another, face developing countries today, but they also stood as a challenge to many economies during the last era of globalization a century ago.

Resource Trade: The End of Geography?

Globalization implies that more and more economic objects become mobile: goods in trade, people through migration, and investment via the capital market. However, for a long time, geography dictated the structure of economic organization at some level because one fundamental set of inputs—natural resources such as agricultural land, forestry, minerals, ores, and fuels—remained immobile even as almost everything else became transportable. Naturally, this has led to speculation about the geographic determinants of economic activity in general and the Industrial Revolution in particular. According to an oversimplified version of this story, countries in Europe—especially France, Germany, and the United Kingdom—were destined to

---

[12] For example, Sachs and Warner (1995) make the case that openness promotes growth. Rodríguez and Rodrik (2000) provide a more skeptical view of the openness measure and whether it correlates with growth.

[13] For example, Vamvakidis (1997) finds that economic growth in the early 20th century was positively related to tariffs, controlling for other determinants; O'Rourke (2000) finds the same for the late 19th century in a small sample of countries. The consensus within economic history seems to be that these are puzzling and provocative results that warrant more attention and efforts to confirm their robustness. Nonetheless, for now they confirm the older assertions of Bairoch (1972) that from a 19th-century perspective it is hard to argue that tariffs were bad for growth, especially considering the impressive performance in that era of such protectionist bastions as the United States.

industrialize because they were lucky enough to have the relevant raw materials, including coal and iron ore (Landes 1969; Jones 1981; Pomeranz 2000).

The late 19th century provides a better range of data to formally test such a proposition. By examining disaggregated data on imports and exports, Wright (1990) exposes the resource-rich content of U.S. net exports during 1880–1930. This is a crucial finding, since it was at this time that the United States entered a rapid growth spurt, overtaking Britain and all other nations in terms of productivity and income per capita, and the sources of that spectacular growth demand explanation. The resource-led switch to industrial activity, in spite of its historic comparative advantage in primary products, allowed the United States to specialize in products with faster total factor productivity growth potential.

In the background here is a story of specialization driven by factor endowments, in the usual Heckscher-Ohlin style. Is such an assumption justified? The Heckscher-Ohlin theory has never worked that well when tested as a factor-content-of-trade model, but Estevadeordal and Taylor (2002) put forward an extended, albeit indirect, test of Wright's hypothesis. In the late 19th century, for a sample of 18 countries, they show that it was only for natural resources (both land and minerals) that the Heckscher-Ohlin theory fit reasonably well, whereas the fit was poor for labor and capital (see figure 2–6). Their results indicate that resources were an important determinant of comparative advantage globally and not just in the United States.

However, already by the dawn of the 20th century, this argument was losing steam. Even resource endowments began to overcome the "tyranny of distance" that had pinned them down for so long. By the mid-to-late 20th century, the lowered cost of transportation for raw materials fostered a group of newly industrializing countries (NICs) that had little in the way of the necessary local resource endowments. Vast amounts of Australia's land were shipped to Japan (because of a major postwar trade treaty in the 1950s) and (later) to the East Asian NICs on bulk carriers. Mineral ores from remote outback regions like the Kimberley and Pilbarra supply foreign steel plants with a vital input and prove that, in this day and age, even mountains can be moved.

But this trade is not so universal that resource endowments no longer matter. In practice, they matter because not every country has established either the required infrastructure or the necessary free commercial policy to reduce domestic resource prices to world levels. Geography surely matters. For example, a landlocked country will be hard-pressed to access Australian ore imports as easily as Japan and the East Asian NICs did in the past 50 years: those countries were fortunate enough to have developed deepwater ports. Thus, the significance of the landlocked dummy in many growth and gravity model equations seems entirely reasonable, although with appropriate transport developments via infrastructure investment, even this constraint can be broken. Ceteris paribus, such investments would not be efficient, but given the extremely low levels of development in poor, landlocked countries (and the attendant low wages), such developments could be beneficial in the right institutional setting.

Why should this matter for long-run outcomes? In a static model it will not matter, but in a dynamic model, specialization can matter for growth if countries can be trapped in slow-growing sectors by comparative advantage. Models such as Matsuyama's (1992) formalize this process. In that case, the intuition is that only one sector (call it "industry") has positive learning-by-doing externalities. The other (call it "agriculture") does not. Thus, any factor—an agricultural revolution, a commercial policy distortion, scarcity of minerals, or abundance of land—that promotes a shift in resources out of manufactures will harm long-run growth.[14]

---

[14] Of course, these kinds of results are built-in: they follow from the assumption that the sectors are asymmetric, and an endogenous growth process exists only in one and not both.

Figure 2–6

Resources and Comparative Advantage, Circa 1910

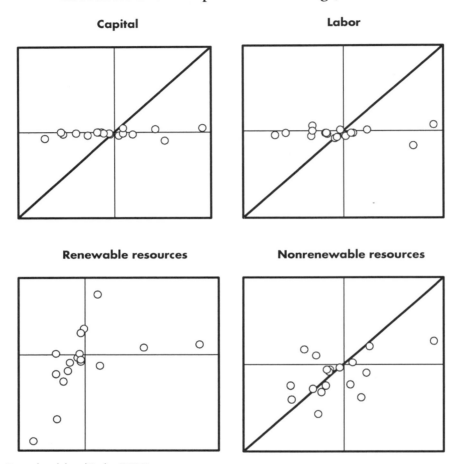

Source: Estevadeordal and Taylor (2002).

Capital Goods Trade: An Import-Led Growth Strategy?

The other type of input trade that history has a great deal to say about is trade in capital goods. One strand of the recent growth literature has recognized that capital goods may be an important channel for determining growth outcomes. De Long and Summers (1991) posit the existence of differential returns for equipment investment across countries arising from differences in commercial policies and other distortions. Jones (1994) embeds this finding in a model in which distortions on capital goods act as a tax on accumulation, and hence slow growth, and makes an example of India. Taylor (1994, 1998a, 1998b) explores the detailed econometrics of the price-investment nexus, using the postwar price-distortion policies in Argentina as a key exemplum. In such cases, tariff policies, if they protect capital goods more than other goods (consumption goods), can create a high relative price of capital, defined as P_K/P_Y, the price of capital goods relative to GDP. This will, in turn, bias the user cost of capital upward: even for the same interest rate, a project must yield a higher output stream to compensate for the expensive capital inputs that must be purchased locally.

Some of the variation in capital goods prices could be attributed to reverse causation (low productivity) coupled with the nontradability of capital goods (structures, for example). Still, Taylor (1998b) shows that in a cross section of countries, much of the variation in P_K/P_Y could be explained by commercial policy and capital controls, as proxied by policy measures such as tariffs and black market premia. This finding is consistent with a view that much capital equipment is tradable (and not just machinery and equipment—even the erecting of structures can be open to bidding from foreign firms).

Recent research that applies these insights to the last great era of globalization serves to strengthen this perspective on growth with tradable capital inputs. Collins and Williamson (1999) find great variation in capital goods prices in 1870–1939, and they use these data in a similar fashion to the postwar studies to see whether capital goods prices explain variations in investment ratios and growth. Indeed, they do, and the association proves to be robust in earlier epochs. An increase of 10 percent in capital goods prices could lower investment ratios by roughly 5 percentage points, a large impact.

To make this point more tangible, consider one of the famous cases of development "failure" from this period within the OECD, namely Australia. Once perhaps the richest economy in the world (if Maddison's [1995] data are to be believed), by the mid to late 20th century, this country had experienced negative growth relative to the OECD as a whole and compared with the United States in the lead. Indeed, such was the concern over this falling back that some commentators feared an Argentine-style outcome, with regression to middle-income status (Duncan and Fogarty 1984).

McLean and Taylor (2001) examine some features of the Australian case, and one fact that stands out is the coincidence of retardation from circa 1914, with a rapid increase in relative capital prices, especially compared with other OECD countries. Figure 2–7 shows this dramatic change and indicates that the origins of the trend can be traced back to the 1890s, a time when Australia embarked on import-substituting industrialization with aggressive use of tariff policy. By the 1920s and 1930s, the tariff's effects were compounded by the increase in global protectionism, leaving Australia, with no comparative advantage in machinery and equipment, facing capital goods prices that had increased by perhaps 50 percent compared with the United States.

This kind of analysis of the dynamic effects of trade policy is now beginning to influence policymaking. In a noteworthy recent example, then Argentine finance minister Domingo Cavallo decided to eliminate tariffs on capital goods and raise them on consumer goods in an attempt to reinvigorate the depressed Argentine economy.[15] Most likely, this policy has been overtaken for the moment by events such as the state's fiscal crisis and de facto default. It will be interesting to see whether this kind of plan will inspire imitators elsewhere. If so, then policy reforms that explicitly recognize the different static and dynamic tradeoffs in the protection of consumption and capital goods could be an important area in years ahead, although it remains to be seen what kind of institutional embedding will make such changes possible.

---

[15] This plan was explicitly intended to boost investment and hence growth, and attract foreign capital—exactly as the above academic research papers argue. It was a radical plan, and not without problems because it required unilateral actions that conflicted with Mercosur commitments. Nonetheless, domestic interests have prevailed, and restarting growth was seen to trump free trade area agreements.

Figure 2–7

The Relative Price of Capital in Five Countries, 1875–1950

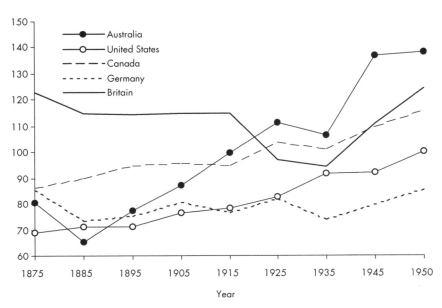

Source: McLean and Taylor (2001).

AND THE WINNER IS . . . ? A LONG VIEW OF POLITICAL ECONOMY AND TRADE

Trading Up or Trading Down? Globalization and Inequality

Trade, according to an old pedagogical device, is best thought of as just another technology. A production process in a factory turns inputs into outputs. But so does trade: the inputs are exports, and what comes out are imports. But like any technology, trade is subject to constant change, shifts that can benefit some countries more than others and some individuals more than others. A new mechanized way to produce textiles upset the Luddites (and had them breaking machines in protest), but the same irritations would have accompanied (indeed, do accompany) the sudden arrival of cheap textiles not from a new-fangled device, but simply out of the machinery of trade.

Similar technological analogies for globalization forces could easily be built around shifts in other markets, be it outflows of capital or inflows of immigrants (demonized for economic impacts as well as racial, ethnic, or cultural bias). But what are the facts? Looking at the views of either side, how accurate is the picture historically? History offers some neglected but relevant case studies.

For example, in the 19th century, beginning with the repeal of the Corn Laws in Europe, the free trade movement was a radical populist movement. It sought to release Old World working classes from low wages and high food prices (and symmetrically, to release landlords from low labor costs and high land rents). Labor exported itself from glutted markets, either literally (by migration) or implicitly (in labor-intensive goods exports); in the opposite direction, cheap food flooded in from the New World, an implicit import of land embodied in goods. As wages, rents, and prices adjusted, the real incomes of rich and poor converged. The other side to the story, of course, is that opposite effects obtained in the trading partners. Ceteris paribus, New World wages had to decline and land rents rise, as income distribution effects worked in the reverse direction (O'Rourke and Williamson 1999).

Lindert and Williamson (2002) provide some guidance on whether the major shifts in globalization and trade have had any temporal or causal association with inequality. These authors find that global inequality *between individuals* has increased over time since circa 1800, as shown in figure 2–8. However, all of this change is accounted for by the rise in *international* rather than *intranational* inequality. That is, the Great Divergence of national economic outcomes has had more to do with global inequality than have any within-country effects of changing economic factors in the past 200 years.

Admittedly, the data underlying these results are highly fragmentary and fragile, especially the attempt to compute global and national income distributions before 1950, and especially before 1900. Although built on heroic assumptions, this is still an original and important exercise in data collection and agglomeration. Taken at face value, the main result is, in and of itself, enough to cast doubt on many of the presumed channels through which today's critics imagine that globalization exacerbates within-country inequality.

For example, if the Heckscher-Ohlin framework is valid, there should be large changes in factor rewards, and hence inequality, whenever there is a major change in trading regime because different countries have great variation in endowments. Even an allowance for differ-

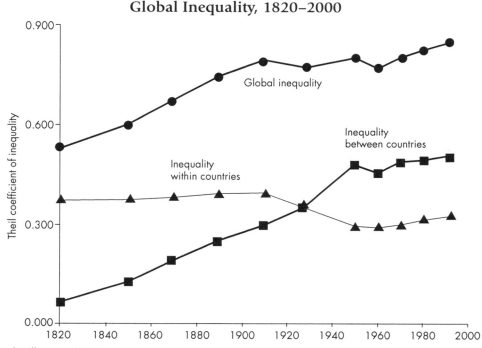

Figure 2-8

Global Inequality, 1820–2000

Source: Lindert and Williamson (2002).

ing technology levels between countries is entirely consistent with this result (Trefler 1993). Yet, the vast ups and downs in world trade integration over 200 years (figure 2–1) and the steady, long-run trend toward higher trade volumes appear to be little correlated with shifts in within-country income distributions (figure 2–8).

Similarly, we could construct arguments based on the rise and fall of international capital flows and labor migration in the 19th and 20th centuries to suggest that within-country inequality ought to have been disturbed by linkages in these markets too—when they functioned well before 1914 and when they did not function for most of the mid 20th century. Yet, again, there is no correlation. World within-country inequality did not systematically rise in the last great age of globalization, then fall during the 20th century anti-global reaction, and then rise again. Simply put, the relationship between globalization and inequality (and certainly between trade and inequality) is not that direct or clear-cut.

There are two possible reactions to the basic evidence. One is to believe that the linkage from trade to inequality is weak or nonexistent. This, I would argue, is an erroneous conclusion. The forces appear to be quite strong and statistically significant in well-focused historical studies that examine econometrically the links between changes in the terms of trade and changes in domestic factor prices. For example, the effects appear to be strong for both the industrial and developing world in the late 19th century (O'Rourke, Taylor, and Williamson 1996; Williamson 2002). It might just be that these effects, although strong, are swamped in quantitative significance by changes in between-country inequality, namely the Great Divergence. That is the message in figure 2–8.

A second conclusion might be, instead, to doubt the extent to which globalization has actually been allowed to proceed to its fullest extent. Perhaps trade would change global inequality if it were allowed to proceed without barriers, but as yet it has not been permitted to reach that level. In those areas of the world that participated in the globalization of the pre-1914 era, trade drove radical shifts in income distribution. In the New World, land rents rose as the land was embodied in food and exported. In Europe, the opposite forces were at work when the food arrived. In the former case, landowners gained, but in the latter they faced large losses in income.

Since this chapter is concerned with the potential implications of globalization for developing countries, it looks for specific historical precedents for the Heckscher-Ohlin story. Such experience was not limited to a few rich countries participating in the global economy of the late 19th century. Similar impacts of trade on income distribution were seen in both labor-rich and labor-scarce developing countries of that era in the Middle East, South Asia, and Latin America. In a labor-abundant country, such as Thailand, for example, opening up to the world economy meant that the poorest laborers gained enormously compared with the owners of scarce land, implying a dramatic leveling of the country's income distribution (Williamson 2002).

The lesson here is that when globalization forces operate, they may have egalitarian impacts in some countries and inegalitarian impacts in others (Wood 1994). However, moving beyond the artificial confines of a nation-state view of the world, the bottom line should be clear. Overall, globalization is one of the few forces that has *offset* global inequality for 200 years, with trade and factor markets allowing identical factors a better chance of earning the same reward in spatially separate locations. Those rewards might have diverged even further had spillovers from the Great Divergence in technology levels been kept more closely confined within the borders of the rich countries. Yet there, too, global technology transfer, although imperfect and incomplete, has prevented even starker inequality, and its mechanisms undoubtedly rely on imitation and adaptation through trade links and inward investment.

Yet, what might seem like good news from a global utilitarian point of view does not, of course, translate into a simple local or regional embrace of open economy policies. The political economy of nation-states drives policies, and if free trade were beneficial, it would not offer a Pareto improvement in welfare terms without redistribution. If such compensation were imperfect, winning coalitions (or minority but powerful lobbies) might be able to block any shift to more open policies.

History shows that such distributional conflicts can be a serious obstacle to trade, even under the most sympathetic circumstances. In continental Europe, powerful landed interests were resistant to the grain invasion from the New World and successfully fought for protection, as compared with the liberal tradition in England, where the landed class was once and for all defeated with the repeal of the Corn Laws in the 1840s. In the New World, owners of the abundant land resource generally could push for lower trade barriers in polities where their voices dominated political discourse (for example, in the South in the United States or in Argentina), compared with other places (for example, in the North in the United States or in Australia). Outcomes usually reflected this voice, the sectional clash of economic interests in the United States being a vivid intranational example of such conflict where the battle lines were clearly drawn (Rogowski 1989).

History thus illuminates present-day challenges that are more acute now that the safety valve of migration is largely closed off. Trade might ease inequality in poor countries if it allows abundant low-skilled labor an out, but it could have the opposite effect on income differentials in rich countries flooded by unskilled labor. The trade-off depends on the observer's worldview, whether it is nationalistic or a global concern for income distribution or other economic objectives. The impacts also spell out clear policies to offset inequitable effects in richer countries, where low-skilled workers face the severest competition from workers in developing countries: policies should aim to educate, train, or otherwise lift skill levels to differentiate local from foreign workers.

As figure 2–8 shows, the far more important determinant of an individual's relative income level is not globalization per se, but rather the Great Divergence. History suggests that the impacts of the Heckscher-Ohlin forces are in the long run of a much smaller magnitude than the massive spreads due to levels of total factor productivity or technology. This historically informed perspective ought to be central to the globalization debate, but it only infrequently surfaces in political discourse, perhaps most famously in the 1994 Perot-Gore debate over NAFTA (in the United States). Perot protested that U.S. workers were doomed because Mexican workers earned a wage one-fifth as high. Gore, obviously primed for that point, shot back that there was nothing to fear at all because Mexican workers were only one-fifth as productive as American workers.

Not merely a talk-show sound bite, this observation captures an enduring feature of the world economy. We know that fundamental differences in raw worker productivities are a longstanding, ineluctable feature of the world economy. As Clark (1987) shows, in 1910 one U.S. textile worker could work as effectively as 1.5 British workers or six Indian or Chinese workers. Open trade will make some marginal differences, but it will not, say, reduce U.S. wage levels to the levels in less developed countries, and the technology-augmented Heckscher-Ohlin model shows why (Trefler 1993).

Whether globalization, broadly construed, will lead to convergence in these worker efficiency levels, and whether trade might be one of its channels, remain to be seen. How large a role can trade play? One way to put an upper bound on that is to imagine trade acting as a perfect substitute for factor market integration, and to ask what such integration would imply. In reality, integration is a much less than perfect substitute, but suppose that the thought experiment stands (Collins, O'Rourke, and Williamson 1999).

Globalization in factor markets, albeit imperfect, could stimulate movement partway toward convergence because differences in physical/human capital intensity are substantial across countries. Yet, according to Hall and Jones (1999), in the language of Ak models, the differences in technology (A) still account for two-thirds of international divergence, and differences in capital intensity (k) for only one-third. Others place even greater emphasis on A (Easterly and Levine 1999).[16] Since, to some degree, k is endogenous, given A, this might underestimate the role of factor convergence versus productivity convergence. Several scholars find evidence of both forces working equally strongly for the OECD (Milbourne 1995; Dowrick and Rogers 2001). If these forces were unleashed at a global level, at least some of the Great Divergence might finally start to reverse. If trade is a channel for this, or even for transmitting technology convergence, then global inequality may owe more to the lack of trade than to its presence.

Convergence Postponed in the 20th Century: Detour or Portent?

Compared with long-run trends in globalization, the 20th-century economic experience has been a historical aberration: the only sustained period in the past several centuries when trends in the growth of world trade, and globalization more generally, were put in reverse.

Some authors, like Polanyi (1944), could write half a century ago with great conviction that indeed the world had entered a new age in which global markets would play second fiddle to the state. Now that statement appears premature, since the forces that unleashed trade—the economic impulse, the institutional foundations, and the technological advances—seem quite durable, even after some of the most disruptive global political shocks history has ever seen. Instead, the past century could be seen as a major hiatus in which the gradual unification of the world economy was put on hold.

Yet, even if technological fundamentals are in place, such as efficient transport infrastructure or essential legal institutions, political will is needed too. The first era of globalization began in an era of highly unrepresentative government (figure 2–9). Did this make the process any easier? Can today's democratically chosen governments afford the long view? It is possible, if the gains from trade are there and the winners adequately compensate the losers in the short run. But the history of trade as a development strategy is the story of an evolving process, in which winners may appear later, losers perhaps earlier, and the payoffs to innovation may be slow and contingent.

All these factors are at odds with planning horizons dictated more by politics and popular opinion in the short run. That being said, the return toward a more globalized system in recent years also parallels a rise in representative government. Thus, at the level of raw correlation, these problems do not appear overwhelming so far, although the political tensions on the street are increasingly palpable.

As the 21st century opens, it seems close to rejoining, at least in some areas, the trend toward global integration that lasted for several centuries before 1913. This is not to say that a

---

[16] In an Ak model, income per capita is $y=Ak$, where A is technology and k is a measure of composite capital (physical and human) per person. Crucially, all such inputs can be accumulated and show no diminishing returns.

Figure 2–9

The Rise of Democracy, 1800–2000

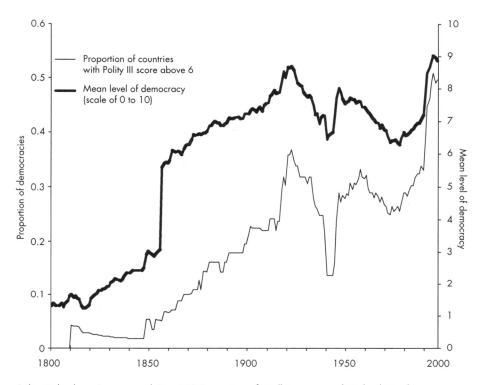

Legend:
— Proportion of countries with Polity III score above 6
— Mean level of democracy (scale of 0 to 10)

Source: Polity III database (Jaggers and Gurr 1995), courtesy of Niall Ferguson and Michael Ward.

future detour, another serious setback to globalization, will not appear. Yet the past provides warnings about the kind of events that may trigger such a backlash, from geopolitical conflicts and distrust to economic policies that disregard inclusion by focusing on the winners from globalization and neglecting the losers. The technological basis for trade is strong; doubt arises as to whether the institutional bases determined by political economy will be allowed to weaken once again.

A successful transition to a globalized world promises more individual freedom, economic and otherwise, and greater opportunities for all in the end. How to get there from here presents plenty of pitfalls. History reveals how costly distractions can be, but also how and why to guard against them.

REFERENCES

Angell, Norman. 1910. *The Great Illusion.* London, UK: W. Heinemann.

Bairoch, Paul. 1972. Free Trade and European Economic Development in the 19th Century. *European Economic Review* 3: 211–45.

Bordo, Michael D., and Hugh Rockoff. 1996. The Gold Standard as a "Good Housekeeping Seal of Approval." *Journal of Economic History* 56(2): 389–428.

Chiswick, Barry R., and Timothy J. Hatton. 2002. International Migration and the Integration of Labor Markets. In M. D. Bordo, A. M. Taylor, and J. G. Williamson (eds.), *Globalization in Historical Perspective.* Chicago, IL: University of Chicago Press.

Clark, G. 1987. Why Isn't the Whole World Developed? Lessons from the Cotton Mills. *Journal of Economic History* 47(1): 141–73.

Collins, William J., Kevin H. O'Rourke, and Jeffrey G. Williamson. 1999. Were Trade and Factor Mobility Substitutes in History? In R. Faini, J. De Melo, and K. F. Zimmermann (eds.), *Migration: The Controversies and the Evidence.* Cambridge, UK: Cambridge University Press.

Collins, William J., and Jeffrey G. Williamson. 1999. *Capital Goods Prices, Global Capital Markets and Accumulation: 1870–1950.* Working Paper 7145, National Bureau of Economic Research, Cambridge, MA.

Crafts, N. F. R. 1985. *British Economic Growth during the Industrial Revolution.* Oxford, UK: Clarendon Press.

De Long, J. Bradford, and Lawrence H. Summers. 1991. Equipment Investment and Economic Growth. *Quarterly Journal of Economics* 106(2): 445–502.

Dickson, P. G. M. 1967. *The Financial Revolution in England: A Study in the Development of Public Credit, 1688–1756.* London, UK: St. Martin's Press.

Dowrick, Steve, and Mark Rogers. 2001. Classical and Technological Convergence: Beyond the Solow-Swan Growth Model. Australian National University, Faculty of Economics and Commerce. Unpublished.

Duncan, Tim, and John Fogarty. 1984. *Argentina and Australia: On Parallel Paths.* Carlton, Australia: Melbourne University Press.

Easterly, William, and Ross Levine. 1999. It's Not Factor Accumulation: Stylized Facts and Growth Models. World Bank, Washington, DC. Unpublished.

Eichengreen, Barry J., and Douglas A. Irwin. 1995. Trade Blocs, Currency Blocs and the Reorientation of World Trade in the 1930s. *Journal of International Economics* 38(1): 1–24.

Estevadeordal, Antoni, Brian Frantz, and Alan M. Taylor. 2003. The Rise and Fall of World Trade, 1870–1939. *Quarterly Journal of Economics* 118.

Estevadeordal, Antoni, and Alan M. Taylor. 2002. A Century of Missing Trade? *American Economic Review* 92(1, March): 383–93.

Ferguson, Niall. 2001. *The Cash Nexus: Money and Power in the Modern World, 1700–2000.* New York, NY: Basic Books.

Findlay, Ronald, and Kevin H. O'Rourke. 2002. Commodity Market Integration, 1500–2000. In M. D. Bordo, A. M. Taylor, and J. G. Williamson (eds.), *Globalization in Historical Perspective.* Chicago, IL: University of Chicago Press.

Fukuyama, F. 1992. *The End of History and the Last Man.* New York, NY: Free Press.

Glaeser, Edward L., and Andrei Shleifer. 2000. Legal Origins. Harvard University, Cambridge, MA. Unpublished.

Gray, John. 1998. *False Dawn: The Delusions of Global Capitalism.* London, UK: Granta Books.

Greider, William. 1997. *One World, Ready or Not: The Manic Logic of Global Capitalism.* New York, NY: Simon and Schuster.

Greif, Avner. 1993. Contract Enforceability and Economic Institutions in Early Trade: The Maghribi Traders Coalition. *American Economic Review* 83(3, June): 525–48.

———. Forthcoming. *Genoa and the Maghribi Traders: Historical and Comparative Institutional Analysis.* Cambridge, UK: Cambridge University Press.

Greif, Avner, Paul Milgrom, and Barry Weingast. 1994. Coordination, Commitment and Enforcement: The Case of the Merchant Guild. *Journal of Political Economy* 102(4, August): 745–76.

Hall, Robert E., and Charles I. Jones. 1999. Why Do Some Countries Produce So Much More Output Per Worker than Others? *Quarterly Journal of Economics* 114(1): 83–116.

Hertz, Noreena. 2001. *The Silent Takeover: Global Capitalism and the Death of Democracy.* London, UK: Heinemann.

Huntington, Samuel P. 1996. *The Clash of Civilizations and the Remaking of World Order.* New York, NY: Simon and Schuster.

Jaggers, K., and T. R. Gurr. 1995. Tracking Democracy's Third Wave with the Polity III Data. *Journal of Peace Research* 32(4): 469–82.

Jones, Charles I. 1994. Economic Growth and the Relative Price of Capital. *Journal of Monetary Economics* 34 (December): 359–82.

Jones, Eric L. 1981. *The European Miracle.* Cambridge, UK: Cambridge University Press.

Klein, Naomi. 1999. *No Logo: Taking Aim at the Brand Bullies.* Toronto, Ontario: Vintage Canada.

Landes, D. S. 1969. *The Unbound Prometheus: Technological Change and Industrial Development in Western Europe from 1750 to the Present.* Cambridge, UK: Cambridge University Press.

Lindert, Peter H., and Jeffrey G. Williamson. 2002. Does Globalization Make the World More Unequal? In M. D. Bordo, A. M. Taylor, and J. G. Williamson (eds.), *Globalization in Historical Perspective.* Chicago, IL: University of Chicago Press.

López-Córdova, J. Ernesto, and Chris Meissner. 2001. Exchange-Rate Regimes and International Trade: Evidence from the Classical Gold Standard Era. U.C. Berkeley, Berkeley, CA. Unpublished.

Maddison, Angus. 1995. *Monitoring the World Economy 1820–1992.* OECD Development Center, Paris.

Matsuyama, Kiminori. 1992. Agricultural Productivity, Comparative Advantage, and Economic Growth. *Journal of Economic Theory* 58: 317–34.

McLean, Ian W., and Alan M. Taylor. 2001. *Australian Growth: A California Perspective.* Working Paper 8408, National Bureau of Economic Research, Cambridge, MA.

Micklethwait, John, and Adrian Wooldridge. 2000. *A Future Perfect: The Challenge and Hidden Promise of Globalization.* New York, NY: Crown Business.

Milbourne, Ross. 1995. Factor Convergence versus Productivity Convergence. University of New South Wales, Sydney, Australia. Unpublished.

Monbiot, George. 2000. *The Captive State: The Corporate Takeover of Britain*. London, UK: Macmillan.

Moselle, Boaz, and Benjamin Polak. 2001. A Model of a Predatory State. *Journal of Law, Economics and Organization* 17(1).

Neal, Larry. 1990. *The Rise of Financial Capitalism: International Capital Markets in the Age of Reason*. Cambridge, UK: Cambridge University Press.

North, Douglass C., and Barry R. Weingast. 1989. Constitutions and Commitment: The Evolution of Institutions Governing Public Choice in Seventeenth-Century England. *Journal of Economic History* 49(4): 803–32.

O'Brien, Patrick K. 1998. Inseparable Connections: Trade, Economy, Fiscal State and the Expansion of Empire, 1688–1815. In W. R. Louis, A. M. Low, N. P. Canny, and P. J. Marshall (eds.), *The Oxford History of the British Empire*. Oxford, UK: Oxford University Press.

Obstfeld, Maurice, and Alan M. Taylor. 2002. Globalization and Capital Markets. In M. D. Bordo, A. M. Taylor, and J. G. Williamson (eds.), *Globalization in Historical Perspective*. Chicago, IL: University of Chicago Press.

Olson, Jr., Mancur. 2000. *Power and Prosperity: Outgrowing Communist and Capitalist Dictatorships*. New York, NY: Basic Books.

O'Rourke, Kevin H. 2000. Tariffs and Growth in the Late 19th Century. *Economic Journal* 110: 456–83.

O'Rourke, Kevin H., Alan M. Taylor, and Jeffrey G. Williamson. 1996. Factor Price Convergence in the Late Nineteenth Century. *International Economic Review* 37(3): 499–530.

O'Rourke, Kevin H., and Jeffrey G. Williamson. 1999. *Globalization and History: The Evolution of a Nineteenth-Century Atlantic Economy*. Cambridge, MA: MIT Press.

———. 2002a. After Columbus: Explaining the European Overseas Trade Boom 1500–1800. *Journal of Economic History*. Forthcoming.

———. 2002b. The Heckscher-Ohlin Model between 1400 and 2000: When It Explained Factor Price Convergence, When It Didn't, and Why. In R. Findlay, L. Jonung, and M. Lundahl (eds.), *Bertil Ohlin: A Centennial Celebration, 1899–1999*. Cambridge, MA: MIT Press. Forthcoming.

———. 2002c. When Did Globalization Begin? *European Review of Economic History*. Forthcoming.

Polanyi, Karl. 1944. *The Great Transformation*. New York, NY: Rinehart.

Pomeranz, Kenneth. 2000. *The Great Divergence: Europe, China, and the Making of the Modern World Economy*. Princeton, NJ: Princeton University Press.

Rodríguez, Francisco, and Dani Rodrik. 2000. Trade Policy and Economic Growth: A Skeptic's Guide to Cross-National Evidence. In B. S. Bernanke and K. Rogoff (eds.), *NBER Macroeconomics Annual 2001*. Cambridge, MA: MIT Press.

Rogowski, Ronald. 1989. *Commerce and Coalitions: How Trade Affects Domestic Political Alignments*. Princeton, NJ: Princeton University Press.

Rose, Andrew K. 2000. One Money, One Market: The Effect of Common Currencies on Trade. *Economic Policy* 15(30): 7–33.

Rousseau, Peter L., and Richard E. Sylla. 2002. Financial Systems, Economic Growth, and Globalization. In M. D. Bordo, A. M. Taylor, and J. G. Williamson (eds.), *Globalization in Historical Perspective*. Chicago, IL: University of Chicago Press.

Sachs, Jeffrey D., and Andrew M. Warner. 1995. Economic Reform and the Process of Global Integration. *Brookings Papers on Economic Activity* 1: 1–118.

Taylor, Alan M. 1994. Tres fases del crecimiento económico argentino. *Revista de Historia Económica* 12(3): 649–83.

———. 1998a. Argentina and the World Capital Market: Saving, Investment, and International Capital Mobility in the Twentieth Century. *Journal of Development Economics* 57(1): 147–84.

———. 1998b. On the Costs of Inward-Looking Development: Price Distortions, Growth, and Divergence in Latin America. *Journal of Economic History* 58(1): 1–28.

Trefler, Daniel. 1993. International Factor Price Differences: Leontief Was Right! *Journal of Political Economy* 101(6): 961–87.

Vamvakidis, Athanasios. 1997. How Robust Is the Growth-Openness Connection? Historical Evidence. Harvard University, Cambridge, MA. Unpublished.

Williamson, Jeffrey G. 2002. Land, Labor, and Globalization in the Pre-Industrial Third World. *Journal of Economic History*. Forthcoming.

Wood, Adrian. 1994. *North-South Trade, Employment, and Inequality: Changing Fortunes in a Skill-Driven World*. Oxford, UK: Clarendon Press.

Wright, Gavin. 1990. The Origins of American Industrial Success, 1879–1940. *American Economic Review* 80(4): 651–68.

Chapter 3

Regionalism and Economic Development

Anthony J. Venables

Effective participation in the world economy is an important—probably necessary—element in a successful development strategy. What is the role of regional integration in this strategy? Should a developing country focus on the world as a whole, or is there scope for concentrating on integration with selected regional partners?

Regional integration could play several different roles. It could provide an alternative to a global strategy. In the 1960s and 1970s, some countries pursued the model of regional integration behind high external tariff walls, but later abandoned that model as a failure. Another possibility is that a country could pursue regionalism in parallel with a liberal external trade policy. Although regionalism is inherently preferential, it may be able to proceed at a more rapid rate, and achieve deeper integration compared with trade relationships with the world at large. Furthermore, regionalism could be a preparatory stage for wider liberalization. A country could develop trade links with partner countries as a stepping-stone to full participation in the global economy.

This chapter argues that regionalism can be a valuable part of a development strategy, although its contribution depends on the form the agreement takes. Choice of partners is important. The benefits from South-South integration schemes are likely to be rather modest—arising, for example, from scale effects—but such agreements are prone to trade diversion and to diverting production structures away from countries' true comparative advantage. The likelihood of trade diversion is less in North-South schemes and in South-South agreements accompanied by external liberalization or inclusion of Northern partners. The depth of integration is also important, with the gains from market integration depending on how far countries are willing to go in removing not just tariffs, but also a wide range of other barriers to economic interaction.

The next section contains a brief discussion of globalization and regionalization by way of background. The chapter goes on to deal with the economic analysis of regional integration schemes. In addition to providing analysis of the relationships between choice of partner, production structure, and trade diversion, it discusses production networks, returns to scale, and agglomeration effects. The chapter also looks at policy choices, including depth of integration.

The author thanks Robert Devlin, Antoni Estevadeordal, and Pravin Krishna for helpful comments.

BACKGROUND

Globalization

The process of globalization is driven by a number of forces, the most important of which are policy change and technical progress. In the past 20 years, average tariffs on manufactures have fallen from around 7 percent to less than 4 percent, and investment and some service sectors have opened in many countries. Technical change has reduced the costs of transport and slashed the cost of communications. Declines in ocean shipping and airfreight rates seem to have bottomed out in the 1960s and 1980s, respectively, but these figures almost certainly understate the true fall in trade costs. Hummels (2000) estimates that the value of time saved by the speeding up of ocean shipping (due to containerization and faster vessels) and increased use of airfreight is equivalent to a tariff reduction of 11–12 percentage points on U.S. imports.

Figures 3–1a and 3–1b show the growth of trade in 1980–98. The former gives trade-to-income ratios, and the latter concentrates on merchandise trade relative to merchandise value added. In figure 3–1a, the ratio of total exports to gross domestic product (GDP) in the low-income countries increased from 12 percent in 1980 to 17 percent in 1998. In middle and high-income countries, the ratio grew less dramatically because of the rising importance of the service sector. Figure 3–1b controls for this by looking just at the ratio of merchandise exports to merchandise value added, which indicates strong growth from the mid 1980s onward, particularly in middle-income countries, for which the ratio doubled from around 30 percent to nearly 60 percent.

Trade-to-income ratios were higher in 1913 than they are today in some countries. For example, the trade-to-GDP ratio in the United Kingdom was 27.3 percent in 1913 and 20.6 percent in 1990, and the ratio of merchandise trade to merchandise value added was 61.5 percent in 1913 and 62.8 percent in 1990 (Feenstra, Lipsey, and Bowen 1997). However, there are good reasons to think that today's trade is different, involving higher levels of two-way trade in manufacturing goods rather than the exchange of manufactures for primary products.

An additional new feature of recent trade flows is the shipping of parts and components as firms increase their outsourcing and become involved in international production networks. Yeats (1998) estimates that 30 percent of world trade in manufactures is trade in components rather than final products. Hummels, Ishii, and Yi (2001) chart trade flows that cross borders multiple times, as when a country imports a component and then re-exports it embodied in a downstream product. They find that for 10 OECD countries, the share of imported value added in exports rose by a third between 1970 and 1990, reaching 21 percent of export value. Much of the growth of this vertically specialized trade is concentrated in a few countries neighboring existing centers in Asia, Europe, and the United States.

Foreign direct investment (FDI) has grown even more rapidly than trade. Between 1985 and 1997, worldwide nominal GDP increased at a rate of 7.2 percent a year, worldwide imports at 9.2 percent, and worldwide nominal inflows of FDI at 17.6 percent (Shatz and Venables 2000). The largest increases were for low and middle-income countries. During 1988–92, industrial countries received FDI inflows at an average annual rate of 0.90 percent of GDP, while the average for developing and transition countries was 0.78 percent. By 1993–99, the inflow rate in developing and transition countries more than doubled to 2.4 percent of GDP, while that for industrial countries increased to 1.3 percent of GDP. An alternative picture of the importance of FDI comes from looking at the sales of foreign affiliates of multinational firms;

Figure 3-1

Growth of Trade, 1980–98

a. Ratio of total exports to GDP

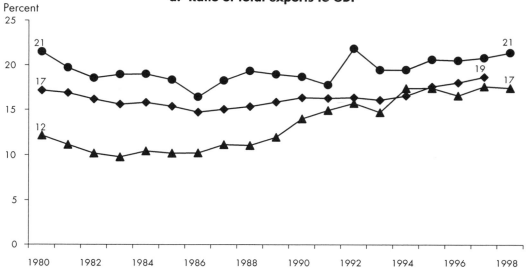

b. Ratio of merchandise exports to merchandise value added

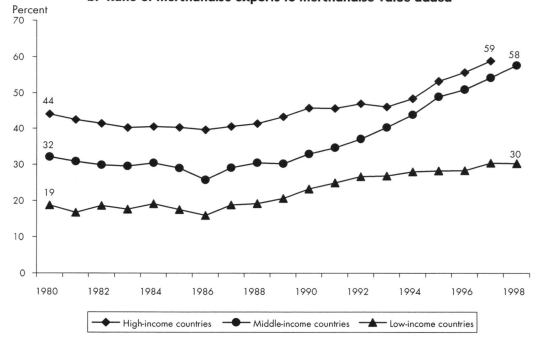

Source: NBER World Trade Database; World Bank (various years).

the overseas production of affiliates of U.S. firms is now three times larger than total U.S. exports.

Regionalism

A process of increasing regionalization has accompanied globalization. Table 3–1 gives the average distance over which selected countries and regions ship their imports. The distance shipped in Asia has declined steadily, largely because of the increasing amount of intra-Asian trade. The values in table 3–1 indicate the importance of regional agreements. The United Kingdom's entry into the European Union in the early 1970s and the later growth of trade within the Americas were both associated with increased regionalism in trade in these areas.

Table 3–2 indicates that although world trade grew by 63 percent (in real terms) between 1980–84 and 1993–97, a number of flows within the Americas grew much faster. Notably, trade between Mexico and the United States more than trebled. U.S. and Canadian exports to Mexico grew by 217 percent and their imports from Mexico grew by 241 percent. Chilean exports to the world as a whole grew almost as fast as those of Mexico (126 and 143 percent, respectively), and bilateral trade between Chile and Mexico grew spectacularly fast. Within Mercosur, trade between Argentina and Brazil approximately quadrupled. By contrast, trade stagnated in the residual "rest of the Americas."

Two factors explain the increasing regionalization of trade. First, trade is increasingly intra-industry, and some of the countries that participate in this trade happen to be close together (notably in Europe). Second, regional integration agreements (RIAs) have grown. In 1999, there were 194 RIAs notified to the General Agreement on Tariffs and Trade/World Trade Organization (GATT/WTO), 87 of which were established after 1990. Previously existing RIAs, such as the European Union, have deepened their integration, and a number of dormant RIAs have been reactivated. Importantly, the 1990s also witnessed the development of North-South RIAs in the bilateral agreements made with the European Union and in the development of the North American Free Trade Agreement (NAFTA).

Table 3-1

Average Distance Traveled by Imports
for Selected Countries and Regions, 1970–97
(Kilometers)

Region or country	1970	1980	1990	1997
NAFTA	5,342	6,162	6,231	5,902
Mexico	4,940	4,988	4,645	4,147
Mercosur	8,755	8,943	8,985	8,119
Latin America	6,954	6,902	6,958	6,197
EU15	2,728	2,549	2,417	2,695
United Kingdom	4,538	3,343	3,140	3,413
Asia	6,910	6,889	6,381	6,071

Note: Values are trade-weighted average trading distances.
Source: NBER World Trade Database.

Table 3-2

Growth of Bilateral Trade Flows in the Americas, 1980–84 to 1993–97
(Percentage change)

Source country	Destination country							
	United States/ Canada	Mexico	Argentina	Brazil	Chile	Rest of the Americas	European Union	World
United States/Canada	81	217	96	101	133	27	29	63
Mexico	241		385	−22	1,558	75	−44	143
Argentina	36	−2		494	338	105	21	53
Brazil	12	41	262		90	70	17	28
Chile	88	249	144	69		173	45	126
Rest of the Americas	−17	119	−17	31	−14	−5	−22	−14
European Union	77	81	99	172	121	42	86	78
World	77	187	103	49	125	23	61	63

Source: NBER World Trade Database.

Trade and Development

The link between trade performance and economic growth is widely accepted and grounded in case studies (see Srinivasan and Bhagwati 1999 for a recent discussion). Recent empirical work on the determinants of growth finds the relationship more elusive. Although a number of cross-country regression studies find a positive relationship between growth and trade, analysts criticize these studies and generally regard the findings as far from robust (Rodríguez and Rodrik 1999). The method of analysis is complicated by the difficulty of measuring openness (or the trade policy stance), and by the high correlation between open trade policies and other institutional features accepted to be conducive to growth.

Dollar and Kray (2001) have a more illuminating approach, identifying a set of developing countries they term the "globalizers." They rank developing countries according to the decline in their tariff rates and the increase in their trade-to-GDP ratio between 1980 and the late 1990s, and select countries that are in the top 40 of both lists. There were 16 such countries, and the two African countries that came closest to meeting the criteria were added, giving Argentina, Bangladesh, Bolivia, Brazil, China, Costa Rica, El Salvador, Ghana, India, Malaysia, Mexico, Nepal, Philippines, Poland, Thailand, Uganda, Uruguay, and Vietnam. (The early trade liberalizers—Chile, Turkey, Hong Kong, Singapore, South Korea, and Taiwan are in the rich-country group, not in this list of globalizers.)

Table 3–3 indicates the greater openness of the globalizers compared with the nonglobalizers (all other developing countries), and gives per capita income growth rates for the past four decades. The striking point is that although the globalizers fared worse than others in the 1960s and 1970s, their performance was dramatically better during the 1980s and 1990s, with annual per capita income growth of 5.3 percent compared with −0.8 percent for the nonglobalizers. It is also noteworthy that the globalizers' exports became increasingly oriented to high-income countries, increasing from 69 percent in 1980 to 78 percent in 1997 (Dollar and Kray 2001). Nonglobalizing middle and low-income countries actually started off with a higher share going to high-income countries, but the share fell from 76 percent in 1980 to 72 percent in 1997.

Table 3-3

Growth and Trade Performance of the Globalizers, 1960s–1990s
(Percent)

Country category	Fall in tariffs, 1980–late 1990s	Increase in trade/GDP, 1980–late 1990s	Annual growth in per capita income			
			1960s	1970s	1980s	1990s
Globalizers	64	92	1.0	1.7	2.6	5.3
Nonglobalizers	29	1	2.2	2.8	0.2	−0.8
High income		50	4.5	3.4	2.5	1.9

Source: Dollar and Kray (2000).

These findings do not establish a causal relationship between trade and growth, nor do they identify particular trade policy instruments as determinants for causing growth, because the countries that liberalized trade also reformed many other domestic policies. However, the findings make a convincing case that full participation in the world economy is an inherent part of modern economic growth. Lindert and Williamson (2001) make this point somewhat differently:

> ...the empty set contains those countries that chose to be less open to trade and factor flows in the 1990s than in the 1960s and rose in the global living-standard ranks at the same time. As far as we can tell there are no anti-global victories to report for the postwar Third World.

ANALYSIS

What is the role of regionalism in development strategy? This chapter argues that regionalism can bring modest opportunities for economies to overcome some of the disadvantages of small size. Increasing returns may be present within firms and within industrial clusters, spurring industrialization through better integration of markets. Regionalism may also provide developing countries with an opportunity to better exploit their comparative advantage (to become "globalizers"). However, this depends crucially on the characteristics of member countries of the RIA. South-South agreements offer limited opportunities. Richer countries in the RIA will typically see their production structures distorted away from their true comparative advantage, as they trade more with poorer partners. Poorer countries are likely to experience trade diversion and possibly real income loss as they import goods from their partners rather than from the rest of the world. North-South agreements typically offer better opportunities, as they promote export growth in line with comparative advantage, and they may also open the way to fuller participation in global production networks.

The remainder of this section lays out the basis of these claims. It begins by looking at the comparative advantage issues, which requires thinking through the way in which gains (or losses) from regional integration depend on partner-country characteristics. It then turns to increasing returns, looking at the possible scale, competition, and agglomeration effects of RIAs. Throughout, the section treats RIAs as preferential tariff liberalizations. The following section looks at some of the other policy changes that might also be involved.

Trade Patterns

Theory

Viner's (1950) study of trade creation and diversion provides the point of departure for analysis of preferential trading arrangements. The analysis shows that while a reduction in tariffs with all trading partners increases welfare, a preferential reduction affecting only partners in the RIA may reduce welfare. The reason is that in addition to creating trade, such a tariff change also tends to divert it, possibly causing import supply to switch from the lowest-cost source to a higher-cost partner country whose exports benefit from preferential market access. This section puts this important idea in an extended context and looks at the way in which trade patterns (and associated production structures) are likely to change because of membership in an RIA. The impact of membership depends on the characteristics of the partner economy. North-South RIAs generate different outcomes compared with South-South ones.[1]

As a framework for thinking about this, suppose that there are three countries. One is large and represents the world average, and the other two (countries 1 and 2) are considering RIA formation. The analysis concentrates on country 1, with country 2 as the partner. In order to study the effects of forming an RIA with partners of different types, country 1 has a particular comparative advantage and a range of different potential partners. The horizontal axis in figure 3–2 gives all the possible partner types, ranked according to their comparative advantage. At the right-hand end of the axis, the endowments of high-income "Northern" countries are abundant in human and physical capital, giving them a comparative advantage in a composite of goods, "good M." At the left-hand end, low-income "Southern" countries have a comparative advantage in "good A." Country 1 has comparative advantage at point I, and the world average is at point R. Thus, if the partner is at point I, the two countries in the RIA have the same comparative advantage. If the partner is in range N, then country 1 forms an RIA with a high-income Northern partner. If the partner is in range HS, then country 1 forms an RIA with a higher-income Southern country; in the range LS, the partner has lower income than country 1.

The vertical axis in figure 3–2 shows the change in country 1's net imports of good M from the rest of the world, from the partner, and in total, as a function of country 1's choice of partner. If country 1 forms an RIA with a partner in set N, the country will experience a large increase in imports of good M from the partner, as indicated by the dashed line, and a fall in imports from the rest of the world, indicated by the solid line. Total imports increase (and so, correspondingly, do exports of A). There are unambiguous welfare gains to country 1 from this change in trade, since it is an increase in imports of good M from a country that has a comparative advantage in good M, relative to country 1 and relative to the rest of the world.

If the partner's comparative advantage is such that it is in set HS, then the qualitative change in the direction of trade is similar, because it is determined by the partner's comparative

---

[1] See Baldwin and Venables (1997) for a technical survey. The literature contains little on choice of partner, and the material here draws on and extends Venables (2000).

Figure 3-2

Trade Creation and Diversion with Different Partners

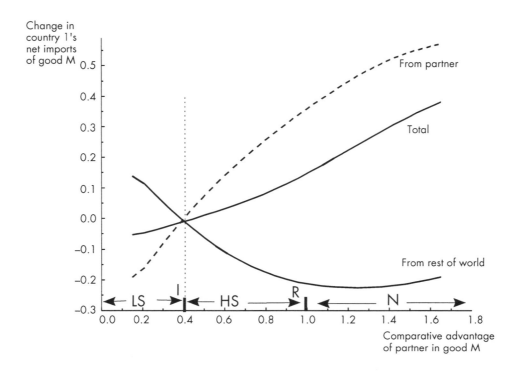

advantage relative to that of country 1. Imports from the partner increase, imports from the rest of the world decrease, and overall imports of M (and exports of A) increase. However, the welfare economics result is quite different. A partner in HS has a comparative advantage in good M relative to country 1, but a comparative disadvantage in this good relative to the world. Since it displaces imports from the rest of the world, Vinerian trade diversion reduces real income. Preferential treatment causes country 1 to divert the sourcing of its imports from the rest of the world (the lowest-cost source of supply) to country 2.

What happens if the partner country has comparative advantage in set LS? In this case, country 1 has comparative advantage in good M, relative to partner country 2, and will increase its exports of good M to country 2, this showing up as a reduction in net imports. Since country 1's increased exports of good M to country 2 raises the price of good M in country 1, there is also an increased flow of imports of good M into country 1 from the rest of the world. This is welfare-improving because country 1 still has an import tariff on these imports.

Figure 3–3 illustrates the welfare effects of these changes, giving full general equilibrium welfare effects, including changes in trade in good A. The U-shaped solid line in figure 3–3 shows the change in country 1's real income. There are gains from forming an RIA with a Northern country as country 1 expands its imports from a country with comparative advantage relative to country 1 and relative to the rest of the world. Turning to South-South agreements, country 1 is likely to gain if it is the intermediate country, but it is likely to lose if it is the

Figure 3-3

Change in Real Income

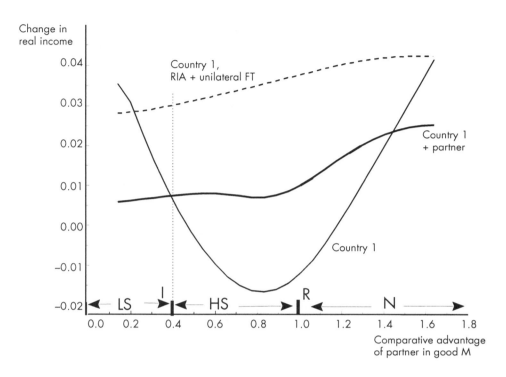

extreme one. Thus, if the partner is in range LS, it is extreme, and country 1 is in the intermediate range between the partner and the world average; country 1 gains as it increases imports of good A from the partner, which has world comparative advantage in this good. However, if country 1 is extreme so that its partner (in range HS) lies between country 1 and the world average, then trade diversion occurs, bringing a welfare loss to country 1.

The other solid line in figure 3-3 gives the welfare change for the RIA as a whole. In South-South agreements, one of the countries has to be extreme, experiencing diversion, so that the RIA as a whole gains little. North-South agreements (with a partner to the right of R) have changes in trade that are in line with global comparative advantage and considerably larger aggregate gains.

Several further points come out of this analysis. First, it is always the extreme country that is prone to diversion. Thus, a South-South integration scheme tends to increase existing income differentials between the two countries, because the agreement diverts the poorer member country's trade to a partner between the poorer country and the world average. The opposite is true for a North-North integration scheme, in which the extreme country has higher income and the agreement diverts its imports to the intermediate country.[2]

---

[2] Thus, Germany starts to import textiles, say, from Portugal, rather than from a country with global comparative advantage in textiles.

Second, in the country that does better in a South-South agreement (the intermediate country), the production structure moves in the opposite direction from what would occur with external trade liberalization. The country does better by exploiting its comparative advantage with the poorer country, not with the rest of the world. In terms of the static model outlined here, this does not damage real income. However, in a dynamic setting in which regional integration provides a way to develop the capacity or efficiency of export industries, perhaps prior to broader trade liberalization, this type of integration is clearly problematic because it develops the wrong sectors.

Third, other trade policy changes can mitigate the effects outlined above. The dashed line in figure 3–3 gives the effect on country 1's income of forming an RIA and implementing unilateral free trade with the rest of the world. This is beneficial for small countries in a perfectly competitive setting. More interestingly, it removes the deep U shape of the effects of RIA membership. Even if country 1's partner is in interval HS, trade diversion does not occur because imports of M are liberalized both from the partner and from the world. This suggests the importance of accompanying South-South RIA formation with liberal external trade policy, or with the inclusion of a large Northern partner.

Empirics

The theory outlined above indicates how changing trade patterns might be associated with welfare gains or losses. Empirical work on trade creation and diversion takes two main forms. One is the use of computable equilibrium techniques to predict the effects of changes in trade policy, and the other is based on ex post empirical studies of changes in trade flows. Neither has focused particularly on the differences between South-South and North-South agreements.

The computable equilibrium studies have the advantage of containing a great deal of microeconomic detail, but their major weakness is that they are not usually fitted to data as carefully or subject to the same statistical testing as econometric models. Computable equilibrium studies typically find gains from regional integration, with trade creation outweighing trade diversion, but the gains are small, usually just a fraction of a percentage of GDP (François and Shiells 1994; Harrison, Rutherford, and Tarr 1994). These gains can be amplified by adding market imperfections, such as increasing returns to scale.

The other technique is to estimate the effects of integration on changes that occurred in the actual volumes of trade with partner and nonpartner countries. Researchers have developed a variety of different econometric models, the most common based on the gravity model that estimates bilateral trade between countries as a function of their GDP and population, the distance between countries, and physical factors, such as sharing a land border and being landlocked or an island. Dummy variables capture whether countries are in a particular RIA, their estimated effect indicating whether there is more or less trade than would otherwise be expected.

Bayoumi and Eichengreen (1997) use this technique and find that the formation of the European Economic Community reduced the annual growth of member trade with other industrial countries by 1.7 percentage points, with the major attenuation occurring over 1959–61, just as trade preferences were phased in. Soloaga and Winters (1999) look at a wide range of RIAs, producing a mixed picture with little evidence of widespread trade diversion. Overall, there appears to be weak evidence that external trade is smaller than it otherwise might have been in at least some of the blocs that have been researched. However, the real income effects of these changes cannot be inferred without information on relative costs and tariff structures, variables that are not incorporated in this sort of aggregate exercise.

Production Networks

The traditional analysis of trade creation and trade diversion worked on the basis that preferential trade agreements would change the magnitude and direction of existing trade flows. However, an RIA might also create new trade flows as countries become involved in production networks, outsourcing different parts of the production process across countries in the RIA. This may occur within multinational corporations (in which case it is known as vertical FDI) or through supply chains external to the firm.

The basis of this sort of trade is factor price differences, so it is more likely to occur in North-South than in South-South RIAs. Furthermore, this trade often involves multiple frontier crossings as components are exported and re-exported embodied in assembled goods. Low transport costs are therefore important, as is security of supply. Rapid transport is also important, particularly in sectors where products are fashion-sensitive or faults have to be detected rapidly. This suggests the importance of proximity, especially for products that cannot be shipped by airfreight.

What is the relationship between regionalism and the empirical importance of production networks? Low border costs and security of supply should be present in an RIA, but not restricted to it. The industrializing Asian economies are important participants in this sort of trade, but they are not in formal RIAs (Yeats 1998).[3] Production networks are also important for some of the transition economies that are closest to the European Union and first in line for full membership. Mexico perhaps provides the best example, because it can exploit its position as an export platform to the United States. FDI flows into Mexico more than doubled in the year following the launch of NAFTA. Blomström and Kokko (1997) argue that this increase was mainly due to firms in non-NAFTA countries taking advantage of preferential access to the larger Northern market. For example, Japan redirected part of its FDI from the United States and Canada toward Mexico, and many projects (for example, in the automobile industry) are intended for the NAFTA continental market.

What are the welfare economics of these changes, and how do they relate to the traditional literature on trade creation and diversion? It is possible (although unlikely) that the changes are associated with trade diversion. Perhaps, in the initial situation, country 1's imports of the good came from the rest of the world, and preferential integration replaced those imports with higher-cost production based on components imported from the partner and assembled in country 1. This would cause a welfare loss, although if final consumption of the product took place largely in the high-wage economy, then that country would experience most of the welfare loss.

Two alternative mechanisms are likely to provide much more important sources of welfare gain for the lower-wage economy. First, the extra labor demand associated with the assembly activity would raise real income because wages paid might exceed the value of the marginal product of labor in its alternative occupation. And increased employment might increase wages, tending to improve the economy's terms of trade. Second, technology transfer would likely result in welfare gains.

Scale, Competition, and Agglomeration

Small economies have a disadvantage in the extent to which they can benefit from economies of scale, and RIA membership offers the potential for overcoming this disadvantage. For some

---

[3] APEC has yet to implement tariff reform.

activities, small economies can achieve benefits through government action—for example, collaboration on large investment projects, such as dams, road networks, or research and development (R&D). However, regional integration will not automatically enable the private sector to achieve potential returns to scale. It will depend on the way in which integration changes market conditions faced by firms, possibly leading to reorganization of the industry and consequent benefits from more intense competition and fuller realization of economies of scale.

Pro-Competitive Effects and Economies of Scale

An example with two integrating economies illustrates the interaction between scale and market structure. The example focuses on a single industry in which firms face increasing returns to scale, have market power, and set price greater than marginal cost. What happens when the two countries liberalize trade with each other?

If firms continue to charge the same prices, the liberalization will have no direct effect. This might happen if the firms collude and agree (implicitly if not explicitly) not to invade each other's markets. In their work on the United States–Canada Free Trade Area, Cox and Harris (1985) put forward an extreme alternative. They hypothesize that domestic firms collude, setting the tariff-inclusive price of imports. A reduction in the tariff then leads to an equal reduction in domestic prices. Furthermore, Cox and Harris suppose that free entry and exit of firms characterizes the industry, and that firms have decreasing average cost (increasing returns to scale). Then, at equilibrium, zero abnormal profits implies that price equals average cost, so any reduction in price brings about an equal efficiency improvement. Some firms exit the industry (possibly through bankruptcy, more likely through mergers and acquisitions) and remaining ones expand, sliding down their average cost curve until they have reached sufficient scale to break even at the new, lower prices. Based on this sort of mechanism, Cox and Harris estimate substantial Canadian gains from the United States–Canada Free Trade Area.

Smith and Venables (1988) take an intermediate position (see also Flores 1997). They model competition between firms as a Cournot equilibrium, in which firms' price-cost markups depend on their market shares. Applying this model in the context of the European Union's Single Market Programme, Smith and Venables argue that a reduction in border measures would increase the share of imports in each country, thereby reducing the dominant positions of domestic firms and increasing the intensity of competition. This change would have a modest effect on prices (a reduction of 1–2 percent in the most concentrated industries) and, through free entry and exit, a similar effect on average costs and welfare. The effects would be larger if the increase in competition were associated with a reduction in internal inefficiencies within firms.

These studies demonstrate the potential gains that can come from regional integration forcing a change in competitive conditions in the industry, and consequent industrial rationalization and fuller exploitation of economies of scale. However, it is important to note that the rationalization occurs because the direct effect of the change is to increase competition and reduce firms' profits. Firms, naturally, have an incentive to resist these changes. It is often argued that national borders provide a way to restrict competition, as firms (tacitly) maintain agreements to restrict sales in each other's markets. A reduction in tariff barriers may not be enough to intensify competition, in which case the real income gains will not be achieved. The European experience suggested that 25 years of free trade was not sufficient to create a fully "integrated" market because national firms retained dominant positions in domestic markets. The Single Market Programme was designed to counter this, and is discussed more fully below.

Pro-Competitive Effects and the Terms of Trade

An additional way in which an RIA may raise welfare is by improving the terms of trade of the partner countries. This can happen in a perfectly competitive framework if the countries concerned are large enough for changes in their trade flows to change the world prices of goods, although in practice this effect is likely to be small. More important, even a small economy might change the price at which it imports goods from the rest of the world if its markets are imperfectly competitive and segmented, so there is no single world price of the good. Membership in an RIA might be expected to increase competition in the domestic market, in which case importers from external countries will experience the same downward pressure on prices. There is some evidence that this has been quite an important effect. Chang and Winters (1999) show that a significant decline in the relative prices of imports from nonmember countries has accompanied Brazil's membership in Mercosur. Even controlling for costs, exchange rates, inflation, and external tariffs, they find that Mercosur membership significantly reduced the relative prices of U.S. goods in the Brazilian market.

Horizontal Foreign Direct Investment

In vertical FDI, firms exploit factor price differences by dividing their production activities between countries. Historically, most FDI has not taken this form, but has instead been horizontal, with firms setting up production plants to supply local or regional markets. (The term "horizontal" refers to the fact that it is duplication of similar activities in different locations, as opposed to the vertical fragmentation of the production chain.) Undertaking such investments typically involves some degree of increasing returns to scale, as firms replace imports with production from local plants. Consequently, these investments are more likely to be made the larger is the local (or regional) market. Since an RIA offers the prospect of supplying the entire regional market from one plant, it is likely to increase horizontal FDI inflows, and there is some evidence that this has occurred.

For example, in Mexico and Europe, a major surge in FDI accompanied the Single Market Programme. The European Commission (1997) finds that the European Union's share of worldwide inward FDI flows increased from 28 to 33 percent in 1982–93. Mercosur also provides evidence of significant expansion of FDI inflows; the share of Mercosur countries in the stock of U.S. FDI increased from 3.9 to 4.4 percent in 1992–95.

Agglomeration

Increasing returns to scale may be external or internal to the firm, suggesting that expansion of one firm might benefit other firms that operate in similar or related activities in the same location. These external economies can arise through a number of different mechanisms. Direct technological externalities, such as knowledge spillovers from firm to firm, might increase external economies. Alternatively, they may be due to pecuniary externalities, arising as changes in quantities interact with market imperfections that prevent marginal benefits from being equal to marginal costs. Expanding an activity with marginal benefit greater than marginal cost creates a positive pecuniary externality, as does contracting an activity with marginal benefit less than marginal cost. Thus, demand and supply linkages between firms can create external increasing returns, as one firm's expansion increases the demand for intermediates produced by imperfectly competitive suppliers, increasing their profits and attracting more firms to the location. Similarly, if one firm's employment expansion draws skilled workers into the area, it may benefit other firms in the area, creating overall increasing returns. Or if one firm's expansion leads to an increase in public investment in activities with increasing returns to scale (such as infrastructure provision), it may benefit other firms and generate overall increasing returns.

One of the consequences of such external returns is that industry is likely to cluster, as firms seek to benefit from the proximity of other firms (Fujita, Krugman, and Venables 1999). The clustering may occur at different levels—perhaps particular functions (for example, the concentration of R&D activity), perhaps the concentration of whole industries (for example, financial services), or possibly the concentration of manufacturing and business services as a whole. Henderson, Shalizi, and Venables (2001) argue that the last of these is particularly likely in developing countries, partly because the relevant sources of increasing returns are likely to be important across a wide range of sectors (for example, infrastructure provision is important for all sectors, and more likely to be patchy in a developing than an industrial country), and partly because regions in developing countries are less likely to run into diminishing returns (due to land use policy or labor shortages) than are regions in high-income countries.

By making it easier to supply customers from a single location, regional integration is likely to promote clustering of activity. Clustering has three main sorts of effects. First, it brings with it efficiency gains, as firms benefit from the externalities created by other firms. Second, an expansion of overall activity levels is likely to follow from these efficiency gains, and cumulative causation may develop, leading to the takeoff of a country's industrial development. Thus, by creating a large internal market, an RIA may act as a catalyst, facilitating the formation of an agglomeration of activity that may be able to achieve a critical mass (Puga and Venables 1998). Notice that this argument is essentially inward-looking, based on expansion of the domestic market. The extent to which such an agglomeration can eventually expand through exports depends also on external trade policy and the region's comparative advantage in the sector.

Third, development of successful agglomeration at the aggregate level also brings with it a potential cost. Agglomeration of activity in one country is likely to be associated with an increase in inequality between countries in the RIA. It is worth linking this with the earlier discussion of integration and comparative advantage. The intermediate country would become the supplier of manufactures to the more extreme country in the RIA, and would experience income gain, whereas the extreme country could lose. Agglomeration effects would likely amplify this, concentrating benefits in just one of the countries. The unequal division of the benefits of an RIA has sometimes been a source of political tension within RIAs (or economic unions more generally), examples including the antebellum United States, East and West Pakistan, and the old East African Economic Community.

Technology Transfer

A major source of benefit from increased openness is better access to technology. Empirical research has linked international technology transfers to both trade and investment flows (see, for example, Keller 2001), although much ignorance remains about the determinants of these transfers. How might regional integration impact such flows? The first point is simply that the potential for technology transfer is much greater within a North-South scheme than a South-South scheme. Second, at least part of the transfer is likely to be through FDI flows, and secure trade relationships might increase investment in production networks and larger markets might encourage horizontal FDI. FDI's effects on local productivity levels typically come from backward linkages, inducing domestic suppliers to improve quality or efficiency; forward linkages, improving distribution and retail networks or developing local downstream production; labor market training; and demonstration effects. A good deal of case study evidence points to the importance of all these mechanisms, although econometric studies show more mixed results (Blomström, Kokko, and Zejan 2000).

Factor Prices, Adjustment, and Political Economy

This chapter has outlined a number of different ways in which membership in an RIA can affect trade flows, production structure, and overall income. What about the internal distribution of these income changes? Factor prices change in response to changes in trade patterns and production structures. In a North-South RIA, the Southern country should experience an increase in its wage-rental ratio (the wage of unskilled workers relative to skilled) as production intensity in the abundant factor expands. A South-South RIA would have been a more complex situation, depending on the characteristics of the partner country. In terms of the earlier example, the extreme country (although it experiences welfare loss due to trade diversion) would see an increase in its wage-rental ratio, as it exploited its comparative advantage with its partner. The intermediate country would see its wage-rental ratio go in the opposite direction as it increased exports of goods in which it had a comparative advantage with the partner, but not with the world as a whole. Thus, for a South-South RIA, factor prices in the poorer economy would move toward their free trade values, while in the richer economy they would tend to go in the opposite direction.

Production networks locate their more labor-intensive stages in labor-abundant economies, tending to raise the wage-rental ratio and move factor prices toward their free trade levels. However, more complex patterns of change in factor prices are possible. It may be the case that activities that relocate are labor-intensive relative to other activities in the Northern economy, but capital-intensive relative to existing activities in the South. In this case, production networks would tend to reduce the wage-rental ratio in both the integrating countries (Feenstra and Hanson 1997).

How does this inform the thinking about the political economy of RIA membership? Some analysts argue that membership in an RIA is a stepping-stone to fuller trade liberalization, as it mitigates the adjustment costs and redistributional implications of reform. This is confirmed, insofar as the impact of an RIA on factor prices is generally less than the impact of full free trade. However, in a South-South agreement, one of the countries—the higher-income one—will see its factor prices moving away from their free trade values. Thus, from a political economy perspective, it is a step away from free trade, not a step toward it.

POLICY CHOICES

A country considering making regionalism part of its development strategy faces a number of choices, including decisions about choice of partner and depth of integration.

Choice of Partner

Much of the earlier analysis addressed the implications of RIA membership among countries with differing characteristics. It found that a South-South RIA offers potential benefits from better exploitation of economies of scale and the opportunity to increase the intensity of competition in local markets. However, it is not clear that South-South RIAs have always been able to achieve these benefits, as they depend heavily on the depth of integration. South-South RIAs enable countries to increase trade according to their comparative advantage relative to each other, although this may be different from their comparative advantage relative to the world as a whole. Thus, the lower-income member suffers trade diversion as it imports goods from a partner with intra-RIA comparative advantage but not global comparative advantage. The higher-income member sees its trade and production structure move in the opposite direction from the way it would if it were exploiting its global comparative advantage. Inequality between the countries likely increases, particularly if agglomeration mechanisms accentuate production changes arising from intra-RIA comparative advantage.

North-South RIAs seem to offer better prospects. One disadvantage is that the likely changes in trade flows are larger, as are changes in production structure and factor prices. However, these changes are in line with countries' global comparative advantage, as well as their intra-RIA advantage. The growth of outsourcing and production networks provide reasons to believe that the potential for exploiting this comparative advantage vis-à-vis a high-income partner is now larger than it has been historically, and the growth of FDI suggests increased opportunities for technology transfer.

In addition to these purely economic arguments, a number of political economy arguments have been put forward in favor of North-South agreements (see World Bank 2000). The most important is that if RIA membership is being used as a commitment to reform (possibly reform going beyond trade), then it is important that the partner country has the means and incentive to punish deviations (for example, by withdrawal of preferential trade access), and that the costs of this punishment are high enough to deter deviation from the reform program.

Depth of Integration

Tariffs and other formal trade barriers between countries make up only a small part of the costs involved in crossing a border. Helliwell (1997) vividly demonstrates the importance of borders in his research on Canadian provinces. Their exports to other Canadian provinces are around 20 times larger than their exports to equivalently located U.S. states, choking off trade by the same amount as would distance of more than a thousand miles.

There are four additional main costs of borders. First, different languages, political and legal systems, cultures, and information flows have associated costs, which this study regards as exogenous and beyond the scope of policy. Second, border formalities involve costs, such as customs administration, administration of tax systems, and frontier delays. Third, product standards raise costs. And fourth, costs arise due to the additional uncertainty that is associated with trading across a border, including uncertainty about trade policy and exchange rate movements.

It is generally difficult to get direct evidence on the magnitude of the costs associated with each of these elements, but it is likely that they have large economic implications. They are real resource costs, unlike tariffs, which are transfer payments. Small trade frictions can have important effects, inhibiting the development of production networks, facilitating firms' segmentation of markets, and frustrating attempts to intensify competition. There is little evidence that currency volatility has a major effect on trade flows, although some authors find that currency union membership has large effects on trade volumes (Frankel and Rose 2000).

Customs Unions and Free Trade Areas

In a free trade area countries are free to set their own external trade policy, whereas in a customs union the RIA as a whole sets a common external policy. The great advantage of a customs union is that because members have a common external tariff, it is possible to have much simpler internal border formalities (possibly none at all). By contrast, a free trade area leaves external trade policy to individual member governments and faces a problem known as *trade deflection*—the redirection of imports from outside countries through the free trade area member with the lowest external tariff to exploit the tariff differential. If unconstrained, trade deflection reduces the effective tariff of every member to that of the lowest plus the transportation cost involved in indirect importing. The usual solution is *rules of origin*, the apparently reasonable requirement that goods qualifying for tariff-free trade should be produced in a member country, rather than just passing through it.

The costs of implementing rules of origin are high. Controls on goods crossing internal frontiers have to be retained to ensure compliance and collect customs duties. Customs authorities (and individual customs officers) may have a good deal of discretion, and the attendant danger is that such discretion might be abused. Rules of origin are particularly complex because they have to take into account tariffs on imported intermediate goods used in products manufactured within the free trade area. The principle is that imports from outside the free trade area should pay the tariff of the country of final sale, but additional value added in free trade area members should be tariff-free.

In practice, calculations are not made on such an exact basis, but instead according to more or less arbitrary rules, typically stating that exports have to derive a certain proportion of their value from local content or undergo certain production processes within the free trade area to obtain duty-free treatment (World Bank 2000). The rules are complex and difficult to negotiate and, since they do not match the exact inputs in each commodity, they introduce further biases and sources of distortion. The European Union's agreement with Poland has 81 pages of small print in its rules of origin section, and NAFTA has some 200 pages (Krueger 1997). NAFTA rules of origin in some sectors have protective effects that shift trade and investment patterns from lower to higher-cost sources. Most clothing produced in Mexico gains tariff-free access to the North American market only if its inputs are virtually 100 percent sourced in North America. In the automobile industry, the origin requirement of 62.5 percent local content has induced Japanese automobile manufacturers with plants in Canada to produce components in the United States rather than import cheaper ones from Japan. Yet, even with complex rules of origin in place, the problem of FTA imports entering through the country with the lowest external tariff is not entirely solved. A low-tariff partner can meet its own requirements from imports and export a corresponding amount of its own production to its partners, in what is called indirect trade deflection (Robson 1998).

Thus, substantial benefits support the formation of a customs union, but only a small minority of RIAs notified to the GATT/WTO are in fact customs unions. The main cost of a customs union is that harmonization of external trade policy means a loss of national autonomy. Political institutions need to be put in place to ensure that these tariffs are set in a consensual way, and tariff revenues generated by the common external tariff have to be distributed among member countries. In the European Union, these revenues are part of the central budget and spent on agreed programs, yet the level of each member's net contribution or receipt from the budget remains contentious. Many developing country customs unions have great difficulties in agreeing on a common external tariff and the distribution of revenues.

Contingent Protection

Contingent protection measures include anti-dumping, countervailing duties (in response to foreign subsidies), and emergency protection to address balance-of-payments problems or protect an industry from surges in imports. Although contingent protection has been abolished within the European Union, it remains applicable in all the European Union's agreements with other countries except the European Economic Area. Some RIAs widely use contingent protection; in Mercosur, Argentina initiated 33 anti-dumping cases on imports from Brazil in 1992–96 (Tavares and Tineo 1998). What are the benefits and costs of removing these measures, as has been done in the European Union, the Canada–Chile free trade area, and the Australia–New Zealand agreement?

Contingent protection provides a major barrier to trade, not only when actually applied to trade flows, but also by its mere existence, which has a chilling effect on trade. For example, the threat of initiation of anti-dumping actions can lead to an immediate fall in trade as importers seek to avoid the costs of posting bonds required by customs authorities while the investigation is ongoing. Empirical estimates of the chilling effect on trade find that threatened exporters often agree to raise prices and maintain historical market shares, so contingent protection becomes an instrument facilitating collusion between domestic and foreign firms (Messerlin 1990; Staiger and Wolak 1989).

These are powerful arguments for abolition of contingent protection, but there are several counterarguments. First, dumping can be predatory when a foreign firm (or cartel) seeks to force domestic competitors out of the market by pricing below cost, with the intention of raising prices after the competition leaves. However, research suggests that predation is very much the exception, not the rule, in anti-dumping cases, and that in most anti-dumping actions, an antitrust authority would not have intervened on competition grounds (Messerlin 1997).[4]

Second, suspension of countervailing duties requires measures to restrain or coordinate industrial subsidies that may have a negative impact on domestic firms. When such subsidies are being used, there are valid economic justifications for the use of countervailing duties (Dixit 1988). However, in general, contingent protection is an inefficient instrument to deal with the effects of foreign subsidies or industrial policies because it imposes additional costs on domestic consumers without greatly increasing the incentives of the foreign government to change its policies. Small countries in particular are unlikely to have much success by pursuing retaliatory policies—they will only end up adding an additional distortion to consumption. The appropriate policy is to draft rules that restrict the ability of RIA members to use industrial policies in ways that are detrimental to the welfare of other member countries. In practice, this may be difficult to achieve; only a limited number of RIAs have done much to discipline the ability of members to provide subsidies.

Border Controls, Public Procurement, and Product Standards

Trading across international borders brings real costs in delays, filling in forms, recertification of products, and so on. There may be policy bias in purchasing; for example, public procurement may favor local producers over imports.

---

[4] Furthermore, if there is predation, the national antitrust authority should be able to address the problem, and this can be done unilaterally—there is no need for international agreement or harmonizing competition regimes.

Good customs administration and the use of standard procedures can reduce border formalities. Much of this is possible independent of RIA membership, by adopting best practices in the area of customs administration and implementing international conventions aimed at trade facilitation. However, it is likely that the needed measures are easier to implement within an RIA because of the inherent simplicity of not collecting duties on internal trade and the development of common approaches and institutions (such as the adoption of standard paperwork).

In the European Union, increasing awareness of the fact that these frictions prevented full market integration—and thereby impeded scale and efficiency effects—was a major motivation for the Single Market or "EC-1992" program. The project involved adoption of almost 300 measures to eliminate intra–European Union barriers, including the following:

- Simplification and in some cases abolition of intra–European Community border controls. For example, a European Union system of administering value-added tax on cross-border transactions replaced border paperwork.
- Progress toward deregulation of the transport sectors in European Union countries, including measures to reduce restrictions on haulers from one country accepting loads in another.
- The opening of public procurement in European Union countries to effective competition from suppliers in all European Union countries. Measures include the requirement that public projects be advertised in publications throughout the European Union.

Variations in national product standards create further barriers to trade. Estimates from Egypt in the early 1990s show that redundant testing and idiosyncratic standards alone imposed taxes equivalent to between 5 and 90 percent of the value of shipments (Hoekman and Konan 1999). Product standards raise complex issues, since countries can genuinely differ on what they regard as acceptable levels. Countries seeking to reduce the barriers created by differing standards can follow two alternative routes—harmonization or mutual recognition.

Harmonization can be achieved by unilaterally adopting the standards of another country or group of countries or by developing a set of common standards. The European Union experience suggests that the latter process is extremely slow and painful (it took more than a decade to reach agreement on the composition of fruit jams and mineral water, and only nine directives on foodstuffs were adopted in 1962–79). Differences in national norms—reflecting national tastes, history, legal regimes, and producer lobbies seeking to restrict competition from imports—made it difficult to achieve the required consensus.

The alternative to harmonization is mutual recognition, under which member countries simply accept that goods that are legally traded in one member state can be legally traded in all. This principle was incorporated into the Single Market Programme and has proved to be a powerful tool for increasing cross-border competition in European markets. However, it raises two difficult issues. First, countries have to be able to agree on the minimum norms that should be met to safeguard public health and safety or maintain the integrity of public networks. Second, there has to be mutual trust in the competence and ability of the national institutions responsible for enforcing the relevant mandatory standards. Thus, even if all members accept the levels at which standards are set, it may require significant institutional strengthening for one country to accept that another's testing and certification procedures are adequate.

Investment Flows

The likely effects of FDI flows in an RIA may refer to flows from outside or from partners within the RIA, as plants move to exploit the comparative advantage of different locations and compete more directly with host-country firms. In practice, there can be substantial barriers to such investment. The barriers take many forms, including absolute barriers to establishment in some sectors or activities, requirements that foreign equity not exceed a certain percentage of the total, domestic content requirements or export requirements, requirements that FDI projects meet targets not imposed on national firms, and obstacles to repatriation of profits.

Little progress has been made on liberalizing these restrictions on a multilateral basis. The OECD's proposed Multilateral Agreement on Investment sought to overcome some of these barriers, establishing, for example, a binding dispute settlement procedure, but the initiative failed. Many bilateral investment treaties are now being established (with something over 1,000 currently in place). These typically specify national treatment (the principle that partner-country residents are treated no less favorably than domestic residents) and specify dispute settlement procedures. There is a strong case for incorporating formal investment codes in an RIA because of the potential importance of both horizontal and vertical FDI. In practice, this has gone furthest in the European Union. NAFTA also contains investment provisions, as does the Asian-Pacific Economic Cooperation (APEC), although the latter are nonbinding.

Liberalization of Services

Trade in services is inherently more complex than goods trade for two reasons. First, in many service activities, problems of asymmetric information are particularly acute; the purchaser does not know the quality of a professional service being purchased until after it has been paid for and consumed. And second, service trade frequently requires consumers and providers to be at the same place at the same time.

The first of these complexities creates a proper need for regulation of such service activities. Service suppliers must obtain certification or licensing in such fields as financial services, law, accountancy, and medicine. However, standards are often set by professional bodies that have an interest not only in creating a reputation for ensuring quality, but also in restricting entry and limiting competition. The second complexity—that service providers typically have to be established in the country they are supplying—is an inherent obstacle to international trade.

The combination of these two considerations has made trade in services difficult to liberalize and notoriously prone to various trade restrictions. Many countries restrict the access of foreign services and service suppliers to domestic markets, and sometimes trade in services is simply prohibited. Rights of supply may be restricted to domestic firms (for example, in domestic transportation and basic telecommunication services), or to domestic residents (for example, in legal, insurance, education, surveying, or investment advisory services). Even if there are no formal prohibitions, there are often major barriers to entry, such as professional standards set in a way that requires foreigners to engage in costly recertification.

This restrictive starting point and the fact that most of the barriers are essentially quantity restrictions (prohibitions and regulations rather than tariffs) mean that gains from opening up trade in services to international competition are likely to be particularly large. Indeed, from a starting point of prohibitive barriers, preferential liberalization cannot divert trade, so a major source of ambiguity about gains from preferential liberalization is absent.

In addition, the fact that the service sector is an input to so many other activities in the economy—production, commerce, trade, and education—makes it particularly important that the sector functions efficiently. Failure to liberalize services when an RIA liberalizes trade in goods can give rise to the phenomenon of negative effective protection. Output does not receive tariff protection, but inputs do (implicitly, in the form of barriers to service trade), thus creating negative incentives for the development of activities that use these services.[5]

If liberalization is to be pursued, it can proceed through various channels. The General Agreement on Trade in Services (GATS) provides a multilateral framework. Most RIAs have not gone much beyond what has been achieved in the GATS, the main exceptions being the European Union and NAFTA. NAFTA has made substantial progress using a negative list system, so all service sectors are covered unless specifically exempted. Other RIAs vary in their coverage of services. In Mercosur, free circulation of services is a long-term objective to be achieved by 2007; progress has been slow, with members still negotiating a framework agreement. ASEAN members have agreed to full liberalization (on a preferential basis) in most services by 2020. The free trade areas between the European Union and Mediterranean countries do not include services, while those with the Central and Eastern European countries do.

Despite the slow progress, there are several reasons to think that RIAs may, for many countries, offer a more effective route to service liberalization than does the multilateral system. First, service liberalization may involve labor mobility. Service providers need to become established locally, and this typically involves temporary if not permanent residence. Politically, this may be easier to achieve in an RIA than on a nondiscriminatory basis. Second, procedures are needed to make sure that quality standards are met. These issues are conceptually similar to those in product standards, such as the agreement on harmonization or, if mutually agreeable standards are in place, on mutual recognition. Achieving these within an RIA may be easier than establishing them for all comers.

CONCLUSIONS

Regional integration may make it possible to go faster with deep integration than could occur through unilateral or bilateral trade liberalization. Removal of trade frictions, simplification of border controls, and service and investment liberalization are possible, and bring with them substantial potential benefits, exposing sectors to increased competition and efficiency. Deep regional integration also offers security of trade flows that is important for encouraging FDI and the development of production networks.

However, regional integration is inherently a second-best policy, likely to be associated with trade diversion and specialization according to regional comparative advantage, which is not necessarily global comparative advantage. The extent to which this occurs depends on the choice of partners. This chapter has argued that these costs will be greatest in South-South regional agreements that can increase inequalities between member countries and distort production away from countries' global comparative advantage. These arguments point to the need to accompany South-South integration with external liberalization, or with inclusion of large Northern partner countries.

---

[5] Estimates for Egypt suggest that trade barriers in services reduced effective rates of protection for manufacturing activities by some 30 percentage points (Djankov and Hoekman 1997).

REFERENCES

Baldwin, R. E., and A. J. Venables. 1997. International Economic Integration. In G. Grossman and K. Rogoff (eds.), *Handbook of International Economics, Volume 3*. Amsterdam, Netherlands: North Holland.

Bayoumi, T., and B. Eichengreen. 1997. Is Regionalism Simply a Diversion? Evidence from the Evolution of the EC and EFTA. In T. Ito and A. O. Krueger (eds.), *NBER East Asia Seminar on Economics, 6, Regionalism versus Multilateral Trade Arrangements*. Chicago, IL: University of Chicago Press.

Blomström, M., and A. Kokko. 1997. *Regional Integration and Foreign Direct Investment: A Conceptual Framework and Three Cases*. Policy Research Working Paper 1750, World Bank, Washington, DC.

Blomström, M., A. Kokko, and M. Zejan. 2000. *Foreign Direct Investment. Firm and Host Country Strategies*. London, UK: Macmillan.

Chang, W., and L. A. Winters. 1999. *How Regional Blocs Affect Excluded Countries: The Price Effects of MERCOSUR*. Discussion Paper 2179, Centre for Economic Policy Research, London, UK.

Cox, D., and R. Harris. 1985. Trade Liberalisation and Industrial Organization. Some Estimates for Canada. *Journal of Political Economy* 80: 456–75.

Dixit, A. K. 1988. Antidumping and Countervailing Duties under Oligopoly. *European Economic Review* 32: 55–68.

Djankov, S., and B. Hoekman. 1997. Effective Protection and Investment Incentives in Egypt and Jordan: Implications of Free Trade with Europe. *World Development* 25: 281–91.

Dollar, D., and A. Kray. 2001. Trade, Growth and Poverty. World Bank Policy Research Working Paper 2587, World Bank, Washington, DC.

European Commission. 1997. *European Union Direct Investment Yearbook 1996*. Office for Official Publications of the European Communities, Luxembourg.

Feenstra, R., and G. Hanson. 1997. Foreign Direct Investment and Relative Wages: Evidence from Mexico's Maquiladoras. *Journal of International Economics* 42: 371–93.

Feenstra, R., R. E. Lipsey, and H. P. Bowen. 1997. *World Trade Flows 1970–79*. NBER Working Paper 5910, National Bureau of Economic Research, Cambridge, MA.

Flores, R. 1997. The Gains from MERCOSUR: A General Equilibrium, Imperfect Competition Evaluation. *Journal of Policy Modeling* 19: 1–18.

François, J., and C. Shiells. 1994. *Modeling Trade Policy: Applied General Equilibrium Assessments of North American Free Trade*. Cambridge, UK: Cambridge University Press.

Frankel, J., and A. Rose. 2000. *Estimating the Effect of Currency Unions on Trade and Output*. NBER Working Paper W7857, National Bureau of Economic Research, Cambridge, MA.

Fujita, M., P. Krugman, and A. J. Venables. 1999. *The Spatial Economy: Cities, Regions, and International Trade*. Cambridge, MA: MIT Press.

Harrison, G., T. Rutherford, and D. Tarr. 1994. *Product Standards, Imperfect Competition and the Completion of the Market in the EC*. Policy Research Working Paper 1293, World Bank, Washington, DC.

Helliwell, J. 1997. *National Borders, Trade, and Migration*. NBER Working Paper 6027, National Bureau of Economic Research, Cambridge, MA.

Henderson, J. V., Z. Shalizi, and A. J. Venables. 2001. Geography and Development. *Journal of Economic Geography* 1: 81–106.

Hoekman, B., and D. Konan. 1999. *Deep Integration, Nondiscrimination, and Euro-Mediterranean Free Trade*. Discussion Paper 2095, CEPR, London, UK.

Hummels, D. 2000. Time As a Trade Barrier. Purdue University, West Lafayette, IN. Unpublished.

Hummels, D., J. Ishii, and K-M Yi. 2001. The Nature and Growth of Vertical Specialization in World Trade. *Journal of International Economics* 54: 75–96.

Keller, W. 2001. The Geography and Channels of Diffusion at the World's Technology Frontier. University of Texas. Unpublished.

Krueger, A. O. 1997. Free Trade Agreements versus Customs Union. *Journal of Development Economics* 54: 169–87.

Lindert, P., and J. Williamson. 2001. Does Globalization Make the World More Unequal? Harvard University, Cambridge, MA. Unpublished.

Messerlin, P. 1990. Anti-Dumping Regulations or Pro-Cartel Law. The EC Chemical Cases. *World Economy* 13: 465–92.

———. 1997. Reforming the Rules of Anti-Dumping Policies. In H. Siebert (ed.), *Towards a New Global Framework for High Technology Competition*. Tübingen, Germany: J.C.B. Mohr (Paul Siebek).

Puga, D., and A. J. Venables. 1998. Trading Arrangements and Industrial Development. *The World Bank Economic Review* 12: 221–49.

Robson, P. 1998. *The Economics of International Integration*. London, UK: Routledge.

Rodríguez, F., and D. Rodrik. 1999. Trade Policy and Economic Growth: A Skeptic's Guide to the Evidence. University of Maryland. Unpublished.

Shatz, H., and A. J. Venables. 2000. The Geography of International Investment. In G. L. Clark, M. Feldman, and S. Gerther (eds.), *The Oxford Handbook of Economic Geography*. Oxford, UK: Oxford University Press.

Smith, A., and A. J. Venables. 1988. Completing the Internal Market in the European Community: Some Industry Simulations. *European Economic Review* 32(7, September): 1501–25.

Soloaga, I., and L. A. Winters. 1999. *Regionalism in the Nineties: What Effect on Trade?* Discussion Paper 2183, Centre for Economic Policy Research, London, UK.

Srinavasan, T. N., and J. Bhagwati. 1999. Outward-Orientation and Development: Are Revisionists Right? Yale University, New Haven, CT. Unpublished.

Staiger, R., and F. Wolak. 1989. *Strategic Use of Antidumping to Enforce Tacit International Collusion*. NBER Working Paper 3016, National Bureau of Economic Research, Cambridge, MA.

Tavares, J., and L. Tineo. 1998. Harmonization of Competition Policies among Mercosur Countries. *Antitrust Bulletin* 43(1, Spring): 45–70.

Venables, A. J. 2000. Gainers and Losers from Regional Integration Agreements. Discussion Paper 2568, CEPR, *http://econ.lse.ac.uk/staff/ajv/jpap4.pdf*.

Viner, J. 1950. *The Customs Union Issue*. Washington, DC: Carnegie Endowment for International Peace.

World Bank. 2000. *Trade Blocs: Policy Research Report*. Oxford: Oxford University Press.

World Bank. Various years. World Development Indicators CD Rom. World Bank, Washington, DC.

Yeats, A. 1998. *Just How Big Is Global Production Sharing?* Policy Research Working Paper 1871, World Bank, Washington, DC.

Chapter 4

The Political Economy of Trade and Economic Integration: A Review Essay

Alícia Adserà and Carles Boix

What are the determinants of trade policy and regional economic integration? What are the institutional and political consequences of trade? After examining the domestic factors shaping trade policy, which have been surveyed by many scholars, the chapter summarizes the less trodden path (at least among economists) of the international or systemic causes of trade openness.[1] The chapter describes the growing literature on the positive impact that free trade has on domestic compensation and hence on the size of the public sector. Finally, it reviews the impact of trade on domestic institutions—mainly the size of nations and the type of political regimes.

TRADE POLICY MODELS

Research on the political and institutional determinants of trade policy undoubtedly represents the lion's share of the literature on the political economy of trade. Here we examine the key work on the domestic and international determinants of trade policy.

Domestic Factors

Most of the recent formal (and systematic empirical) research on the causes of trade policy has dwelled on two types of domestic factors: the distribution of individual preferences, which describes the choice set on which policymakers act and hence the probability attached to each policy outcome, and the institutional structure of the political system, which constrains the choice set by defining the expressed and aggregated preferences.

Individual Preferences

In general, the current literature on trade policymaking models individual preferences as the result of the consequences that trade policy has on each agent, given how the latter derives

---

[1] Nelson (1988); Hillman (1989); Magee, Brock, and Young (1989); Magee (1994); Alt and Gilligan (1994); Rodrik (1995); Alt and others (1996).

income and, in particular, the factor or sector composition of the assets held by each individual. This broad analysis uses the existing economic models of trade—Heckscher-Ohlin, Ricardo-Viner, and (more sparingly) models with increasing returns to scale and imperfect competition.

THE HECKSCHER-OHLIN MODEL. In the Heckscher-Ohlin model, trade policy has distinct distributional consequences for the owners of the factors of production (capital, land, and labor). As a result, the model predicts that the position each individual takes over trade depends on the factor composition of the individual's assets.

The Heckscher-Ohlin model rests on three assumptions. First, it assumes that the factors of production move costlessly across sectors and, as a result, factor returns are equalized throughout the economy, moving together across the industries in which they are deployed. Second, a country exports (imports) products that intensively employ factors in which it is relatively abundant (scarce). Third, changes in the price of any product affect the returns to the factors that are used intensively in the production of that product. It follows that free trade benefits the owners of abundant factors and, absent compensation, harms the owners of scarce factors. Hence, the position over trade policy will follow factor or class lines. The owners of abundant factors will favor free trade. Conversely, the owners of scarce factors will be protectionist.

THE RICARDO-VINER MODEL. The Ricardo-Viner model abandons the assumption that factors move costlessly across the economy, and characterizes trade interests. In this model, the level of factor specificity is high to the point that at least one factor cannot move between sectors of the economy. With high levels of asset specificity, the distributional consequences of trade policy take place along sector or industrial lines, and the model predicts the formation of political coalitions along export versus import-competing industries.

Economists have traditionally treated the question of asset specificity as a function of time and characterized the Ricardo-Viner model as the short-run version of the long-run Heckscher-Ohlin model. The logic of this argument is simple and parallel to similar distinctions made in macroeconomic theory about the behavior of prices. Whereas very few assets can be transferred without any costs in the short run, in the long run no assets are specific. If this theoretical claim is true, then the Heckscher-Ohlin model should explain long-run historical events and Ricardo-Viner predictions should fit short-run positions. As noted by Alt and Gilligan (1994), however, the temporal integration of both models may be misleading, given the likelihood that specificity is endogenous to the political process. Once sectors that are heavily specific jockey for and eventually secure state protection for their declining industries, the long-run incentive to move to a new industry disappears. Policymakers, who are concerned about their political support, continue to protect those sectors, so that, in the politics of trade, short-run interests trump long-run positions.

INCREASING RETURNS TO SCALE. A number of recent models depart from the assumption of constant returns to scale that underlies both the Heckscher-Ohlin and Ricardo-Viner models. Trade models based on increasing returns to scale lead to very different and in fact rather blurred predictions about the redistributive consequences of openness. For example, in models with product differentiation and monopolistic competition, trade is predicted to occur mainly along intra-industry lines between regions of similar factor endowments rather than along inter-industry lines. In general terms, trade openness forces a reduction in monopoly power and thus should be especially welcomed by consumers and fought by concentrated industries.

EMPIRICS. The empirical evidence in support of each model is still ambiguous. Rogowski (1989) offers a powerful analysis of trade policymaking mainly in the last two centuries using the Heckscher-Ohlin model. Particularly for the 19th century, he finds that trade coalitions among capital, labor, and land factors vary according to the abundance or scarcity of each factor. Magge, Brock, and Young (1989) show that in a cross section of national tariff rates, a long-run Stolper-Samuelson model explains about 75 percent of the variation. Balistreri (1997) and Beaulieu (1996, 1997) find factor type to be more relevant than industry or employment in explaining Canadian voter patterns and trade attitudes. Kaempfer and Marks (1993) and Scheve and Slaughter (2001) report similar results for the United States.

By contrast, Ricardo-Viner models are employed by Magee (1980) for the United States, Irwin (1994, 1996) for early 20th century British elections, and Frieden (1991) for Latin America. Combining both approaches, Hiscox (2001) shows that the dominance of either factor-based or industry-based coalitions has varied over time, as a function of variation in the level of asset specificity, in the 19th and 20th centuries in Australia, Canada, France, Sweden, the United Kingdom, and the United States.

Structure of the Political System

In deciding whether to act in the political arena, say, to shape trade policy, individuals engage in a calculation about the expected benefits of their action. This calculation includes the gross benefits of achieving their ideal trade policy as well as the costs of political action.

COLLECTIVE ACTION. To model the costs and structure of political action, the literature on the formation of trade policy relies heavily on Olson's (1965, 1982) theory of collective action.[2] Findlay and Wellisz (1982) and Hillman (1989) model trade policy as a function of the size of lobbying resources spent by contending organized interests to influence policymakers. Magee, Brock, and Young (1989), Grossman and Helpman (1994), and Mayer and Li (1994) find that the amount of resources (campaign contributions) that special-interest groups transfer to politicians affects trade policy.

Combining the literature on the costs of collective action and the origins of preferences over trade policy, table 4–1 describes the main models in the literature. With no collective action problems and purely mobile factors, trade policies should be based on classes or factors. As the costs of collective action become high (and factors remain mobile), free riding is pervasive, and no trade policy coalitions emerge—individuals have only exit options in the form of job relocation, emigration, or capital flight. With specific factors and low costs of collective action, there is a multiplicity of interest groups and active consumer groups. In this situation, all industries could collude in a generalized logroll that leaves each one worse off (since the costs of protection would escalate). The standard trade policy models based on influence and lobbying would take place with specific factors and high collective action costs: highly concentrated sectors (based on geography or the number of owners) would be able to overcome these costs and lobby policymakers successfully.

POLITICAL INSTITUTIONS. In contrast to research based on collective action theory, the literature on the impact that constitutional structures may have on trade is still in its infancy. Mayer (1984)

---

[2] In 1927, before Olson formulated his theory of collective action, Pareto had linked protectionism to certain organizational asymmetries since, as quoted in Alt and Gilligan (1994: 379), "a protectionist measure provides large benefits to a small number of people, and causes a very great number of consumers a slight loss."

Table 4–1

Models of Trade Policymaking as a Function of Factor Specificity and Collective Action Costs

Type of factor	Collective action costs	
	Low	High
Mobile	Factor-based policies	Pervasive free riding No trade policy coalitions
Specific	Many interest groups	Standard trade policy models (Pareto, Schattschneider, Olson, influence, and lobbying models)

provides a benchmark. Employing a Heckscher-Ohlin model of trade preferences (in which there are neither lobbies nor political parties), Mayer applies the median voter theorem to derive the trade policy outcome. Assuming that the distribution of wealth is skewed and therefore the median voter has a higher labor/capital ratio than the economy as a whole, the model predicts tariffs whenever imports are labor intensive (since they would transfer wealth from capital to labor). Hence, Mayer's model implies positive tariffs in industrial countries and negative tariffs in developing countries.

Alt and Gilligan (1994) attribute different policy effects to "majoritarian" and "non-majoritarian" institutions. Majoritarian voting mechanisms, such as presidential elections or referendums, tend to mirror the preferences of the median voter and facilitate the formation of broad-based factor coalitions. By contrast, nonmajoritarian institutions, such as an insulated bureaucracy or a legislature elected on the basis of geographically differentiated constituencies, may bolster the growth of specific interests. Insulated bureaucrats are clearly much easier to lobby than politicians accountable to the whole electorate. Similarly, if the legislature is composed of representatives elected in small, sector-specific districts, sector-based lobbies may have direct access to the policymaking process.

Empirical analysis has tested this distinction in the case of the Reciprocal Trade Agreements Act of 1934 in the United States, which moved the locus of decisionmaking on trade policy from Congress to the president. According to Lohmann and O'Halloran (1994), the delegation of authority to the president eliminated protectionist logrolling and made more salient the costs of tariffs to consumers that would otherwise have been neglected because they were dispersed across electoral districts. As convincingly shown by Hiscox (1999), however, a pure institutionalist account fails to explain why these institutions were changed in the first place. The answer is that the array of interests that favored rules friendly to free trade had previously become dominant in the political arena.

International Factors

Although the extent of protectionism has varied across nations, the degree of trade openness has fluctuated historically at the world level as well. The Franco-British trade agreement of

1860 initiated a wave of commercial treaties that generalized a free trade regime across Europe during the following two decades. However, by the late 1870s and 1880s, this "liberal interlude," to use Bairoch's (1993) term, gave way to the reintroduction of protectionist tariffs in Germany and France. Subsequently, Italy, Portugal, Spain, and Sweden reimposed high tariffs in the last decade of the 19th century. The 20th century had the same pattern of policy ebbs and flows. Word War I precipitated the generalized introduction of barriers to trade—some of which remained after 1919—and the Great Depression of 1929 constituted a definitive turning point away from global free trade. However, after 1945 free trade was progressively restored across the globe.

Shifts in domestic preferences across borders explain part of the international trends in trade policy; the protectionist backlash of the 1880s took place in direct response to the collapse in world grain prices. But the existence of international temporal dynamics seems to call for nondomestic factors to obtain a satisfactory explanation. We examine three possible (yet not necessarily exclusive) explanations: worldwide change in transportation and communication costs; strategic interaction of countries; and the role of international regimes facilitating the generation and maintenance of free trade.

Changes in Technology

A substantial literature has linked the generalized adoption of free trade policies to an exogenous change in the technology of production and transportation.[3] In a nutshell, the argument is as follows. As the invention of new and cheaper means of transportation and communication leads to a significant fall in the costs of trade, domestic and world prices converge and the distortionary effects of protective barriers rise. These distortions take place in two ways. First, protectionist measures have purely distributional consequences: consumers (producers) of goods with domestic prices higher than international prices are hurt (benefited) by a closed economy. Second, protectionist measures have damaging effects for aggregate social welfare. By distorting prices, protectionism leads to the inefficient allocation of resources and hinders producers' incentives to adopt new technologies and match their international competitors. As the opportunity costs of protection climb, policymakers become more interested in dismantling barriers to trade.

The historical impact of exogenous changes in trade costs is undeniable. The expansion of trade in the 19th century seems to have been associated with the construction of railroads, which reduced land transportation costs by 85–95 percent; the introduction of steamships; the opening of canals; and improved communications. Similarly, trade expanded again after World War II, helped by supertankers, extensive trucking, airfreight, and the systematic use of telephones and data processing. Still, this explanation faces three problems. First, technological change may well be endogenous to, rather than just a cause of, government policy (North and Thomas 1973; North 1990). Second, a fall in trade costs unleashes distributional conflicts (among different domestic interests) that may result in the maintenance of the protectionist status quo. Third, the liberalizing response of policymakers to the growing loss of welfare takes for granted the rather questionable assumption that the former are benevolent or that their utility function places enough weight on social welfare to make it responsive to the shift in international prices.

---

[3] For a summary, see Frieden and Rogowski (1996).

Free Trade as a Strategic Game

According to classical trade theory, engaging in unilateral free trade is always the best solution. Whether this strategy may be embraced depends on its internal distributional consequences (and the fact that a mechanism of compensation from the winners to the losers cannot be put in place—an issue we examine in the subsection on protectionism).

Still, consider the possibility that free trade may not be the best policy to be pursued unilaterally. Rather, some degree of protectionism may constitute the best strategy for every country, given that other countries decide to move away from free trade.[4] In this case, trade policy (including free trade) becomes affected by a structure that resembles a game-theoretic situation. Each state's decision becomes conditional on the decisions of other states, and, under certain conditions, a generalized protectionist regime at the international level may be put in place, even against the first preference of each actor. Broadly speaking, political economists and international relations theorists have modeled this type of situation as either a prisoner's dilemma or a coordination game.[5]

In a prisoner's dilemma game, the noncooperating equilibrium (the equilibrium in which both parties defect to protectionism) dominates the cooperative (or free trade) outcome, although each party or country would separately benefit more from the latter one. The noncooperative result arises because each country has defection (following unilateral protectionism while exploiting the good, liberal behavior of the other country) as its individual dominant strategy. In their willingness to exploit each other, both countries end up in a suboptimal, protectionist regime. As Scitovsky (1942) intuits, such a strategic structure may lead to an escalating tariff war in which countries find that a further increase in tariffs constitutes the best response to previous protectionist moves by other countries. In the coordination game, instead, there are several Pareto-efficient equilibria, and the actors face the problem of picking one of them collectively. In the case of trade policy, they respond with free trade to a free trade offer and with protectionism to a protectionist strategy.[6]

Hegemonic Theory and the Creation of Free Trade Regimes

With the structure of interstate cooperation affected by collaboration or coordination problems, international political economy theorists have advanced three alternative mechanisms to explain the emergence of cooperation or free trade: self-emerging cooperation; hegemonic theory; and interstate or regional institutions. We discuss the first two in this subsection, and deal with the third in the following subsection.

Although states may be submerged in a prisoner's dilemma situation, cooperation (free trade) can still emerge under certain conditions: when the game is repeatedly played by the

---

[4] For an analysis of the reasons that make protectionism a best response, see Ray (1998, chapters 17 and 18). It is also worth noting that what makes protectionism an "optimal" response is not necessarily that it is so according to economic theory. It is enough that policymakers believe it to be optimal for our discussion to hold.

[5] For other possible games modeling interstate choices, see the summary in Hasenclever, Mayer, and Rittberger (1997).

[6] For the sake of simplicity, we do not consider here a variant of the coordination game, the battle of the sexes game, in which actors prefer coordination outcomes to noncoordination, yet value different coordination values differently. For the first application and discussion of this game to the area of international cooperation and regimes, see Krasner (1984). Knight (1992) develops a unified bargaining model that accommodates the prisoner's dilemma and coordination games.

same players in an infinite or quasi-infinite horizon; when the number of players is sufficiently small; and when the payoff structure is well-known (Axelrod 1981, 1984; Keohane 1984).

Alternatively, since these conditions are relatively stringent, some researchers explain cooperation as an outcome imposed by a hegemonic power on other states. Drawing on Kindleberger's (1973: 305) work on the Great Depression, in which he argues, "for the world economy to be stabilized, there has to be a stabilizer, one stabilizer," several international relations theorists have coined a theory of hegemonic stability, according to which a single power dominating the world would be likelier to provide and guarantee collective goods, such as a free trade regime (Gilpin 1975; Krasner 1976; Keohane 1980). The Pax Britannica of 1870–1914 and the Pax Americana of the postwar period are examples of hegemonic periods associated with free trade.

The theory of hegemonic stability has been criticized on several counts. On the one hand, its empirical underpinnings seem fragile. First, its set of cases is rather limited— although, as Rogowski (1989) suggests, it is possible to extend it to the cases of classical Athens, imperial Rome, and 17th-century Netherlands. Second, it overstates the extent to which free trade was in place in the last third of the 19th century (McKeown 1983). Lastly, it wrongly collapses the interwar years (a time that had no single dominant power) into a single period in which free trade waned even before 1929 (Bairoch 1993).

On the other hand, the logical foundations of the theory of hegemonic stability have been called into question as well. First, the theory does not state why the dominant power should favor free trade.[7] Second, it does not spell out the conditions under which the dominant force would exercise its power. For example, the United Stated clearly did not exercise it in the interwar period, but did after 1945. Third, some analysts criticize the game theoretic foundations of the theory. According to Snidal (1985), in the first elaboration of hegemonic theory, the provision of free trade (among other policy outcomes) was equated to the provision of a public good. Yet, in the area of free trade, the attribute of nonexcludability is not present: those states that remain closed can be excluded from the advantages of the free trade regime.

Although the use of hegemonic theory has receded, it has not lost its theoretical knack. In his analysis of the varying rate of success of regional integration across the world, Mattli (1999) shows that the European Union and the Zollverein prospered because, in addition to generating real gains for their members, they were sustained by Germany and Prussia. By contrast, in the absence of a leading nation, attempts at integration in Europe and other continents foundered in the late 19th century.

Regional Trade Agreements

Regional trade agreements (RTAs) are not distributed symmetrically across the world.[8] They are well extended and stable among industrial countries, but have only emerged among developing countries and across industrial and developing countries in recent years. Ray (1998) attributes this pattern to two variables: the similarity, in terms of factor composition, of different products; and the depth in consumption or input variety in each country.[9]

---

[7] Rogowski (1989) provides a way to fill this gap in a parsimonious manner. Generally speaking, the leading power has been abundant in capital, which exhibits high returns, and therefore is able to pursue and impose a policy of free trade.

[8] We use the term "regional trade agreement" to refer to preferential trade agreements, free trade agreements, customs unions, and common markets.

[9] See also de Melo and Panagariya (1993).

It is only when both factors are met that RTAs easily emerge. North-South or industrial-developing RTAs hardly exist (NAFTA is probably an exception) because the factor endowments of the two areas are too dissimilar. This is paradoxical because traditional trade theory predicts free trade particularly among countries that can realize enormous trade gains. However, the very dissimilitude between countries implies that the distributional consequences within them may be too harsh—and hence the domestic population, especially in rich countries, will block a free trade arrangement. Still, as Devlin and Estevadeordal (2001) point out, North-South integration has progressed as stable rules for market access have been set up and foreign investment flows have increased.

By contrast, industrial countries, which generally trade in products that are differentiated in some dimension (such as brand) yet similar in factor composition, meet the two conditions. The distributional consequences (through a rearrangement of factor prices) are not blunt enough to block a free trade arrangement. Yet, countries can reap the benefits of expanded markets and the reduction of monopolistic practices.

Finally, in developing countries, factor composition may be similar (with a heavy presence of unskilled labor and land), but trade constitutes a minimal fraction of the national product. Whenever RTAs are established, they are conceived as a way to create large-scale markets that will facilitate import-substitution industrialization strategies. Still, these agreements are threatened by the possibility of increasing returns to scale leading to tipping models and the geographical concentration of an industry in a single country. As soon as economies of scale and agglomeration effects manifest themselves, RTAs will rapidly collapse. In fact, since countries probably anticipate the risk that industries will not develop equally across the regional area, they impose conditions that water down their agreements.

TRADE AND DOMESTIC COMPENSATION

In exploring the consequences that the international economy has on the domestic political arena, a growing literature shows that higher levels of trade systematically lead to a larger public sector across both industrial and developing nations. This section looks at domestic compensation, endogenizing politics, and the puzzle of protectionism.

Domestic Compensation

In a pathbreaking article, Cameron (1978) observes that the best predictor of an increase in the size of the public sector as a share of gross domestic product (GDP) in 1960–75 was the degree of economic openness (the sum of exports and imports over GDP) in 1960 among OECD countries. Rodrik (1998) corroborates this association for industrial countries and extends it to the level of government consumption and trade openness for the world sample. Garrett (1998, 2001) confirms these findings, showing that trade openness is associated with higher levels of government consumption and overall spending for world cross sections in the mid 1980s and the mid 1990s.[10]

---

[10] However, Garrett (2001) shows that, at least for the mid 1990s, the relationship breaks down for high-spending countries.

The theoretical mechanisms that underlie the statistical relationship are still the object of considerable debate. Broadly speaking, there are two types of explanations for the correlation between trade and size of the public sector. On the one hand, for scholars such as Cameron (1978), trade openness shapes the structure of the economy in a way that facilitates the formation of organizations and interests that impose high redistributive demands on the state. As a result of having a small domestic market and fierce competition in exports, export-based countries specialize in a reduced number of sectors, led by companies large enough to contend with the fluctuations in the world market. High levels of industrial concentration facilitate the formation of strong and centralized employers' associations and labor unions. A high degree of unionization and a relatively centralized union system then expand the public sector in two ways. First, they contribute to the formation of strong social democratic and labor parties, which in turn pursue aggressive redistributive agendas based on the expansion of the welfare state. Second, they lead to a structure of centralized wage bargaining at the national level. Strongly centralized union movements strike corporatist deals with national governments, in which unions offer wage moderation in exchange for expansionary policies geared toward full employment and increased public expenditure in areas such as unemployment benefits, health, or pensions.[11]

On the other hand, in his analysis of small, corporatist European states, Katzenstein (1985) insists that higher levels of trade integration (coupled with a high level of sector concentration in the economy) lead to growing risks, related to the volatility of the international business cycle, which in turn put pressure on policymakers to develop publicly financed compensatory programs in favor of the exposed sectors.[12] Rodrik (1998) takes up and extends these ideas in a formal setting. According to Rodrik, since more open economies have higher exposure to the risks derived from turbulent world markets, public expenditure, set by a state purely conceived as a social planner, grows to stabilize aggregate income and deliver social peace and political stability.

The model works as follows. First, greater openness increases rather than reduces domestic volatility and risk. Although the world market is less volatile than any domestic economy, particularly in a small country, openness to trade normally implies specialization in production due to the law of comparative advantage. Accordingly, holding all other things constant, small, open economies are less diversified than large economies. Second, assuming that an economy cannot purchase insurance from the rest of the world, domestic welfare varies with fluctuations in domestic production.[13] Third, any economy has three sectors—a private tradables sector, a private nontradables sector, and the government—whose income streams feed into a representative household. The government sector is a "safe" sector from the international economy; that is, its employment and income levels are uncorrelated with world-driven shocks. As a result, if one of the policymakers' objectives is minimizing the risk borne by the household as a result of external shocks, expansion of the public sector should be correlated with higher levels of trade openness.

---

[11] In a related idea, Aukrust (1977) models the tradables sector as an international price taker and employs public spending to buy the acquiescence of the nontradables sector to low wage increases, therefore ensuring the overall competitiveness of the national economy.

[12] For a first attempt to point to domestic compensation under a free trade regime as a mechanism to minimize risks, see Bates, Brock, and Tiefenthaler (1991).

[13] Purchasing private insurance is, according to Rodrik, unfeasible due to either conflicts between capital market openness and other objectives of government policy, or incentive and sovereign-risk problems restricting the range and extent of financial instruments available to governments.

Endogenizing Politics

The current models of trade and domestic compensation neglect the importance of political conflict in two ways. First, they (implicitly) attribute the level of trade openness to parameters exogenous to the political decisions of domestic actors, thus forgetting the political-economic models of trade policy. Second, they describe the growth of the public sector as an automatic and, in some cases, functional requirement of having a free trade regime, thus neglecting the literature on the redistributive consequences of public spending (Esping-Andersen 1990; Holsey and Borcherding 1997). In Rodrik (1998), for example, households do not differ on the sources of income, and the government sector, completely unlinked from the external economy, can expand as much as necessary (with the only constraint imposed by the distortionary effects of taxes) to minimize the volatility inherent in trade openness.

Adserà and Boix (2002) address this unrealistic description of the political-economic setting. They develop a model in which voters have heterogeneous preferences in both trade and tax policy dimensions due to their exposure to trade and the variability of their potential trade gains. Politicians then make two decisions. First, two parties run for office, offering two alternative economic strategies: the protectionist party supports a protectionist regime; the free trade party defends a program that combines free trade and domestic compensation. Second, the model goes on to allow politicians to choose, given the set of policy alternatives available to them, the political regime they would impose—either a democracy or an authoritarian regime.

Solving the model, any mechanical correlation between trade openness and domestic compensation breaks down. Domestic compensation emerges as just one possible strategy to build a free trade coalition: its use to secure low tariffs is neither necessary nor sufficient. It is not necessary because free trade may be achieved without increasing public spending—basically by employing an authoritarian strategy that represses all trade losers. It is not sufficient because policymakers can impose a protectionist solution through either elections or an authoritarian regime. Adserà and Boix (2002) empirically corroborate these different political outcomes by employing a panel of 65 developing and industrial nations for 1950–90, using data for public revenue as a share of GDP.

The Puzzle of Protectionism

To the extent that it has been publicized, the finding that free trade and domestic compensation constitute an empirical regularity in the political economy of trade policy surprises both the standard scholarly literature in economics and public opinionmakers. However, in hindsight, it is the persistence of protectionism rather than the free trade–compensation outcome that appears to be the most striking phenomenon, given what we know from trade theory. As repeatedly noted by trade theorists, trade policy is an inefficient tool for redistributing income. Any form of direct compensation achieves the objective of preserving the welfare of the import-competing sector while in fact minimizing the total deadweight loss for the economy. Therefore, if compensation is Pareto optimal with respect to protectionism, we need to understand why the "puzzle of protectionism" actually occurs. Rodrik (1995: 1471) suggests at least three ways to reconcile what he terms "the political efficiency of trade policy with its economic inefficiency for redistributive purposes." After summarizing them, we suggest two additional explanations.

First, the persistence of protectionism may be due to the fact that the total excess burden may be lower than under alternative, more efficient mechanisms (such as production subsidies) once the costs involved in the political choice of the mechanism (for example, those generated by competing lobbies) are also taken into account.

Second, protectionist outcomes may emerge in a context of incomplete information. In a highly influential model, Fernández and Rodrik (1991) assume that trade reform, which always increases aggregate welfare, is adopted or rejected through majority vote. Whenever trade reform (in favor of more openness) increases the income of a majority and that information (about who benefits) is available to the winners, trade reform is adopted. Trade reform does not happen, however, once there is an unequal distribution of information among voters about the individual consequences of trade reform.

Consider a case in which most of the voters know they will gain for sure. The remaining voters only know that overall welfare will increase (by a certain amount), but they are uncertain about their individual gain. Still, they can estimate their expected benefit from reform—the difference between the overall increase and the part that goes to the known winners. This situation makes the individuals in the second group identical ex ante and prone to reject reform because the chances of a positive gain are slim.[14] This model explains status quo bias—uncertain voters simply block change—and therefore requires the additional assumption that protectionism was dominant in previous periods to explain its current persistence. Rodrik (1995) notes that this is not an unreasonable claim, in part because trade tariffs are an excellent tax handle among poor nations; there seems to be a built-in bias in favor of protectionism across countries (for purely fiscal or revenue-collection reasons). Furthermore, the model does not seem to deal well with an alternative position between the status quo and trade reform plus compensation (the model is simply about voting for or against reform). An example of the failure of the second option and therefore the persistence of protectionism requires the introduction of a new factor that addresses the question of credibility.[15]

The third way to reconcile political efficiency with economic inefficiency is to note that protectionism may occur in the context of voting in a multidimensional space. Mayer and Riezman (1989) place voters in an array in three-dimensional space according to their preferences on trade, consumption, and income taxes. With multidimensional voting, there is a minimal probability of having an equilibrium, and therefore the outcome depends on the strategy of an agenda setter, who may prefer inefficient tariffs. However, it is unclear why the agenda setter would choose an inefficient instrument if what finally matters is the welfare of voters.

We add two possible suggestions to the models suggested by Rodrik. First, the preference of protectionism over free trade plus compensation may be related to the inability of free traders to credibly commit to a compensation package. For example, in Fernández and Rodrik's model, the majority that is certain to gain may promise the remaining voters a compensation package that would make them at least as well off under the new regime as they were in the status quo arrangement. The compensation is feasible given the positive aggregate consequences of the reform. However, once the reform is passed and the veil of ignorance has disappeared, the majority that wins has no incentive to approve the compensation plan. Anticipating this, the uncertain minority will block the reform. The result should hold in a more general model. Even when winners and losers are known ex ante and the winners are a minority that needs to

---

[14] The status quo vote occurs with a risk-neutral, rational, and forward-looking individual. It is exacerbated by the introduction of risk aversion.

[15] Feenstra and Lewis (1991) and Coate and Morris (1993) also model protectionism as an outcome of a political arena with uncertainty.

commit to compensation policies to buy the support of the median voter to open the economy, the issue of credibility may finally jeopardize the openness result.

Second, protectionist sectors are endogenous to protectionist policies. Once they have achieved the passage of a tariff, import-competing sectors have no incentive to reallocate their assets to export-competing industries. This may explain as well why protectionist policies are preferable to losing economic sectors. The alternative mechanism of compensation may not be equally attractive to the import-competing sectors because in many cases it may not ensure their persistence—and therefore their political capacity to receive government support.

THE IMPACT OF TRADE ON DOMESTIC POLITICAL INSTITUTIONS

Spurred by the breakup of Yugoslavia, the Soviet Union, and Czechoslovakia, as well as the growing secessionist movement across Europe, a formal literature has developed to examine the political and economic causes of political integration. The level of trade integration plays an important role in this new literature. In Wei (1991a, 1991b), growing levels of openness (and thus the realization of trade gains) must be secured by a process of political integration. Still, the expansion of states generates a more inefficient provision of public goods. The parameter (trade gains or public goods provision) that weighs heavier in the policymakers' decision is conditional on economic development. At higher levels of development, the economic benefits from facilitating trade play a larger role and thus political integration becomes likelier. At lower levels of development, the costs of inefficient government may outweigh the benefits of economic integration.

By contrast, Casella and Feinstein (1990) and Alesina and Spolaore (1997) treat the level of trade integration as independent of the process of political integration. In Casella and Feinstein, political integration has two opposite effects: political and legal unification reduces transaction costs and thus boosts economic integration; at the same time, the provision of public goods becomes farther removed from local preferences. Alesina and Spolaore also consider a location model, but they explore how different types of political regimes affect the chances of political integration. As the size of the nation grows, the average utility provided in public goods declines because more citizens are located far from the capital of the state (where public goods are generated). Still, the level of political integration varies with the type of political regime. When the provision of public goods and political integration are determined under a democratic setting, the number of small nations increases because voters located at the borders have an incentive to form separate nations. Conversely, under authoritarian regimes, controlled by self-interested individuals whose objective is to maximize net tax revenues, more political integration occurs. Given this setup, the level of economic integration or globalization also shapes the number of nations. As free trade increases, the need to establish unified political institutions to secure trade gains falls and the number of nations in turn increases.

In Bolton and Roland (1997), interindividual income differences substitute for differences in geographical location, and an optimal taxation model, as in Meltzer and Richards (1981), decides the tax rate. Different patterns of income distribution across regions in a given country affect the choice of secession or unification by their populations. If each region has a different income distribution, the median voter in each one may decide to vote for separation, precisely to achieve a policy that is closer to that voter's ideal point. Trade again affects the decision of voters: if trade gains can be realized even after secession, the incentives to sustain a unified country decline. Bolton and Roland (1996) further explore the role of factor mobility in the decisions of countries. Perfect factor mobility leads to the equalization of fiscal policies across countries and thus cements political unions. Conversely, with fixed factors, heterogeneity in preferences and policies remains and secessionist claims escalate.

Although this new formal literature on trade and the size and number of nations seems to match important developments in international political economy, at least three questions need further research.[16] First, with the exception of Wei (1991a, 1991b), the literature treats the level of trade integration as exogenous to political decisions. In doing so, it implicitly embraces a purely economic view of trade integration, according to which growing efficiency gains and price convergence driven by technological shocks force free trade on policymakers, while disregarding the political sources of openness.[17] Second, little attention is given in any model to the impact of trade integration on demand management policies. As shown in Romer (1993) and Campillo and Miron (1997), the incentives to pursue monetary expansion and hence inflation are much lower in open economies. Higher levels of trade integration ease the costs of forming a monetary union.[18] Third, the possible effects of trade integration on nations are modeled with no regard to the heterogeneity of either factor or sector trade interests in each nation. Any model that treats voters as a homogeneous set of actors in the trade policy dimension must be necessarily incomplete.

Predictions over the impact of trade openness on the type of political institutions are extremely mixed in the literature. On the one hand, it sees trade liberalization as generally incompatible with democracy because it imposes considerable losses on key economic sectors. Recently, authoritarian regimes or policymakers that are isolated from public opinion have pursued trade openness (Fernández and Rodrik 1991; Haggard 1990; Stokes 1999). Yet, on the other hand, the fact that trade and democratic regimes came hand in hand in such disparate periods as 19th-century England and ancient Greece has not gone unnoticed by some authors (Rogowski 1989).

Boix and Garicano (2001) develop a model to explain democratization, which can be easily extended to explain the interaction between democracy and trade policy. In their model, decisions over the political regime take place in economies characterized by two parameters: the degree of wealth inequality between individuals and the extent to which productive assets are specific to the country in which they are located. Economic equality promotes democracy in the following way. As modeled in Meltzer and Richards (1981), in a democratic system, in which the median voter sets the tax rate, the level of taxation (to fund redistributive transfers) increases with the level of inequality. Hence, for high levels of inequality, the richest segment of voters (who suffer net losses) may have an incentive to impose an authoritarian system and reduce taxes to zero. As the distribution of capital becomes more balanced across individuals, the potential redistributive impact of democracy diminishes to the point that the repression costs of imposing a dictatorship become higher than the tax rate voted by the median voter, and the probability of a peaceful transition from an authoritarian regime to universal suffrage

---

[16] For an empirical test of the relationship between the size and number of nations and different levels of international economic integration, see Alesina, Spolaore, and Wacziarg (2000).

[17] Alesina, Spolaore, and Wacziarg (2000: 1284) seem to suggest that as the average number of countries increases, and given that small countries benefit the most from trade openness, support for a more open trade regime will go up. However, this discounts the possibility that free trade and protectionist strategies develop in a strategic game resembling a prisoner's dilemma game. Even if each small nation may prefer free trade, an open trade regime may not be an equilibrium. Historically, the breakup of the Austrian-Hungarian empire clearly did not lead to a free trade regime in interwar Central Europe.

[18] For a review of this issue, see De Grauwe (1997).

increases. However, a decline in the specificity of capital curbs the redistributive pressures from noncapital holders. As capital can be more easily moved away from its country of origin, tax rates decline in equilibrium and the likelihood of democracy also rises.

In the context of this model, it is easy to show that trade openness affects the choice of a political regime conditional on the distribution of factors in the economy. To see the varying effects of trade, assume two types of countries, A and B, with two types of agents: skilled workers, who use a relatively well developed technology and therefore earn high wages; and unskilled workers, who operate a bad technology and receive low wages. Countries vary in the distribution of types. Whereas in country A skilled workers are the scarce factor (and unskilled workers are the abundant factor), in country B skilled workers constitute the abundant factor. In country A, unskilled workers clearly benefit from an expansion in trade. As the demand for them goes up, their wages increase and wage compression takes place. With inequality declining, previous redistributive tensions ease and the probability of democracy goes up—such as in Britain in the 19th century. In country B, by contrast, any decline in tariffs hurts the poor class. As the demand for skilled workers increases, wage dispersion goes up, political pressures for redistribution grow, and an authoritarian backlash becomes more likely—as in most Latin American countries in the second third of the 20th century.

CONCLUSION

The past two decades have witnessed extraordinary activity in formal and empirical research on the political determinants and consequences of trade policy. Still, several areas are in need of further work. First, analysts should develop models that integrate the domestic and international determinants of trade policy. Second, further research is needed to understand why free trade, on its own or sustained by compensation policies toward the losing sectors of the economy, is so hard to come by across the globe. Third, there is fertile ground for better integration of the (joint) choice of fiscal and trade policies. Finally, more work is required to expand the literature on how trade flows shape domestic preferences and hence domestic political institutions.

REFERENCES

Adserà, Alícia, and Carles Boix. 2002. Trade, Democracy and the Size of the Public Sector. *International Organization* 56(2, Spring). Forthcoming.

Alesina, Alberto, and Enrico Spolaore. 1997. On the Number and Size of Nations. *Quarterly Journal of Economics* 112 (November): 1027–56.

Alesina, Alberto, Enrico Spolaore, and Romain Wacziarg. 2000. Economic Integration and Political Disintegration. *American Economic Review* 90 (December): 1276–96.

Alt, James E., Jeffry Frieden, Michael J. Gilligan, Dani Rodrik, and Ronald Rogowski. 1996. The Political Economy of International Trade: Enduring Puzzles and an Agenda for Inquiry. *Comparative Political Studies* 29(6, December): 689–717.

Alt, James E., and Michael Gilligan. 1994. The Political Economy of Trading States: Factor Specificity, Collective Action Problems and Domestic Political Institutions. *Journal of Political Philosophy* 2(2): 165–92.

Aukrust, Odd. 1977. Inflation in the Open Economy: A Norwegian Model. In L. Krause and W. Salant (eds.), *Worldwide Inflation*. Washington, DC: Brookings Institution.

Axelrod, Robert. 1981. The Emergence of Cooperation among Egoists. *American Political Science Review* 75 (June): 306–18.

———. 1984. *The Evolution of Cooperation*. New York, NY: Basic Books.

Bairoch, Paul. 1993. *Economics and World History. Myths and Paradoxes*. Chicago, IL: The University of Chicago Press.

Balistreri, E. 1997. The Performance of the Heckscher-Ohlin-Vanek Model in Predicting Endogenous Policy Forces at the Individual Level. *Canadian Journal of Economics* 30: 1–17.

Bates, Robert H., Philip Brock, and Jill Tiefenthaler. 1991. Risk and Trade Regimes: Another Exploration. *International Organization* 45: 1–18.

Beaulieu, E. 1996. Who Supported the Canada-U.S. Free Trade Agreement: Factor or Industry Cleavages in Trade Policy? Unpublished.

———. 1997. Factor or Industry Cleavages in Trade Policy? An Empirical Test of the Stolper-Samuelson Theorem. Unpublished.

Boix, Carles, and Luis Garicano. 2001. Democracy, Inequality and Country-Specific Wealth. University of Chicago, Chicago, IL. Unpublished.

Bolton, Patrick, and Gerard Roland. 1996. Distributional Conflicts, Factor Mobility, and Political Integration (in Unification and Separation in Europe). *American Economic Review* 86 (May): 99–104.

———. 1997. The Breakup of Nations: A Political Economy Analysis. *Quarterly Journal of Economics* 112 (November): 1057–90.

Cameron, David R. 1978. The Expansion of the Public Economy: A Comparative Analysis. *American Political Science Review* 72: 1243–61.

Campillo, Marta, and Jeffrey A. Miron. 1997. Why Does Inflation Differ across Countries? In Christina D. Romer and David H. Romer (eds.), *Reducing Inflation: Motivation and Strategy*. Chicago, IL: University of Chicago Press.

Casella, A., and J. Feinstein. 1990. *Public Goods in Trade: On the Formation of Markets and Political Jurisdictions*. Working Paper in Economics E-92-12, Hoover Institution, Stanford University, Palo Alto, CA.

Coate, S., and S. Morris. 1993. On the Form of Transfers to Special Interests. University of Pennsylvania, Philadelphia, PA. Unpublished.

De Grauwe, Paul. 1997. *The Economics of Monetary Integration*. New York, NY: Oxford University Press.

de Melo, Jaime, and Arvind Panagariya (eds.). 1993. *New Dimensions in Regional Integration*. New York, NY: Cambridge University Press.

Devlin, Robert, and Antoni Estevadeordal. 2001. What's New in the New Regionalism? In Victor Bulmer-Thomas (ed.), *Regional Integration in Latin America and the Caribbean: The Political Economy of Open Regionalism*. London, UK: Institute for Latin American Studies, ILAS Series.

Esping-Andersen, Gosta. 1990. *The Three Worlds of Welfare Capitalism*. Cambridge: Polity.

Feenstra, R. C., and T. R. Lewis. 1991. Distributing the Gains from Trade with Incomplete Information. *Economics and Politics* 3: 21–40.

Fernández, Raquel, and Dani Rodrik. 1991. Resistance to Reform: Status Quo Bias in the Presence of Individual-Specific Uncertainty. *American Economic Review* 81(December): 1146–55.

Findlay, R., and S. Wellisz. 1982. Endogenous Tariffs, the Political Economy of Trade Restrictions, and Welfare. In J. Bhagwati (ed.), *Import Competition and Response*. Chicago, IL: University of Chicago Press.

Frieden, Jeffry A. 1991. *Debt, Development, and Democracy: Modern Political Economy and Latin America, 1965–1985*. Princeton, NJ: Princeton University Press.

Frieden, Jeffry A., and Ronald Rogowski. 1996. The Impact of the International Economy on National Policies: An Analytical Overview. In Robert O. Keohane and Helen V. Milner (eds.), *Internationalization and Domestic Politics*. Cambridge, UK: Cambridge University Press.

Garrett, Geoffrey. 1998. Governing in the Global Economy: Economic Policy and Market Integration around the World. Yale University, New Haven, CT. Unpublished.

———. 2001. The Distributive Consequences of Globalization. Yale University, New Haven, CT. Unpublished.

Gilpin, Robert. 1975. *U.S. Power and the Multinational Corporation*. New York, NY: Basic Books.

Grossman, Gene M., and Elhanan Helpman. 1994. Protection for Sale. *American Economic Review* 84 (September): 833–50.

Haggard, Stephan. 1990. *Pathways from the Periphery*. Ithaca, NY: Cornell University Press.

Hasenclever, Andreas, Peter Mayer, and Volker Rittberger. 1997. *Theories of International Regimes*. New York, NY: Cambridge University Press.

Hillman, A. L. 1989. *The Political Economy of Protection*. Chur, Switzerland: Harwood Academic Publishers.

Hiscox, Michael J. 1999. The Magic Bullet? The RTAA, Institutional Reform, and Trade Liberalization. *International Organization* 53(4): 669–98.

———. 2001. Class versus Industry Cleavages: Inter-Industry Factor Mobility and the Politics of Trade. *International Organization* 55(1): 1–46.

Holsey, Cheryl M., and Thomas E. Borcherding. 1997. Why Does Government's Share of National Income Grow? An Assessment of the Recent Literature on the U.S. Experience. In Dennis C. Mueller (ed.), *Perspectives on Public Choice: A Handbook*. New York, NY: Cambridge University Press.

Irwin, D. 1994. The Political Economy of Free Trade: Voting in the British General Election of 1906. *Journal of Law and Economics* 37: 75–108.

———. 1996. Industry or Class Cleavage over Trade Policy? Evidence from the British General Election of 1923. In R. Feenstra, G. Grossman, and D. Irwin (eds.), *The Political Economy of Trade Policy: Papers in Honor of Jagdish Bhagwati*. Cambridge, MA: MIT Press.

Kaempfer, W., and S. Marks. 1993. The Expected Effects of Trade Liberalization: Evidence from U.S. Congressional Action on Fast-Track Authority. *The World Economy* 16: 725–40.

Katzenstein, Peter. 1985. *Small States in World Markets. Industrial Policy in Europe*. Ithaca, NY: Cornell University Press.

Keohane, Robert O. 1980. The Theory of Hegemonic Stability and Changes in International Economic Regimes, 1967–1977. In Ole Holsti and others (eds.), *Change in the International System*. Boulder, CO: Westview Press.

———. 1984. *After Hegemony. Cooperation and Discord in the World Political Economy*. Princeton, NJ: Princeton University Press.

Kindleberger, Charles P. 1973. *The World in Depression, 1929–1939*. Berkeley, CA: University of California Press.

Knight, Jack. 1992. *Institutions and Social Conflict*. New York, NY: Cambridge University Press.

Krasner, Stephen D. 1976. State Power and the Structure of International Trade. *World Politics* 28: 317–47.

———. 1984. Global Communications and National Power: Life on the Pareto Frontier. *World Politics* 43: 336–66.

Lohmann, Susanne, and Sharyn O'Halloran. 1994. Divided Government and U.S. Trade Policy: Theory and Evidence. *International Organization* 48(Autumn): 595–632.

Magee, Stephen P. 1980. Three Simple Tests of the Stolper-Samuelson Theorem. In Peter Oppenheimer (ed.), *Issues in International Economics*. London, UK: Oriel Press.

———. 1994. Endogenous Protection: A Survey. In D. C. Mueller (ed.), *Handbook of Public Choice*. Cambridge, MA: Basil Blackwell.

Magee, Stephen P., William A. Brock, and Leslie Young. 1989. *Black Hole Tariffs and Endogenous Protection*. Cambridge, UK: Cambridge University Press.

Mattli, Walter. 1999. *The Logic of Regional Integration: Europe and Beyond*. New York, NY: Cambridge University Press.

Mayer, Wolfgang. 1984. Endogenous Tariff Formation. *American Economic Review* 74 (December): 970–85.

Mayer, Wolfgang, and J. Li. 1994. Interest Groups, Electoral Competition, and Probabilistic Voting for Trade Policies. *Economics and Politics* 6: 59–77.

Mayer, Wolfgang, and R. Riezman. 1989. Tariff Formation in a Multidimensional Voting Model. *Economics and Politics* 1: 61–79.

McKeown, Timothy. 1983. Hegemonic Stability Theory and 19th Century Tariff Levels in Europe. *International Organization* 37: 73–91.

Meltzer, A. H., and S. F. Richards. 1981. A Rational Theory of the Size of Government. *Journal of Political Economy* 89: 914–27.

Nelson, D. 1988. *The Political Economy of U.S. Automobile Protection.* NBER Working Paper 4746, National Bureau of Economic Research, Cambridge, MA.

North, Douglass. 1990. *Institutions, Institutional Change and Economic Performance.* Cambridge, UK: Cambridge University Press.

North, Douglass C., and Robert Paul Thomas. 1973. *The Rise of the Western World: A New Economic History.* Cambridge, UK: Cambridge University Press.

Olson, Mancur. 1965. *The Logic of Collective Action.* Cambridge, MA: Harvard University Press.

———. 1982. *The Rise and Decline of Nations.* New Haven, CT: Yale University Press.

Ray, Debraj. 1998. *Development Economics.* Princeton, NJ: Princeton University Press.

Rodrik, Dani. 1995. What Does the Political Economy Literature on Trade Policy (Not) Tell Us That We Ought to Know. In G. Grossman and K. Rogoff (eds.), *Handbook of International Economics, Volume 3.* Amsterdam, Netherlands: Elsevier Science.

———. 1998. Why Do Open Economies Have Bigger Governments? *Journal of Political Economy* 106: 997–1032.

Rogowski, Ronald. 1989. *Commerce and Coalitions. How Trade Affects Domestic Political Alignments.* Princeton, NJ: Princeton University Press.

Romer, David. 1993. Openness and Inflation: Theory and Evidence. *Quarterly Journal of Economics* 107: 869–904.

Scheve, Kenneth F., and Matthew J. Slaughter. 2001. What Determines Individual Trade-Policy Preferences? *Journal of International Economics* 54(2, August): 267–92.

Scitovsky, T. 1942. A Reconsideration of the Theory of Tariffs. *Review of Economic Studies* 9: 89–110.

Snidal, Duncan. 1985. Coordination versus Prisoners' Dilemma: Implications for International Cooperation and Regimes. *American Political Science Review* 79(December): 923–42.

Stokes, Susan. 1999. What Do Policy Switches Tell Us about Democracy? In Adam Przeworski, Susan C. Stokes, and Bernard Manin (eds.), *Democracy, Accountability, and Representation.* New York: Cambridge University Press.

Wei, Shang-Jin. 1991a. Federation or Commonwealth: A Viable Alternative to Secessions? University of California, Berkeley, CA. Unpublished.

———. 1991b. To Divide or to Unite: A Theory of Secessions. University of California, Berkeley, CA. Unpublished.

PART III
POLICIES AND INSTITUTIONS

Chapter 5

Trade Policy Regimes and Development Strategies: A Comparative Study

Sam Laird and Patrick A. Messerlin

Over the past two decades, nearly all developing countries and transition economies have undertaken important changes in their trade regimes, often as part of World Bank-International Monetary Fund programs. Recently, further changes in trade regimes have been driven by participation in regional trade agreements (RTAs) and in the General Agreement on Tariffs and Trade/ World Trade Organization (GATT/WTO). However, while greater openness appears to have produced useful gains, not all countries have benefited equally from the reforms. This study attempts to distinguish between important elements of the reform programs, taking account of the linkages with other economic policies, and to derive some indicators of trade policy performance that might be used in developing more precise guidelines for future reforms.

The study looks at the relative importance of reforms in different regions and corresponding trade performance. The first section describes the overall economic performance of a number of countries in Latin America, Europe, and Asia. The second section reviews Latin American trade policies over the past 20 years, and the third section provides an international comparison and develops indicators that could serve as guidelines for monitoring progress. The fourth section discusses the links between trade and other economic policies.

ECONOMIC PERFORMANCE IN SELECTED COUNTRIES

The overall economic performance of Latin America has been somewhat less satisfactory than that of the Pacific Asian region, particularly in the 1970s and 1980s, although there was marked improvement in the 1990s until the Brazilian crisis. Table 5–1 gives the real growth in GDP from 1965–70 to 1997–98 for a number of countries in Latin America, Europe, and Asia, chosen to represent a range of policy choices and performance.[1] Chile has been the lead performer in Latin America, but Argentina and the Dominican Republic had increased economic growth in the 1990s. The Latin American countries also performed well prior to the debt crisis of the early 1980s, which had only a minor effect on countries in Pacific Asia.

Overall growth is reflected in per capita incomes. While Latin American incomes were considerably higher than those of the Pacific Asian countries up to 1985, by the late 1990s,

---

[1] The effects of the East Asian crisis already show up in the 1997–98 data for Pacific Asia.

Table 5-1

Real Growth in GDP in Selected Countries, 1965–98
(Percent)

Country/region	1965–70	1970–75	1975–80	1980–85	1985–90	1990–95	1995–97	1997–98
Argentina	4.0	3.1	2.8	−2.5	−0.5	6.6	6.8	3.9
Brazil	7.8	10.3	6.7	1.1	2.0	3.1	3.0	0.1
Chile	4.6	−1.4	7.3	0.9	6.7	8.7	7.5	3.4
Colombia	5.9	5.7	5.4	2.2	4.5	4.5	2.4	0.6
Dominican Republic	9.0	9.0	4.9	2.3	2.8	4.2	7.7	7.3
Mexico	6.2	6.3	7.1	1.9	1.7	1.5	6.0	4.8
Latin America (average)	6.2	5.5	5.7	1.0	2.9	4.8	5.6	3.4
Korea	10.5	8.1	7.1	8.1	10.0	7.5	5.9	−5.8
Singapore	12.9	9.5	8.5	6.2	8.4	9.1	7.8	1.5
Thailand	9.1	5.7	8.0	5.4	10.3	8.6	2.1	−9.4
Indonesia	6.3	7.8	7.9	5.6	7.1	7.8	6.3	−13.2
Asia (average)	10.9	7.8	7.8	6.6	9.6	8.4	5.2	−4.6
Poland	—	—	—	0.1	1.1	2.7	6.4	4.8
Romania	—	—	7.4	3.1	−3.0	-2.1	-1.5	−7.5
Turkey	—	5.7	2.8	4.9	5.6	3.2	7.2	2.8
Central Europe (average)	—	5.7	5.1	2.7	1.2	1.3	4.1	0.0

Note: Values are based on GDP at market prices (1995 U.S. dollars).
Source: World Bank (2000).

income levels in Pacific Asia ($11,449) were 50 percent higher than those in Latin America ($7,622) (World Bank 2000). Income growth in the Central European countries has lagged behind even Latin America since the late 1990s. The growth rate in Chile's income levels has been only slightly below the average in Pacific Asia since 1985, and above it in 1995–97.

Pacific Asia's export performance was also better than that of Latin America in 1980–95. Latin America was able to lift its performance in 1995–97, with strong results in Mexico, Argentina, and the Dominican Republic (table 5–2). Latin American and Central European countries had comparable performance in 1990–95, while Poland's strong exports sustained a superior European performance over other regions in 1997–98.

Extensive debate has focused on the link between openness and economic performance (Sachs and Warner 1995; Rodrik 1999). Although analysts generally accept that trade liberalization makes a positive contribution to economic growth, at least in the medium-to-long term, some criticize the econometric evidence. Rodrik, in particular, emphasizes the importance of governance rather than openness per se. Even economists who accept the general proposition recognize that the short-term effects need not be positive (Mosley 2000). In practice, there is likely a considerable overlap, with more open economies also undertaking institutional reforms. The evidence from the countries covered by this study fits the general pattern, with a moderate positive correlation between growth in real gross domestic product (GDP) in the selected countries in the 1990s against their trade/GDP ratios for the same period (figure 5–1).

Figure 5–2 plots the aggregate export performance of Latin America and Pacific Asia (exports of goods and services in current U.S. dollars, indexed at 1995=100) and their real exchange rates in 1980–98. (The real exchange rate is the U.S. dollar rate adjusted by the

Table 5-2

Growth in Exports of Goods and Services, 1980–98

(Percent based on current dollars)

Country/region	1980–85	1985–90	1990–95	1995–97	1997–98
Argentina	0.3	8.1	11.1	11.2	0.5
Brazil	4.9	4.9	8.4	6.0	−0.7
Chile	−5.5	17.9	13.6	3.6	−8.8
Colombia	−3.3	14.0	7.2	7.6	−5.2
Dominican Republic	0.8	6.7	25.6	11.0	6.0
Mexico	6.9	9.1	12.8	16.8	6.3
Latin America (average)	3.5	8.5	11.3	11.5	2.1
Indonesia		8.6	12.6	9.3	−13.3
Korea	9.0	19.2	15.0	5.8	−5.0
Singapore	2.8	19.3	17.0	2.7	−17.6
Thailand	2.8	26.3	19.2	1.5	−9.0
Asia (average)	5.3	20.3	16.6	3.7	−10.7
Poland	−4.1	7.8	13.4	5.5	9.2
Romania	−2.0	−10.2	8.1	2.9	−4.4
Turkey	25.2	13.6	11.7	19.2	4.9
Central Europe (average)	2.0	5.8	12.0	11.6	5.7

Source: World Bank (2000).

Figure 5-1

Trade/GDP and GDP Growth, 1990–98

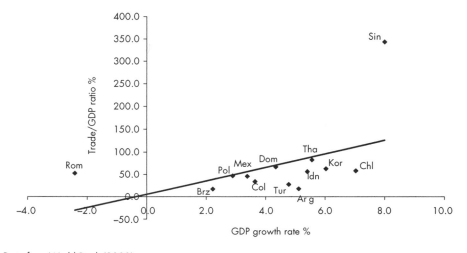

Source: Data from World Bank (2000).
Note: Countries in the sample are listed in table 9–1.

Figure 5–2

Real Exchange Rates and Exports, Latin America and Asia, 1980–98

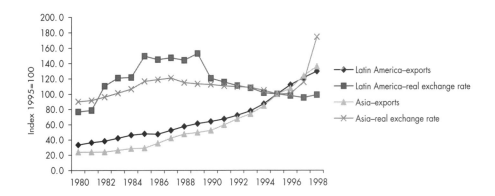

relative movements in inflation, measured by GDP deflators.) The figure shows a significant negative correlation in the 1990s, implying that a real appreciation is associated with a negative movement in exports of goods and services.

We also regressed the export index in figure 5–2 against real exchange rates and the aggregate economic growth of major industrial economies in 1981–98. Table 5–3 shows that the aggregate export performance of the selected countries is positively affected by GDP growth in the industrial countries and negatively affected by their real exchange rates. Since the data are in index form (1995=100), the interpretation of the coefficients is that relative to the base year, 1995, a 1-point movement in the index of GDP in the industrial countries will call forth an increase of 2.27 points in the exports of goods and services in the selected developing countries. By contrast, a 1-point appreciation of the real exchange rate in the selected countries will cause a decrease of 0.46 points in their exports.

Table 5–3

Factors Affecting Export Performance in the Sample Countries, 1981–98

Variable	Coefficient	t-value
Constant	−90.15	4.08
Real exchange rate	−0.46	3.45
GDP growth in industrial countries	2.27	14.24
R^2	0.93	
F statistic	113.04	
Degrees of freedom	17	

Note: Values are from ordinary least squares regression; the dependent variable is the export index. The countries in the sample are listed in table 9-1.
Source: Authors' calculations.

The main message from this analysis is that, while developing countries can do little about the economic performance of industrial countries, developing countries can operate on their own export performance in several ways. First, they can affect the real exchange rate by trying to control or liberalize movements in their nominal exchange rate, directly or indirectly (for example, through monetary policies). Similarly, an autonomous or policy-induced increase in foreign direct investment (FDI) inflows would likely cause an appreciation under a floating currency regime, and vice versa.

Second, developing countries could operate on price movements in their own countries by using macroeconomic and microeconomic policies that affect investment, technology, industry, and trade. For example, trade policies impact efficiency in the allocation of resources, technology, and productivity. Adoption of new technologies may be the key to improving productivity—and hence unit prices and international competitiveness. Although transparent and predictable trade policies are helpful in attracting FDI, which is often associated with new technologies, other governance factors also affect the attractiveness of a host country for FDI.

LATIN AMERICAN TRADE POLICIES

From Import Substitution to Outward Orientation

Until the reforms that began in the 1980s, Latin America (like many developing regions) was characterized by a high degree of government intervention and state ownership. In trade policy, policymakers thought that import protection and import substitution industrialization (ISI) were needed to generate jobs and provide income stability. They used infant industry (economy) arguments to justify shutting out foreign trade by means of exchange controls, multiple exchange rates, quantitative import restrictions or prohibitions, high tariffs, subsidies, and tax breaks. Export restrictions or taxes channeled raw materials to domestic processing industries (in the transition economies, they have been used in the past to ensure food supplies). There was widespread xenophobia about foreign investment, and many countries placed legal and constitutional obstacles in the way of foreign participation in the development of natural resources and financial and other services.

A particularly important consequence, the ISI policies created an anti-export bias: import protection reduces the demand for foreign currencies (apparently saving foreign exchange), but this inevitably pushes up the exchange rate, making exports more expensive and reducing their international competitiveness. Specifically, ISI policies had strong negative effects in agriculture—an area of comparative advantage in Latin America (Krueger, Schiff, and Valdez 1988)—exacerbating rural poverty and encouraging the drift to urban areas. In industry, tariffs were generally high, unbound, and set in tiers that escalated with the level of processing, although they were often irrelevant because of the prevalence of nontariff measures (from minimum prices to quantitative restrictions).[2] Moreover, there were so many tariff exemptions that the published tariff often bore little resemblance to the duties collected.[3] The tariffs,

---

[2] Papageorgiou, Michaely, and Choksi (1990) provide an excellent review.
[3] For example, in Argentina, the average nominal tariff was reduced from 98 to 49 percent in the Martinez de Hoz period (1976–81), and stood at more than 30 percent in 1988, but the ratio of duties collected to total imports was close to 2 percent for all the years between 1970 and 1988.

import restrictions with liberal exemptions, and tax breaks for key sectors created a policy mix that was so complex as to be partly self-defeating. Industry lost touch with international markets, falling behind in the adoption of newer technologies and international competitiveness.

The lack of any discernable growth and high inflation in the 1980s paved the way for a break with the past. Per capita incomes were declining, unemployment soared, and social programs were threatened. In a number of cases, there were serious balance-of-payments crises (Indonesia, Mexico, and Nigeria); in Latin America, there was acute hyperinflation (Argentina, Bolivia, and Peru). Following the growing disillusion with the failure of past policies (or at least a recognition that the ISI model had run its course), many countries noted the achievements of the fast-growing economies in East Asia, which were either open (Singapore and Hong Kong) or had begun reforms much earlier (Korea and Chinese Taipei), albeit with different emphases in key elements.

Today, the trade policy situation is much clearer than in the pre-reform period. Developing countries have eliminated most nontariff barriers and tariff exemptions, applied lower most-favored-nation (MFN) rates, and adopted more uniform tariff structures. However, much remains to be done.

Trade Liberalization and Domestic Growth: First Evidence

Table 5–4 gives an overview of the changes and their impact on growth. It presents applied (rather than bound) MFN tariff rates before and after the main reforms for a small group of countries. All the countries in the sample show a positive relation between reduced protection and increased growth rates (table 5–1). This relation is captured by "tariff liberalization gross elasticities," defined as the increase or decrease in the growth rates (before and after tariff liberalization) with respect to the decrease in tariff protection.[4] The gross qualification is intended to convey that tariff changes are likely to be accompanied by regulatory reforms in other domains (for instance, reduction of nontariff measures, liberalization of financial transactions, better macroeconomic policies, and general governance), which are generally (although not necessarily) consistent with tariff reductions.

Gross tariff elasticities can be estimated for the short and long run. Short-run estimates are based on changes in the growth performance between the five-year periods immediately preceding and following the liberalization; long-run estimates are based on the average growth rates for the entire periods available before and after liberalization. It seems reasonable to give precedence to gross elasticities in the short run because trade is only one growth factor among several. The impact of any tariff liberalization is likely to decrease with time, assuming all other things constant and the absence of indirect effects of liberalization on technical progress, and competitive market structures.

Table 5–4 provides three major results. First, all the short-run elasticities except one are negative, as expected. For instance, in Argentina, a 1-percent tariff decrease is associated with a 0.36-percent increase in the growth rate. The exception is Mexico, which exhibits a positive (although small) short-run elasticity. Setting data problems aside, two reasons may explain the

---

[4] It is crucial to relate changes in growth rates to *changes* in the level of protection. Relating growth rates to the *level* of protection (as Bairoch [1993] did in examining the European liberalization of the 1860s) is not the relation suggested by economic analysis, and indeed it leads to a result—the European tariff liberalization of the 1860s–1970s leading to recession—that is not observed if changes are taken into account (Messerlin 1985).

Table 5-4

Gross Tariff Liberalization Elasticities for Selected Countries, 1980s and 1990s

| Country | Pre-reform | | Post-reform | | Short-run elasticity with respect to | | | Long-run elasticity with respect to | | |
	Average tariff rate	Year	Average tariff rate	Year	Growth	Exports of goods	Exports of goods and services	Growth	Exports of goods	Exports of goods and services
Argentina	30.0	1989	12.2	1992	-0.359	-0.172	-0.152	-0.245	-0.262	-0.261
Brazil	51.0	1988	12.5	1996	-0.117	-0.434	-0.371	0.319	-0.127	-0.125
Chile	20.0	1985	11.0	1992	-0.902	-3.313	-3.640	-0.673	-2.140	-2.461
Colombia	31.0	1987	11.5	1996	-0.329	-1.853	-1.989	0.172	-1.447	-1.642
Mexico	22.6	1986	12.5	1993	0.047	-0.525	-0.634	0.382	-0.653	-0.757
Indonesia	27.0	1985	20.0	1994	-0.642	-3.437	-3.680	0.694		
Korea	24.0	1984	9.0	1995	-0.114	-1.338	-1.426	0.343	-0.481	-0.551
Thailand	44.0	1991	23.1	1995	-0.341	-1.777	-1.680	0.112	-1.090	-0.985
Poland	18.3	1989	9.3	1995	-0.195	-0.232	-0.683	-0.449	-0.968	-1.002

Note: Values for elasticities are simple averages for all products, including agriculture, except for Poland (which is a trade-weighted average).
Source: Authors' calculations.

Mexican anomaly: macroeconomic problems and the already existing *maquiladora* regime. In any case, this result is interesting because it fits well with the insistence of the Mexican authorities to conclude the NAFTA agreement.

Second, the highest elasticities are those observed for Chile, which has a uniform MFN tariff—another observation tending to support the superiority of the uniform tariff formula over a product-discriminatory tariff liberalization (Tarr 2001). This result likely mirrors the existence of other liberalization measures in Chile (a uniform tariff is such a bold approach that it is unlikely to be limited to tariff matters).

Third, long-run elasticities may be positive—once again, not such a surprising result because many factors other than trade liberalization play a role in domestic growth. Long-run elasticities are negative in only three cases: Argentina, Chile, and Poland. In the Chilean case, this result re-emphasizes the robustness and simplicity of the Chilean trade policy in the long run (enhancing the expectations of further liberalization in Chile, as recently underlined by the reduction in MFN tariffs from 11 to 9 percent with little opposition). By contrast, the Polish case may reveal the expectations related to the Polish accession to the European Union (Poland will have to adopt lower European Union tariffs). Positive long-run elasticities are consistent with economic analysis for the remaining eight countries, to the extent that some reversal in tariff liberalization is observed in the other countries of the sample, particularly if antidumping measures are included. That leaves Argentina as the only country in the sample with a negative long-run elasticity despite a (slight) reversal in tariff protection between 1992 and 2000.[5]

Gross tariff liberalization elasticities can also be computed with respect to changes in export performance. Table 5–4 presents the results for exports of goods only, and for exports of goods and services. Negative elasticities are the rule, a result consistent with economic analysis showing that tariffs on imports are de facto taxes on exports.

Multilateral Framework and Domestic Goals

Prior to the Uruguay Round, Latin American interest in GATT was largely aimed at improving access to foreign markets, including by securing legitimacy for special and differential treatment. At the beginning of the Uruguay Round, the position of the Latin American countries began to evolve. GATT members, such as Argentina, Colombia, and Mexico, began to play an active and positive role in the Uruguay Round negotiations. Initially, they adopted a strategy of asking for credit for their previous unilateral actions on trade liberalization, which they undertook in connection with World Bank lending programs. This was not a successful move, both because industrial countries did not believe that there would be a reversal of the ongoing trade liberalization, and because Latin American governments were increasingly convinced that trade liberalization was good for the implementing country. In addition, since 1986, some 15 Latin American countries have joined the GATT/WTO, binding all their MFN tariffs at ceiling levels ranging from 20 to 50 percent and, in some cases, making binding commitments on nontariff measures.

In the Uruguay Round itself, all Latin American GATT members made comprehensive ceiling-binding commitments, normally around 35 percent. The main exceptions to the 35

---

[5] The tariff reversal consisted of the merger of tariffs and the statistical tax (hence, the reversal was more apparent than real).

percent ceiling binding were Peru, which bound across the board at 30 percent, and Costa Rica, which bound at 40 percent. Overall in the Round, the Latin American countries cut their bound rates by 24.5 percent (Guzman and Laird 1998). However, these concessions were to bind at rates substantially above current applied tariff rates, leaving scope for tariff increases.

Apart from tariff reforms, the Latin American countries also committed themselves to the multilateral rules-based system, which the Uruguay Round was extending in such areas as services and trade-related intellectual property rights (TRIPs), as well as to tightened disciplines in other areas (see Safadi and Laird 1996).

Regionalism Old and New

Prior to the reforms of the last 10-15 years, tariff preferences were widespread throughout the region. But they were established bilaterally or among groups of countries under the Asociación Latin-Americano de Integración (ALADI) umbrella with different product coverage, limited degrees of preference, and often production-sharing agreements. All these agreements failed for several key reasons (de Melo and Dhar 1992): many products were excluded from the coverage of the agreements, high rates of protection were maintained against third countries, and there was little scope for economies of scale. Thus, the early regional arrangements essentially led to amplified trade diversion, and reduced rather than increased welfare (Langhammer and Hiemenz 1991).

Paralleling the autonomous reform process in Latin America and the increased GATT/WTO membership in the 1980s and early 1990s, RTAs have flourished in Latin America—mirroring a worldwide movement to which the European Union has by far been the largest contributor, the hub for a host of RTAs (Crawford and Laird 2001; Messerlin 2001). Among the more important of these new or reformulated RTAs are Mercosur (and its FTAs with Bolivia and Chile), the Andean Community, the Central American Common Market (CACM), the G3 (Mexico, Colombia, and Venezuela), and the Caribbean Rim Agreement. Several Latin American countries are also participants in the Asia-Pacific Economic Cooperation (APEC), although this is not as yet a preferential trade agreement, espousing open regionalism. Last but not least, there is the plan for a Free Trade Area for the Americas (FTAA) by 2005 that could subsume all existing free trade agreements in the region and carry trade liberalization further than previously imagined.

All these new RTAs differ markedly from those of the 1960s. They not only cover tariff liberalization covering almost all products, but they also aim at comprehensive agreements in the areas of investment, intellectual property, rules of origin, antidumping duties, sanitary standards, dispute settlement, and competition policy. Beyond the questions related to their sheer complexity and overlap, these new RTAs raise two key strategic issues for Latin American countries.

First, do RTAs with industrial countries have greater credibility than intradeveloping country RTAs? This question of increased credibility, as well as improved market access and even political stability, echoes the problems behind the candidatures of Central European countries to the European Union. Available evidence from these cases does not strongly support the credibility argument in favor of RTAs with industrial countries. For instance, tariff increases from European Union partners have preceded the Europe Agreements. They have been unsuccessful in reducing the skyrocketing use of antidumping measures, both between the members of the agreements and between the members and outsiders. Their complexities (for instance, on rules of origin) have generated transaction costs higher than small tariffs (moreover, these costs tend to be appropriated by trade intermediaries, fueling rent-seeking tactics). They have generated increases in applied tariffs by developing countries against their neighboring nonmembers (in an attempt to minimize losses of tariff revenues due to decreases in their tariffs vis-à-vis industrial hubs). Lastly, for most of these agreements, there is no evidence of large FDI inflows that could be directly attributed to them. However, Hartler and Laird (1999) show that Turkey's MFN tariff was reduced by half and the implementation of a number of measures under the Customs Union Agreement has been beneficial to Turkey and third countries. The main exception is agriculture, where both Turkey and the European Union have high levels of protection. Evidently, much depends on the details of the case, and it cannot be assumed that engaging in an RTA with industrial countries is necessarily welfare increasing.

Second, how easy will it be for Latin American countries to multilateralize the existing RTAs in which they participate? For instance, to what extent will the combination of the FTAA and an RTA with the European Union be close to worldwide free trade for the Latin American countries that would decide to join these two envisaged RTAs? If they were close to worldwide free trade, then Latin American countries might be induced to multilateralize them rapidly in the context of WTO Rounds of liberalization—an incentive that could be shared by other developing countries in the world, such as those in the Middle East and North Africa (Hoekman and Messerlin 2002).

TRADE POLICY REGIMES: AN INTERNATIONAL COMPARISON

Evolution of Trade Policies

There are some indications that trade policies have moved more slowly in Latin America than elsewhere. For instance, the use of nontariff measures has declined in many countries (Michalopoulos 1999; Laird 1999). However, nonautomatic licensing is still relatively frequent in Latin America (often related to the administration of tariff quotas in the agricultural sector); variable levies, associated with the use of price band systems, are important in Chile and Colombia; and prohibitions are still current in Brazil. Counterbalancing this decline in nontariff measures, there has been an increase in the use of administrative measures, such as anti-dumping, where certain Latin American countries (Argentina, Brazil, and Mexico) are among the most intensive users. Lastly, export regimes have survived in many Latin American countries, in sharp contrast with the Pacific Asian countries, which have mostly dismantled their export regimes since 1995, with the nearly complete elimination of the export processing zone instrument.

To gain an understanding of these moves in relative terms, we attempt to construct indices to allow broad comparisons between the trade policies of various countries. This approach highlights the determinants that producers and traders take into consideration when deciding to export to (or invest in) foreign markets. Firms export more to or from markets subjected to the best trade policies (even if they still do not fit the free trade ideal) than to other markets, and trade policies compete with each other to attract trade (and investment) flows. The approach has two additional advantages: it provides useful lessons to countries for improving their existing trade policy, and it does not require knowledge of the absolute costs related to trade policies (which is hard to find), but a mere ranking of the trade policies examined.

When looking at foreign markets, firms consider a wider range of features than free trade. First, they consider whether the examined trade policy is simple to understand and predict. Second, they determine whether it will guarantee secure access in the future. And they analyze the policy's openness in terms of market access (the free trade component). In order to address these concerns, we considered three indices—simplicity, irreversibility, and openness—for a reference set of 39 countries (including 10 in Latin America), based on data from WTO (2001), UNCTAD's TRAINS database, and the OECD.

Simplicity Indices

Building the Indices

Simplicity indices aim at capturing the information and other transaction costs that a trade policy imposes. They are intended to determine the extent of effort that producers, traders, and investors need in order to understand the trade policy of a country. The simplicity index in agriculture relies on six basic indicators.

1. Does the tariff schedule of the country examined include many tariff lines, meaning that more effort most be devoted to find the correct tariff line to be used, or that there are more risks of errors by or conflicts with the country's customs authorities than would be the case with a tariff schedule consisting of a more limited number of tariff lines?

2. What is the percentage of non-ad valorem bound tariffs? A low percentage would imply that greater effort is required to assess the real level of protection because specific tariffs or combined specific ad valorem tariffs entail a level of protection that varies with world prices.

3. What is the standard deviation of bound tariffs? A high deviation requires more effort to find out the exact tariff rate. Risks in the face of different rates are high, and the consequences potentially more costly than for a low standard deviation. A zero standard deviation signals a uniform tariff policy that has two advantages. First, it minimizes the information and transaction costs of foreign exporters for determining the nominal tariff rate (unique by definition). Second, it does not disturb the country's comparative advantage (the effective rate of protection of each industry is equal to the unique nominal tariff rate), so that foreign investors have no reason to make complex calculations in order to know the effective tariff rates that their production will face, if located in the country.

4. What is the percentage of non-duty-free tariffs? A high percentage would imply greater risks of facing different tariffs (hence, information costs).

5. How many product groups are affected by the export subsidy reduction commitments signed by the country in question under the Uruguay Agriculture Agreement (UAA)? A small number would suggest a less complicated assessment of the support granted to the domestic producers of the examined country.

6. How many tariff quotas are included in the country's UAA commitments? A high number would imply the need for greater efforts to investigate the impact of these tariff quotas.

This list does not exhaust all possible indicators of simplicity. Indicator 1 would be improved with information on the existence and magnitude of changes in the number of lines during recent years (in order to capture the possible reshuffling of the tariff schedule for protectionist purposes) and on the number of tariff schedules that reflect preferential agreements involving the country examined. Indicator 2 would be more complete with evidence on seasonal tariffs and/or the number of public authorities (ministries and agencies) in charge of trade issues. Indicator 4 would be improved by information on low tariffs (say, lower than 3 percent) in order to get a sense of the extent to which trade barriers matter and to understand the rationale for such a wasteful allocation of resources (collecting low tariffs often does not even cover the administrative costs of customs). Indicator 6 could be improved with information on the management of tariff quotas—in particular, whether they are granted on a first come, first served rule or on another rule (underscored by OECD [2001], a first come, first served rule tends to have a protectionist impact).

The simplicity index in industry relies on five basic indicators. The first four are similar to the first four indicators for agriculture. The fifth indicator consists of the frequency of nontariff measures. A high frequency would require greater efforts to investigate the exact impact of these nontariff measures in the export market.

The first four indicators for industry could be improved in ways similar to those for agriculture. Indicator 5 would be improved with data on the number of customs officers (or enforcement officers in other government departments involved in NTM management) per dollar of imports, in order to capture the intensity with which nontariff measures could play an effective role as a trade barrier on imports. However, there is no systematic information available in this area.

For each country, each basic indicator receives a score from 1 to 10, which reflects the decile to which the country belongs for that indicator. For instance, the highest grade (10) is given to those farm trade policies pertaining to the decile with (1) the smallest number of tariff lines, (2) the lowest percentage of non-ad valorem bound tariffs, (3) the lowest standard deviation of bound tariffs, (4) the lowest percentage of non-duty-free tariffs, (5) the smallest number of product groups affected by export subsidies, and (6) the smallest number of tariff quotas. In manufacturing, the same scoring system is applied for the first four common indicators with agriculture, and the highest grade (10) is given to trade policies pertaining to the decile with the lowest frequency of nontariff measures for indicator 5.

Then, for each country, aggregated indices for agriculture and industry are calculated as simple averages of the corresponding basic indicators. This (admittedly crude) method provides indices for the 39 countries and six regions (North America, Latin America, Europe, Pacific Asia, Southeast Asia, and Africa). The simplest trade policy would receive an index of 10 (it should be stressed that an index of 10 does not mean that the trade policy is perfectly simple, but merely that it is among the simplest available in the reference sample of 39 countries), and the most complicated an index of 1. As simplicity indices of 10 and 1 do not necessarily exist (because they are the simple average of several basic indicators), the average simplicity index for the whole set of countries is used as the reference figure.

Results

Table 5–5 shows that the seven Latin American countries for which there is information (there is no information available for Chile, Jamaica, and Peru) enjoy a simpler trade policy in agriculture than the reference average for the 39 countries.[6] Only Colombia exhibits a trade

---

[6] Table 5–5 gives summary results by aggregated index. Detailed results by indicator are available from the authors.

policy less simple than the reference set. The European countries (Norway and the European Union) have the poorest performance in simplicity in farm matters, reflecting the many instruments included in their agricultural policies. Interestingly, table 5–5 shows no result by country that would be at odds with the general perception from the past 20 years of analyses and negotiations in the farm sector.

Table 5–5 shows that the situation in industry is dramatically different. Latin American countries have a markedly more complicated trade policy than the reference average for the whole sample of countries. In particular, the three largest Latin American countries (Argentina, Brazil, and Mexico) have the most complicated trade policies of all the countries in the sample (with Turkey, but the observations for this country date from 1997, that is, at the time when the customs union signed with the European Union had not yet simplified Turkey's trade policy). Three small Latin American countries (Jamaica, Costa Rica, and Chile) have an index higher than the average index of the reference sample of countries.

The sharp contrast between the situation of Latin American countries in farm and industry matters is striking, all the more so because of the negligible difference between the world simplicity indices in agriculture and industry. This implies a converse shift in other countries. Of course, European countries provide the best illustration of this converse situation, although their relative performance in simplicity of industry is mediocre (close to the world average).

Of course, simplicity is not synonymous with openness. Certain countries have a simple trade policy because they are open, as best illustrated by Iceland in industry, or Hong Kong, China in agriculture and industry. But simplicity does not necessarily imply openness. For instance, the European Union trade policy in industry is relatively open but complicated; trade policies of African countries tend to be relatively simple but not open; and India and (to a lesser extent) Sri Lanka exhibit relatively complex, closed trade policies.

This observation raises two key issues for improving trade policies. The first is the need to pay attention to the divergence between the measures of simplicity and openness—in particular, complex but open trade policies—since the lack of simplicity is likely to erode the benefits from open market access. Second, detailed information based on the basic indicators shows the main sources of the lack of competitiveness in Latin American trade policies vis-à-vis the policies of the rest of the world: the number of tariff lines in certain Latin American tariff schedules, the share of non-duty-free bound tariffs, and the frequency of nontariff measures.

Irreversibility Indices

Building the Indices

The irreversibility indices aim at capturing the risks that an existing trade policy could be reversed rapidly and substantially. Irreversibility is a major dimension of trade policy envisaged by producers, traders, and investors—and by GATT/WTO with the concept of bindings.

The irreversibility index in agriculture relies on four indicators. Greater irreversibility in trade policy implies the following:

1. A smaller share of unbound tariffs in the tariff schedule. Unbound tariffs exempt the country from the most stringent WTO discipline, that is, the need to renegotiate any increase in a tariff above the binding ceiling rate.

Table 5-5

Aggregate Indices for Agriculture and Industry, Selected Countries and Regions, Late 1990s

Country/region	Region	Agriculture			Industry		
		Simplicity	Irreversibility	Openness	Simplicity	Irreversibility	Openness
Canada	NA	7.8	9.0	9.3	8.2	8.6	9.8
United States	NA	6.7	7.0	9.1	7.4	7.5	9.4
Argentina	LAC	7.0	10.0	6.8	5.0	7.2	6.4
Brazil	LAC	7.0	10.0	8.0	5.2	7.6	6.9
Chile	LAC				7.2	7.2	8.4
Colombia	LAC	6.8	8.3	5.6	6.4	6.8	7.5
Costa Rica	LAC	8.5	8.5		7.4	8.1	8.4
El Salvador	LAC	10.0	9.0		6.8	8.6	8.5
Jamaica	LAC				8.0	8.0	7.0
Mexico	LAC	7.8	8.0	7.9	5.2	7.2	6.9
Peru	LAC				6.8	6.8	6.9
Venezuela	LAC	7.0	7.5	6.3	6.6	6.8	7.1
European Union	E	4.8	6.8	7.0	6.6	6.3	9.6
Iceland	E	6.5	8.0	6.7	8.8	7.5	9.1
Norway	E	3.5	5.8	5.0	8.8	5.8	8.4
Switzerland	E	5.7	5.5	7.4	5.8	6.1	10.0
Turkey	E	3.8	5.5	6.3	4.6	5.0	7.8
Czech Republic	E	6.8	8.5	8.7	7.2	7.8	9.3
Hungary	E	5.2	3.5	8.6	6.0	5.8	7.6
Poland	E	4.8	5.0	7.1	6.4	5.8	8.9
Romania	E	4.8	7.5	3.5	6.2	5.5	7.5
Australia	PA	9.2	9.8	8.9	7.2	8.7	9.1
Hong Kong	PA				8.4	8.4	10.0
Indonesia	PA	7.8	10.0	7.4	6.6	8.0	8.3
Japan	PA	8.6	9.7	7.7	8.8	8.7	9.6
Korea	PA	6.2	8.0	6.0	8.0	7.1	9.1
Malaysia	PA	8.0	7.3	8.2	6.6	7.5	7.8
New Zealand	PA	9.8	8.8	8.1	7.6	8.6	9.3
Philippines	PA	7.8	8.3	6.7	7.6	7.6	8.7
Singapore	PA	10.0			8.2	9.1	10.0
Thailand	PA	6.8	9.0	6.5	6.4	7.2	7.8
India	SEA	7.0	8.0	3.0	5.8	6.0	4.0
Sri Lanka	SEA	7.0	10.0	6.8	6.4	7.6	7.9
Cameroon	A				7.8	7.8	7.3
Chad	A				7.8	7.8	7.3
Gabon	A				8.0	8.0	7.4
South Africa	A	6.3	6.3	8.5	7.0	7.0	7.0
Tunisia	A	7.3	7.0	3.4	6.2	6.0	5.9
Zimbabwe	A				7.0	7.0	6.7
Number of observations		31	30	28	39	39	39
Minimum index		3.5	3.5	3.0	4.6	5.0	4.0
Maximum index		10.0	10.0	10.0	8.8	9.1	10.0
North America	NA	7.3	8.0	9.2	7.8	8.1	9.6
Latin America	LAC	7.7	8.8	6.9	6.5	7.4	7.4
Europe	E	5.1	6.2	6.7	6.7	6.2	8.7
Pacific Asia	PA	8.2	8.9	7.4	7.5	8.1	9.0
Southeast Asia	SEA	7.0	9.0	4.9	6.1	6.8	5.9
Africa	A	6.8	6.7	6.0	7.3	7.3	6.9
All countries		7.0	7.8	6.9	7.0	7.3	8.1
All countries except							
Latin America		6.8	7.6	7.0	7.2	7.2	8.3
Industrial countries		7.2	7.8	7.5	7.8	7.7	9.4
Developing countries		6.9	7.9	6.6	6.6	7.1	7.4

Source: Authors' calculations.

2. A smaller standard deviation in the fill rates of tariff quotas. A wide dispersion reflects the impact of quota management methods, assuming that the tariff quotas included in the UAA (3 to 5 percent of domestic consumption) are so small that they should be fulfilled at a similar (presumably high) rate.
3. A smaller average use of export subsidy outlays.
4. A smaller percentage of tariff lines potentially subjected to special agricultural safeguard provisions.

The list misses the most relevant information on domestic farm policies, for instance, the existence of (legal or de facto) trade monopolies or farm boards, the risks of reversibility associated with sanitary and phytosanitary standards, labeling procedures, and nontrade concerns. For example, environmental policies may be perverse if, as is the case in the European Union, they may favor farmers who have been the initial polluters.

In industry, the index relies on five indicators:

1. A smaller share of unbound tariffs in the tariff schedule (as in agriculture)
2. A smaller number of tariff lines with bound tariffs higher than 15 percent (because high unbound tariffs generate either higher risks of reversal or risks of larger reversals)
3. A smaller difference between the bound and applied tariffs
4. A smaller frequency of core nontariff barriers (NTBs)
5. A smaller number of antidumping cases (per hundred million dollars of imports) initiated during the period 1995–99.

The economic rationale of all these indicators is obvious, although there are some apparent data problems.[7] As for simplicity, the list of indicators could have been more complete. For instance, a country that has no antidumping regulations is treated the same as one that has the regulation but has initiated antidumping cases, although the potential risk of irreversibility may be quite different, at least in the short run. As a result, it would have been useful to add to indicator 4 an indicator on the existence of antidumping regulations adopted under the Uruguay Anti-dumping Agreement.

Results

The results in table 5–5 appear plausible, although the picture in manufacturing for Central European countries (Czech Republic, Hungary, Poland, and Slovakia) and Gabon seems too optimistic. (This may be due to the fact that, for these countries, the frequency of their core NTBs has been arbitrarily set to the regional average; see footnote 7.)

Irreversibility indices provide the same global results as the simplicity indices, although they are slightly less marked: the Latin American countries exhibit a noticeably higher level of

---

[7] For example, in some instances, applied tariffs are higher than bound tariffs for certain countries (indicator 3). This may result because observations on bound and applied tariffs are for different years or because of trade-weighted averaging. Moreover, differences between bound and applied tariffs should ideally be assessed differently whether they are calculated over a small share of unbound tariffs or over a large share. A score of 1 has been attributed to all countries with a share of unbound tariffs larger than 50 percent (independent of the observed difference between bound and applied tariffs for the country in question). Indicator 4 (frequency of core nontariff barriers) is not available for all countries. The European Union frequency has been applied to Central European countries, and the regional average to the Latin American, Pacific Asian, and African countries for which a specific observation is missing.

irreversibility than the reference sample of countries in agriculture (European countries have the lowest level), whereas the converse situation prevails in industry. Chile is the only exception in industry, with an index higher than the world average. The contrast between large and small Latin American countries that was visible for simplicity does not hold clearly for irreversibility.

Detailed results by basic indicator (not shown) suggest that trade policies can lack irreversibility for different reasons. Three basic indicators explain the less-than-average indices of Latin American countries: the large number of tariff lines with bound tariffs higher than 15 percent (more than 99 percent of the Latin American tariff lines are in this situation, with the exception of Brazil [97.4 percent]); the large difference between bound and applied tariffs (the record being held by Jamaica with 41.2 percent); and the intensive use of antidumping measures per hundred million dollars of imports (Argentina and Peru being 18 times more aggressive than the United States and 11 times more aggressive than the European Union in antidumping enforcement).

Openness Indices

Building the Indices

The level of protection is another key dimension examined by producers, traders, and investors when making their decisions, and we attempt to capture this with the openness index. The openness index in agriculture relies on nine indicators. Greater openness in farm trade policy implies the following:

1. A smaller average bound tariff as estimated by the OECD
2. A smaller average bound tariff as estimated by the World Bank[8]
3. A smaller average applied tariff
4. A smaller share of tariffs lower than 15 percent
5. A smaller share of tariffs lower than 100 percent
6. A smaller escalation index (the ratio of the average tariff on semi-processed goods with respect to the average tariff on unprocessed products, as calculated by WTO 2001, in order to take into account the magnification of nominal protection introduced by the escalation process
7. A lower producer support estimate mirroring production subsidies (drawn from OECD)
8. A lower final post-Uruguay Round budgetary outlay commitment on export subsidies
9. A higher fill rate of the tariff quotas.[9]

The openness index in industry relies on eight indicators. Greater openness in manufacturing trade policy for a given country implies the following:

1. A smaller average bound tariff
2. A smaller average applied tariff

---

[8]Bound tariffs in agriculture often have a specific tariff component that is difficult to quantify in ad valorem terms; therefore, we rely on the two available estimates provided by the OECD and the World Bank.

[9]There is so little information on the average applied tariffs in agriculture that, unfortunately, it has been impossible to introduce this indicator.

3. A smaller share of peak tariffs (higher than 15 percent)
4. A smaller escalation ratio (the ratio of the average tariff on finished products with respect to the average tariff on raw materials, as calculated by WTO 2001)
5. A smaller standard deviation of the applied tariffs (because a narrow range of tariff rates minimizes the risk and magnitude of effective protection)
6. A smaller frequency of core NTBs
7. A smaller use of antidumping actions (per thousand dollars)
8. An indication of whether the country has signed the information technology agreement (ITA), reflecting the country's openness to technical progress, which is key for liberalizing services.

Since several Latin American countries are aggressive users of antidumping actions, an additional interesting piece of information would have been the average antidumping duty, or the ad valorem equivalent of antidumping measures.

Results

Table 5–5 provides a summary by region. According to detailed results by basic indicator (not shown), Latin American countries have average openness performance (compared with the reference sample) in agriculture, but significantly lower than average in industry. In industry, there is a clear division between small countries (Chile, Costa Rica, and El Salvador) that are more open than the sample average, and large countries (Brazil, Mexico, and Argentina) that exhibit significantly lower indices than the world average.

Policy Lessons

The approach described here is not only useful to better assess the existing situation. It also provides useful lessons for improving existing trade policy by helping each country to assess the major weaknesses of its current policy. Thus, each country decides which remedy is most urgent and whether to undertake action in a unilateral or multilateral framework. For instance, should a country focus on the simplicity dimension of its trade policy, or should it also deal with the irreversibility or openness aspects? For each aspect, what is the precise source of problems, hence the priority instrument for improvement? Such questions are often overlooked when adopting trade policy. For instance, many difficulties in trade facilitation flow from the implementation of complex trade policy. Solving the problem at its source (simplifying trade policy) is a more efficient action than creating a problem by adopting a complex trade policy, and then investing in ways to deal with the problems it creates (Maur and Messerlin 2001).

The three indices are correlated to a certain extent, but differently in agriculture and industry.[10] The trade policies of most Latin American countries lag behind those of the rest of the sample—Chile being the main exception, with, in several instances, certain small Latin American countries (El Salvador and Jamaica). The fact that the Latin American country positions are better in agriculture than in industry reflects two converging forces: the more protectionist approach of

---

[10] The lower level of quality for agricultural data compared with data on industry does not allow the combination of indices for agriculture and industry. This is even truer for services, where data are so poor that it has been impossible to conduct a similar exercise of scoring and calculating indices by country and region.

Latin American trading partners in agriculture, coupled with the Latin American comparative advantages in this activity, which induce these countries to have a more liberal trade policy. Of course, this situation is not satisfactory for Latin American consumers (who would benefit from less protection in industry) and producers (who would benefit from less protection in Latin American trading partners).

This approach is useful from a policy perspective because it provides insight on the areas where improvements in policy should be made and on the environment in which such improvements should be made. This second point deserves more attention than usually granted. Openness is an issue that is best dealt with through WTO negotiations because a country can then compound the benefits from its lowered protection by the gains from lowered protection among its trading partners. By contrast, simplicity is a feature that could be addressed through unilateral actions because it permits a full return from the level of openness granted by previous trade negotiations. It seems counterproductive to erode granted trade concessions and their potential benefits by implementing a complicated trade policy, the ultimate consequence of which is to restrict market access. In such a case, the country bears the political costs of liberalization, without realizing the economic gains. Irreversibility may be a feature that needs multilateral disciplines, but it also has a purely domestic component in terms of subsidies and broadly conceived national treatment.

In sum, decomposing trade policy into features that have different (unilateral or multilateral) tones suggests a subtle approach to trade liberalization. For instance, simplifying its trade policy would be unlikely to provide large benefits to Chile, which already ranks high in this domain. By contrast, simplification would be productive for Argentina and Mexico; for instance, Mexico should reduce the number of tariff lines, and Argentina should reduce nontariff measures. Adding services would reinforce this contradiction, to the extent that privatization of services undertaken in Latin American countries is equivalent to liberalizing these services, an assumption that many economists and observers would challenge. In effect, too many of these privatizations have consisted of moving public monopolies into private hands without a substantial opening of the markets involved.

TRADE POLICIES AND OTHER ECONOMIC POLICIES

Latin America has had a long history of populist policies, leading to overly expansive macroeconomic policies relying on deficit financing, generalized controls, and a disregard for basic economic equilibria (Dornbusch and Edwards 1991). Policymakers, rejecting monetarist orthodoxy and influenced by structuralist supply-side solutions, thought that idle capacity would provide leeway for the economic expansion needed to improve living standards without running inflationary risks. This was done by deficit financing, covered by foreign borrowing. When bottlenecks arose, usually from a lack of foreign exchange, devaluation was initially rejected because of the likely adverse consequences for inflation and living standards. It was also argued that devaluation would not work because of institutional rigidities. For example, under existing systems of land tenure, it is easy to avoid increasing agricultural production in response to price incentives (increasing output would have required the possibility of creating larger farms). If agricultural production were increasing, the gains would be offset by a decline in the terms of trade. Moreover, in the absence of equivalent domestically produced goods, imports would not fall. Thus, it was argued that devaluation would not improve the trade balance, but rather lower real incomes and accelerate inflation. Nevertheless, each time the economic situation deteriorated, governments were usually forced to resort to price realignments, devaluation, exchange controls, and import restrictions.

In Latin America, more than most other developing regions, fixed or managed exchange rate policies have often been used as a nominal anchor to help combat inflation. The risk attached to such policies is that, when real exchange rates appreciate, there is a negative effect on export competitiveness and export performance, affecting the overall balance-of-payments position. This occurred in Mexico until the tequila crisis of 1994, in Brazil up to 1998, and most recently in Argentina. Thus, Latin American countries (and the selected European countries) have persistently run current account deficits (table 5–6). Although Pacific Asian countries faced a similar problem until the 1990s, they have had greater success in controlling deficits than has Latin America.

In order to combat the deterioration in trade performance and balance of payments as a result of real exchange rate appreciation, countries in Latin America often used import restrictions in the past. However, with the tightening of WTO disciplines and Latin American countries' increased participation in regional trade agreements, the option of using trade policy for balance-of-payments reasons has become more difficult. In any case, trade measures do nothing to address the domestic deficits that underlie current account imbalances, and likely inhibit the type of structural change necessary to resolve such problems. Therefore, in the past 10–15 years, governments have increasingly addressed such macroeconomic problems with fiscal and monetary measures.

Several economic indicators explain the nature of the problem. For example, Latin American (and European) countries have taken a less strict fiscal stance than the selected Pacific Asian countries, which have more often run fiscal surpluses. Within Latin America, only Chile and the Do-

Table 5–6

Current Account Balance, Selected Countries and Regions, 1980–98
(Percentage of GDP)

Country/region	1980	1985	1990	1995	1997	1998
Argentina	−6.2	−1.1	3.2	−1.9	−4.1	−4.9
Brazil	−5.5	−0.1	−0.8	−2.6	−3.7	−4.3
Chile	−7.1	−8.6	−1.6	−2.3	−5.0	−5.3
Colombia	−0.5	−4.5	1.2	−5.0	−5.4	−5.7
Dominican Republic	−10.9	−2.1	−4.0	−1.5	−1.1	−2.1
Mexico	−4.7	0.4	−2.8	−0.4	−2.1	−4.1
Latin America (average)	−5.8	−2.7	−0.8	−2.3	−3.6	−4.4
Indonesia		−2.2	−2.6	−3.2	−2.3	4.2
Korea	−8.5	−0.8	−0.8	−1.7	−1.7	12.6
Singapore	−13.3	0.0	8.5	17.3	15.8	20.9
Thailand	−6.4	−4.0	−8.5	−8.1	−2.0	12.8
Asia (average)	−9.4	−1.8	−0.9	1.1	2.4	12.6
Poland	−6.0	−1.4	5.0	0.7	−4.0	−4.4
Romania			−8.5	−5.4	−6.1	−7.6
Turkey	−5.0	−1.5	−1.7	−1.4	−1.4	0.9
Europe (average)	−5.5	−1.5	−1.7	−2.0	−3.8	−3.7

Source: World Bank (2000).

minican Republic have run surpluses since 1990. In Latin America, fiscal deficits have been financed both by overseas borrowing and by printing money, giving rise to periods of high inflation and even hyperinflation. The Central European countries have, at times, experienced similar problems, which are rare in the Pacific Asian countries that have generally had less than single-digit inflation since the mid 1980s. In general, the Latin American countries had greater success in tackling inflation in the late 1990s, although it has persisted above 10 percent in Colombia and Mexico.

Latin America's need for foreign borrowing to finance development has been occasioned by the relatively poor rates of domestic savings and investment. In the past 20 years, the GDS/GDP and GDI/GDP ratios in Latin America (and the selected European countries) have typically been 10–15 percentage points lower than those of Pacific Asia.[11] For example, the GDS/GDP and GDI/GDP ratios were 21.3 and 19.9 percent, respectively, in Latin America in 1997, and the corresponding figures for Pacific Asia were 33.7 and 37.1 percent, respectively. Developing and transition economies have also had a poor record in attracting FDI and indeed have often followed policies that explicitly rejected inward FDI flows. However, these policies changed in the 1990s, and recent data show that Latin America had some success in increasing foreign investment in the 1990s (table 5–7).

Prior to the change in foreign investment policies, Latin America—and other developing regions—relied on sovereign borrowing from international financial institutions and foreign banks (although less so from banks since the debt crisis of the early 1980s). This has led to a huge debt servicing commitment. The debt service/gross national product ratios of Latin American countries are comparable to those of other regions, but, reflecting their poorer trade performance, Latin American ratios of total debt service to exports of goods and services have typically been around 15 percentage points higher than other regions, for example, 35 percent in 1998, compared with 21.7 percent for Pacific Asia and 18.1 percent for the European countries.

Latin America's performance resulted in lack of confidence in the region, which is also reflected in relatively high real interest rates, 10–18 percent in the 1990s, compared with 5–8 percent for Pacific Asia. If the private sector has to pay such high interest rates for borrowing for capital investments, this must also affect Latin America's international competitiveness. Competitiveness is factored into export performance through relative prices that are a component of real exchange rates.

Thus, macroeconomic policies impinge on trade performance through a number of channels. High inflation, as a result of lax fiscal and monetary disciplines, directly affects all prices in the domestic economy. High interest rates, which result from uncertainty, and high foreign borrowing affect factor prices. And relative price movements are a component in the real exchange rate. In addition, using the nominal exchange rate as an anchor to control domestic inflation may result in a real appreciation with negative effects on export performance. If import restrictions or import taxes are used to tackle balance-of-payments deficits, they will also cause an anti-export bias and, by locking in structural weaknesses, make adjustment more difficult.

OVERALL EVALUATION

WTO commitments have helped to lock in autonomous reforms, and have contributed to the predictability and transparency of trade regimes (governance issues), although they have done

---

[11] GDS is gross domestic savings and GDI is gross domestic investment.

Table 5-7

Foreign Direct Investment, 1980–98

Country/region	1980	1990	1997	1998
Percentage of GDP				
Argentina	0.9	1.3	2.8	2.1
Brazil	0.8	0.2	2.4	4.1
Chile	0.8	1.9	7.0	5.9
Colombia	0.4	1.1	5.2	3.0
Dominican Republic	1.4	1.9	2.8	4.4
Mexico	1.0	1.0	3.6	2.6
Latin America (average)	0.9	1.2	4.0	3.7
Indonesia	0.2	1.0	2.2	−0.4
Korea	0.0	0.3	0.6	1.7
Singapore	10.5	15.2	10.2	8.6
Thailand	0.6	2.9	2.5	6.2
Asia (average)	2.8	4.8	3.9	4.0
Romania		0.0	3.5	5.3
Turkey	0.0	0.5	0.4	0.5
Poland		0.1	3.4	4.0
Europe (average)	0.0	0.2	2.4	3.3
Millions of dollars				
Argentina	788	1,836	4,924	4,177
Brazil	1,544	324	18,608	29,192
Chile	213	654	3,354	1,840
Colombia	51	484	4,894	2,509
Mexico	2,090	2,634		
Dominican Republic	93	133		
Latin America (total)	4,779	6,064	31,780	37,718
Indonesia		1,093	4,499	−400
Korea	−20	−264	−1,605	616
Singapore	1,138	3,541	4,988	4,110
Thailand	187	2,303	3,356	6,811
Asia (total)	6,176	6,674	11,238	11,137
Romania	0	−18	1,224	2,040
Turkey	18	700	554	573
Poland		89	4,908	6,365
Europe (total)	18	771	6,686	8,978

Source: World Bank (2000).

little to further open Latin American markets. Some advances have been made through regional trade agreements, despite important exclusions. The new WTO agenda and ongoing negotiations in RTAs may lead to further changes, but there is an impression that trade reforms have stalled, and the evidence on simplicity, irreversibility, and openness provided above shows that there is considerable variation among countries. Much remains to be done on simplifying and opening up trade regimes and locking them in. Moreover, although the analysis has focused on trade policy, good governance requires actions on the entire legal framework of a country. Privatization programs tend to focus too little on effective competition, weak government procurement procedures, and the lack of a strong competition policy in all but a few countries. Therefore, markets are less contestable than is desirable, and this impacts the international competitiveness of domestic production.

To understand the evolution of trade policy in Latin America, it is important to take macroeconomic policy into account. The relatively high level of inflation in the region led some countries to adopt fixed exchange rates or managed floats, which, together with other policies, caused real exchange rate appreciation with negative effects on export competitiveness. Latin America's savings/investment ratios are low compared with those in Pacific Asia. Past policies pushed up the cost of borrowing for domestic investment and made it difficult for Latin America to attract FDI, the key to improving productivity and competitiveness.

Finally, while the majority of developing countries have much to do to complete their trade reform programs, they continue to face the problem of protectionism in major markets (Laird 1999; Messerlin 2001). Apart from high, escalating tariffs on certain key exports of the developing countries, they have increasingly resorted to administrative protection—antidumping policies and export restraint agreements. Developing countries face nontariff barriers to their exports of chemicals, iron and steel, other basic manufactures, textiles and clothing, and electronic goods. In addition, quotas, surcharges, variable levies, subsidies, and state trading have distorted agricultural trade. This result partly reflects the absence of developing countries in the GATT rounds. Hence, it is important for these countries to participate actively in the post-Doha WTO work program in order to further their interests in removing barriers to trade.

REFERENCES

Bairoch, Paul. 1993. *Economics and World History: Myths and Paradoxes*. Chicago, IL: The University of Chicago Press.

Crawford, J. A., and S. Laird. 2001. Regional Trade Agreements and the WTO. *North American Journal of Economics and Finance* 12: 193–211.

de Melo, J., and S. Dhar. 1992. *Lessons of Trade Liberalization in Latin America for Economies in Transition*. Policy Research Working Paper Series 1040, The World Bank, Washington, DC.

Dornbusch, R., and S. Edwards (eds.). 1991. *The Macroeconomics of Populism in Latin America*. London, UK, and Chicago, IL: The University of Chicago Press.

Hartler, C., and S. Laird. 1999. The EU Model and Turkey—A Case for Thanksgiving? *Journal of World Trade* 33(3) June: 147–66.

Hoekman, Bernard, and Patrick A. Messerlin. 2002. Harnessing Trade for Development and Growth in the Middle East. Council on Foreign Relations, New York, NY.

Krueger, A., M. Schiff, and A. Valdez. 1988. Agricultural Incentives in Developing Countries: Measuring the Effects of Sectoral and Economy-wide Policies. *World Bank Economic Review* 2(7).

Laird, S. 1999a. *Multilateral Market Access Negotiations in Goods and Services*. CREDIT Research Paper no. 00/4, University of Nottingham, Nottingham, UK.

Laird, S. 1999b. Regional Trade Agreements—Dangerous Liaisons? *The World Economy* 22(9): 1179–200.

Laird, S., and R. Guzman. 1998. Trade Measures in Manufacturing Trade. In Montague J. Lord (ed.), *The Handbook of Latin American Trade in Manufactures*. New York: Edward Elgar.

Langhammer, R., and U. Hiemenz. 1991. *Regional Integration among Developing Countries: Survey of Past Performance and Agenda for Future Policy Action*. UNDP-World Bank Trade Expansion Program Occasional Paper no. 7, Trade Policy Division, World Bank, Washington, DC.

Maur, J.C., and P. A. Messerlin. 2001. Which Free Trade Agreement in South Eastern Europe? UK Department for International Development (DFID), London, UK, and Stability Pact Secretariat, Brussels, Belgium.

Messerlin, P. A. 1985. Les politiques commerciales et leurs effets en longue période: le cas français (1837–96). In B. Lassudrie-Duchene and J. L. Reiffers (eds.), *Le protectionnisme*. Paris, France: Economica.

———. 2001. *Measuring the Costs of Protection in Europe: The EU Commercial Policy in the 2000s*. Washington, DC: Institute for International Economics.

Michalopoulos, C. 1999. Trade Policy and Market Access Issues for Developing Countries. World Trade Organization, Geneva, Switzerland.

Mosley, Paul. 2000. Globalization, Economic Policy and Convergence. *The World Economy* 23(5): 613–34.

Organisation for Economic Co-operation and Development (OECD). 2001. *The Uruguay Round Agreement on Agriculture: An Evaluation of Its Implementation in OECD Countries*. Paris, France: OECD.

Papageorgiou, D., M. Michaely, and A. Choksi. 1990. *Liberalizing Foreign Trade in Developing Countries: The Lessons of Experience*. Washington, DC: World Bank.

Rodrik, D. 1999. *The New Global Economy and Developing Countries: Making Openness Work (Policy Essay 24)*. Washington, DC: Overseas Development Council.

Sachs, J., and A. Warner. 1995. Globalization and Economic Reform in Developing Countries. *Brookings Papers on Economic Activity* 1: 1–117.

Safadi, R., and S. Laird. 1996. The Uruguay Round Agreements: Impact on Developing Countries. *World Development* 24(7) June: 1223–242.

Tarr, D. 2001. On the Design of Tariff Policy: Arguments for and against Uniform Tariffs. In *Trade Policy for Developing Countries in a Global Economy: A Handbook*. Washington, DC: World Bank.

World Bank. 2000. World Development Indicators CD-ROM, World Bank, Washington, DC.

World Trade Organization (WTO). 2001. *Market Access: Unfinished Business, Post-Uruguay Round Inventory and Issues*. Geneva, Switzerland: World Trade Organization.

Chapter 6

Regional Integration Instruments and Dimensions: An Analytical Framework

Ramon Torrent

Regional integration is sometimes presented as a unidirectional process, proceeding in stages from the creation of a free trade area to wider and deeper forms of integration. This chapter applies a different approach: regional integration follows various paths that may lead in different directions, even if these paths all share some common elements.

The chapter focuses more on the nature of regional economic integration (REI) processes than on their economic consequences. This nature is defined essentially by the legal instruments that support and provide the framework for each process (keeping in mind that the same law can lead to different practices). The chapter does not aim to deepen the analysis of the various aspects of regional integration, but to contribute to the overall understanding of it by developing an analytical framework (or road map) for discussion and research oriented toward policymaking. It builds on preexisting material already known to most specialists, while emphasizing aspects that are often overlooked.

REI aims to mold social and economic preconditions in order to reach its objectives using certain instruments. Its development can be analyzed in terms of different dimensions, allowing for the establishment of a typology of regional integration processes. The chapter discusses these topics, emphasizing the different instruments and dimensions, and makes recommendations for strengthening regional integration.

PRECONDITIONS AND OBJECTIVES OF REGIONAL INTEGRATION

Preconditions

Regional integration does not begin in a vacuum. It is conditioned by a diversity of factors. Page (2000) considers the following:

- Geography, including ease of communications, a precondition frequently not met even between neighboring countries (for example in South America)
- Population, although experience proves that difference in size between member states does not necessarily create an obstacle to successful integration
- The size of the economy and income per capita

- Political congruence, at least in the European process (including its successive expansion) and in the birth of Mercosur
- Common background or sense of community, as in the case of the Caribbean Community (CARICOM).

Two major factors impact the strength of REI processes. First, the credibility and effectiveness of the rule of law supporting integration are important. REI processes cannot be guaranteed solely through regional institutional arrangements. Particularly in Europe, experience has shown that strength results from a general attitude of respect for the rule of law among member states. Thus, this attitude becomes an extremely important precondition for integration, as so many cases in Latin America—where this attitude does not exist—seem to show.

Second, the public expenditure and tax capacity of member states are also important factors. If public income relies heavily on duties, trade policy becomes, in fact, subordinate to fiscal policy. And a low level of public expenditure makes it more difficult for member states to cope with negative consequences of integration. It is worth mentioning that within the European Union, disputes on public spending are kept within reasonable limits. This is not only because a regional competition policy exists, but also because all member states have the budgetary capacity to fund huge aid programs within established limits.

Objectives

The recent literature adequately discusses the economic and political objectives served by regional integration (and their intended or unintended effects). From an economic point of view, integration is mainly an instrument of development (or of competitiveness and growth). This ultimate goal is pursued through a series of intermediate objectives, commonly analyzed from two standpoints. First, competition and scale develop as the larger market permits economies of scale and brings producers in member countries into closer contact with each other. Second, regional integration changes the pattern of trade and the location of production (World Bank 2000). A dynamic perspective is needed to discuss these dimensions because the net benefits of the dynamics of integration, coupled with the so-called nontraditional effects, such as signaling and lock-in, can be several times larger than their static reallocation effects (Devlin and Ffrench-Davis 1999).

It is now accepted that "integration is political" (World Bank 2000). The broader political objectives are commonly summarized as follows (Page 2000; World Bank 2000; Bouzas 1999):

- Intraregional and extraregional security
- Bargaining power in the global/multilateral system
- Locked-in internal policy reforms, not only in the areas directly covered by each REI process, but also in other related areas.

As regards strictly economic objectives, when the attraction of foreign direct investment from third countries becomes the main goal of participating in preferential trade agreements, this policy's systemic global consequences must be carefully analyzed and should not be discussed in terms of the usual creation/diversion alternative applied to trade. This policy may be legitimate for developing countries and for South-South agreements in which all members wish to attract foreign direct investment from industrial countries. But in North-

South agreements, industrial countries should always be able to state why they share the objective of channeling foreign direct investment to one specific developing country while excluding the rest, particularly its neighbors. In terms of broader political objectives, politically correct language should not hide that regional integration has been and is often used, on all continents, as an instrument of influence by dominant or powerful countries. Any evaluation of the relation of regional integration to the multilateral system must take this possibility into account.

Objectives can change during the development of the process. The European Community's history and the European Union's birth are undoubtedly the best examples of this. At first, the objectives were predominantly internal (peace and security); external objectives (such as greater presence in the international arena) acquired increasing importance only in the 1980s and 1990s. A change in objectives can give life to the process and revitalize the political will behind it. But it can also create confusion (not only in public opinion, but also among politicians who might lose sight of the goal of the process). It can also lead to trying to fit new objectives within a framework that was originally designed to meet other goals, and does not necessarily adapt well to the new ones. The European experience illustrates both dangers.

New objectives can be generated from within the integration process itself. This can happen if specific institutions (such as the European Commission) are charged with the task of generating initiatives and proposals. But the experience of Mercosur seems to show that there is no need of formal institutions for this type of development. If high-ranking officials are endowed with an excessive degree of autonomy, they may push initiatives that interest them personally rather than the governments that orient and direct the process and whom they should serve. This development also risks inflating the number of decisions taken at the regional level, which might exceed the capacity of member states to assimilate them.

In any case, it should not be forgotten that regional integration, however important, is only a means to an end and should not become an end in itself. The objectives of member states' whole political systems are broader than those served by integration. Integration may be a success in itself without necessarily being a success in terms of those broader objectives. The evolution of the European Union during the 1990s provides the best real case for discussion, including the monetary union. It has been a success in terms of integration as it has had a great deal of effective content, strength, and dynamism. But it has had rather disappointing results in economic terms and has led to a growing disaffection among citizens with regard to European institutions.

INSTRUMENTS OF REGIONAL ECONOMIC INTEGRATION

Regional integration is a common endeavor of a plurality of states that requires them to use the available instruments in order to influence social and economic reality. This chapter classifies these instruments in three categories: legislation (rules); public activities (including subsidizing specific economic activities carried out by private operators); and income redistribution through budgetary transfers. As REI processes are an international phenomenon, they also make use of the traditional diplomatic instruments of dialogue and cooperation. For analytical purposes, these instruments must be neatly differentiated from the techniques used to create them and the institutional arrangements used to guarantee their adequate implementation. The subject matter of the instruments defines the content of regional integration; techniques and institutional arrangements affect its strength and dynamism, but not its content.

The following example highlights this distinction. Both the North American Free Trade Agreement (NAFTA) and the European process deal with government procurement by enacting rules. Although the instrument (the rules) is similar and affects recipients (public administrations and private operators) of the norms in a similar manner, the technique used is completely different. NAFTA inserts the rules in the constitutive treaty; the European process gradually defines rules through a specialized organization. Various institutional arrangements (regional institution's role and judicial control) guarantee implementation of the rules.

Two Integration Techniques

Two techniques enact regional rules and provide a framework for regional public activities. The traditional distinction between "intergovernmental" and "supranational" aims at defining them. But it has been used too loosely, in particular as a tool for comparing the European process (the incarnation of supranationality) with other processes. On the one hand, the European process has an extremely high degree of intergovernmentalism. To take just two examples, the elimination of tariffs within the zone was achieved essentially through an intergovernmental method, while the European Monetary System was, from beginning to end, an intergovernmental mechanism based on an agreement among Central Banks with absolutely no intervention from the European Community. On the other hand, supranationality is an important element for the World Trade Organization (WTO).

Thus, it is better to replace that terminology with the more neutral of the two techniques that can be used by an integration treaty (as a matter of fact, by any international treaty) in order to enact rules. The techniques are to previously insert rules into the treaty that must be complied with by member states or to institute a mechanism for creating laws within the framework of the agreement.

For example, the European Community—a legal entity with its own competency—provides the paradigm for using the second technique. However, the European process still relies just as much on the first one. The treaty itself contains a set of rules imposing far-reaching and serious obligations on member states when they exercise their own competencies; these obligations are underscored by the general overarching obligation of nondiscrimination as regards nationality in any area covered by the treaty. NAFTA, by contrast, relies exclusively on the first technique. Many bilateral agreements of the European Community (alone or jointly with member states) with third countries also rely on the second technique to create a joint institution able to produce additional law that deepens the content of the agreement.[1] There are advantages and disadvantages to both techniques. The first tends to give strength and credibility to the risk of inflexibility and lack of capacity for adaptation; the second tends to have the opposite effects.

---

[1] This supranational development, often forgotten, proves that the distinction between intergovernmentalism and supranationalism has been much abused (and that the conclusion that supranationalism is difficult to conceive outside the European context is not well-founded). For example, the framework agreement between the European Community and its 15 member states and Mexico, signed in 1997, was "filled up" later by two decisions of the Joint Council and not by independent, supplementary agreements. The choice of internal procedures followed by the different parties before their representatives in the Joint Council adopt the decisions depends on each party's constitutional characteristics. In some cases, they resemble those used in the approval of international agreements; in others, they differ entirely.

The Institutional Arrangements

Institutional arrangements (including dispute settlement and judicial control) are not in themselves instruments of integration. I would argue that they are, in any case, instruments of the instruments. The markets are successfully integrated to one degree or another by the rules liberalizing trade in goods or capital movement (or for harmonizing standards). Institutional arrangements help to increase or decrease the effectiveness of these rules and facilitate their adaptation.

A comparative examination proves that, as long as the rules are effective, integration can proceed successfully (or risk failure), regardless of the institutional arrangements adopted in each process. NAFTA and the European process share some successes despite their completely different approaches to institutions. And Mercosur, which is institutionally light, shares some of the same failures as the institutionally heavy Andean Community.

This argument applies even to policies governing regional competition. It appears that it cannot exist without the regional institutions or bodies to implement it. However, the example of the European Economic Area proves just the opposite. The European Economic Area Treaty includes provisions on competition policy, but their implementation is left to the institutions on both sides of the agreement: the preexisting ones on the European Community side and the new European Free Trade Association (EFTA) Surveillance Authority and EFTA Court on the EFTA side. Thus, here again, there is a clear-cut distinction between the instruments (common regional rules) and the institutional arrangements (left to each part) for implementation.

The existence or lack of a regional budget must also be discussed as a problem of institutional arrangements and not of proper instruments. Regional public activities can be implemented through regional or national budgets, or through a combination. Two examples from the European experience are illustrative. First, the Common Foreign and Security Policy (as it appeared in the Maastricht Treaty, not the present policy) provided two alternative forms of budgetary implementation: through the European Community budget and through national budgets. Second, the future of the Common Agricultural Policy depends partly on whether present implementation through the European Community budget is maintained or at least partially transferred and financed through national budgets. Each alternative has serious consequences for the strength and dynamism of the process.

Regional Rules

Regional rules can cover any social and economic situation. From an analytical perspective, it is best to analyze the subject matter of the rules under the heading of content rather than under instruments for regional integration. The analysis of rules as instruments must relate to the three main approaches (or instrumental ways) of international rules for promoting integration. The first is to impose obligations on liberalization and access to markets. The second is to impose certain obligations of nondiscrimination on the legal framework applicable to transactions and operations covered by the agreements—basically most-favored-nation (MFN) status or national treatment (NT) obligations—while leaving domestic legislation intact. The third is to create uniform legislation establishing a common legal framework for transactions and operations covered by the agreement. These three approaches differ legally and in terms of their political and economic implications.

The obligations that accompany liberalization are strictly limited in scope to international transactions. Obligations as regards treatment (in particular if they apply to treatment of foreign firms and professionals after their establishment in the host country), as well as uniform or harmonized rules, apply essentially to internal transactions. They are more intrusive politically (and, as a consequence, much more difficult to tackle) than the former. But many argue that integration cannot rely solely on liberalization obligations to make sense in legal terms. Furthermore, it is becoming even clearer from a strictly economic perspective that market integration is not achieved by liberalizing access as long as internal rules continue to differ.

The two latter types of rules pose a political dilemma. Uniform rules serve integration goals extremely well, but are difficult to set up for three reasons. First, they are technically difficult to agree upon because of the different legal traditions and contexts of the parties, making it difficult to agree even on terminology and definitions. Second, they are intrusive in relation to the internal political process, insofar as they are locked in by international law, which precludes policy changes that may follow a switch of domestic governments and political majorities. Third, they threaten the adaptability of the regional scheme because they are more difficult to change than domestic rules since they require a consensus (or a qualified majority) among all parties.

Obligations regarding treatment drastically reduce these difficulties by allowing much greater discretionary power related to domestic legislation, provided that content is nondiscriminatory. But such obligations pose other difficulties. Uniform rules follow the same logic and have the same scope at the international and domestic levels. This is not the case with international obligations on treatment (in particular on treatment of enterprises). These obligations have a sort of double universality. They apply to all sectors, and they cover all aspects of the legal framework applicable to enterprises.[2] On the domestic front, however, there is not a single rule or set of rules that has this double universality. Different rules apply to different sectors (energy or air transport, for example) and to different aspects of the legal framework (from company law to taxation, through labor conditions or expropriation, for example). With the sole exception of the European Community, experience shows that far-reaching obligations of treatment of enterprises can be accepted only if they are accompanied by a list of exceptions. But this list of exceptions tends to expand geometrically as the number of parties to the agreement increases. In the end, the list of exceptions overwhelms MFN and NT.[3]

Public Activities

States do more than merely enact and implement general legislation. For example, they finance and manage public services, such as education; build physical infrastructure; and subsidize specific economic activities. I refer to these as public activities and not as policies because policies can also be implemented exclusively through general rules (on environment, social and labor standards, or education, for example).

The same distinction applies at the regional level. Public activities can play a relevant role in certain regional integration schemes. Some analysts argue that regional public activity must be carried out to avoid regional integration becoming simply a politically correct remake of market liberalization. Here again, the subject matter for these activities fits best under contents. What must be emphasized under instruments is that such activities may be needed in order to enact liberalizing rules. The European Community's Common Agricultural Policy is again the main example.

---

[2] When the obligation of treatment applies to goods, its scope is much narrower.

[3] This was one of the main reasons for the failure of the OECD's 1995–98 negotiations on a Multilateral Agreement on Investment.

In the 1950s, when the European Community Treaty was negotiated, agriculture posed two major problems as a sector. First, national budgets heavily subsidized it, and this would create huge distortions for competition if intrazone trade were liberalized. Second, public intervention was linked to the existence of producer organizations and systems of price controls that clearly infringed on the principles of free competition and antitrust. The alternatives were either to exclude agriculture from the scope of the treaties or to regard the issue as part of the common policies. Member states chose to create a specific set of common rules for agricultural markets that would be inconceivable outside the realm of agriculture. Throughout the history of the Common Agricultural Policy, these rules have involved price controls, public purchases, and buffer stocks, as well as cartels with ceilings on production and penalties for exceeding them.

Leaving aside their merits in terms of economic policy, public activities can have positive effects on the integration process. I shall not refer to the impact of creating powerful sector lobbies in favor of regional action, because critics can neutralize this effect. I refer here to the definition and management of such policies, which keeps regional integration going, even during periods of stagnation, and the fact that regional integration is about real economic life and not simply about politics.

Income Redistribution through Budgetary Transfers

All public activities may affect income distribution. Income redistribution becomes a specific regional instrument when it targets specific categories of beneficiaries defined in terms of their income or some other broad economic characteristic. This instrument is typically European.

Internally, an embryonic income redistribution policy based on personal criteria dates back to the 1950s (the social fund). But this instrument only became meaningful (also in budgetary terms) in the 1980s and 1990s, when it included the comparative situation of geographically defined collectives, specific areas within member states (structural funds), and whole countries (cohesion fund). Externally, the first round of European Community agreements with Mediterranean countries in the 1970s and 1980s included budgetary commitments. Later on, this practice was abandoned and foreign aid was taken out of the agreements (except for the African, Caribbean, and Pacific [ACP] states), and the European Community dealt with it autonomously.

Diplomatic Instruments

As an international phenomenon, regional integration relies on the typical international diplomatic instruments of dialogue and cooperation. Their use may promote the emergence of a proper regional policy (implemented through legislation or public activities), but this is not necessarily or commonly the case.

These instruments are diplomatic in origin, and extend to all other areas covered by each process, in particular the economic areas. This development goes beyond regional integration, as the number of international forums on all areas of economic, social, and political life has multiplied. Their effects on integration are greatly enhanced when they are able to effectively involve social and economic actors, in particular in businesses, promoting exchanges and common activities among them. This is a significant difference between the current negotiations for the Free Trade Area of the Americas (FTAA) and the negotiations between the European Union and Mercosur. In the first case, these actors were effectively involved; in the second case, they were not.

THE DIMENSIONS OF REGIONAL INTEGRATION

Regional integration develops within a multidimensional space, and does not necessarily move forward continuously. It has four main dimensions: external, content, strength, and dynamism.

External Dimension

Customs unions are sometimes presented as deepening free trade areas (FTAs). This is misleading, however, because customs unions also widen FTAs. They define a policy at the regional level that FTAs leave to individual member states: trade relations with third countries. But it is best not to compare customs unions and FTAs in terms of deepening or widening. It is better to view them from a different perspective or dimension, as different ways of inserting REI processes into the global system. The same approach must apply to any other area covered by an REI process (such as services, capital, right of establishment and treatment after establishment, and movement of workers).

The analysis of this dimension must refer to the number of matters that are dealt with at the regional level in relation to third countries. This is essential, for example, in the case of the European process. It is often forgotten that the European Community has not developed a unified external policy in matters as important as services, the right of establishment of foreign firms, or the so-called reform of the global financial architecture.[4] These are all matters in which individual member states continue to develop different, and even contradictory, policies.

The external dimension is of paramount importance in these processes (in particular South-South agreements), where the main goal is that of increasing the bargaining power of members and, in general, improving conditions for insertion into the global system. In general, the existence or absence of an external dimension permeates the whole approach to integration. When there is no external dimension, the process tends to focus on policy restraints (because domestic policies could endanger intrazone liberalization). When there is an external dimension, the focus turns to policy building (that is, a common external policy), at least as a reaction to third-country demands.

Analysis of an REI's external dimension is essential in order to evaluate its effects on the global system and other countries. Often, such a discussion centers on the misuse of trade policy instruments, and some conclude that customs unions are more likely to be misused than FTAs in order to inhibit trade liberalization. If the discussion centers on WTO compatibility, it often becomes a debate on the quantitative meaning of the General Agreement on Tariffs and Trade (GATT) article XXIV, on the notion of substantially all trade. I suggest looking at REI processes in terms of their possible misuse as regards their structural contribution (good or bad) to the global architecture.

In this regard, the existence or absence of an external dimension of REI processes seems relevant with regard to two of the main specific problems created by the multiplication of preferential agreements (and, in particular, by individual countries' multiple membership in

---

[4] This explains why member states continue to sign separate investment treaties with third countries and are members of the WTO or parties to many agreements with third countries, jointly with the European Community. The reforms introduced by the Treaty of Nice will modify the scope of the European Community's external competencies.

them). The first concerns the risks of diversion of trade and investment. The participation of a country in different FTAs has the effect (and, in some cases, the conscious goal) of multiplying the risk of diversion of trade and investment. By limiting such a possibility, customs unions positively contribute to building global architecture. The second problem is that of transforming the global system into a spaghetti bowl of intertwined agreements, whose negative effects have already been abundantly discussed. By hypothesis, customs unions limit the scope of such a development by compelling all their members to go together in their trade relations with third countries. By contrast, FTAs allow each member to choose any third country to create an additional FTA, multiplying the spaghetti effect.

Discussion of these problems should abandon or refine the usual recourse to alternative geometrical or mechanical comparisons (concentric circles or hub and spokes). Indeed, a hub-and-spokes model becomes a concentric circle when the hub is constituted by an REI process. The typical example is the agreements linking the European Community (alone or jointly with all member states) to third countries, but this would also be the case of NAFTA within an FTAA that was NAFTA-minus in terms of content. The essential point in these two cases is that all members of the REI process are in the same position in relation to third countries. This does not create any specific problems as regards architecture.

The real architectural problem is that of multiple memberships in REI processes by different members. Then the problem is one of overlapping, rather than concentric, circles. In the second comparison, the issue is whether a vehicle can adequately function when the spokes connect the outer points of the wheel to different hubs.

Effective Content

Width x Depth

The width of any international agreement or organization (including regional ones) can be defined in terms of the number and scope of the areas it covers. Depth refers to the degree in which these areas are subject to common rules or public activities. An example taken from the multilateral level helps to differentiate both notions. The General Agreement on Trade in Services (GATS) is wide because it covers all service sectors and all aspects of post-establishment treatment of foreign firms; but it is not deep (and unequally deep at any rate) because the market access and national treatment commitments in members' respective schedules are quite limited.

Apparently, width can easily be determined by looking at the subject matter of the different regional instruments that are being used. This apparent ease does not exist in relation to rules because the width of rules must be analyzed in terms of a matrix: vertically when referring to sectors (such as agriculture or financial services) and horizontally (taxation, competition, and labor standards). Depth is not easy to determine, in particular in relation to rules. The best criterion for determining depth is the extent to which member states remain free to regulate specific topics differently; the more they do, the shallower the process will be in terms of depth. Application of this criterion requires careful analysis of the relevant legal provisions for establishing actual regulatory meaning, especially because ambitious language may often mask a lack of actual regulatory effect.

For analytical purposes, the distinction between width and depth is perfectly sound but can also be misleading. Indeed, width and depth are not independent characteristics of integration. What matters is the content of the process, and width and depth are but two aspects of it that must be considered jointly. Reality offers us plenty of examples of bilateral economic agreements that are wide in terms of scope, but with no depth in terms of obligations or effective cooperation. They end up being little more than political declarations of intent.

Content versus Effective Content

As REI processes occur within a multilateral system in which members have already accepted obligations, to get to actual REI value added requires analyzing the effective content of the processes and not merely their content. Effective content must be defined as regional content minus multilateral obligations. Here again, reality offers plenty of examples of bilateral/regional agreements that attempt to increase their content by simply restating already accepted bilateral and multilateral obligations, or even falling short of this. This strategy seems risky. It creates confusion, reduces transparency, and weakens the multilateral system without making any meaningful contribution to integration.

An example is Mercosur's 1997 Montevideo Protocol on services, sometimes presented as proof of Mercosur's ambitions. It might be better to view this as proof of Mercosur's inability to advance further in the integration process. The Protocol is certainly wide, but it has little depth; and, in any case, it falls short of specific obligations already accepted by its four member states in the GATS framework because it does not incorporate their respective schedules of commitments. Thus, its effective content is negative (although its MFN clause does not allow for exceptions).[5]

Strength

As with width and depth, I suggest analyzing the strength of an REI process by examining two aspects jointly: the credibility and effectiveness of the law of integration and member states' political commitment (broadly defined). Here again, both aspects are better understood as multiplying each other rather than simply adding up. Many examples show that mere political commitment is not enough to strengthen an REI process if it is not accompanied by at least some credibility as regards the law of integration. However, legal mechanisms cannot compensate for the absence of political commitment. The strength of the process tends to be 0 if either its legal or political components is 0 (even if the other one is positive).

Credibility and Effectiveness of the Law

REI can undoubtedly proceed on the basis of the previously outlined fourth instrument (dialogue and cooperation), without any specific law of integration. But if REI is supported or regulated by law, then the law must be credible and effective. If it is not, the process becomes a failure and could be successfully replaced by de facto integration.

No law is 100 percent credible and effective; credibility and effectiveness are always a matter of degree. A high degree of credibility can be achieved through different mechanisms. However, credibility is not necessarily linked to the existence of a regional mecha-

---

[5] Sectoral annexes and schedules of commitments were later added but neither the Montevideo Protocol nor the addition of the sectoral annexes and the lists of commitments have yet entered into force, pending ratification. Therefore, Mercosur's effective content on this topic continues to be negative with reference to WTO's commitments.

nism of law enforcement. It seems to depend more on the existence of a general attitude of respect for the rule of law in member states and the perceived interest (political as well as economic) in strengthening integration. At this point, it is worth recalling that within the framework of the European Community Treaty, until recently, the Court of Justice of the European Community has not had any effective mechanism at its disposal to enforce its decisions. Reprisals among member states are absolutely forbidden, even in cases where one of them violates European Community law. The system has always worked essentially based on voluntary compliance by member states (including compliance with the Court's decisions).

Political Commitment

The degree of political commitment of member states to the REI process may be difficult to measure with precision. However, its existence is absolutely necessary. Political commitment is political in that it can go further than the effective economic content of integration, thereby strengthening the process. An example is the common actions on the part of the three remaining member states of Mercosur when the fourth member, Paraguay, was in political crisis and its democracy was at risk. Another example is the intervention by the United States when Mexico was in a serious financial crisis. These actions (in areas not properly covered by the processes) strengthened Mercosur and NAFTA, respectively.

If political commitment exists, the diplomatic instruments of dialogue and cooperation may be an effective means of enhancing integration. If it does not, they become counterproductive in the long run because of the (correct) public perception that integration has become a purely rhetorical affair.

Dynamism and Capacity for Adaptation

A region can be defined as a group of countries that has created a legal framework of cooperation covering an extensive economic relationship, with the intention that it will be of indefinite duration, and with the possibility foreseen that the region will evolve or change because countries' economic structures change, and with them the nature of their linkages (Page 2000).

The capacity to adapt (the ability to change the instruments of integration in terms of content or to add new ones) is only one aspect of REI processes, not a defining characteristic. In the first place, the need for adaptation depends on the goals pursued and the adequacy of the initial instruments. In the second place, the capacity to adapt (or too much of it) can endanger the strength of the process (and, in particular, its credibility). Much of the history of regional integration in Latin America could be written based on this second perspective.

The capacity to adapt has to do essentially with mechanisms to create laws and the swiftness with which the new or reformed laws can adapt to new circumstances. Does the new or reformed law require a new treaty? Alternatively, does the treaty provide for some mechanism of adaptation? The distinction between the static and dynamic nature of regional integration processes depends on the answers to these questions.

A comparison of NAFTA, the European Community, and Mercosur reveals three major differences. First, NAFTA has a static character. It is a comprehensive agreement that is once and for all; there is no explicit mechanism to create laws. Adaptation must come from new agreements that modify or supplement the initial one. Second, the Treatises establishing the

European Community are twofold in character. They have a solid, static nature because they are classical international Treatises, creating (once and for all) far-reaching obligations for member states (just like NAFTA), but they also create a specific mechanism for producing new law, which gives them a dynamic nature. Furthermore, the practice of periodic revision and modification of the founding Treatises has boosted their dynamic nature. Third, Mercosur risks having neither a static nor a dynamic nature. From the static point of view, it does not have the wide, deep, and strong set of obligations typical of NAFTA and the Treatises that establish the European Community. Mercosur is dynamic, but its dynamism remains largely virtual because its mechanisms for creating laws do not work well.

The need for dynamism (or adaptability) is linked to the other three dimensions. First, if there is an external dimension to the process, the need for adaptation comes from outside, from other participants in the global system and its multilateral institutions. A customs union's commercial policy (or other external policies, if they exist) cannot remain unchanged over time; it must be adapted. This need is not present in the case of FTAs, where each member adapts its commercial policy on its own.

Second, as far as content is concerned, the need for adaptation arises if the REI process includes regional public activities or income redistribution. These must be defined, adjusted, and implemented. Adaptation is also linked to the question of deepening (more than to the question of widening because it is unikely that, by adapting, an REI process could cover areas not covered in the initial treaty). If the agreement is static (like NAFTA), all provisions affecting depth must be included in the initial treaty. If the agreement is dynamic, the initial treaty may be limited to defining some relatively open or broad rules or obligations, leaving deepening to the future.

Third, adaptability is related to strength. The static nature of an REI process certainly contributes to strengthening it; but an adequate dynamic nature can also contribute to it if, by adapting, it can avoid becoming obsolete in legal terms. A dynamic nature can also enhance legal adequacy and, consequently, prevent violation.

TYPOLOGY OF REGIONAL ECONOMIC INTEGRATION

A complex typology of REI processes can be constructed by combining preconditions and objectives, instruments, and dimensions. Instead of engaging in this purely abstract exercise, I outline a few types that can be useful in discussing actual integration processes.

The first type is a no-rules, purely political framework for de facto economic integration. This model can be reasonably successful in some cases and absolutely irrelevant in others. The best example of success is the first 25 years of the Association of Southeast Asian Nations (ASEAN).[6] It was built on the basis of solid geographical-historical preconditions. It has had a significant external dimension, as well as internal strength via political commitment and dynamism. The best examples of failures are probably the trade and cooperation agreements negotiated by the European Community with countries in Latin America and Asia that lack any effective content.

The second type is that of the pure FTA. It has no external dimension and is static. It has some, but not much, effective content, which is normally limited to trade in goods (usually

---

[6] Of course, ASEAN did not fit the model exactly because it had rules on preferences, but these rules were just an accessory to the main nature of the agreement.

with significant exceptions), and without much depth (it does not attempt to create uniform rules). Finally, the degree of political commitment is low. This model roughly fits many of the regional agreements within the WTO.

These agreements should be discussed in terms of their internal and external effects. Such a discussion would go beyond the scope of the present chapter. As far as their global systemic effects are concerned, these agreements tend to be inconsequential because their effect on trade is nearly nonexistent; nevertheless, they represent noise that muddies the clarity of international economic relations. If they are effective, they might allow for multiple memberships in different integration schemes by different members so that they risk multiplying the trade and investment diversion effects. If they link industrial with developing countries, they might have distorting effects on other developing countries (neighboring countries, in particular) that are not parties to the agreement.

In the third type of REI process, institutions strengthen the community of states. This process typically integrates states with relatively small populations and territories that have some sense of shared history and culture. The key motivation of the integration process is not so much the actual and potential intensity in intraregional economic relations; external considerations weigh relatively more. One of the main arguments for integration is the need for institutional strengthening in order to maximize the allocation of scarce human resources while also enhancing the capacity for regulatory and economic policy formulation (Jessen and Rodriguez 1999). The paradigm could be CARICOM, but some African schemes would also roughly fit the model.

Precisely because both human resources and institution-building capacity are so scarce, these processes face two main challenges. First, they have to adequately define the extent of their external dimension. Second, they must make the right choices as regards their effective content (rules versus public activities), while maintaining or increasing political commitment among member states.

The fourth type of REI process is a broad-based, halfway internal economic area with strong rules and no public activities. It shares the characteristic of not having an external policy dimension with the second type, and, consequently, shares some of its systemic risks. But this type has more ambitious objectives and more effective content, going much further than trade in goods, although it does not cover many aspects of economic relations. It is strong in terms of law and political commitment. The model has two main varieties: static and dynamic. The main example of the static variety is NAFTA. The main example of the dynamic variety could be the European Economic Area created by an agreement between the different EFTA countries (except Switzerland) and the European Community and its 15 member states.

The fifth model is the strong, broad-based, internal plus external, static plus dynamic, incomplete general integration process. It corresponds to the one launched by the European Community Treaty in the 1950s. This type is based on strong geographical/historical foundations. It has a definite external policy dimension, but is incomplete because, as far as third countries are concerned, 15 national policies continue to target many aspects, even in the purely economic area. It has a high effective content that has increased over time, but its width and depth and the number and importance of its public activities should not be exaggerated. The legal strength of the process is remarkable and explains a great part of its success. This has been achieved mainly through voluntary compliance by member states. The degree of political commitment to the process has always been high, but it has suffered visible erosion during the past 15 years, particularly in terms of public opinion. The process has a strong static foundation (the far-reaching obligations imposed on member states by the Treatises), but it is also dynamic because it has a well-lubricated mechanism of law creation and treaty reform that leads to an increase in the content of the process. The Andean Pact/Community and Mercosur could be analyzed as more or less successful/unsuccessful examples of this fifth type.

FAVORING THE PROGRESS OF REGIONAL INTEGRATION

Taking Care of the External Dimension

REI processes may or may not have an external dimension. When they do have such a dimension, its consolidation is at least as important, and sometimes more so, than internal widening or deepening. A strong external dimension lends credibility to the process and strengthens it, legally as well as in terms of the political commitment of its members. It also provides stability to the multilateral system. The experiences of the European Community and Mercosur tend to support this argument. One of the few absolute dogmas in Brussels regards the exclusive competence of the European Community in the area of foreign trade. The day-to-day management of the Customs Union has kept the Community alive and functioning even during its worst periods of stagnation.[7] By contrast, uncoordinated actions on the part of member states in the Mercosur process have eroded its foundations and credibility.

To achieve consolidation, 100 percent uniformity is not necessarily the main goal; a common or single policy would be sufficient. Even the European Community maintained differentiated national frameworks within the common imports framework for decades (not only for textiles, toys, and bananas, but, more significantly, for automobiles). Sector national exceptions, permanent or transitory, are perfectly legitimate provided that the Community agrees to and manages them. Indeed, REI schemes with an external dimension should have some mechanism to expeditiously adapt their common external framework to members' specific sector problems. The principle of free circulation of imports among members after they have entered the common customs territory is just as important as the principle of uniformity. The absence of this principle prevents Mercosur, for example, from becoming a proper customs union, much more than differences in the external framework do.

Rules-based REI processes pose an important external problem even if they do not have an external dimension: the hierarchy between regional and multilateral rules. From the standpoint of regional agreements, there are three possibilities: the agreement is silent on this question, the agreement recognizes the primacy of the multilateral agreement, or the agreement establishes its primacy over the multilateral agreement.

Internally, European Community law and the jurisprudence of the Court of Justice of the European Community in general respect the primacy of international law. However, externally, all bilateral agreements that the European Community has negotiated with third countries fall within the first possibility (remain silent). By contrast, NAFTA falls within the other two. As a general rule, its article 103 establishes that it prevails over other overlapping multilateral agreements; but its specific articles on standards (articles 713 and 903) seem to recognize the primacy of international agreements.

This problem is not only legal; it is primarily political because it points to a basic policy choice: favoring either the unilateral/bilateral/regional approach or the multilateral. This problem should be addressed directly and not as a sideline, as in NAFTA—which produced contra-

---

[7] This is management in the regulatory sense because customs authorities continue to be national.

dictory results when done on a case-by-case basis. Policymakers should go beyond the rhetoric about the primacy of the multilateral system, and introduce a conformity clause into regional agreements regarding multilateral agreements.[8]

Choosing the Right Content

Regional integration should always be multilateral-plus. This idea is not new, but it is often overlooked in practice, in terms of both substance and procedure. In substance, regional rules on services often fall short of schedules for specific commitments on GATS. In procedure, mechanisms to create laws and settle disputes are much less powerful than those of the WTO. There is a need to increase awareness regarding existing multilateral obligations, and to deepen research on the overlap between multilateral and regional agreements in order to determine the benefits of the latter's effective content.

From the internal perspective, experience with Mercosur, and even the European Community, proves that too much content is a potential danger, especially in dynamic processes. It could weaken the process if rule production at the regional level exceeds the capacity of domestic systems and the demands from citizens and businesses to assimilate them. When the potential danger becomes a reality, a drastic redefinition and narrowing down of the agenda are the only way to avoid a progressive degeneration of the process.

Five considerations guide the development of content, helping to avoid confusion and pursue attainable goals. First, the notion of nontariff barriers is dangerous because it covers two areas that differ completely from political, legal, and economic points of view: direct and indirect barriers to trade. Direct barriers to trade (or measures at the border) exclusively apply to imports and exports (quotas, taxes—including anti-dumping duties—and licenses). Indirect barriers to trade result from the application to all trade (internal as well as external) of internal rules that may differ between members. Direct barriers to trade should disappear with regional integration; indirect barriers, by contrast, will never disappear completely unless the REI process ends up as a 100-percent uniform state. Therefore, the goal regarding indirect barriers should be to eliminate well-identified, relevant ones.

Second, the idea that indirect barriers to trade and to other operations and transactions can be eliminated through two alternative methods (harmonization or mutual recognition) is dangerously confusing. This consideration refers to indirect barriers created by different domestic standards. In Brussels jargon, what is referred to as mutual recognition is the addition of two factors. The first is obligations imposed by the treaties on member states that prohibit trade restrictions resulting from the application of standards when they are not justified. The second is harmonizing standards in variable detail when they are justified (which happens in many cases). It is better to forget about the myth of mutual recognition. The true alternative lies between not applying standards, harmonizing standards, and conflicting standards.

Third, the WTO's notion of trade in services generates enormous confusion. It is preferable to follow the approach of both the European Community Treaty and NAFTA, and limit the chapters on services to provision of services (the European Community's terminology) or cross-border trade in services (NAFTA's terminology), while dealing separately with investment (in services and all other sectors).

---

[8] See Torrent (1998, chapter 9) for a more in-depth discussion about such a conformity clause.

Fourth, concerning investment, the European Community Treaty's approach of distinguishing between cross-border movements of capital (linked/not linked to establishment), establishment (not necessarily linked to cross-border movement of capital), and various aspects of post-establishment treatment seems preferable to mixing them all together under the label of investment.

Fifth, well-designed regional public activities can foster integration more than can ambitious rules that may not be effectively applied. Such activities can also be the means to achieve real multilateral-plus integration.

Gaining Both Strength and Adaptability

If REI schemes are not mere political frameworks for de facto economic integration, the law that creates and regulates them must be strong and credible. In addition, they must have some capacity to adapt to new problems or unforeseen circumstances, as well as built-in adequate legal instruments so as to avoid mere de facto solutions that are contrary to the law. Adaptability and strength can go together. Along with adequate legal mechanisms, a well-developed capacity to adapt helps to avoid violations of the law and strengthens it. But the capacity to adapt can only rest on a sufficiently solid, static foundation.

The question of how to strengthen the law of integration while increasing the capacity to adapt constitutes a dilemma for discussion beyond the limits of this chapter. A fruitful discussion of this subject must begin by abandoning assumptions about supranationality and so-called impossibilities deriving from national constitutions (like those that so often have prevented a reasonable discussion of this topic in the framework of Mercosur). Fast-track mechanisms to ratify international agreements or to internalize decisions of regional bodies are within the realm of any national constitution, as are mechanisms to create laws like those of the WTO when its bodies approve waivers or accept new members into the organization. Future applied research should focus on these mechanisms.

REFERENCES

Bouzas, R. 1999. Regional Trade Arrangements. Lessons from Past Experiences. In M.R. Mendoza, P. Low, and B. Kotschwar (eds.), *Trade Rules in the Making*. Washington, DC: Brookings Institution Press.

Devlin, R., and R. Ffrench-Davis. 1999. Towards an Evaluation of Regional Integration in Latin America in the 1990s. *The World Economy* 22(2), March.

Jessen, A., and E. Rodriguez. 1999. The Caribbean Community: Facing the Challenges of Regional and Global Integration, ITD-INTAL Working Paper, Inter-American Development Bank, Washington, DC.

Page, S. 2000. *Regionalism Among Developing Countries*. MacMillam Press/Overseas Development Institute, London.

Torrent, R. 1998. *Derecho y práctica de las relaciones económicas en la Unión Europea*. Editorial CEDECS, Barcelona.

World Bank. 2000. *Trade Blocs: Policy Research Report*. Oxford: Oxford University Press.

Chapter 7

Regional Integration and the Rule of Law: Some Issues and Options

Marise Cremona

This chapter addresses the role of law and the importance of the rule of law in the context of trade and regional integration. The intention is to raise and clarify a number of key issues and options, rather than to offer a detailed analysis of existing arrangements. As states increasingly engage in a complex variety of regional and subregional/bilateral trade initiatives, different rule of law considerations emerge. The term "rule of law" takes on, or is given, different meanings in different contexts. The chapter makes explicit some of these different senses of the term in the context of a number of different interacting legal regimes. On the one hand, it considers the impact on the *domestic legal order* of the contracting states, from both substantive and procedural perspectives. Substantive impacts include changes to domestic law and legal structures; procedural impacts include enforcement and dispute settlement issues. On the other hand, states are concerned with the legal implications of projected or actual specific regional commitments for their preexisting bilateral and multilateral commitments, especially their World Trade Organization (WTO) commitments. Both cases involve a more or less formal interaction between different legal regimes: domestic and regional, and regional and bilateral/multilateral.

The chapter reviews the different senses in which the term "rule of law" is used, and its importance as a foundation for political, economic, and social development at the domestic level; as such it has become a focus for development and assistance policies, especially for the European Union. The chapter then evaluates the rule of law demands made by membership of the WTO, and the legal relationship between regional integration agreements (RIAs) and multilateral (especially WTO) commitments. This is not only a question of legal compatibility per se, but also of the forum/fora within which compatibility is addressed, and before which questions of conflict may be resolved.

The chapter looks at the different minimum rule of law requirements for different levels and intensities of regional integration, the appropriate legal and institutional framework at the regional or international level, and the more or less deep impact that RIAs have on substantive legal obligations within the domestic legal order. The degree of impact depends not only on the scope of the obligation, but also on its nature and legal force. Increased appreciation of the demands that RIAs make on the domestic legal system, and, conversely, of the dependence of a successful RIA on effective implementation and enforcement, has turned attention to conditionality, whereby subscription to the rule of law by a potential contracting (or member) state becomes a threshold requirement for the establishment of regional integration relationships.

Finally, the chapter examines the legal implications of different international dispute settlement procedures, including judicial and nonjudicial dispute settlement and enforcement mechanisms. In the following discussion, where examples are chosen from experience and policy in the European Union, these are intended to serve as illustrative of practice only, and not as normative goals.[1]

THE RULE OF LAW AND POLITICAL AND ECONOMIC DEVELOPMENT

The term "rule of law" is a much-used phrase, often employed without paying attention to its substantive content (McLeish 1993). Looking at definitions and descriptions of what is meant by the rule of law in both general and specific contexts, it is hard to avoid lists of virtues (or values or ideals), the logical connections between which can appear arbitrary. It is also a phrase or concept that is growing in currency; where once reference used to be made to the twin virtues of democracy and human rights, now the reference is more likely to be to a trinity: democracy, the protection of human rights, and the rule of law. One reason for this is the increased realization of the part played by the rule of law in achieving both stable democracy and effective protection of human rights. The European Union has recently referred to the rule of law alongside human rights, democracy, good governance, and transparency as the "core values embraced by the European Union and its Member States."[2]

At its most basic, the rule of law refers to a state where power is exercised according to and accountable to the law. The equivalent French expression *l'Etat de droit* or German *Rechtsstaat* emphasizes the link between law and state (and state institutions) within a constitutional system of government. According to Oxford University Press's *Dictionary of Law*, the Diceyan concept of rule of law embodied "three concepts: the absolute predominance of regular law, so that the government has no arbitrary authority over the citizen; the equal subjection of all (including officials) to the ordinary law administered by the ordinary courts; and the fact that the citizen's personal freedoms are formulated and protected by the ordinary law rather than by abstract constitutional declarations." (Dicey 1885)

In practice, the rule of law in the context of regional integration has a number of different dimensions. First, it is linked to the values of democratic government and human rights guarantees. Second, it is also seen as a prerequisite for economic and social development. Both these political and economic aspects are bound up with *institutional development*, most especially the institutions of central and local government, but also the institutions of a functioning civil society. They are also essentially concerned with *procedure*, and the specific legal virtues of certainty, predictability, stability, clarity and transparency, consistency, and coherence. The rule of law is thus closely connected to the objective of good governance as a prerequisite for both political and economic development.

---

[1] The European Union encompasses the European Community, the European Atomic Energy Community, and additional policies and initiatives developed outside the European Community framework, in particular the Common Foreign and Security Policy and Police and Judicial Cooperation in Criminal Matters. This chapter uses the term "European Union" to refer to the Union as a whole, including the totality of these different policies, and the term "European Community" to denote specifically European Community competencies, such as trade or development policy.

[2] Common Strategy of the European Union on the Mediterranean Region adopted by the European Council at Feira, Portugal, 19–20 June 2000.

In its political dimension, linked to democracy and human rights, the rule of law emphasizes due process and equality before the law and signifies that a state possesses certain key features: independent constitutional and judicial authorities; properly functioning public administration at the local and central government level; a well-qualified, functioning, and independent judiciary; an accountable law enforcement structure; an adequate, well-trained, and disciplined police force; and an independent media. In this sense, the rule of law underpins such goals as equality (nondiscrimination), minority rights, executive accountability, and anti-corruption measures. The European Commission summarizes its view of the rule of law as follows:

> The primacy of the law is a fundamental principle of any democratic system seeking to foster and promote rights, whether civil and political or economic, social and cultural. This entails means of recourse enabling individual citizens to defend their rights. The principle of placing limitations on the power of the State is best served by a representative government drawing its authority from the sovereignty of the people. The principle must shape the structure of the State and the prerogatives of the various powers. It implies, for example:
>
> * A legislature respecting and giving full effect to human rights and fundamental freedoms
> * An independent judiciary
> * Effective and accessible means of legal recourse
> * A legal system guaranteeing equality before the law
> * A prison system respecting the human person
> * A police force at the service of the law
> * An effective executive enforcing the law and capable of establishing the social and economic conditions necessary for life in society.[3]

The rule of law also has an economic development dimension; the existence of a transparent and effective legislative and regulatory framework, as well as of the necessary institutions, is regarded as a prerequisite for both domestic and foreign investment. A functioning legal system means more than an independent judiciary; it implies a legal system that can play its part in formulating and working out the regulatory choices that are at the heart of modern economies. In this sense, the rule of law means not only that these regulatory choices are accountable to legal procedures, but also that legal institutions are a necessary part of the legal foundation for economic transition and development.

RIAs create both opportunities and challenges for the rule of law. This chapter shows that the demands made by different types of RIAs require the development of both political and legal institutions, frameworks, and procedures that will support the rule of law within the domestic system. This is one way in which an RIA supports the economic and social development of its members. However, the nature of RIAs, in particular those that envisage a high degree of economic integration, poses challenges for the rule of law at the domestic level as traditionally understood, and requires the creation of new rule of law mechanisms at the regional level. More specifically, where political accountability becomes more distant from individual citizens (as it may when decisions are taken at the regional level), the need for legal

---

[3] Commission Communication of 12 March 1998 on democratization, the rule of law, respect for human rights, and good governance: the challenges of the partnership between the European Union and the ACP, COM (1998) 146, 4.

accountability becomes even more important. It is for this reason, among others, that dispute settlement is an important element of the rule of law picture.

This link between RIAs and the rule of law can be seen in the development and technical assistance policies of the European Community as well as in the broader foreign policy objectives of the European Union as a whole. One of the explicit objectives of the European Community's development cooperation policy is the development and consolidation of democracy and the rule of law, respect for human rights, and fundamental freedoms.[4] The Commission has recently referred to "the European Community's development priority of promoting institutional capacity-building, good governance and the rule of law."[5] Article 11 of the Treaty on European Union states, as one aspect of the Union's objectives for its common foreign and security policy, that it aims "to develop and consolidate democracy and the rule of law." As this shows, the rule of law may be an objective of the external policy of the European Community and the European Union outside the specific context of development policy.

A specific agreement between the European Community and a third country may expressly state the rule of law to be an objective of cooperation, intended to underpin its broader development and integration objectives. The new Cotonou Convention between the European Community and the 77 African, Caribbean, and Pacific states, for example, includes the rule of law as an objective of cooperation, specifically referring to access to justice and the professionalism and independence of judicial systems.[6] The European Community's Agreement with South Africa states that "development cooperation shall contribute to South Africa's harmonious and sustainable economic and social development and to its insertion into the world economy and to consolidate the foundations laid for a democratic society and a state governed by the rule of law in which human rights in their political, social and cultural aspects and fundamental freedoms are respected."[7] In the Economic Partnership, Political Coordination and Cooperation Agreement between the European Community and Mexico, the parties agree to focus cooperation inter alia on "training and information measures designed to help institutions function more effectively and to strengthen the rule of law."[8] The Stabilisation and Association Agreement between the European Community, its member states, and the former Yugoslav Republic of Macedonia includes a provision that specifically refers to "the consolidation of the rule of law" in the context of institution building at all levels of the administration in general and in law enforcement and the machinery of justice in particular, focusing on the independence of the judiciary, the improvement of its effectiveness, and training of the legal professions.[9]

The rule of law is also prioritized as a key element of democratization and good governance in Community development and technical assistance programs, as well as in the context

---

[4] Article 177(2) EC.

[5] Communication from the Commission to the Council and the European Parliament - The European Union's role in promoting human rights and democratisation in third countries, 8 May 2001, COM (2001) 252 final.

[6] Cotonou Convention, Article 33(1)(c).

[7] Agreement on Trade, Development and Cooperation between the European Community and its Member States and the Republic of South Africa, OJ 1999 L 311/3, Article 65(2).

[8] Economic Partnership, Political Coordination and Cooperation Agreement between the European Community, its Member States, and the United Mexican States COM (1997) 9527 final OJ 1997 C 350/6, Article 39(2)(b).

[9] Stabilization and Association Agreement between the European Community, its member states and the former Yugoslav Republic of Macedonia, signed March 2001, Article 74. A similar clause is found in the Stabilisation and Association Agreement with Croatia, Article 75. These agreements are likely to serve as a model for further stabilization and association agreements, which are ultimately envisaged with the Federal Republic of Yugoslavia, Albania, and Bosnia-Herzegovina.

of regional dialogue.[10] As the Commission points out, institutional capacity building is central to this objective.[11] This means that, whereas in some earlier instruments reference is made to democracy and good governance rather than explicitly to the rule of law, support for the rule of law may nevertheless be treated as an objective.[12]

More recent programs make explicit the importance of the rule of law for development. For example, in its communication on the follow-up to the Rio Summit of June 1999 between the European Union, Latin America, and the Caribbean, the Commission identifies as a priority "new positive measures" with the aim of "support for democratic political systems, contributing in particular to the consolidation and modernization of the rule of law, through support for the media and press freedom."[13] The European Community's Economic and Social Committee refers to "the importance of 'good public management' and strengthening institutions supporting the rule of law" within European Union–Latin America/Caribbean cooperation programs.[14]

In fact, the rule of law now appears as an objective in all the "geographically based" Community programs, including those just mentioned relating to Latin America, the Mediterranean region, the candidate states of Central and Eastern Europe, Southeastern Europe, and the former Soviet Union and Central Asia. Within the program of assistance for the Mediterranean countries, support for sustainable economic and social development expressly includes "the development of cooperation in areas relating to the rule of law, such as cooperation in judicial and criminal matters, the strengthening of institutions which guarantee the independence and effectiveness of the judicial system, the training of national security services and civil protection."[15] The program of technical assistance for the partner states in Eastern Europe and Central Asia (TACIS) is defined as "a programme to promote the transition to a market economy and to reinforce democracy and the rule of law in the partner States" (Article 1), and support for the rule of law is included alongside reinforcement of the legal and regulatory framework.[16]

---

[10] For a recent summary of support for human rights and democracy within European Community external policy, see Commission Communication COM (2001) 252 final, *supra* note 6.

[11] Institutional capacity building, good governance, and the rule of law are identified as "priority fields" for European Union development policy according to the Communication from the Commission to the Council and the European Parliament - The European Community's Development Policy, 26 April 2000, COM (2000) 212.

[12] For example, Council Regulation 443/92/EEC of 25 February 1992 on financial and technical assistance to, and economic cooperation with, the developing countries in Asia and Latin America OJ 1992 L 52/1, Art. 5.

[13] Commission Communication, 31 October 2000, COM (2000) 670 final, 7. These measures include a proposal for a European Union-Latin America/Caribbean discussion forum for the promotion and protection of human rights, based on experience gained in Central America where a committee of independent experts was set up under the San José Dialogue to discuss human rights. The group has been asked to submit a report with conclusions and proposals for action to the 2002 European Union-Latin America Summit: COM (2001) 252 final, Annex 1.

[14] Opinion of the Economic and Social Committee on 'Relations between the European Union, Latin America and the Caribbean: socio-economic interregional dialogue' OJ 1999 C 169/49, at para 2.3.

[15] Regulation 1488/96/EC on financial and technical measures to accompany the reform of economic and social structures in the framework of the Euro-Mediterranean partnership (OJ 1996 L 189/1), as amended by Regulation 2698/2000 (OJ 2000 L 311/1), Art 2 and Annex II. See also Regulation 257/2001/EC (OJ 2001 L 39/1) on the implementation of measures to promote economic and social development in Turkey, under which cooperation projects and operations may include "any form of cooperation seeking to defend and promote democracy, the rule of law, human rights ..." (Art. 4(1)(h)).

[16] Council Regulation 99/2000/EC concerning the provision of assistance to the partner states in Eastern Europe and Central Asia OJ 1999 L 12/1, Art. 2(2) and Annex II. See also the TACIS program annual report for 1999, COM (2000) 835 final.

Again, in the context of Southeastern Europe, the current European Union assistance program specifies Community assistance for the creation of a legislative and institutional framework to underpin (inter alia) the rule of law, alongside other objectives, such as economic development and reform and regional cooperation.[17]

In addition to these geographically based programs, the European Community may base assistance on instruments that provide a basis for Community operations that contribute to the general objective of developing and consolidating democracy and the rule of law and to the objective of respecting human rights and fundamental freedoms.[18] The Treaty of Nice, when it enters into force, will amend the European Community Treaty to provide a new explicit legal base for "economic, financial and technical cooperation measures" with third countries (not therefore limited to development policy), a general objective of which will also be the development and consolidation of democracy and the rule of law, respect for human rights, and fundamental freedoms.[19] Thus, cooperation in matters of the rule of law should play an increasing role in the European Community's external policies and agreements, within and beyond development policy.

These Community instruments demonstrate an appreciation that the rule of law is not just or even mainly a matter of constitutional law. It requires functioning institutions and independent agencies, and not only those that are directly related to government. The growth of a rule of law "culture" depends on the strengthening of civil society institutions, including universities, the media, and professional organizations. This has implications for the planning and targeting of technical assistance programs.

This section has briefly explored the way in which the rule of law operates within a domestic legal order. Without effective legal norms, economic reforms will not be able to take root; the development of a substantive legal infrastructure is necessary for a modern market economy. However, the rule of law has an even more fundamental role to play. The enactment of legislation in such areas as corporate law, accountancy, taxation, and antitrust will not of itself encourage investment (domestic or foreign) in the absence of such principles as the transparency and stability of laws and effective anticorruption controls. The rule of law is thus seen, by the European Union and its member states, among others, as a prerequisite for economic, social, and political development, and as such has become a key element in the European Community's technical and financial assistance programs and development, cooperation, and association agreements. Many of these agreements are themselves RIAs. A later section of this chapter examines the rule of law implications for such regional arrangements. The following section places RIAs in the context of the multilateral trading system typified by the WTO.

THE RULE OF LAW AND THE MULTILATERAL TRADING SYSTEM

For the majority of states, membership of an RIA takes place against the background of WTO membership. Indeed, the European Union regards WTO membership as an informal precondi-

---

[17] Regulation 2666/2000/EC on assistance for Albania, Bosnia-Herzegovina, Croatia, the Federal Republic of Yugoslavia, and the Former Yugoslav Republic of Macedonia OJ 2000 L 306/1, Art 2(2)(b). This Regulation replaces the former OBNOVA Regulation for the region.

[18] There are two such Regulations: Regulation 975/1999/EC OJ 1999 L 120/1, which covers operations within the field of development cooperation, and Regulation 976/1999/EC OJ 1999 L 120/8, which covers all other third countries.

[19] Article 181a(1) European Community Treaty as amended by the Treaty of Nice (not yet in force).

tion for the conclusion of a free trade agreement with a trading partner. This section examines the rule of law implications of WTO membership and then turns to the question of the interrelationship between such multilateral obligations and regional agreements.

There is no doubt that the WTO places greater rule of law demands on a member than the General Agreement on Tariffs and Trade (GATT) did in 1947. The GATT in 1947 was based on the contractual model discussed later in the context of rule of law requirements for regional integration. Its institutional dimension was limited, it did not envisage any legislative mechanism at a regional level, and it did not entail substantive domestic legislative commitments. Its most distinctive feature from this perspective was perhaps the fact that although the GATT disciplines of most favored nation (MFN) and national treatment were nonnegotiable, the degree of trade liberalization to which the contracting parties were committed (bound rates of duty) was negotiated on an individual basis at the time of entry and again in subsequent rounds.

The WTO, by contrast, includes a package of agreements, some of which, notably the Agreement on Trade-Related Aspects of Intellectual Property Rights (TRIPS), impose substantive legal commitments at the level of domestic law. These include not only standards of protection for intellectual property rights, but also adequate enforcement mechanisms. The Agreement on Sanitary and Phytosanitary Measures (SPS) requires adherence to international standards, the operation of risk assessment mechanisms, and inspection and approval procedures. Not only does the SPS agreement thus require the development of regulatory institutions and frameworks; by accepting that importing WTO members may justifiably (subject to conditions) apply their SPS standards to imports, the agreement creates a demand for equivalent domestic standards within exporting members.

More generally, since there is no space here to discuss these developments more fully (see Jackson 1998), the evolution of the WTO into a more rule-based system—in both the substantive content of its rules and in its dispute settlement procedures—presupposes that its members have a sufficiently developed legal framework to apply the rules and to protect their interests through legal challenge. These trends are likely to continue. In the context of the projected new round, the European Union has recognized the demands that this places on developing country members and the need for capacity building and assistance in the negotiation as well as the implementation stages.[20] The choices that will be made in forthcoming negotiations, in connection with proposed new regimes for investment or competition, for example, carry with them the need for institutional and procedural infrastructures. The rule of law implications of various economic integration agreements and methodologies are thus increasingly relevant to WTO membership.

The WTO also has an impact on the form taken by RIAs between its members. The widening membership and scope of the WTO has meant that countries negotiating an RIA will see the WTO level of commitment as a floor, a foundation on which the RIA will build as a "WTO plus" (Echandi 2001: 408). There is nothing to prevent two or more of the parties to a multinational agreement such as the WTO from concluding a subsequent bilateral treaty as long as the later agreement does not interfere with the rights of other parties or make it impossible to fulfill the objectives of the prior multilateral agree-

---

[20] European Community Commission, 'EC position in relation to the development dimension of a new Round of multilateral trade negotiations,' Memorandum for Joint ACP-EU Ministerial Trade Committee in Nairobi, 2 October 2001.

ment.[21] Compliance with these conditions in the case of RIAs concluded between WTO members in practice requires compliance with Article XXIV of the GATT and Article V of the General Agreement on Trade in Services (GATS). Certain basic parameters are thus set with respect to coverage, timing, and the scope of trade liberalization envisaged.

The RIA may make express reference to the intention to comply with WTO rules (a statement that would inform interpretation of the agreement in case of dispute).[22] In case of incompatibility, the subsequent agreement would not thereby be rendered invalid, but there would be a breach by the parties of their obligations under the earlier agreement. Such issues of compatibility may thus be resolved either under the dispute settlement procedures of the earlier multilateral agreement (the WTO) or in the context of the application of the subsequent bilateral agreement (for example, a challenge to the legality of an act adopted under the subsequent agreement on the grounds that it was incompatible with the earlier multilateral agreement).[23] An RIA agreement may expressly preserve the rights of third parties under earlier treaties concluded by parties to the RIA.[24] In addition, many agreements contain a clause recognizing the fact that both parties have existing RIA commitments.

The European Community's Agreement with Mexico illustrates the interrelationship between bilateral and multilateral agreements outside the WTO with countries that are already members of RIAs. The Agreement is explicit about the intention of the parties to operate within a WTO-compliant framework. In addition, the Decision adopted by the Joint Council in March 2000 for the implementation of trade aspects of the Global Agreement with Mexico provides:

> Nothing in this Decision shall preclude the maintenance or establishment of customs unions, free trade areas or other arrangements between either of the Parties and third countries, insofar as they do not alter the rights and obligations provided for in this Decision.[25]

A mechanism for consultation within the Joint Committee resolves issues arising out of free trade and customs union agreements and "on other major issues related to the Parties' respective trade policies with third countries." Mexico's membership of the North American Free Trade Agreement (NAFTA) did not require special provision because a free trade area does not constrain its members' trade policy toward third countries. Rather, it may be seen as a stimulus toward the conclusion of the bilateral agreement with the European Community.

---

[21] Under Article 41(1) of the Vienna Convention on the Law of Treaties, "Two or more of the parties to a multilateral treaty may conclude an agreement to modify the treaty as between themselves alone if: (a) the possibility of such a modification is provided for by the treaty; or (b) the modification in question is not prohibited by the treaty and: (i) does not affect the enjoyment by the other parties of their rights under the treaty or the performance of their obligations; (ii) does not relate to a provision, derogation from which is incompatible with the effective execution of the object and purpose of the treaty as a whole."

[22] Article 6 of the Stabilisation and Association Agreement between the European Community, its member states, and the former Yugoslav Republic of Macedonia states: "The Agreement shall be fully compatible with the relevant WTO provisions, in particular Article XXIV of the GATT 1994 and Article V of the GATS."

[23] See discussion by Saggio AG in case C-149/96 *Portugal v Council* [1999] ECR I-8395.

[24] For example, see Article 307 EC.

[25] See above, note 9 at Article 23. The Global Agreement itself is not yet in force; however, the Interim Agreement on Trade came into force in July 1998, and Decision 2/2000 of the Joint Council of the Interim Agreement on Trade and Trade-Related Matters brought into effect the free trade provisions of the agreement and came into force on 1 July 2000, OJ 2000 L 157/10.

For an individual country, therefore, membership of more than one RIA or of the WTO and an RIA entails not only the adoption of new substantive obligations. The country's domestic legal system has to accommodate the demands of both sets of commitments and needs mechanisms for adjudicating between them in cases of conflict. In some cases, the agreements contain provisions dealing with these issues, but their impact within the domestic legal order is a matter for each state (Cremona 2001).

RULE OF LAW REQUIREMENTS FOR REGIONAL INTEGRATION

Different models of RIAs all present different rule of law requirements, and the choices among them depend on many considerations, economic and political no less than legal. However, the legal aspect is not just a matter of a choice among different options, selecting the better solution from a rule of law perspective. Equally important are the challenges that RIAs pose for the rule of law as traditionally understood, and the need to create new rule of law mechanisms at the regional level.

The rule of law thus operates at two levels: the *regional/international* and the *domestic* levels. It is important, however, not to assume that transferring powers to an RIA institution will somehow cure defects in the rule of law at the domestic level. On the contrary, RIAs impose greater demands, directly and indirectly, on the institutional framework necessary to support the rule of law at the domestic level. It is in part for this reason that, increasingly, rule of law conditions are imposed, either on accession to an existing RIA or on the creation or progression of a relationship.

The Rule of Law at the Regional Level

An RIA requires choices to be made as to the appropriate institutional and legal structures for its management. Different levels of regional integration require an assessment of the rule of law needs for each. To some extent, the different levels correspond to the classic distinction of economic analysis between a free trade area, a customs union, and a common market (El-Agraa 1996). However, from the perspective of legal integration and the rule of law, it is more helpful to locate different stages on a continuum between contractual and constitutional models of integration, and to identify some of the parameters that determine the nature of a particular RIA.

The paradigm of the contractual model is the simple free trade agreement, which experience shows does not require the establishment of a formal organization: the European Free Trade Association (EFTA), for example, operates on the basis of treaty-based obligations with a minimal institutional structure. Both cooperation and enforcement are intergovernmental in character, and dispute settlement is dealt with through the EFTA Council (there are no independent law-making institutions and no court of justice). Under the EFTA model, the organization itself does not have legal personality or treaty-making power, so that further free trade agreements are negotiated either by the EFTA members individually (as was the case between the European Community and the individual EFTA states during the 1970s) or as a group (for example, the agreement between the four EFTA states[26] and Mexico signed in November 2000,

---

[26] Iceland, Liechtenstein, Norway, and Switzerland.

or the European Economic Area Agreement between three of the four EFTA states and the European Community). The GATT, until 1994, was likewise based on a contractual rather than an institutional model. In terms of the rule of law, these contractual arrangements operate within an international law context. They do not seek to create their own *sui generis* legal order, but operate within the broader framework of international law. Characteristically, then, decisionmaking and dispute settlement are consensual, and the agreements do not impact directly on their members' domestic constitutions or legal orders.[27]

At the other extreme, perhaps, is the European Community, the constitutive Treaty of which "constitutes the constitutional charter of a Community based on the rule of law."[28] This constitutional model of regional integration impacts directly on the legal orders of the member states: the European Court of Justice has identified the essential characteristics of the Community legal order as its primacy over the laws of the member states and the direct effect of a whole series of provisions that are applicable to their nationals and the member states themselves.[29] The implications of the Court's statement are that the Treaty, as interpreted by the Court, needs to provide the constitutional framework for lawmaking and law enforcement. Rule of law concerns, such as administrative accountability, due process, and judicial dispute settlement, need attention.

For example, in 1986, the European Court of Justice decided that although the Treaty did not explicitly provide for judicial review of acts of the European Parliament, it must nevertheless be possible to challenge acts of the European Parliament that have legal effect vis-à-vis third parties. The Court's reasoning was based on the fact that the Community was "a Community based on the rule of law, inasmuch as neither its Member States nor its institutions can avoid a review of the question whether the measures adopted by them are in conformity with the basic constitutional charter, the Treaty."[30] This example illustrates, first, the type of question that needs answering (the scope of legal challenge and the appropriate enforcement mechanisms), and, second, the importance of an independent court to uphold the institutional balance within this constitutional model.[31]

For the European Union, this has not of course been a controversy-free process. As the European Community has widened the scope of its activities and, through the European Union, extended into foreign and even security policies, questions of the legitimacy or democratic deficit of the Community and Union structures are raised (Snyder 1996; Craig and Harlow 1998; Weiler 1999). Particularly problematic have been issues of transparency, access to documents, rights of participation in the decisionmaking process, and limits imposed on individual (and nonstate entity) rights to judicial review. There is no space to enter into these arguments here. However, their existence points to an important conclusion: the creation of deeper forms of regional integration not only requires consideration of specific rule of law–type questions,

---

[27] I do not mean by this that these agreements always have a dualist relation to domestic legal orders; rather, the impact of the agreement within the domestic legal order of each member depends on that member's constitutional position, not on the agreement itself.

[28] Per ECJ in *Opinion 1/91* (draft EEA Treaty) [1991] ECR 6079, at para 21.

[29] Ibid.

[30] Case 294/83 *Parti Ecologiste 'Les Verts' v. European Parliament* [1986] ECR 1339 at para 23. The Court has also held that the European Parliament can bring an action itself, in order to defend its prerogatives: case C-70/88 *European Parliament v. Council* (Chernobyl) [1990] I-2041. Since these cases, the Treaty provisions have been amended to reflect the Court's rulings: see Art. 230 EC.

[31] The institutional balance is between the Council (representing the member states), the European Parliament (representing the peoples of the European Union), and the Commission (representing, in a sense, the Community interest).

such as the extent of judicial review at the regional level, it also puts into question the rule of law within the constituent member states.

Not all regional integration arrangements fall within either the contractual (EFTA-style) model or the constitutional (European Union–style) model. When the Community and the EFTA states decided to create the European Economic Area, they had in mind something that went beyond the simple European Community–EFTA free trade agreements, but that did not go as far as full European Union membership for the EFTA states.[32] Although the European Economic Area is a free trade area and not a customs union, it nevertheless shares some of the depth of integration found in the European Community's common market. The integration structure envisaged was expressed in terms of both homogeneity and dynamism with respect to the European Community's own legal order (Cremona 1994).

The European Economic Area was intended both to mirror and track European Community legislative developments. This imposed institutional requirements that had not been necessary under the simpler free trade regimes, as well as mechanisms to be set up on the EFTA side to ensure that the EFTA states would "speak with one voice" to their European Community interlocutors within those joint institutions. Most strikingly, the European Economic Area required the establishment of an EFTA Court and EFTA Surveillance Authority in order, inter alia, to enforce the strong competition (antitrust) provisions of the European Economic Area. A separate EFTA Court was required because the European Court of Justice took the view that the Community's own rule of law would be compromised by the creation of a joint court.[33]

Clearly, many different models of RIAs are possible. However, there are some parameters concerned in different ways with the extent to which competencies are transferred from the national to the regional level. Three such determinants are the level of intensity of legal integration, the external or international dimension of integration, and the substantive scope of integration.

The first determinant is represented by the balance between negative and positive integration. Negative integration requires the abolition of specific state (and nonstate) barriers to trade and other economic activity. Rule of law issues here relate primarily to enforcement and dispute settlement: the level at which enforcement takes place (regional and/or domestic) and the extent to which private enforcement is envisaged. Are dispute settlement procedures primarily political and negotiated, or are they of a more judicial character? An RIA at the contractual end of the spectrum is likely to be based primarily on negative integration techniques, and its effect on national law to be less direct.

By contrast, positive integration envisages the enactment of positive rules at a regional level (deregulation at the national level may thus be replaced by re-regulation at the regional level). Arrangements with a positive integration dimension will thus inevitably require more developed institutional structures and raise rule of law issues of legislative and administrative accountability and the legitimation of secondary as well as primary norms (Joerges and Vos 1999). More specifically, positive integration requires choices to be made, both in the source of the norms and in the mechanisms used for harmonization. Will a particular regulatory model, for example, be imported or will existing practice be adapted and used as a foundation? Imported norms may be proven and reliable in their own context, but may not be appropriate in a different legal (or economic) environment.

---

[32] European Economic Area Agreement, OJ 1994 L1/1.

[33] *Opinion 1/91* (draft EEA Treaty) [1991] ECR 6079.

Furthermore, it is important to develop a rule of law "culture," with its necessary institutional infrastructure; a gradual and experiential development of appropriate norms will be more likely to produce a robust system than the wholesale adoption of an external model. Harmonization techniques vary, encompassing different combinations of mutual recognition, minimum standards, and fully developed rules; within each of these methodologies, there is always a tension between the requirements of uniformity and diversity. Harmonization itself implies a degree of uniformity, but the ability to manage a degree of diversity is important, not only in order to reflect the specific preferences, traditions, and priorities of different member states within the RIA, but also because the resulting competition among norms entails fruitful testing of those norms within the context of market integration (Esty and Geradin 2000).

The second determinant in the transfer of competencies from the national to the regional level is the extent to which the RIA is to become an international actor and speak with the single voice of the organization. A customs union needs to establish mechanisms for setting the external tariff, negotiating preferential tariffs, and settling classification and other relevant issues with its trading partners; a free trade area does not need to create these mechanisms at the regional level. The transfer of decisionmaking implied by the more intensive forms of RIAs (such as customs unions) thus applies to external policy as well as to internal legal norms. For the European Union, the transfer of external negotiating power in fields such as services, investment, and intellectual property rights—going beyond traditional external trade norms—has proved (and is still) contentious, raising questions as to both political and legal control over executive discretion.

The third determinant relates to the substantive scope of integration envisaged. Integration involving access to labor markets and/or direct impacts on private law (harmonization of employment or consumer protection law, for example) leads inter alia to debate over the participation by nonstate entities in the regional lawmaking process and the rights of interested parties to challenge executive and legislative decisions. A competition policy that is enforced at the regional level requires not only an executive capable of investigation and enforcement and liaison (cooperation) between regional and national enforcement agencies, but also mechanisms of challenge. This also suggests that the same institutional model should not be imposed throughout a complex RIA; different aspects of the system (foreign policy, market regulation, and social policy) lend themselves to different models of governance.

The Rule of Law at the Domestic Level

The parameters just outlined are relevant also when considering the rule of law implications of RIAs within the domestic legal order. Negative integration imposes obligations on state and/or nonstate actors, and the questions that arise primarily concern enforcement. To what extent are such obligations to be enforced at the national level (in national courts)? Will norms be enforceable by individuals against the state only, or also against other individuals? To the extent to which they are so enforced, are the choices as to (for example) administrative or judicial enforcement to be left to national legal systems or determined at the regional level?

European Union law is remarkable for the extent to which it has insisted that the answers to these and similar questions are a matter for European Union law itself; even the member states' so-called "national procedural autonomy" in law enforcement has been eroded. A member state has even been found to be in breach of its Treaty obligations by failing to ensure compliance with negative integration obligations by private parties within its territory.[34]

Where the RIA encompasses positive integration measures—that is, where the institutional mechanisms set up by the RIA produce new legislative (and nonlegislative policy) initiatives—then additional demands are made on the national legal order. And the demands presented by an RIA with an agenda of ongoing integration (such as the European Union) are different from those of a specific substantive agreement (such as TRIPS). These include, but are not limited to, the question of institutional capacity to cope with the implementation of incoming norms. Rule of law issues also arise concerning active and effective national participation in the decisionmaking process at the regional level, for example, about how national parliamentary and nonstate interests are represented and how the national position should be formed and presented. An RIA requires working out relations between foreign ministries, line ministries, and other agencies, and putting coordinating structures in place.

What constitutional mechanisms exist for implementation? An active and powerful RIA may put great pressure on parliamentary procedures and time, and may lead to the increased use of secondary legislative techniques; such techniques and strategies pose constitutional and rule of law questions at the domestic level. Implementation of externally agreed norms requires regulatory choices (especially where a minimum-standards harmonization technique is used). The domestic legislative structure needs to respond to these, to engage in impact assessment and the kinds of information and training needed in any law reform scenario.

The scope of the commitments entered into within the RIA will obviously affect the nature of the implementation process, and this will also be a function of the level of development of the preexisting domestic infrastructure. At the simplest level, a free trade agreement requires a functioning customs system and border controls, as well as a functioning system of internal indirect taxation. Mutual recognition provisions require reliable certification and testing systems. A national treatment obligation is likely to be less intrusive than a commitment to harmonize standards or regulatory regimes. In some cases, new agencies, such as a new regulatory body, may need to be created, and rule of law questions will arise relating to its powers, level of independence, accountability, and enforcement capabilities. The reach of modern RIAs may extend beyond traditional international trade laws, deep into domestic areas of law, including contract, consumer protection, and financial services. They thus impact all citizens, not only those engaged in foreign trade. Impact assessment encompasses not only the effects of opening markets, but also the effects of regulatory change or imposition of new regulatory commitments.

Furthermore, these developments may arise not only from the strict legal requirements of a particular RIA agreement, but also from the convergence that may emerge from close regional cooperation, sometimes termed "soft harmonization." To take one example, in the field of competition policy, the European Community Treaty creates a regional-level regime; it does not make demands per se on wholly domestic competition policies or regimes (except that they should not obstruct the Community regime). And yet, every European Union member state now has in place a domestic anti–monopoly and restrictive practices regime that is (to variable degrees) shaped by the European Community regime (Maher 1996).

A fundamental rule of law consideration concerns the impact of an RIA, and international legal norms within the agreement itself or created under it, within the domestic legal order

---

[34] Case C-265/95 *Commission v. France* [1997] ECR I-6959 at paras 30-31.

(Jackson 1992). Two essentially constitutional questions are especially important. The first relates to the hierarchy of norms within the national legal system and the extent to which international norms may take precedence over domestic norms, even possibly domestic constitutional law. The second relates to the extent to which international norms may create rights for individuals enforceable through national courts. The two questions are clearly connected, in the sense that the effective enforcement of individual rights derived from international norms will depend on the hierarchical relationship between those international norms and domestic law.

Although these two potential characteristics are not an inevitable feature of all international norms, an additional question arises as to the extent to which a specific RIA will allow national constitutional choice in this respect. A potential new member of the European Union knows that there is no choice in the matter: European Community Treaty norms take precedence over even national constitutional law;[35] the issue of whether a European Community law (primary or secondary) creates individual rights enforceable in national courts is a question to be decided at the Community level, by the Court of Justice, not by the constitutional laws of individual member states.[36] These are essential characteristics of the new legal order created by the European Community Treaty.[37] Indeed, for the European Union, this goes even further: the binding character and ability to create individual rights of *other RIAs* entered into by the European Community itself are matters for the Court of Justice, even as regards their effect within national legal orders of the European Union member states. A potential new member may therefore have to include amendment of its constitution in order to accommodate these principles, as part of the legal adjustment required of membership (one of the obligations of membership referred to in the third Copenhagen criterion—discussed in the following subsection).

By contrast, NAFTA, the EFTA, and the WTO do not impose a specific answer to these questions on their members (Cottier and Schefer 1998). Where the question is left open, the parties need to consider their own constitutional requirements and traditions. The legal system of a state may give automatic legal effect to international obligations; they become part of the national legal order as soon as the constitutional ratification processes have been completed. Other systems require a domestic legislative act of some form in order to give effect to international treaty obligations in national law. This latter case does not necessarily refer only to a once-and-for-all transposition of a particular RIA. If the institutional structure of the RIA is such that binding decisions will be adopted in the future (by a joint council, joint committee, or association council, for example), then the national transposing legislation will need to take account of this process and either provide for a (simpler) transposition process or remove the need for it altogether. An open-ended delegation to an independent rule-making body without any provision for domestic scrutiny raises rule of law questions akin to those already mentioned.

However, it is not only domestic constitutional norms that are relevant, but also issues of reciprocity.[38] To what extent do the parties wish to ensure not only reciprocity of substantive obligation, but also reciprocity of enforcement procedures? It is possible to argue that perfor-

---

[35] Case 11/70 *Internationale Handelsgesellschaft mbH v. Einfuhr-und Vorratsstelle für Getreide und Futtermittel* [1970] ECR 1125 at para 3; case 106/77 *Amministrazione delle Finanze dello Stato v. Simmenthal SpA* [1978] ECR 629 at paras 17-22.

[36] Case 26/62 *NV.Algemene Transporten Expeditie Onderneming van Gend en Loos v. Nederlandse Administratie der Berlastingen* [1963] ECR 1; case 106/77, above note 36.

[37] *Opinion 1/91* (draft EEA Treaty) [1991] ECR 6079. See also *Brunner v. The European Union Treaty* (judgment of the German Federal Constitutional Court) [1994] CMLR 57, and comments by Everling (1994) and Weiler (1995).

[38] Case C-149/96 *Portugal v Council* [1999] ECR I-8395.

mance of obligation is the key issue, and the question of how that obligation is performed is of secondary importance. But from the rule of law point of view, it is of great significance whether individual citizens are able to enforce state obligations directly, and whether automatic priority will be given to RIA obligations by national courts. The right of individuals to challenge acts of the administration is normally included as a constituent of the rule of law. The consideration here is whether the grounds for such a challenge could or should include failure to comply with an obligation entered into by the state under a specific RIA. There are implications here for domestic legal structures: the individual enforcement of international obligations in national courts requires adequate administrative law processes and procedures,[39] and development of judicial understanding of the legal nature and scope of the RIA in question. Such a decision would also have the effect of making the enforcement process judicial, an issue that the next subsection discusses further.

Conditionality and the Rule of Law

Given the demands that modern RIAs impose on the legal systems of their members, especially but not only those RIAs at the constitutional end of the spectrum, it is not surprising that conditions may be imposed, either by the existing members of a regional integration arrangement with respect to prospective new members, or by one of the parties with respect to the prospective conclusion of a new bilateral agreement. Conditionality takes different forms, including economic thresholds and political requirements, and the rule of law may appear as an aspect of both political and legal conditionality. Joining a well-established and deeply integrated existing RIA will not only be a matter of agreeing to accept the existing level of commitment (negotiating the terms of entry and being prepared to sign the contract). The existing members will need to be assured that the prospective new member shares the common objective, will reliably implement its obligations, and has the capacity to play a full part in the development of policy.

The European Union, for example, opens the possibility of membership to those European countries that subscribe to its founding principles, which include the rule of law. The Treaty of Amsterdam 1997 amended the Treaty on European Union so that for the first time accession formally depends on the fulfillment of qualitative political criteria and not merely being a European state. Under Article 49(1) of the Treaty on European Union: "Any European State which respects the principles set out in Article 6(1) may apply to become a member of the Union." Article 6(1) refers to "the principles of liberty, democracy, respect for human rights and fundamental freedoms, and the rule of law." Although this formal amendment of the Treaty took place in 1997, the Community has imposed de facto conditions (with a rule of law dimension) on membership since 1993. At the historic meeting of the European Council in Copenhagen in June 1993, the member states declared the following:

> The associated countries in Central and Eastern Europe that so desire shall become members of the European Union. Accession will take place as soon as an associated country is able to assume the obligations of membership by satisfying the economic and political conditions required.

---

[39] Case C-213/89 *R. v. Secretary of State for Transport, ex parte Factortame Ltd. and others* [1990] ECR I-2433.

The following conditions were set out for the associated states:

(i)   Stability of institutions guaranteeing democracy, the rule of law, human rights, and respect for and protection of minorities
(ii) The existence of a functioning market economy as well as the capacity to cope with competitive pressure and market forces within the Union
(iii) The ability to take on the obligations of membership, including adherence to the aims of political, economic, and monetary union.

The Copenhagen criteria, as they are known, were drawn up with respect to the Central and Eastern European states, but they have since been applied to other candidates, including Turkey, Malta, and Cyprus, and there is no doubt that they would be applied to applicants from Southeastern Europe (van Westering 2000; Smith 2000).

In this context, the rule of law is explicitly included in the first (political) criteria; however, there is also a rule of law dimension to the third criteria, "the ability to take on the obligations of membership." Acceptance of the *acquis communautaire* entails the necessary institutional infrastructure to manage membership and to participate in Union decisionmaking and implementation processes. To this extent, these criteria are not only about establishing values as membership criteria, but also about setting conditions without which membership in a highly complex regional organization is not a viable proposition.

Rule of law conditionality also appears in a bilateral context. It may form one aspect of a series of conditions attached to the progress of economic integration with a country or group of countries. For the European Union, conditionality in this sense has been most fully worked out in relations with the countries in Southeastern Europe (Smith 1998; Cremona 1999).[40] In April 1997, the Council of Ministers adopted "Conclusions" (a policy statement) on the application of conditionality to its relations with Southeastern Europe, which still form the basis of its policy. Both general and country-specific conditions were attached to trade relations, financial assistance, and the evolution of contractual relations.

For the purposes of this chapter, it is of interest to note the specific criteria attached to the dimension of conditionality headed "human rights and rule of law." These include freedom of expression, including independent media; effective means of redress against administrative decisions; access to courts and right to fair trial; and equality before the law and equal protection by the law.[41] In addition, the criteria for assessing compliance with "democratic principles" include the separation of powers and accountability of the executive, and the assessment of progress toward market economy reform includes the establishment of "a transparent and stable legal and regulatory framework."

The new Partnership Agreement between the European Community and the African, Caribbean, and Pacific states (Cotonou Convention) also declares the importance of the rule of law as an instrument of development:

> Respect for all human rights and fundamental freedoms, including respect for fundamental social rights, democracy based on the rule of law and transparent and accountable governance are an integral part of sustainable development.

---

[40] The countries that form part of this process are Albania, Bosnia-Herzegovina, Croatia, the Federal Republic of Yugoslavia, and the former Yugoslav Republic of Macedonia.

[41] Council Conclusion of 29 April 1997 on the application of conditionality with a view to developing a coherent European Union strategy for relations with the countries in the region.

… The structure of government and the prerogatives of the different powers shall be founded on the rule of law, which shall entail in particular effective and accessible means of legal redress, an independent legal system guaranteeing equality before the law and an executive that is fully subject to the law.[42]

The rule of law is included, alongside democratic principles and respect for human rights, as a subject of political dialogue and objective of the Agreement, as well as an essential element of the Agreement, serious breaches of which may justify suspension of the Agreement.[43] It is increasingly common for the rule of law to be included—alongside democratic principles and respect for human rights—in such "essential elements" clauses in European Community agreements.[44]

DISPUTE SETTLEMENT AND THE RULE OF LAW

The previous section demonstrated that enforcement of RIA obligations at the national level is closely connected to the legal relationship between international and national law. This section focuses on issues of dispute settlement (and therefore enforcement) at the regional level. The Latin American experience has suggested that strong dispute settlement mechanisms are more important to the success of RIAs than the establishment of supranational decisionmaking bodies (Echandi 2001: 405).

An initial distinction needs to be made between political and judicial enforcement. On the face of it, this distinction seems clear. However, experience, not least within the WTO, has shown that in practice there is a continuum rather than a straight bipolar distinction. Dispute settlement under the 1947 GATT was essentially nonjudicial; dispute settlement under most of the European Community's free trade agreements is based on the attempt to negotiate a solution through discussion in the political forum of a joint committee or the equivalent, with the possibility of recourse to arbitration.[45] Dispute settlement under the European Community Treaty, by contrast, is essentially judicial.[46] The word "essentially," of course, points to a less clear-cut distinction: the 1947 GATT operated on the basis of independent panel reports; enforcement under the European Community Treaty involves a frequently extended administrative phase during which negotiations between a member state and the Commission may resolve the dispute without recourse to the Court.

More significantly, should dispute settlement under the WTO be characterized as judicial or nonjudicial? To adopt Jackson's (1998: 60) more appropriate terminology, is the approach negotiation or diplomacy-oriented, or rather juridical, or rule-oriented? The Appellate Body, in particular, seems to adopt a rule-oriented approach. However, the Ministerial Conference and the General Council (political or diplomatic bodies) have exclusive authority to adopt inter-

---

[42] Cotonou Convention, Articles 9(1) and (2).

[43] Cotonou Convention, Articles 9(2) and 96(2).

[44] For further examples, see Agreement on Trade, Development and Cooperation between the EC and its Member States and the Republic of South Africa, OJ 1999 L 311/3, Article 2; Stabilisation and Association Agreement between the EC, its Member States and the former Yugoslav Republic of Macedonia, Article 2 (not yet in force).

[45] See, for example, the Europe Agreement establishing an association between the European Community and its member states and Poland, OJ 1993 L 348/2, Article 105.

[46] Articles 226-228 EC.

pretations of the WTO Agreement and its Annexes, and reports of dispute settlement panels and the Appellate Body require adoption by the Dispute Settlement Body (DSB).[47] Recommendations or rulings by the DSB are to be "aimed at achieving a satisfactory settlement of the matter"[48] in accordance with the parties' rights and obligations, rather than primarily ensuring that "the law is observed."[49]

Negotiation is still an important part of the dispute settlement process.[50] In advocating a rule-oriented approach, Jackson is careful not to equate this with rule of law in that "rule orientation implied a less rigid adherence to 'rule,' and connotes such fluidity in rule approaches," giving room to accommodate some bargaining or negotiation (Jackson 1998: 61). Nevertheless, the attractions of a rule-oriented approach to dispute settlement are clearly linked to the rule of law virtues of greater credibility, transparency, certainty, and predictability. To the extent that the economic integration envisaged in an RIA is of benefit to its participants, they will have an interest in its more effective and predictable enforcement through a rule-oriented system.[51] In addition, a rule-oriented system is less liable to be undermined by domestic special interests and may be attractive for states in a weaker bargaining position (equality before the law).[52] These advantages arguably outweigh the potential benefits of a system that allows a more flexible approach to enforcement. If flexibility is desired, then building it into the agreement's substantive provisions through differentiation and asymmetry of obligation is the more transparent and rule of law–oriented solution.

Despite the European Community's support for strengthening the WTO's rule-based and dispute settlement systems, there is nevertheless a certain caution as to the role of the WTO Understanding on Rules and Procedures Governing the Settlement of Disputes (Dispute Settlement Understanding, DSU):

> There are very distinct limits to how far dispute settlement procedures will go in solving problems between members or adapting the rules to new circumstances not foreseen at the time of negotiation. Dispute settlement can never and should never replace agreements negotiated by Governments representing their countries and ratified by Parliaments. Judiciary or quasi-judiciary institutions should not decide the manner in which the WTO responds to the challenges of today's world. Governments must take the required policy decisions. …[53]

As this passage indicates, there will always be tension between the resolution of disputes through a prearranged dispute settlement process, more or less juridical in nature, and the use of ad hoc intergovernmental processes. This tension reflects further rule of law issues surrounding dispute settlement processes, including the appropriate standard of review, the approach to treaty interpretation, and judicial activism and creativity.

One aspect of this tension concerns the relationship between dispute settlement at a multilateral level and enforcement (through the courts) at a regional or even national level.

---

[47] WTO Agreement, Article IX:2.

[48] DSU, Article 3(4).

[49] Article 220 EC.

[50] Case C-149/96 *Portugal* v *Council* [1999] ECR I-8395 at paras 36-39, referring to Article 22 of the DSU.

[51] Predictability is important to private actors (for example, investors) as well as to governments.

[52] It should of course be recognized that inequalities operate also within a judicial system, especially at the level of available expertise.

[53] Introductory Statement on behalf of the EU to Trade Policy Review Body, July 2000 at p.18.

Does the existence of a specific dispute settlement procedure established within a particular RIA preclude the enforcement of obligations under that agreement through the courts? The European Court of Justice has held that it does not, in the context of a bilateral free trade agreement:

> The mere fact that the Contracting Parties have established a special institutional framework for consultations and negotiations inter se in relation to the implementation of the agreement is not in itself sufficient to exclude all judicial application of that agreement.[54]

However, when the issue was raised in the context of the WTO, the Court of Justice took the view that direct enforcement of WTO rules through the Community (or national) courts would unduly constrain the Community's executive in reaching a satisfactory settlement of the issue within the framework of the DSU:

> To accept that the role of ensuring that those rules comply with Community law devolves directly on the Community judicature would deprive the legislative or executive organs of the Community of the scope for manoeuvre enjoyed by their counterparts in the Community's trading partners.[55]

Thus, the European Community's rule-oriented judicial enforcement mechanism may give way to the demands of reciprocity, executive discretion, and negotiation (van den Broek 2001).

Dispute settlement procedures at a regional (or multilateral) level will generally involve only the parties to the agreement in question, whether as complainant or defendant. Some RIAs, especially those adopting a constitutional model, may include the possibility of actions being brought by one or more of the institutions set up by the agreement. Individuals or other interest groups or agencies in general do not have the right to bring complaints. Even within the European Union, rights for these nonprivileged applicants to challenge Community legislative acts before the European Court of Justice are limited and do not exist at all with respect to member state actions (Harding 1980; Craig 1994).[56] Hence, enforcement at the national level is important. These issues are particularly sensitive where the agreement covers matters of direct interest to (and possibly directly affecting the legal interests of) private parties.

To take competition law as an example, the existence of a credible dispute settlement procedure is one reason the European Commission puts forward for preferring the WTO to (for example) the OECD as a forum for the development of a possible competition agreement.[57] Nevertheless, the Commission also resists any idea that international dispute settlement should be open to private parties; dispute settlement under any new agreement should (in the Commission's view) remain intergovernmental.[58] The Community envisages an agree-

---

[54] Case 104/81 *Hauptzollamt Mainz* v *Kupferberg* [1982] ECR 3641 at para 20.

[55] Case C-149/96 *Portugal* v *Council* [1999] ECR I-8395 at para 46.

[56] See, for example, case T-585/93 *Stichting Greenpeace Council v. Commission* [1995] ECR II-2205; on appeal case C-321-95P [1998] ECR I-1651.

[57] Commission Communication of 17 June 1996, 'Towards an International Framework of Competition Rules', COM (96) 284.

[58] However, it argues that the criteria for an effective *domestic* competition policy should include scope for private party challenge to a competition authority's decision. This approach reflects the current position in relation to antidumping measures.

ment that would impose obligations on the state parties, requiring enactment of domestic legislation, but that would not directly create rights or obligations for private parties.[59] Others are skeptical as to the suitability of the WTO as a forum for resolving the problems of competition policy (Tarullo 1999: 450). Even if WTO-based dispute settlement were limited to ensuring that members' domestic competition laws complied with the agreed framework of "core principles and common approaches," difficult issues would arise where a dispute ultimately challenged the legitimacy of an approach or a decision of a national authority in a specific case.[60] In addition, possible rights of intervention for private parties or agencies showing a legitimate interest in the outcome would need to be determined.

Finally, in considering dispute settlement and enforcement, the issue of sanctions or penalties for noncompliance is important. Is a declaration of noncompliance sufficient, or should a penalty be imposed? If a penalty is imposed, should it be a judicial sanction (for example, a fine[61]), or should retaliatory action by the injured party be possible? Should full compliance be required, or should it be possible to pay for noncompliance with compensation? To some extent, the answers to these questions reflect the rule-oriented or diplomacy-oriented approach to dispute settlement, in that a rule-oriented system is less likely to allow for retaliation or compensated noncompliance.[62] For a smaller or less powerful injured party, compelling full compliance would be more helpful than the possibility of retaliatory action or suspension of obligations, which may have little economic impact on a stronger defaulting party. In an institutionally based RIA, other methods of enforcement would be possible: regular monitoring reports, for example, or publishing lists of defaulters.

CONCLUSION

The objective of this chapter has been to highlight the importance of the rule of law as a prerequisite for successful regional economic integration. The rule of law, including robust institutions and procedures, is an integral part of political, economic, and social development at the domestic level. In this sense, the rule of law encompasses not only the constitutional requirements of (for example) an independent judiciary and the accountability of the executive to legal process; it also signifies a legal infrastructure sufficient to underpin the modern market economy and institutions—both governmental and nongovernmental—capable of engaging in the ongoing process of legal experimentation, development, and dialogue.

---

[59] Submission from the European Community and its member states to the WTO Working Group on "the relevance of fundamental WTO principles of national treatment, transparency and most favoured nation treatment to competition policy and vice versa," 12 April 1999, WT/WGTCP/W/115. The implication is that private parties, as well as being denied recourse to the WTO dispute settlement procedure, would not be able to enforce the envisaged agreement in national courts.

[60] The Commission is clear that there should be no review of individual decisions, but it suggests exploration of the possibility of a panel review in cases of an alleged "pattern of failure" to enforce competition laws in cases affecting the interests of other members (Commission Discussion Paper on Trade and Competition, 19 March 1999).

[61] See Article 228 EC and case C-387/97 *Commission v Greece* [2000] ECR I-5047.

[62] Under the European Community system, retaliation is not permitted: Joined Cases 90/63 and 91/63 *Commission v Luxembourg and Belgium* [1964] ECR 625; Case 232/78 *Commission v France* [1979] ECR 2729. Not only may fines be imposed on defaulting member states by the Court of Justice (see note 62); the Court has also developed the remedy of state liability in damages to the extent that failure to comply with Community law in breach of an individual right has caused quantifiable damage: cases C-6 & 9/90 *Francovich v. Italian State* [1991]ECR I-5357.

From this perspective, engaging in regional economic integration initiatives poses challenges for a domestic legal system. The chapter has surveyed a number of the issues that arise within a variety of models of RIA, and, in particular, the rule of law requirements at the regional level. These models vary according to the depth of integration envisaged, their scope, the level of institutional development at the regional level, and dispute settlement procedures. Choices need to be made in establishing or developing an RIA, not only as to the projected level of integration or liberalization and appropriate institutional structures, but also concerning implementation methods and enforcement within the domestic legal order; the nature and legal force of the obligations to be imposed; the relationship between domestic, regional, and multilateral legal orders; and the creation of an effective dispute settlement process.

The more intensive models of RIA, especially those that create independent lawmaking institutions and rule-oriented dispute settlement, both require greater attention to rule of law issues at the regional level and pose challenges for the rule of law at the domestic level. The RIA itself will require a level of legal development (how much will of course depend on the model of RIA adopted), not only to comply with specific obligations, but also to play a full part in the decisionmaking processes of the regional body. It is therefore dangerous to regard membership of an RIA as somehow an alternative or a substitute for developing adequate rule of law mechanisms at the domestic level. However, domestic constitutional norms may need to be rethought in the light of regional integration commitments and processes. Whatever model of RIA is contemplated, existing and potential member states cannot ignore the need to consider the implications for the rule of law of the choices made, and the demands that these will place on domestic legal structures.

REFERENCES

Cottier, Thomas, and Krista Nadakavukaren Schefer. 1998. The Relationship between World Trade Organization Law, National and Regional Law. *Journal of International Economic Law* 1: 83.

Craig, Paul. 1994. Legality, Standing and Substantive Review in Community Law. *Oxford Journal of Legal Studies* 14: 507.

Craig, Paul, and Carol Harlow (eds.). 1998. *Lawmaking in the European Union.* The Hague, Netherlands: Kluwer.

Cremona, Marise. 1994. The 'Dynamic and Homogeneous EEA': Byzantine Structures and Variable Geometry. *European Law Review* 19: 508.

———. 1999. Creating the New Europe: The Stability Pact for South-Eastern Europe in the Context of EU-SEE Relations. *Cambridge Yearbook of European Legal Studie*s 2: 463.

———. 2001. Rhetoric and Reticence: EU External Commercial Policy in a Multilateral Context. *Common Market Law Review* 38: 359.

Dicey, Albert Venn. 1885. An Introduction to the Study of the Law of the Constitution. *Dictionary of Law.* London, UK: Oxford University Press.

Echandi, Roberto. 2001. Regional Trade Integration in the Americas during the 1990s: Reflections of Some Trends and Their Implication for the Multilateral Trade System. *Journal of International Economic Law* 4(2, June): 367–410.

El-Agraa, A. M. 1996. International Economic Integration. In D. Greenway (ed.), *Current Issues in International Trade.* London, UK: Macmillan.

Esty, Daniel C., and Damien Geradin. 2000. Regulatory Co-opetition. *Journal of International Economic Law* 3(2): 235–55.

Everling, U. 1994. The Maastricht Judgement of the German Federal Constitutional Court and Its Significance for the Development of the EU. *Yearbook of European Law.* 14: 1.

Harding, Christopher. 1980. The Private Interest in Challenging Community Action. *European Law Review* 5: 354–61.

Jackson, John H. 1992. Status of Treaties in Domestic Legal Systems: A Policy Analysis. *American Journal of International Law* 86(2, April): 310–40.

———. 1998. *The World Trade Organisation: Constitution and Jurisprudence.* London, UK: RIIA, Pinter.

Joerges, Christian, and Ellen Vos (eds.). 1999. *EU Committees: Social Regulation, Law and Politics.* Oxford, UK: Hart Publishing.

Maher, Imelda. 1996. Alignment of Competition Laws in the EC. *Yearbook of European Law* 16: 223.

McLeish, Kenneth (ed.). 1993. *Bloomsbury Guide to Human Thought.* London, UK: Bloomsbury Publishing.

Smith, Karen. 1998. The Use of Political Conditionality in the EU's Relations with Third Countries: How Effective? *European Foreign Affairs Revie*w 3(2): 253–74.

———. 2000. The Conditional Offer of Membership as an Instrument of EU Foreign Policy: Reshaping Europe in the EU's Image. *Marmara Journal of European Studies* 8: 33.

Snyder, Francis (ed.). 1996. *Constitutional Dimensions of European Economic Integration*. The Hague, Netherlands: Kluwer.

Tarullo, Daniel K. 1999. Competition Policy for Global Markers. *Journal of International Economic Law* 2(3): 445–55.

van den Broek, Naboth. 2001. Legal Persuasion, Political Realism, and Legitimacy: The European Court's Recent Treatment of the Effect of WTO Agreements in the EC Legal Order. *Journal of International Economic Law* 4(2, June): 411–40.

van Westering, Jolanda. 2000. Conditionality and EU Membership: The Cases of Turkey and Cyprus. *European Foreign Affairs Review* 5: 95.

Weiler, J. H. H. 1995. Does Europe Need a Constitution? Reflections on Demos, Telos and the German Maastricht Decision. *European Law Journal*. 1: 219.

———. 1999. *The Constitution of Europe*. Cambridge, UK: Cambridge University Press.

Chapter 8

Institutional Models of Regional Integration: Theory and Practice

Walter Mattli

This chapter analyzes and illustrates two institutional dimensions of regional integration. The first I call the vertical dimension of regional institutional arrangements; it distinguishes primarily between two models, the intergovernmental institutional model and the supranational institutional model of regional integration. The second is the horizontal dimension of regional institutional arrangements; it describes the process of delegating policy tasks from regional intergovernmental organizations to private sector agencies to achieve faster and deeper economic integration. The study considers the relevance of the various institutional models in light of integration processes in Europe, Latin America, and the Arab world, as well as the role of institutional leadership in regional integration.

VERTICAL DIMENSION

Intergovernmental Institutional Model

The vertical dimension captures the extent to which policy authority and tasks have migrated from the national level to the regional or global level. At one end of this continuum is the intergovernmental institutional model, which holds that integration can best be understood as a series of bargains among the heads of governments of the leading states in a region. These political leaders, jealous of their national sovereignty, carefully circumscribe any sacrifice of sovereignty that may become necessary in order to attain common goals. Large states exercise a de facto veto over fundamental changes in the rules of integration. As a result, bargaining tends to converge toward the lowest common denominator of large state interests.

However, due to the complexity of the integration process, the incentives for unilateral defection may be considerable, especially if cheating is difficult to evaluate. Logically, if cheating is endemic, there are no gains from regional cooperation. It is thus in the member states' self interest to delegate authority to common institutions to enable them to monitor compliance with treaty obligations and to sanction defections. Such institutions may also help to create a shared belief system about cooperation in the context of differential and conflicting sets of individual beliefs that would otherwise inhibit the decentralized implementation of

The author is grateful for comments by Robert Devlin, Antoni Estevadeordal, Jay Smith, Ramon Torrent, and participants at the conference on regional integration and trade in the development agenda.

integration treaties. Common regional institutions may perform the valuable function of mitigating the incomplete contracting problem by applying the general rules of the integration treaty to a myriad of unanticipated contingencies. This obviates the need for member states to make exhaustive, costly agreements that anticipate every dispute that might arise among them (Garrett 1992).

This considerable range of tasks notwithstanding, common institutions in the intergovernmental model serve primarily a technical-servant role, that is, they faithfully implement the collective internal market preferences of the member states. In sum, in the intergovernmental model, institutions are agents on a "short leash" from the principals (that is, the member states' governments). As such, they are essentially ineffective in forcing sovereign states to adopt a pace of integration that does not conform to the states' own interests and priorities; they simply assist in the execution of treaty provisions and rules formulated by the member states of a regional group.

Supranational Institutional Model

At the other extreme is the supranational institutional model, which describes a situation in which political actors in several distinct national settings are persuaded to shift their political activities and expectations toward a new and larger center, whose institutions possess or demand jurisdiction over the preexisting states. The primary players in the integration process are above and below the nation-state. Actors below the state include economic interest groups and political parties. Above the state are supranational regional institutions. These supranational institutions promote integration, foster the development of interest groups, and cultivate close ties with them and with fellow technocrats in the national civil services. In other words, the supranational model of regional integration stipulates that regional institutions are not simply technical-servant agents of the member states, but strategic, rational actors in their own right, frequently with internalized mandates to promote regional integration according to the aims set forth in integration treaties.

In sum, whereas the intergovernmental institutional model of regional integration holds that institutions are agents on a short leash from their agents (the member states), the supranational model depicts institutions as agents on a long leash, that is, as more independent and sophisticated strategic actors. At least four factors determine the length of the agents' leash, that is, the relative autonomy of supranational institutions:

- Distribution of preferences among member state principals and the supranational agents
- Institutional rules governing policymaking among the members of regional groups
- Information available to member governments and supranational agents
- Ability of supranational institutions to build transnational constituencies within the member states.

The first two factors imply that a supranational institution can exploit member state differences to shirk within certain limits and avoid sanctions. This ability depends, in turn, on the institutional decision rules established for applying sanctions, overruling legislation, and changing agents' mandates. Generally, the greater the scope of majority voting and the more diverse the policy preferences among the member states, the greater the autonomy of supranational institutions.

The third and fourth factors further limit member states' ability to tightly control supra-national institutions. Information asymmetry in favor of supranational institutions may result from the highly technical nature of the issues dealt with by these institutions. Finally, the influence of supranational institutions is greatest in situations where they can establish linkages with and rely on constituencies of subnational institutions, interest groups, or individuals that can act to bypass the member governments or place pressure on them.

HORIZONTAL DIMENSION

The horizontal dimension is concerned with analytically and empirically tracing the process of delegation of policy tasks from regional intergovernmental organizations to private sector agencies to accelerate the process of economic integration.

Frequently, the most successful regional institutional arrangements tend to be hybrid forms of governance; they are characterized by a blend of private and public ordering, so as to partake of the virtues of both approaches while minimizing their defects. The key advantages of private agents are superior information, technical expertise, and flexibility. Public oversight and intervention can help to ensure openness, transparency, and legitimacy of policymaking (Abbott and Snidal 2001). For example, politicians may choose to move from a strategy of detailed harmonization of economic policies, through intergovernmental negotiations, to a speedier and more flexible strategy that divides policy work between public and private agents. Governments could focus, for example, on specifying the "essential requirements" that products must meet in terms of health, safety, environmental and consumer protection, leaving the task of developing detailed technical specifications that meet the essential requirements to private technical institutions.

Careful institutional design is as crucial here as it is in the context of the vertical dimension. Whether independence of private experts and public accountability can be made complementary and mutually reinforcing depends, to a large extent, on the structure of the relationship between elected politicians and technical experts. Democratic regimes must allow electorally accountable leaders to override the decisions of experts when such decisions have broad political and economic implications. However, the interference must be transparent; it must follow well-defined procedures and should entail high political costs if it is not objectively justified.

VERTICAL DIMENSION IN PRACTICE

Minimal Institutionalism in Practice

Intergovernmental or minimalist institutional arrangements impose only a small cost on political leaders in terms of foregone sovereignty. This, no doubt, explains their general popularity. Indeed, virtually all integration schemes in developing countries have been of the minimalist type. The drawback of such arrangements is that even slight political opposition of the member states or simple anticipation of such opposition can undermine the effectiveness of the arrangements. The combination of unanimous decisionmaking and strict control by the member states inevitably leads to situations where the actions of common institutions do not exceed the preferences of the least integration-minded member state (the veto player) on any given issue or at any given moment.

Thus, it is not surprising that minimalist institutionalism has poorly served regional integration. It has encouraged states to pass a myriad of resolutions without much regard to issues of implementation and compliance.

Arab Integration

The Arab League Pact of March 1945 was supposed to promote cooperation in economic and financial affairs, communications, cultural affairs, extradition issues, and social and health matters. In 1950, the members of the Arab League signed a joint defense and economic cooperation treaty providing for collective security measures, including a Joint Defense Council and a Permanent Military Commission. Many specialized agencies and permanent committees were set up under the umbrella of the League to promote intra-regional cooperation (Musrey 1969; Flory and Agate 1989; Luciani and Salame 1988; Haseeb and Makdisi 1981; Clements 1992).

Despite these many initiatives, the number of tangible results has been small. Hudson (1999: 11–12) observes that "[t]he League's efforts to foster economic integration have been generally ineffectual and its military and collective security functions never materialized." Luciani and Salame (1988) note that about 80 percent of the 4,000 resolutions that were unanimously adopted by the Arab League have never been implemented. The authors also cite the impressive number of treaties signed under the auspices of the Arab League: "Applied they would have created a very high level of pan-Arab integration. This is obviously not the case." (Tibi 1999: 92–106)

Periodic summit meetings of Arab heads of state have served as an alternative approach to Arab integration. The advantage of this parallel approach is that it brings together key decisionmakers. However, the political will of these leaders to sustain the process of integration was never strong. Sayigh (1999: 255) puts it bluntly: "The Arab politicians who express enthusiasm about economic integration but secretly remain at best lukewarm toward it—and these probably represent the majority—are essentially worried that if economic integration were seriously and purposefully sought, it would lead to political integration. And political integration is anathema to them as a class. Here lies one of the main blockages to economic integration." In the absence of maximalist commitment institutions, there simply is no effective commitment mechanism that can force member states to live up to the promises laid out in integration treaties.

In 1989, the heads of state of the Maghrib countries convened in Marrakesh to launch a Maghrib Arab Union (UMA). The treaty of Marrakesh provided for regular meetings (two per year) of the heads of state. At the third meeting, the leaders signed agreements on a wide range of issues, including an agricultural common market, investment guarantees, phytosanitary coordination, elimination of double taxation, land transit, and transport measures (Soudan 1990). During the fourth meeting, Algeria proposed the creation of a free trade area by 1992 and a common market by 1995.

The member states also endowed the Union with a set of common institutions, such as the Presidential Council, a secretariat, a consultative committee composed of members from each state's parliamentary body, a tribunal of 10 judges, the Maghribi Bank for Investment and Foreign Trade, as well as many functional commissions (Zartman 1999: 179–80).

Despite its appearance, the integration process remains firmly in the hands of governments, and the institutionalist arrangement of the UMA is best described as minimalist. Unsurprisingly, the results have been meager for the most part. Few common policies are operative due to the failure of member states to adopt implementing measures. The only institution to show any real activity to date has been the Presidential Council. Zartman (1999: 182) sums up the Union's performance as follows: "As it nears the end of its first decade, the UMA shows no greater overall integration than it did at any of its birthdays. Indeed, compared to the plans and timetables, it is behind and stagnating."

Latin American Integration

Similar to Arab integration, recent regional integration in Latin America closely follows the intergovernmental model with its (de jure or de facto) minimalist commitment institutions. For example, executive power within Mercosur is with the governments rather than with a European-style Commission. Chapter 1 of the Protocol of Ouro Preto describes the structure and role of the various Mercosur institutions. The highest decisionmaking body is the Mercosur Council, made up of the foreign and finance ministers of the four countries. Each country holds the presidency of the Council for six months on a rotating basis. The Council meets at least once every six months with the four presidents present. There are two decisionmaking bodies beneath the Council: the Mercosur Group—the main executive body composed of officials from the four governments—and a trade commission to review trade policy and examine complaints. Other institutions are a Parliamentary Commission to represent the four countries' legislatures, a Consultative Forum for private sector businesses and trade unions, and a purely administrative Mercosur Secretariat based in Montevideo. An annex to the Protocol sets out the trade commission's complaint procedure: The four partners will attempt to solve complaints and trade disputes through consensus. If there is no consensus or a decision is not upheld, the complainant can initiate proceedings under the 1991 Protocol of Brasília. A tribunal with one judge from each of the countries in dispute and a third independent judge decides the cases.[1]

This minimalist institutional arrangement has repeatedly shown its weaknesses. In a recent evaluation of Mercosur, Bouzas (2001) points to many deficiencies at the implementation stage, especially since 1995. In the area of nontariff barriers, little progress is reported. The implementation of common trade policies has also lagged. The CET has only been partially implemented, and many "temporary" exceptions have been authorized. The deepening agenda agreed upon in Montevideo in December 1995 has made virtually no progress.

In April 2000, the presidents of the member states pledged to relaunch the deepening project. They agreed to harmonize economic statistics and set common targets for inflation and public debt. They signed a deal to bring automobiles into the Mercosur agreement; however, sugar, another contentious item, was not included. Overall, progress has been excruciatingly slow. Also notable is that the leaders failed to agree on a common policy on antidumping. Many other objectives remain unfulfilled, including eliminating nontariff barriers, allowing free trade in services and government purchases, as well as getting rid of the many exceptions to the common tariff.

Several of the problems afflicting Mercosur today can be traced back to Brazil's 35-percent devaluation in January 1999, which put an end to the exchange rate stability that had spurred trade within the group. Argentina and Brazil have since been involved in a series of noisy trade disputes over products, ranging from autos and shoes to chicken and sugar. Mercosur's ad hoc dispute settlement mechanism, which remained untested until 1999, has since been activated to adjudicate one or two cases. This can hardly be called an effective dispute resolution mechanism. The crux of the problem is that, fearing an erosion of sover-

---

[1] On Mercosur, see Coffey (1998) and Roett (1999).

eignty, the presidents of Brazil and Argentina have preferred to resolve their disputes in personal meetings.

In sum, it is apparent that Mercosur will languish without the injection of a substantial dose of supranationalism. Unilateral defection, noncompliance, and enforcement problems will persist in the absence of serious institutional commitment mechanisms.[2]

Supranationalism in Practice: The European Union

The European Union possesses the most far-reaching supranational institutions of any recent regional integration scheme. Two European Union institutions, in particular, are responsible for monitoring and enforcing Community obligations: the Commission and the European Court of Justice. An important task of the Commission is to see that individuals, companies, and member states do not act in ways that run counter to the Treaties or to European Union secondary law.[3] For example, if firms enter into an agreement that restricts competition, the Commission may seek a voluntary termination of such an agreement or issue a formal decision prohibiting it and inflicting fines on the parties to the agreement. It can also take member states to task by demanding termination of an infringement, or by taking the matter to the Court of Justice for a final decision.[4]

The Court also plays a key monitoring and enforcement role in integration. Most notably, it has improved the effectiveness of the European Union's enforcement mechanism through two judge-made doctrines: supremacy and direct effect (Burley and Mattli 1993). The supremacy doctrine holds that European Union law has primacy over national legislation; the direct effect doctrine provides that European Union law is directly applicable to the citizens of the member states without prior intervention by their governments.

Direct effect authorizes private parties (firms and individuals) to enforce treaty obligations against member governments (vertical enforcement) and also against private parties (horizontal enforcement).[5] Recently, individuals have even been empowered to pursue legal actions against member governments that fail to implement community directives (that is, secondary legislation) correctly or in a timely fashion.[6] This direct participation by private parties in the enforcement of the Treaty of Rome, a treaty of international law, is without precedent. It has

---

[2] It is worth noting that effective central monitoring and third-party enforcement are also absent from the Association of Southeast Asian Nations (ASEAN). Similar to the Arab and Latin American cases, the member states have been unwilling to transfer any decisionmaking authority to such regional institutions. Disputes are handled through political, rather than administrative or juridical, arrangements. The ineffectiveness of such a mechanism has been vividly illustrated by recent friction between Singapore and Malaysia over trade in petrochemical products. For a description of the ASEAN dispute resolution mechanism, see chapter 6, "Pacific Settlement of Disputes," of the 1976 Treaty of Amity and Cooperation, reprinted in Nagi (1987, appendix).

[3] Treaty and secondary law has been considerably broadened in scope over the years. It was originally confined to issues dealing with trade in a narrow sense. Today it regulates a wide range of areas, including competition, intellectual and commercial property, public procurement, state aid, telecommunications, banking, financial services, company accounts and taxes, indirect taxation, technical rules and standards, consumer protection, health and safety, transport, environment, research and development, social welfare, education, and even political participation.

[4] Besides the Commission, member states also have the right to bring cases to the Court. In practice, however, legal proceedings initiated directly by member states against each other are relatively rare. See Everling (1984).

[5] See case 36/74, B.N.O. Walrave and L. J. N. Koch v. Association Union Cycliste International, *ECR*, 1974, 1405; and case 149/77, Gabrielle Defrenne v. Société Anonyme Belge de Navigation Aerienne Sabena, *ECR*, 1978, 1365.

[6] See case 152/84, Marshall v. Southhampton and South West Hamshire Area Health Authority (Teaching), *Common Market Law Review* 1 (1986), p. 688; and case 152/84, *ECR*, 1986, 737.

greatly improved the Court's role as central monitoring agent. By the same token, it has increased the Court's caseload. In response, the European Union added a new institution, the Court of First Instance, to its enforcement system in 1988. This new Court was established to hear and give judgment on a number of specific types of legal action, particularly on complaints or disputes arising from the European Union's competition policy (Archer and Butler 1992: 37). In a notable step to further the Court's effectiveness, the European Union empowered the European Court of Justice to impose heavy penalties on member states that fail to comply with Court rulings (Mattli and Slaughter 1995, 1998).

It is of central importance to understand that the Court's modus operandi, especially during the 1960s and 1970s, diverged significantly from what the signatories of the Treaty of Rome had in mind. The remarkable process by which the Court incrementally managed to carve out its own space of relative policymaking autonomy is worth narrating in some detail because it holds valuable institutional lessons for regional integration schemes beyond Europe.

A quick perusal of the Treaty of Rome articles suggests that the founders intended the Court and its staff to interact primarily with other community organs and the member states. Articles 169 and 170 provide for claims of noncompliance with community obligations to be brought against member states by either the Commission or other member states. Article 173 gives the Court additional jurisdiction over a variety of actions brought against either the Commission or the Council by a member state, by the Commission, by the Council, or by specific individuals who have been subject to a Council or Commission decision directly addressed to them. Almost as an afterthought, Article 177 authorizes the Court to issue "preliminary rulings" on any question involving the interpretation of Community law arising in the national courts. Lower national courts can refer such questions to the European Court of Justice at their discretion.

In practice, the Article 177 procedure served as a channel of corporate pressure and demands for deeper integration. It established the framework for the constitutionalization of the Treaty by providing links between the Court and subnational actors—private litigants, their lawyers, and lower national courts.[7] Referrals to the European Court of Justice under Article 177 rely on the initiatives of private actors who deem government regulation incompatible either with existing Community rule or with the spirit of the Treaty of Rome.

From its earliest days, the European Court of Justice waged a campaign to enhance the use of Article 177 as a vehicle enabling private individuals to challenge national legislation. The Court was concerned that if the enforcement mechanism turned primarily on Articles 169 and 170, few cases would be referred to it—since states do not like to sue each other for fear of retaliation—and overall compliance with European Union law would be low. The Article 177 mechanism, however, ingeniously shifted the vanguard of Community law enforcement (and creation) to cases involving primarily *private* parties.[8] It thus removed the Court from the overtly political sphere of direct conflicts between the member states, or even between the Commission and member states.

An early example of this mechanism is the famous *Van Gend & Loos* case of 1963. Through an Article 177 reference, a private Dutch importer raised the question whether he was entitled to directly invoke the common market provision of the Treaty of Rome against the Dutch

---

[7] Constitutionalization describes the process by which the Treaty of Rome evolved from a set of legal arrangements binding on sovereign states into a vertically integrated legal regime conferring judicially enforceable rights and obligations on all legal persons and entities, public and private, within the European Union.

[8] The number of Article 177 cases in the Court's docket grew steadily through the 1970s, from a low of nine in 1968 to a high of 119 in 1978, averaging more than 90 a year from 1979 to 1982.

government's attempt to impose customs duties on some of his imports from Germany.[9] Over the explicit objections of the member states, the Court proclaimed that "the Community constitutes a new legal order...for the benefit of which the states have limited their sovereign rights, albeit within limited fields, and the subjects of which comprise not only member states but also *their nations*...Community law therefore not only imposes obligations on individuals but it also intended to *confer upon them rights* which became part of their legal heritage."[10] The effect of this case was that firms and private individuals that stood to gain from European integration could now push their governments, through the Article 177 procedure, to live up to paper commitments by pointing to Treaty provisions that supported an activity they wished to undertake; a national court would then certify the question of how Community law should be applied to the European Court of Justice, and if the Court's interpretation of a Treaty obligation implied a conflict between national law and Community law, national courts would have to set aside domestic rule.

Another example of how the Article 177 procedure helped to strengthen integration is given by the role played by large French firms in forcing the Conseil d'Etat, the politically influential supreme administrative court of France, to accept the judge-made doctrines of direct effect and supremacy of Community law.[11] Until the beginning of the 1980s, the French Conseil d'Etat felt little pressure to endorse direct effect and supremacy. Two of its major partners, Germany and Italy, had supreme courts that refused to comply fully with the jurisprudence of the European Court of Justice. In 1984, however, the Italian Constitutional Court authorized lower national judges to declare national law incompatible with treaty obligations without having to refer the case to the Constitutional Court.[12] The German Federal Constitutional Court announced in 1986, in the *Solange II* case, that it would no longer control the constitutionality of Community legal acts.

The legal context in which corporate interests in France now found themselves put them increasingly at a competitive disadvantage relative to firms operating in member states where supremacy and direct effect doctrines were fully accepted. According to Plötner (1996: 29), "solid economic reasons [existed rendering]...full integration of Community law into French law paramount. How could the Project of 1992 become effective if the almost three hundred directives intended to transform it into legal reality were not to be directly enforced by the Conseil d'Etat?" He adds: "[T]he impossibility of referring to certain community regulations was bound to represent a serious economic disadvantage [to French firms] in comparison to their European competition. In the long run, this could have led to a movement of forum shopping, combined with some delocalization of head offices." (Plötner 1996: 24)

To remedy this situation, major import and export-oriented companies in France launched systematic attacks on government decisions that they believed were contrary to Community law. Their aim was to provoke a chain of verdicts by the European Court of Justice condemning France for breach of Community law. This increased the pressure on the French government and the Conseil d'Etat to comply with Community rule. The strategy was successful, and the Conseil d'Etat was forced to confirm direct effect of Community directives.[13]

---

[9] Case 26/62, *N.V. Algemene Transport & Expeditie Onderneming Van Gend & Loos v. Nederlandse Administratie der Belastingen*, ECR, 1963, p. 1.

[10] *Ibid.*, p. 12, emphasis added.

[11] This section draws on Mattli and Slaughter (1998).

[12] Italian Constitutional Court decision 170/84, Granital, [1984] CMLRev 756.

[13] *Ibid.*, 27. Reporting on the Netherlands, Claes and de Witte (1995) note similar pressures by Dutch business companies seeking to enforce in the early years of the Community the competition rules of the Treaty of Rome before national courts. For another interesting case, see Rawlings (1993).

In sum, the effectiveness of the European Court of Justice as a promoter of integration can be traced back to factors responsible for the long leash between agent and principal. First, the Court did not act alone, but relied on important subnational groups. The European Court of Justice made these actors aware of the opportunities offered to them by the Community legal system. The Court, in fact, created these opportunities by giving pro-Community constituencies a direct stake in the promulgation and implementation of Community law. As a result, individuals (and their lawyers) who could point to a provision in the Community treaties or secondary legislation that supported a particular activity they wished to undertake—from equal pay for equal work to lifting customs levies—were able to invoke Community law and urge a national court to certify the question of whether and how Community law should be applied to the European Court of Justice.

Second, the member states' control mechanism proved limited both in scope and credibility in the case of the Court. Judges hold terms of six years and cannot be dismissed during their tenure. Court decisions are taken secretly by majority vote (neither actual votes nor dissenting views are made public), rendering it difficult for member states to single out the views of individual judges for sanctioning. The Council of Ministers requires a qualified majority to overrule Court decisions, and, in many cases, a unanimous vote, which poses a formidable institutional hurdle. Finally, a revision of the Court's powers requires a revision of the treaties by unanimous vote and ratification by national parliaments. However, a treaty revision is politically difficult to organize (especially if policy preferences among the member states vary). The threat of such a revision is therefore a relatively ineffective, noncredible means of member state control.

Third, the Court benefited from informational asymmetry resulting from the technical legal obscurity of its decisions. In other words, the Court operates in the realm of law, a realm that proved impervious to political interference not only due to "the mask" of technical discourse, but also "the shield" of domestic norms of rule of law and judicial independence.

HORIZONTAL DIMENSION IN PRACTICE

The New Approach: Moving toward Hybrid Regional Governance

Beginning in the 1960s, the European Union attempted to achieve market integration by harmonizing national legislation. Government elites and supranational bureaucrats would spend many years drafting highly detailed directives and regulations. By the early 1980s, the old harmonization approach had run its course; it had become excruciatingly slow and cumbersome with the increasing complexity of the subjects covered. Furthermore, with the quickening pace of technological change and the shortening of product cycles, the technical details in directives and regulations were often obsolete by the time the legal acts were finally promulgated. In the 1985 White Paper on the completion of the internal market, the Commission acknowledged, "relying on a strategy based totally on harmonization...would take a long time to implement, would be inflexible and could stifle innovation."[14]

In other words, the old approach had laid bare some of the procedural inadequacies and organizational limits of regional public governance, most notably the excruciatingly slow pace

---

[14] Commission of the European Communities, *Completing the Internal Market: White Paper from the Commission to the European Council*, COM (1985) 310 Final, p. 18.

of adopting common standards and, in some cases, lack of technical expertise and financial resources to deal with ever more complex and demanding transnational standards issues. These institutional failures led to a much greater involvement of private-sector actors in regulatory matters, as illustrated in the European Union's New Approach.

The cornerstone of the New Approach was the retreat of the Community legislature from the field of technical specification and the delegation of regulatory functions to private sector bodies, namely European standardization organizations.[15] However, this delegation does not mean that governments have capitulated to these private bodies; instead, governments have redefined their role; they have been (re-)asserting their authority by imposing on private standardizers important organizational changes to comply with public interest safeguards.

Under the New Approach, European Union legislation is limited to laying out in directives mandatory requirements in health, safety, environmental, and consumer protection. These directives cover entire sectors rather than single products. The elaboration of the technical specifications that satisfy the essential requirements is delegated primarily to the European Committee for Standardization (Comité Européen de Normalisation, CEN) and the European Committee for Electrotechnical Standardization (Comité Européen de Normalisation Eléctronique, CENELEC).[16] The national authorities are obligated to recognize that products manufactured according to the standards of these private organizations are presumed to conform to the essential requirements specified in directives (European Union law); they must allow these products to circulate freely in the European Union market. However, European standards remain voluntary. Producers who develop alternative technical solutions that meet the levels of safety or health specified in directives cannot be excluded from the market. However, these producers have the burden of proving that their standards do, indeed, reach the required safety and health levels.

Institutional Infrastructure of the New Approach

Success of the New Approach was no foregone conclusion; it depended on a complex set of conditions, most critically the interconnectivity of the regional and national levels of standardization organizations. That is, for the New Approach to work, the two institutional levels needed to be tightly linked and highly complementary.

In order to understand this interconnectedness of the regional and national levels, it is necessary to examine the organizational structure and the modus operandi of CEN and CENELEC. CEN was established in 1961 as a nonprofit regional association producing voluntary European standards in a broad range of areas.[17] CENELEC was set up in 1972 as an association that produces electrotechnical and electronic engineering standards. Both CEN and

---

[15] *New Approach to Technical Harmonization and Standards*, Council Resolution, OJ 1985 C 136.1. See also website www.newapproach.org.

[16] The Commission signed an agreement with CEN and CENELEC in 1984, recognizing them as European Standardization Bodies. A third organization is the European Telecommunications Standards Institute (ETSI). It was established in 1988 to develop standards in telecommunications and related fields. ETSI is a nonprofit organization that is funded entirely by the subscriptions of its 400 members, which are firms and organizations with an interest in the creation of European telecommunication standards.

[17] The areas include mechanical engineering, building and civil engineering, health technology, biology and biotechnology, quality certification and testing, environment, health and safety at the workplace, gas and other energies, transport and packaging, consumer goods, sports, leisure, food, materials (iron and steel), and chemistry.

CENELEC are partially funded by the Commission, and their members are the national standardization bodies in Europe.[18]

The institutional structure of CEN and CENELEC is similar. Both have a general assembly composed of delegations from the national members, an administrative board that acts as the agent of the general assembly, a president that chairs the assembly and the administrative board, and a secretary-general who runs the central secretariat, which is responsible for the day-to-day management of the association, including the meetings of all technical committees, circulation of all necessary documentation, and maintenance of up-to-date records of standardization activities.

A technical board is responsible for monitoring, coordinating, and controlling the standards programs. It advises on all matters concerning the organization, working procedures, coordination, and planning of standards work; monitors and controls the progress of standards work; examines proposals for new projects; creates and disbands technical committees; imposes or releases standstill obligations; and organizes technical liaison with intergovernmental organizations, international organizations, and European trade, professional, technical, and scientific organizations. It also decides, on the basis of national voting, on ratification of draft standards prepared by technical bodies.

The hard work is, of course, done in the technical committees (as well as subcommittees and working groups). At the end of 2000, CEN had 274 active technical committees that had issued a total of 6,666 European standards and related documents and were working on 8,842 items. CENELEC had produced a total of 3,633 standards. It is worth noting that, in the mid 1980s, the total number of European standards was less than 100. In short, the growth of European standards has been staggering.

Does this imply that national standards-developing organizations (SDOs) are becoming obsolete? The answer is "no." Paradoxically, the trend toward European standardization has not weakened national SDOs, but magnified their importance. The national organizations, which, for the most part, are private sector associations—although they receive state subsidies—constitute the veritable backbone of European standardization; they provide the resources, technical expertise, and main institutional infrastructure to support the production of regional standards.

For example, national SDOs select up to three national delegates to a given CEN technical committee. At the same time, they establish so-called mirror committees at the national level that are open to all domestic groups interested in a specific standardization item. The mirror committees brief the national delegates, ensuring that all national interests affected by European standardization are taken into consideration. During the public inquiry stage, the mirror committees debate the contents of draft standards and prepare comments that convey the national point of view. In the final stage of the process, the mirror committees decide on how the national delegates should vote. After the formal approval of a European standard, national SDOs implement the standards as national standards, either by publication of identical texts or by endorsement; conflicting national standards must be withdrawn (Schepel and Falke 2000: 135–150; De Vries 1999).[19]

---

[18] To qualify, applicants must be active in one of the countries of the European Conference of Postal and Telecommunications Administration (CEPT) and agree to contribute to ETSI's work and to use its standards. Several major American companies are ETSI members.

[19] The national transposition of European standards is an obligation for CEN members; however, the application of these standards remains voluntary and thus depends on the acceptability of the standards to those who are expected to use them.

In short, national SDOs produce hundreds of national consensus positions each year, and select and instruct thousands of individuals who serve in delegations to promote the national views in the various committees. Furthermore, because CEN, with its small secretariat in Brussels, has neither the facilities nor the staff to house committees and working groups, the national bodies house and manage them. For example, if the secretary of a CEN technical committee is German, the committee will be housed in the German National Standards Institute. In other words, the actual work of European standardization is done in a decentralized way, with national bodies keeping a close eye on regional committees; that is, they monitor all regional standardization activities and inform potentially interested parties in their countries of new regional initiatives and opportunities. National SDOs are the main financial supporters of CEN and CENELEC.[20]

Paradoxically, the trend toward regional standardization in support of the New Approach has in no way weakened national standardization bodies, let alone rendered them obsolete. The progressive deepening of European integration is, to some extent, premised on the existence of strong, coherent, and centralized national organizations that are capable of aggregating domestic preferences and projecting them with a single voice onto the regional stage. In the area of standards, integration has not undermined national structures, but has strengthened them to optimize the interconnectivity between national and regional levels.

However, the New Approach also leads to a second question: Is the authority of governments being undermined because of the delegation of regulatory power to private sector standardizers? In the early years of the New Approach, many observers questioned its legitimacy and even its legality. Some argued that private standards bodies, dominated by business interests, would be blind to broader social issues, and that the delegation of powers to these private actors would render legislative control over their decisions impossible (Joerges, Schepel, and Vos 1999). Partly in response to these criticisms, member state governments of the European Union have (re-)asserted their authority over the past decade by strengthening their control over standardizers and by engineering subtle, but critical, changes in the procedures and structure of private European SDOs.

For example, they have forced the SDOs to accept the participation of consumer organizations and other groups. The member states issued a declaration in April 1992, emphasizing that the involvement of "social partners...at every stage of the standardization process and at every level of [European] Standardization Bod[ies]...—from Working Group to General Assembly—is a political precondition for the acceptability and further development of European standardization."[21] At the end of the same year, yielding to political pressure, CEN introduced a new category of membership, so-called Associate Members, to integrate into the CEN structure social partners such as the European Association of Consumer Representation in Standardization (ANEC)[22] and the European Trade Union Technical Bureau for Health and Safety (TUTB).[23]

Furthermore, the member states have been improving control over standardization by changing the structure of their financial support for European standardizers, gradually cutting back on general lump-sum subsidies, and switching to project-based financing. They also have increased the practice of employing independent experts to monitor regional standardization

---

[20] CEN, for example, receives 46 percent of its budget from its members (primarily national SDOs); the Commission contributes 41 percent; and sales of documents and specific contracts add anther 11 percent.

[21] OJ C 96 of 15 April 1992, 23.

[22] ANEC stands for *Association de Normalisation Européenne pour les Consommateurs*.

[23] TUTB was established in 1989 by the European Trade Union Confederation (ETUC) to monitor the drafting, transposition, and application of European legislation regulating the work environment.

and determine whether European standards satisfy the essential requirements (Joerges, Schepel, and Vos 1999: 23; Egan 1998: 500).

Lastly, the member states have adopted a series of European Union directives that provide for continuous supervision of the implementation process of standards. For example, the Directive on General Product Safety gives national administrations considerable discretion to impose restrictions on the free circulation of products that they find harmful to consumers, notwithstanding conformity with European standards.[24] Similarly, the Product Liability Directive offers national courts leeway to determine whether a product meets "legitimate consumer expectations" and whether standards reflect the latest scientific and technical knowledge.[25]

In sum, "European standardization [today]...does not operate in a legal vacuum but is in varying intensity embedded into legal frameworks and constantly fed and controlled through networks of non-governmental and governmental actors." (Joerges, Schepel, and Vos 1999: 49–50, 59–61) This fusion of private and public elements in a joint form of governance has conferred on European standardization the high degree of legitimacy that it lacked in the 1980s.

How successful has European standardization been in promoting economic integration? For several sectors, it is too early to tell. New Approach directives must first be adopted and European standardizers then have to produce supporting standards. This all takes time. Nevertheless, preliminary results suggest that the new technique is doing much better overall than earlier approaches. This explains the eagerness of the Commission to apply it more broadly. Indeed, in 1995, the Commission issued a "Communication on the Broader Use of Standardization in Community Policy," announcing plans to extend the New Approach to such areas as biotechnology, environmental policy, and telecommunications. More recently, it decided to begin applying the new technique in the areas of food safety, defense, and services.[26]

However, the positive overall assessment hides considerable variation across sectors in the effectiveness of the New Approach. A detailed account of these differences is not possible here. Instead, I will summarize some of the evidence from interviews and two recent studies.[27] The New Approach seems to be working best in sectors in which the level of regional trade is already high, where there are few dominant manufacturers, and where economies of scale make it advantageous for firms to cover the entire European Union market.

Consider the example of electrical power tools. Before the adoption of the New Approach, most electrical products—especially tools deemed to represent a health and safety threat—were governed by a multitude of national regulations, guidelines, and certification procedures. Many of these national rules have since been superseded by three New Approach directives and corresponding European standards.[28] This change was possible, in part, due to the strong support of industry in Europe, which is dominated by a few global companies. Significantly, the number of manufacturers of electrical power tools has shrunk considerably over the past decade as the larger companies, such as Bosch of Germany and Black & Decker of the United States, bought smaller firms and consolidated their positions as European and

---

[24] Directive 92/59/EEC, 1992 OJ L 228/24.

[25] Directive 85/374/EEC, 1985 OJ L 210/29.

[26] "New Areas of Standardization," *CEN Newsletter* 9 (December 2000), 1–3.

[27] The interviews were conducted at the Commission of the European Union, ANEC, and the European Organization for Testing and Certification (EOTC), all in Brussels, and the Corporate Standardization Department at Philips in Eindhoven, April 5–15, 2000. The two studies are Atkins (1998) and Pelkmans, Vos, and Di Mauro (2000).

[28] The three directives are the Low Voltage Directive, the Machinery Directive, and the Electromagnetic Compatibility Directive.

global leaders. Bosch and Black & Decker have market shares of 35 and 20 percent, respectively, in the European Union, followed by AEG, with 7 percent, and Metabo, with 6 percent. These few large players share similar views about the importance of a single market and have collaborated in the production of European standards.

Other areas that are considered success stories under the New Approach for similar reasons include air reservoirs, pacemakers, and gas cookers. However, in some sectors (for example, cement), there are few suppliers, but economies of scale can be achieved within national markets, and other factors, such as high transportation costs, discourage intra-European Union trade. In these cases, success has been more elusive.

Sectors with many small and medium-sized enterprises (SMEs) and little existing trade are difficult to tackle because they lack concerted industry support, and vested interests tend to fight to keep markets apart. The classic example is the carpet market. The European carpet industry is comprised of hundreds of SMEs. Each country has a variety of regulations for carpets, especially regarding fire safety. Testing methods vary across countries rendering comparability of results impossible, and local fire brigades are often authorized to make final decisions regarding the choice of carpet to be used in public places. Under the Construction Products New Approach Directive, carpets have to meet essential safety requirements for fire resistance, impact noise rating, thermal insulation, and specific slipperiness requirements. However, few relevant European standards have been adopted, and progress is certain to remain slow.

INSTITUTIONAL LEADERSHIP

Theories of regional integration and international relations more generally view opportunistic defection from treaty obligations as the critical collective-action problem impeding cooperation. However, coordination problems are equally important in international cooperation and are of particular relevance in the study of regional integration. One reason is that regional integration schemes often go beyond the removal of border barriers (shallow integration) and include efforts to adopt common regulations and policies. Lawrence (1996: 7) aptly notes:

> "[m]ost theorizing about regionalism [in economics] considers these arrangements in the context of a traditional paradigm in which trade policy is characterized by changes to barriers at the border. Regional arrangements are modeled either as customs unions...or as free trade areas...But although the removal of internal border barriers is certainly an important feature, focusing only on these barriers overlooks much of what regional arrangements are about. The traditional perspective is at best incomplete and at worst misleading. In many cases these emerging arrangements are also meant to achieve deeper integration....Once tariffs are removed, complex problems remain because of differing regulatory policies among nations."

For example, one key element of the European Union's effort to create a common market is the promulgation of coordination equilibria, from common health and safety standards to the harmonization of excise taxes and adoption of common macroeconomic policies.

In sum, the problem with traditional collaboration (as represented by the famous prisoners' dilemma game) is that, in pursuing its self-interest, each state imposes costs on the other independent of the other's policy, whereas in the coordination game each imposes costs or benefits on the other *contingent on the other's policy*. The collective action problem is that neither state can choose its best policy without knowing what the other intends to do, but there is no obvious point at which to coordinate (Snidal 1985; Stein 1983).

In regional integration, the presence of an institutional focal point may help to overcome coordination dilemmas (Mattli 1999). The institutional focal point is a state (a regional leader) whose membership or cooperation in the group is perceived, by all or by a majority within the group, as more important to the group than that of any other state. Adaptation to the policies of the leader makes both political and economic sense; that is, it is likely to be the least costly change within the group. For example, switching to German safety standards is, in the aggregate, less costly to the European Union than switching to Dutch standards.

Cost considerations aside, benevolent regional leaders can also help ease distributional issues that arise as coordination games are played over time. Repeated play makes coordination more difficult because it gives states incentives to be more concerned with the *distributional consequences* of coordination. For some, switching costs may be heavier than for others. Thus, questions of fairness and equitable distribution of the gains from cooperation will need to be addressed to prevent discontent from derailing the integration process. A dominant member state of a regional grouping may be able and willing to assume the role of regional paymaster, easing distributional tensions and thus smoothing the path of integration.[29] The coordination game suggests that successful integration requires the presence of an undisputed leader among the group of countries seeking closer ties. Such a state serves as the focal point in the coordination of rules, regulations, and policies; it also helps ease distributional tensions by assuming the role of regional paymaster.

The history of regional integration schemes seems to confirm that coordination problems are relatively easily solved in the presence of a regional leader, such as Germany in the European Union, Prussia in the Zollverein, or the United States in the North American Free Trade Agreement. Coordination problems are likely to be insurmountable in the absence of an undisputed leader, such as, for example, in the case of the Middle German Commercial Union, the Association of Southeast Asian Nations, or the Andean Pact. Likewise, coordination difficulties arise when two or more potential leaders belong to the same group. For example, within the Asian-Pacific Economic Cooperation, the United States and Japan are contending leaders. Their differing economic institutions and policy preferences in development, money, trade, and other domains make coordination difficult.[30] To be sure, leadership problems are not necessarily insurmountable in Latin America, but it is a key component in defining the success of any current or future regional initiative in the region

---

[29] Note that this account is different from hegemonic stability theory (see, for example, Keohane 1984). The latter is based on an analysis of public goods, a special case of the prisoners' dilemma, and deals with the implications of free riding. By contrast, the present account refers to the coordination game, where the issue is not free riding, but how to overcome distributional inequities.

[30] For an extensive discussion of these examples, see Mattli (1999).

REFERENCES

Abbott, Kenneth, and Duncan Snidal. 2001. International "Standards" and International Governance. *Journal of European Public Policy* 8(3): 345–70.

Archer, Clive, and Fiona Butler. 1992. *The European Community Structure and Process.* New York, NY: St. Martin's Press.

Avery, William, and James Cochrane. 1972. Innovation in Latin American Regionalism: The Andean Common Market. *International Organization* 27: 181–223.

Bouzas, Roberto. 2001. MERCOSUR Ten Years After: Learning Process or DÉJÀ-VU? FLASCO, Argentina. Unpublished.

Burley, Anne-Marie, and Walter Mattli. 1993. Europe before the Court: A Political Theory of Legal Integration. *International Organization* 47: 41–76.

Claes, Monica, and Bruno De Witte. 1995. *The European Court and National Courts – Doctrine and Jurisprudence: Legal Change in Its Social Context – Report on the Netherlands.* RSC Working Paper no. 95/26, European University Institute, Florence, Italy.

Clements, Frank. 1992. *Arab Regional Organizations.* London, UK: Transaction Publishers.

Coffey, Peter (ed.). 1998. *International Handbook on Economic Integration: MERCOSUR.* Boston, MA: Kluwer Academic Publishers.

Devlin, Robert, and Antoni Estevadeordal. 2001. What's New in the New Regionalism? In Victor Bulmer-Thomas (ed.), *Regional Integration in Latin America and the Caribbean: The Political Economy of Open Regionalism.* London, UK: Institute for Latin American Studies, ILAS Series.

De Vries, Henk. 1999. *Standards for the Nation: Analysis of National Standardization Organizations.* Boston, MA: Kluwer Academic Publishers.

Egan, Michelle. 1998. Regulatory Strategies, Delegation and European Market Integration. *Journal of European Public Policy* 5: 487–508.

Everling, Ulrich. 1984. The Member States of the European Community before Their Court of Justice. *European Law Review* 9: 215–41.

Falke, Joseph, and Harm Schepel (eds.). 2000. *Legal Aspects of Standardisation in the Member States of the EC and of EFTA: Country Reports.* Volume 2. Luxembourg: Office for Official Publications of the European Communities.

Flory, Maurice, and Pierre-Sateh Agate (eds.). 1989. *Le système régional arabe.* Paris, France: Éditions du Centre National de la Recherche Scientifique.

Garrett, Geoffrey. 1992. International Cooperation and Institutional Choice: The European Community's Internal Market. *International Organization* 46: 533–60.

Griffin, Keith, and Ricardo Ffrench-Davis. 1965. Customs Unions and Latin American Integration. *Journal of Common Market Studies* 4: 1–21.

Haseeb, Kahir El-Din, and Samir Makdisi. 1981. *Arab Monetary Integration.* London, UK: Croom Helm.

Hojman, David. 1981. The Andean Pact: Failure of a Model of Economic Integration? *Journal of Common Market Studies* 20: 147–56.

Hudson, Michael. 1999. Arab Integration: An Overview. In Michael Hudson, *Middle East Dilemma: The Politics and Economics of Arab Integration*. New York, NY: Columbia University Press.

Joerges, Christian, Harm Schepel, and Ellen Vos. 1999. *The Law's Problems with the Involvement of Non-Governmental Actors in Europe's Legislative Processes: The Case of Standardization under the "New Approach"*. EUI Working Paper Law no. 99/9, European University Institute, Badia Fiesolana, San Domenico (Florence).

Kearns, Kevin. 1972. The Andean Common Market: A New Thrust at Economic Integration in Latin America. *Journal of Inter-American Studies* 14: 225–49.

Keohane, Robert. 1984. *After Hegemony*. Princeton, NJ: Princeton University Press.

Lawrence, Robert. 1996. *Regionalism, Multilateralism, and Deeper Integration*. Washington, DC: Brookings Institution.

Luciani, Giacomo, and Ghassan Salame. 1988. *The Politics of Arab Integration*. New York: Croom Helm.

Mattli, Walter. 1999. *The Logic of Regional Integration: Europe and Beyond*. Cambridge: Cambridge University Press.

Mattli, Walter, and Anne-Marie Slaughter. 1995. Law and Politics in the European Union. *International Organization* 49: 183–90.

———. 1998. Revisiting the European Court of Justice. *International Organization* 52: 177–209.

Middlebrook, Kevin. 1978. Regional Organization and Andean Economic Integration, 1967–75. *Journal of Common Market Studies* 17: 62–82.

Musrey, Alfred. 1969. *An Arab Common Market*. New York: Praeger Publishers.

Nagi, R. 1987. *ASEAN 20 Years*. New Delhi, India: Lancers Books.

Pelkmans, Jacques, Ellen Vos, and Luca DiMauro. 2000. Reforming Product Regulation in the EU: A Painstaking, Iterative Two-Level Game. In G. Galli and J. Pelkmans (eds.), *Regulatory Reform and Competitiveness in Europe*. Cheltham: E. Elgar.

Plötner, Jens. 1996. *The European Court and National Courts - Doctrine and Jurisprudence: Legal Change in Its Social Context - Report on France*. Working Paper, RSC no. 95/28, European University Institute, Florence, Italy.

Rawlings, Richard. 1993. The Eurolaw Game: Some Deductions Form a Saga. *Journal of Law and Society* 20: 309–40.

Roett, Riordan. 1999. *MERCOSUR: Regional Integration, World Markets*. Boulder, CO: Lynne Rienner Publishers.

Sayigh, Yusif. 1999. Arab Economic Integration: The Poor Harvest of the 1980s. In Michael Hudson (ed.), *Middle East Dilemma: The Politics and Economics of Arab Integration*. New York, NY: Columbia University Press.

Snidal, Duncan. 1985. Coordination versus Prisoners' Dilemma: Implications for International Cooperation and Regimes. *American Political Science Review* 79: 923–42.

Stein, Arthur. 1983. Coordination and Collaboration: Regimes in an Anarchic World. In Stephen Krasner (ed.), *International Regimes*. Ithaca, NY: Cornell University Press.

Soudan, Françoise. 1990. Commentaire. *Jeune Afrique* 1544 (August 1).

Tancer, Shoshana. 1976. *Economic Nationalism in Latin America: The Quest for Economic Independence.* New York: Praeger.

Tibi, Bassan. 1999. From Pan-Arabism to the Community of Sovereign Arab States: Redefining the Arab and Arabism in the Aftermath of the Second Gulf War. In Michael Hudson (ed.), *Middle East Dilemma: The Politics and Economics of Arab Integration.* New York, NY: Columbia University Press.

Vargas-Hidalgo, Rafael. 1978. The Crisis of the Andean Pact. *Journal of Common Market Studies* 27: 213–26.

Zartman, William. 1999. The Ups and Downs of Maghrib Unity. In Michael Hudson (ed.), *Middle East Dilemma: The Politics and Economics of Arab Integration.* New York, NY: Columbia University Press.

Chapter 9

Trade Policy Institutions: A Comparative Analysis

Jacint Jordana and Carles Ramió

In the context of globalization, the central role played by states on the international scene may not be disappearing; however, it does need to be transformed through the use of new public intervention instruments that enable states to play a more strategic role (Evans 1997; Weiss 1998). The growing complexity and interdependence of foreign trade policies in the 1990s was a striking example of that transformation, since the countries with more effective public institutions were those that managed to take the greatest advantage of the network of multilateral and bilateral agreements and treaties. One of the crucial elements in the process was the growing international consolidation of new policies and institutions to promote foreign trade, such as the creation of the World Trade Organization (WTO) in 1995. There was also an enormous increase in the internal implications of foreign trade, due both to the logic of opening up trade and because the treaties now take into account many more aspects than previously.

This chapter analyzes and compares the role of institutional structures and rules in the formulation of foreign trade policy at the national level, taking into account the new challenges governments face—in terms of their management capacity—and the growing complexities of the policy. We do not attempt to explain trade policy outputs, but only how institutions shape the trade policy process. The analytical approach falls within the coordinates of New Institutionalism in the way it views comparative political economics (Hall and Taylor 1996). We explore how the existence of certain institutions helps to perpetuate or overcome political or economic problems. This is a position that situates the institutions as a dependent variable, with sufficient explanatory capacity to justify a detailed analysis (Peters 1999). The institutions are mechanisms for adding preferences, although their dynamics go beyond the mere sum of interests, since the expression of the preferences is subject to and transformed by the peculiar features of each institutional structure (Immergut 1998).

In many developing countries, including most Latin American ones, institutional performance remains weak. Severe difficulties arise when trying to generate greater technical capacity in the departments responsible for foreign trade policy, ensure greater internal coordination between government bodies, or develop balanced formulas for societal and business participation in decisionmaking. Therefore, institutional structures that might have been fairly adequate

The authors thank Roberto Bouzas and Diana Tussie for their helpful comments on earlier versions of this chapter, and Gemma Tor for research assistance.

barely 10 years ago are now facing serious difficulties, insofar as they have not managed to renew themselves and adapt to the demands of the new international environment. All these factors mandate the introduction of improvements and reforms, and it is important to identify the essential issues to be addressed when an institutional modernization initiative is envisaged. It is necessary to reinforce the technical information and the strategic management capacity in the main organization responsible for foreign trade policymaking. The government has to manage the growing needs for interdepartmental coordination imposed by the increasing involvement of many productive and tertiary interests in international trade treaties. It must also be able to filter and structure the particular interests of the societal and business players of the country to ensure that national interest prevails.

There are many ways of responding to these challenges. We concentrate on a central question that affects all of them: the influence of formal institutional design on the possibilities of solution and improvement. By institutional design, we mean the following basic aspects: the organizational structure of governments and the distribution of functions related to foreign trade policymaking; the coordination and consultation mechanisms among public bodies and institutions; the rules of selection and motivation of public workers; and the rules for participation of private interests in the decisionmaking process.

The analysis of formal institutional design includes the processes of institutional change as well. The theoretical literature contains excellent proposals for institutional mechanisms, but the applied analysis must carefully consider the conditions that allow the institutions to play the part for which they were designed. Since new institutions are not usually constructed in a void, but within an existing institutional context, the processes of institutional change are the real battlefields for establishing new institutions. When the possibilities of success are limited, it is necessary to consider introducing less intense dynamics of change, with smaller innovations, and adapting them to existing institutional forms.

Thus, it seems more prudent to search for a specific institutional design for each country, rather than setting up general modernization guidelines. A specific design will better fit the conditions and restrictions that influence the formation of foreign trade policy. When making decisions about institutional changes or reforms to answer the initial questions posed, it is better to adjust to the peculiarities of each country, while at the same time aiming to transform them, insofar as they are effective for promoting and reinforcing public policy.

One basic restriction is that there are many hidden costs in changing an organizational model once the country has followed a particular path of institutional development for a long period of time. The weight of path dependency is vital for understanding why many countries prefer modernizing existing institutional arrangements and adjusting them to the new needs, rather than breaking with the past and creating a completely different organizational structure (Pearson 2000). Only during exceptional political moments or crises is it likely that political leaders will choose to assume the costs of radically transforming an existing institutional structure, and promoting an organizational innovation that breaks with tradition and distributes power at the heart of government in a new way (Cortell and Peterson 1999).

In addition to the political costs, there is a risk that a deep institutional change will not achieve its aims and may even lead to a worse situation than the previous one (Lanzara 1999). An institutional change that only goes halfway, for example, may lead to a greater fragmentation of responsibilities among government agencies and thus further complicate the decisionmaking process. The chapter looks more closely at this problem, which is undoubtedly one of the most widespread difficulties in bringing about institutional reform.

INSTITUTIONAL STRUCTURES

Broad Organizational Options

Examining how governments manage trade policy at present throughout the world reveals four organizational models that link foreign trade policy to other key areas of government policy. The first model, perhaps the most traditional one, concentrates on foreign relations and international trade in a single ministerial department, exploiting the diplomats' experience and their international networks. The second model, which brings together policies for the productive sectors (agriculture and industry) and foreign trade, links the producers' exporting needs with the instruments for commercializing their products abroad. The third model integrates trade policy with domestic and foreign economic policy, giving priority to the coherence of the whole macroeconomic policy of the country. The fourth model keeps foreign trade policy isolated from the other ministries and then makes great efforts to coordinate the existing positions in the government.

Table 9–1 describes the advantages and disadvantages of the foreign trade policy organizational models. It is difficult—if not impossible—to identify one of the models as clearly superior to the others. There are specific examples of success and failure—in terms of performance and technical capacity—in the world for each model, and nothing excludes the choice of a specific model a priori.[1] The influences that lead to modernization or stagnation are complex and depend to a large extent on the particular conditions of each country, and institutional design is a key variable (Zysman 1994). That does not mean, however, that a discussion of the characteristics of each model is irrelevant.

We start from the viewpoint regarding the government as a unitary, rational player, which is an oversimplification, and begin to analyze the "black box" of its decisionmaking process. Many factors help explain the problems of institutional performance facing the organizational solutions adopted by each country. Using the logic of "agent-principal," the problem of organizational design for trade policy at the ministerial level could represent a dilemma for the principal (the head of the government) in the sense that, by entrusting a particular agent (minister) with different tasks, the principal has to be sure that these tasks are complementary. The reason is that, if those tasks are substitutive (promoting one limits the development of the other), the incentives may become weak and ineffective. However, if the tasks are complementary, mutual benefits could emerge (Dixit 1998, 1999b).

We consider four countries to illustrate certain key elements in the efficiency of the models. Each one can be identified with a fairly "pure" configuration of each of the models. First, Australia is a country that is extremely oriented toward opening up and liberalizing trade. Australia has brought foreign relations and foreign trade together in one ministry through two separate, closely interconnected vice ministries (both are members of the cabinet). British influence is still felt here, although at a distance.

Second, the case of Malaysia concentrates industry and foreign trade in the same ministry with a series of departments specializing in international integration and negotiation. Reference to such cases as Japan and Korea, which share the same model, is inevitable. In all cases,

---

[1] For a discussion of the virtues of institutional variety in the developing world, see Rodrik (2000).

Table 9–1

Advantages and Disadvantages of the Foreign Trade Policy Organizational Models

| | Foreign trade policy ministry location | | |
Foreign relations	Industry	Economy	Isolated
Advantages			
• Coherence of foreign policies (a single intermediary) • Overseas foreign relations networks • Less risk of hijacking by private players • Traditional institutional logic	• Coherence of industry and foreign trade policies • Maintenance of traditional institutional logic	• Coherence of internal economic and foreign trade policy • Maintenance of traditional institutional logic	• Exclusivity of trade policy (autonomy) • Involvement of presidency in foreign trade • Less risk of hijacking by private players
Disadvantages			
• Diversity of objectives • Predominance of political motivations • Low involvement of presidency in foreign trade	• Diversity of objectives (not giving priority to foreign trade) • Foreign trade and foreign relations duality • Higher risk of hijacking by private players • Low involvement of presidency in foreign trade	• Diversity of objectives (not giving priority to foreign trade) • Foreign trade and foreign relations duality • Low involvement of presidency in foreign trade	• Effort expended on coordination • Possible disconnection of foreign trade from country's long-term development policies • Possible institutional weakness of foreign trade • Ministerial struggles

the aim when defining this option is to support policies that promote the export capacity of large industrial groups (de Franco, Eguren, and Baughman 1988).

Third, in Spain, the foreign trade department is integrated into the ministry of the economy, within a vice ministry. The integration of the foreign trade policy of the European Union has favored its conversion into a highly specialized organization. Its main mission is to prepare and defend Spain's positions when the European Union takes decisions in the field of foreign trade, encouraging economic integration in Europe (Carderera 1997).

The fourth case is the United States, where the organizational option is to place all responsibility for foreign trade in an isolated department. The figure of the U.S. trade representative is defined as a high position in the departmental organization chart (equivalent to a member of the cabinet), but it has hardly any bureaucratic management structure. The task of this figure is to coordinate—at all levels—representatives of specialized spheres of the administration, processing information and building a unified position (Brock 1992). The U.S. model is the option of not having an agent take charge of a set of complementary tasks, but of commissioning an agent to carry out one exclusive task so that different tasks do not become substitutive. The reason for that option may be because the U.S. political and administrative system, characterized by extreme fragmentation of its power cores (multiple principals), makes it difficult to commission a set of multiple tasks, including trade policy, to an agent while ensuring compatibility (Palmer 1995).

In many studies, it is often implicitly assumed that U.S. political and economic institutions are more efficient, and that therefore this is the ideal model for other countries in the region (with less efficient models) to imitate.[2] However, that view, which grants preeminence to the option of isolating the management of trade policy organizationally, is easily questioned because there are other successful institutional models with different styles. Organizational characteristics make a significant contribution to the formation of public preferences. Some policy options may predominate more easily than others, depending on how the hierarchical and coordination structures are established within the government. This is why favoring coherence between trade and other policies may require an organizational model that aims to serve one of the particular political or economic needs of the country and is also linked to a particular long-term development strategy.

The cases of Malaysia and Australia, each with its own development strategy, clearly show that commitment, following two different organizational models. Each model integrates complementary tasks because it complements the existing development strategy. A substitutive relation between objectives in the same department—which reduces the effectiveness of the incentives—may appear when there is no clear link between a particular development option and the organizational model. Such was the case in Spain during the 1960s, when the foreign ministry still held many responsibilities as regards trade policy, and other ministries designed strategies for integration with Europe (Viñas 1980).

There are advantages to keeping foreign trade policy management isolated because of the autonomy and flexibility it produces, although it may involve considerable additional cost in terms of coordination, as happened in the United States in the 1980s, when different departments fought over policy leadership. There may also be a risk of disconnection with a country's long-term development strategies if the policy orientation does not receive ongoing support from the highest branches of government.

From the point of view of the principal, we believe that the choice of a model depends basically on two criteria: the principal's will to establish a well-outlined development strategy and the capacity to monitor the agent's actions. The principal will be able to choose a particular option, depending on how those elements are assessed, and assume the risks involved. For example, a principal who is particularly interested in promoting a development strategy will be able to opt for a more integrating model, even at the risk of the emergence of substitutive tasks (the greater the monitoring capacity available, the smaller the risk). By contrast, a principal who decides to give priority to monitoring the agent will tend to reduce the degree of integration (avoiding commissioning multiple, theoretically complementary tasks as much as possible), and assume greater risk in terms of promoting a deficient global development strategy for the country.

The dilemma posed for the principal arises from the set of specific tasks to be faced by the organization in charge of directing foreign trade policy, which, no doubt, includes a large component of management of inter and intrasectoral conflict. The organizational model chosen must be capable of defending itself from pressures to protect revenue, especially if the ministry is carrying out a process of opening up trade. But the model must also be capable of making commitments with companies and economic sectors on a timescale long enough to generate intertemporal compensations (Laffont 1999). In this context, the credibility of its commitments depends on the stability of the development strategy it is pursuing, as well as the amount of information available on the long-term evolution of the business environment. Both elements can be favored by complementary tasks within a ministry (that differ according

---

[2] See Baldwin's (1996) criticism.

to the model adopted), but there is also a risk that problems of consistency in trade conflict management may arise due to the weakness of the institutions and strong pressure from interest groups. In that context, the principal has to assess the extent to which it is possible to adequately monitor those distortions and correct them if necessary, bearing in mind that accountability may be easier to require of an agent who does not have too many multiple tasks.

At the same time, the logic of choice for the principal cannot be reduced simply to the basic dilemma faced. The weight of institutional dependence on the past is usually crucial in terms of one option or another, since the change in model adds a further major risk to the ones the principal must assume in any option. The difficulties involved in changing a model can be substantial; for Latin America, they can give rise to situations that make the initial conditions worse.

Trade Policy Coordination and Participation Structures

Given the present complexity of trade policy, simply defining functions and laying out organizational structures does not provide enough elements to analyze a government's capacity for adequately managing it. Other elements that are also part of the institutional framework have to be considered in order to understand the extent to which formal structures affect foreign trade policy management. There are formulas for coordination between government bodies that are interested in participating in foreign trade policy formulation. Intergovernmental coordination is always a difficult task, requiring strenuous efforts, but when it functions properly, it yields valuable results in the decisionmaking process. In addition, there are mechanisms for private sector participation, which are needed to balance the capacity of the most powerful interest groups to influence policy. The participatory bodies of the private players, which collect and integrate economic and social interests in the process of drafting policy, can be combined with intergovernmental coordination structures or separated in specific bodies.

Of the countries selected as references for the four different models, the United States makes the greatest use of all types of coordination mechanisms. Since the country maintains an isolated foreign trade model, there is a constant need for connection between the different departments that are in some way involved in trade policy. In the United States, the coordination system functions through a structure with different hierarchical levels, highly specialized at the foundation (with many expert committees and groups), and integrates issues as the hierarchical level of representation rises until reaching the participation of the top official (the U.S. trade representative) in the cabinet.

In that complex multi-level coordination structure, members of the U.S. trade representative's office coordinate the sessions, although they depend basically on the contributions and work of the participants, who come from different departments and agencies. The work is complemented by the information provided by the International Trade Commission, an independent public agency that serves as a think tank to analyze the impact of changes in foreign trade on the U.S. economy (this agency also undertakes anti-dumping measures on behalf of the government). Relations with the private sector are maintained aside from the government decisionmaking process and are formalized through a structure of advisory committees set up by Congress to help involve trade and economic interests in the formation of policy (the trade advisory committee system). More than 40 committees structure participation, specialized according to sectors and policies. However, the most notable one is the Advisory Committee on Trade Policy and Negotiations, whose members are appointed by the president and whose function is to synthesize the work of the other committees and assess the trade policy of the country as a whole (Brock 1992).

Other countries, such as Malaysia and Australia, also have important coordination structures, although they are far smaller than those in the United States. As they are models that integrate public policies in a single organization (industry and foreign affairs, respectively), they have less need for interdepartmental coordination. Also, as congresses play a minor part in the formulation of trade policy within this type of political system, they do not need a highly sophisticated system to guarantee the participation of private interests.

In the case of Malaysia, interministerial committees, some standing and others ad hoc, discuss foreign trade policy issues, generally coordinated by the Ministry of International Trade and Industry. Private participation is structured through consultative committees, where the more active business associations, geared primarily toward exports, predominate. This scheme fits in well with the country's economic development strategy.

Australia has a mixed policy advisory committee with the participation of public and private players (business and trade unions). The civil servants of the Ministry of Foreign Affairs and Trade also establish many informal relations, especially at the more specific sector level. In both Malaysia and Australia, however, the core of decisionmaking is clearly in the ministerial department that takes on the responsibility for policy, and the capacity for influencing other players (public and private) is quite limited (above and beyond their capacity to use the asymmetrical information available). The case of Spain is an extreme example of the absence of formal participation. It is implicitly understood that private interests reach the government through the ministries of agriculture and industry, which then pass on their positions, somewhat filtered, to the Ministry of the Economy.

The institutional participation of nongovernmental players in the trade policy decisionmaking process, through advisory councils or committees, could be interpreted as an incentive offered by the government to private interests. The government establishes this type of incentive to reward those who have private information. This, in turn, motivates those with this private information to reveal it when they declare their positions (Dixit 1999a). However, the asymmetries of information are particularly important in developing countries. The public sector often lacks the necessary information resources—for example, government think tanks—to monitor policy effects and guarantee that economic lobbies are not introducing distorted information when defending their interests through the participation structures set up by the government. This means that the institutionalized participation mechanism is vulnerable to the phenomenon of adverse selection. In other words, idealized forms of participation, without national adaptations, could also have a negative effect on principal development strategies.

Nevertheless, that mechanism still has enough potential to make it an attractive practice despite the danger we have mentioned. The U.S. trade policy management model is a good example of private sector participation through the creation of advisory committees (Brock 1992). Insofar as the composition of the advisory committees is established by the government, which appoints their members, it has the capacity to bring in representatives of different economic sectors ("winners" and "losers" in the liberalization process), or even the spokespeople of other social sectors (such as trade unions or NGOs). This, in turn, reduces the influence of the business groups with the most to lose from the opening up of markets, and could lead to collective action.

Moreover, the system of integration of interests is often a formula for fostering the establishment of prior agreements among the businesses themselves. The classic informal influence of specific interests on the government through more traditional formulas does not disappear altogether. But when participatory mediation works, it is limited to a certain degree by the dynamic of the new formal structures, whereby the players' positions are discussed openly (which is still an indirect benefit). In other words, it represents a modest attempt to shape private preferences in the trade policy process.

Institutional Transformations in Latin America in the 1990s

Table 9–2 presents some basic institutional characteristics of trade policymaking in a sample of Latin American countries. The countries have great diversity in their degree of formalization and in other aspects, but we tried to identify the best match in terms of the predominant organization model. However, in many cases, the present configuration is more a combination of basic models than a "pure" one. An explanation is that, in recent years, the organizational options adopted have varied frequently in the direction of one model or another, but the changes have not been carried out completely. This is because of their political fragility or the difficulty of bringing institutional change to a successful conclusion. This, in turn, produces a high degree of fragmentation of responsibilities in foreign trade policy. In general, these are not transitory processes, but fairly stagnant situations, which usually generate devastating power struggles between ministerial trenches. In these circumstances, it is easy to identify a reason why performance has not improved satisfactorily in many countries. The following are some examples of fragmentation of responsibilities (see table 9–2):

- *Degree of fragmentation.* High, more than two ministries are involved in decisionmaking for trade policy; medium, two ministries are involved; low, a single ministry leads.

Table 9–2

Main Organizational and Institutional Characteristics of Trade Policymaking in Latin America

Country	Predominant organization	Degree of institutional fragmentation	Degree of formalization of coordination	Network of private players	Degree of formalization of participation
Argentina	Foreign	High	Medium	Broad and scattered	Medium
Bolivia	Foreign	Medium	Medium	Concentrated	High
Brazil	Foreign	Low	Medium	Broad and scattered	Medium
Colombia	Isolated	High	Medium	Concentrated	Medium
Costa Rica	Isolated	Low	Medium	Broad and scattered	Low
Chile	Foreign	Low	High	Concentrated	High
Dominican Republic	Industry	Medium	Medium	Broad	High
Ecuador	Industry	High	Medium	Concentrated	Medium
Mexico	Economy/ industry[a]	Low	High	Broad	High
Nicaragua	Industry	Medium	Low	Concentrated	High
Peru	Industry	Medium	High	Concentrated	Low
Uruguay	Foreign	High	High	Broad	High

[a] There is a deputy minister of industry and trade within the ministry of the economy.

- *Degree of formalization of ministerial coordination.* High, there is a committee that reconciles diverging interests between ministries; medium, there is a committee, but with slight coordinating capacity; low, there is no coordination body between ministries.
- *Network of private players.* Broad and scattered, numerous players take part in the process of drafting trade policy, but none predominate; broad, numerous players take part, but some may be clearly dominant; concentrated, few players take part.
- *Degree of formalization of participation.* High, there are formal channels through which the private sector can participate and have influence; medium, there are formal but ineffective channels for private sector participation; low, there are no formal channels for the participation of the private sector.

In 1997, Bolivia created a new foreign trade ministry, separate from the ministry of industry, with the aim of giving greater priority to foreign trade policy, as well as foreign investments. The idea was to establish an isolated structure with a strong and dynamic agenda on all trade issues. However, in the mid 1990s, the foreign ministry, the only department with a stable staff, strengthened its management capacity in international economy and even created a vice ministry of economic relations. Despite the creation of the ministry of foreign trade, the foreign ministry maintained its powers through the political influence of its officials and the control it exercised over the positions of representation of the country abroad. This is how a complex situation of overlapping functions arose, with frequent technical coordination problems, that resulted in political friction.

A similar example is the case of Ecuador, where entry into the WTO in 1996 was viewed as an opportunity to introduce institutional changes in foreign trade policy management. A new foreign trade and investments law created an interministerial coordination body, and mandated giving a greater boost to the ministry of foreign trade, industrialization, and fisheries, as the department responsible for opening up the country to trade. A World Bank program backed the initiative and provided resources to enhance technical capacity (World Bank 1998). Nevertheless, the foreign ministry maintained its capacity to carry out international negotiations in the economic sphere and eventually came into conflict with the reform of the ministry of foreign trade, as they had to agree on many issues together. This led to severe clashes and fights, such as the one for control of the Free Trade Area of the Americas (FTAA) negotiations.

There are many other cases in the region of similar problems with incomplete institutional reforms. For example, in Colombia and Costa Rica, despite having a well-defined coordination and agenda control role, the ministries of foreign trade (created in 1990 and 1997, respectively) have to face constant tensions and pressures from other, more powerful ministries. Moreover, they have had to defend themselves from their foreign ministries' ambition to absorb them. The cases of Argentina and Uruguay are also noteworthy. Their respective ministries of the economy are responsible for strategic leadership in foreign trade policy, but the implementation of the strategy outside the country is the responsibility of their diplomatic representatives abroad. This leads to power sharing, conflict generation, and occasional confusion, and a strong need for constant coordination. A similar situation occurs in Peru, the Dominican Republic, and Nicaragua, although, in these cases, the strategic leadership is not located in the ministries of the economy, but in another ministry, usually industry.

These examples provide a brief panorama of the problems that have arisen in the region as a result of incomplete institutional reforms. Other countries that have not promoted institutional changes have also been limited in their ability to face the new demands of foreign trade policy in the new era of growing market liberalization. However, competence improves when the ministries develop greater technical capacity and have expert units within their own departments that manage to defend themselves. Not all the countries in the region have had the same problems with institutional performance. Chile is the outstanding case in terms of overcoming this problem. At times, in the cases when no reforms have taken place, new problems of organizational fragmentation have also emerged due to the growing complexity of foreign trade policy and the involvement of new players with interests in the sphere. However, in these circumstances, as in the cases of Brazil, Chile, and Mexico, fragmentation usually tends to be less than the serious disintegration resulting from incomplete reforms.

In Latin America, the institutional structures for formal coordination between government bodies are few and far between. Conflicts between ministries frequently arise and, since there is no entity where they can be resolved, they often result in confrontations between ministers, on occasion, even forcing the president to intervene. However, there is a notable use of interministerial coordination formulas in Chile, with its International Economic Negotiations Inter-ministerial Committee; in Colombia, with the Higher Council and a system of technical committees; and in the Dominican Republic, with the Trade Negotiations Committee. In addition to the coordination bodies, these countries have developed mechanisms for consultation with the private sector that complement the decisionmaking process within the government. In general, coordination formulas are linked to a particular model, since each country follows different organizational criteria. For example, Mexico and Uruguay also have interministerial committees, although they are concentrated in the operational coordination between the departments most involved, fundamentally, in both cases, the foreign and economy ministries. Surprisingly, none of the cases occurs among the countries with a more fragmented decisionmaking process.[3]

Not all the countries in the region have the same degree of formalization in terms of private sector participation. In recent years, a frequent model for private sector participation in foreign trade policy has involved mixed structures, which combine participation by different government bodies with representatives of business associations, chambers of commerce, and other private groups. They are generally consultative forums, basically advisory in character, with little discussion or analysis of the more technical issues. These new entities for participation can carry some weight in the formation of policy, or simply provide a space for the organizations to meet and relate without having any effective influence.

There are few successful cases where institutional innovations oriented toward structuring private participation have managed to consolidate and adopt an operational style in accordance with the aims of their initial design. Often the country's political elite has not embraced the institutional innovations (they may not have been tangible enough), and there consequently has been a process of devaluation of the new participation mechanisms, without generating changes in the traditional way of informally influencing political decisions.

HUMAN RESOURCES

Civil Service Models

To define a human resource management system as an institution means focusing attention on how rules, regulations, values, and processes make up a particular way of doing things in terms

---

[3] We might argue that the lack of committees is because although institutional fragmentation is not desired by anyone, it is often the result of incomplete reforms. Given that the designs for reform usually concentrate responsibilities in a single ministry, introducing interministerial coordinating committees did not make too much sense.

of the programs an organization proposes to its employees. In other words, specification of the rules of the game means assessing the operation of the spheres of selection, training, and remuneration, paying attention to the (implicit and explicit) rules and regulations, and the underlying values. Thus, a civil service model is understood as an interrelated set of rules, principles, and values; structures; routines; and processes.

More important than its isolated components, the outstanding feature of the concept is the way components mutually reinforce one another, which explains both their actual composition and their possible resistance to change. In its dimension as an institution, the human resource management system generates a kind of "logic of appropriateness," which lays out the parameters for the activities of the players involved. The set of elements that make up the institution help the players interpret the situations they are facing or determine what their appropriate role should be (March and Olsen 1989; Peters 1999; Tolbert and Zucker 1983).

The human resource management systems in public administrations formally make up a civil service model and are determined by two main factors: client systems versus professional systems, and closed systems versus open systems. The first sets personal and political trust against the criterion of professional capacity when it comes to choosing public employees. In most administrative models in industrial countries, the criteria of professional worth prevail, with the exception of the most senior posts, which are usually occupied by people selected by criteria of political trust with a temporary link with the administration. The clientelism and politicization of most of the administration is to be found in many developing countries. That model is also present in the historical tradition of the industrial countries, where it was sometimes called the "spoils system," although they have gradually abandoned it over the years. The spoils system consists of public employees being renewed after elections when the winning party rewards its followers by appointing them to public posts.

The second factor, closed systems versus open systems, is the direct opposition of a model based on the principle of the polyvalence of public employees (referred to as "career civil servants") to one inspired by the principle of specialization. The closed civil service model begins with the idea that the public employee is connected with the administration for life, occupying different posts, thus laying out his or her professional career. The European administrations faithfully represent the principles of the closed civil service model. The open civil service model is based on differentiation between various posts in the administration, which means making a detailed study of each one with the aim of recruiting the ideal personnel. The administrative system of the United States is the one that best reflects the criteria of the open civil service model. It is noteworthy that different institutional models support these two factors (clientelism versus professionalism and closed system versus open system), motivate different behaviors, and, in turn, encourage or promote certain values and standards (Prats 1996).

One vital aspect to consider is the social and political reality in which the civil service systems emerge, as well as the established administrative tradition from which they draw their essential characteristics and from which the main features of their operation emerge. The established administrative traditions are divided into two broad models: the Anglo-Saxon and the continental. A feature of the two administrative traditions is the relation established between society and the public machines. If the Anglo-Saxon models develop in an environment that is close to pluralism, characterized by a civil society that is reasonably independent of public intervention, the continental models tend to be designed in a context of statism (where the public sector develops a major role as promoter of civil society, with clearly interventionist activity), or alternatively, in one of corporatism, where the structuring of large sectors of society conditions the activity of the government in a relationship of mutual support. Thus, if a stable, continuous civil service model at the service of a strongly interventionist state were consolidated in a context of political instability, its dynamic would be different than if it were consolidated in a stable one, with a highly structured civil society that limits the direct activities of the public machines.

Some of the recent modernization programs applied in developing countries have probably judged the success of one model by the parameters of the other, forgetting the specific way it functions in relation to its context. To condemn the functioning of a civil service model designed fundamentally to provide stability and security for its deficiencies in efficiency and economy is as inappropriate as trying to introduce formulas that ignore the reality where they are to be applied.

As far as the introduction of a new model for civil service, or rather its conversion, is concerned, we also have to deal with a set of elements mentioned in recent literature. The introduction of an institutionalized human resources management model in developing countries must avoid incorporating any negative conception of bureaucracy, where public employees view themselves as divorced from the pursuit of the common good and more concerned with internal elements than results (Niskanen 1971). In other words, it must not emulate cases where public bureaucracies do not respond to the needs of present day societies and do not reflect their power relations (Pierre and Peters 2000). The authors of the New Public Management try to overcome that conception by trying to have managerial principles take priority over bureaucracy; they criticize many of the rules that define an institutionalized civil service model (Aucoin 1990). They propose breaking with the stability principle, making the forms of hiring staff more flexible, and encouraging reciprocal permeability between the public and private sectors, putting an end to the entropy of public employment (Maor and Stevens 1997; Boyne, Jenkins, and Poole 1999).

However, one of the main challenges for the renovation of a civil service model is to design a modern institution, disconnected from the inefficiencies of classic bureaucracies, but without falling into the de-institutionalization proposed by the New Public Management (Durant 1998). If the basic aim is to prevent the continuation of clientelism, deprofessionalization, and the takeover of public apparatuses by particular private interests (Ramió 2001), the New Public Management proposal might not help. The reason is because it is based on empowerment, giving power to public managers to take relatively autonomous decisions and to play an active part in defining the public interest (Moore 1998). It could reinforce a clientelist model without any important achievements in terms of efficacy and efficiency (Peters and Pierre 2000).

It is important to keep in mind that developing countries do not have corporative values like those in consolidated administrative models (Barker and Wilson 1997), which enable the introduction of the idea of discretion in Yeatman's (1997) sense. In developing countries, it is essential to boost the concept of ethical infrastructure to the maximum (OECD 1996). Moreover, without a corporative model, there is a greater risk of replacing senior public employees with external consultants who infiltrate decisionmaking circles, especially in developing countries, with the negative effects of decapitalizing their own human resources even more and even occupying decisionmaking spheres to the exclusion of the political dimension (Saint-Martin 1998).

The Civil Service in Latin America: Clientelism versus Professionalism

The civil service in Latin America offers a wide spectrum of situations. Some countries lack general civil service models, but have civil service in some professional groups (for example, the diplomatic corps abroad). Over the past decade, other countries (for example, Bolivia, the Dominican Republic, and Mexico) have tried to implement a civil service system globally or partially. Still other countries had a historic civil service model; the military dictatorships of the 1980s distorted it and civil service systems are now being restored (for example, in Chile and Argentina).

Despite such enormous differences, there are some similarities. In general, the Latin American systems respond more to client and political stimulus as opposed to professional; and the economic and social status incentives for public servants are low. These two elements imply a considerable turnover of employees, who quickly exchange posts in the public sector for posts in the private sector. This, in turn, means that the public sector can never take advantage of the professional capacity, technical education, and experience invested in its staff. Another similarity in relation to emerging civil service systems is the way they provide a replica (mimetic isomorphism) of the open civil service model, derived from a more generic attraction to the administrative model of the United States. However, the introduction of these young civil service systems runs up against a political reality, which bears little or no relation to the United States.

The problems of human resource development in institutions linked to foreign trade policy are similar to those of other public employees: a low level of professionalism derived from the clientelism in the selection processes, and low economic incentives, which hinder specialization and professional competence. Given that in most countries diplomats are one of the few groups of civil servants with a professional career, two models of human resources related to foreign trade policy are evident: locating foreign trade policy in the foreign ministries, and locating foreign trade policy in isolated trade ministries or linking it to the economy or industry ministries.

In institutional models that locate foreign trade policy in the foreign ministries, diplomats are usually in charge of foreign trade policy. In some cases, the diplomatic corps operates in a similar way to the industrial countries, while in other cases, there is precariousness in the application of the principles of capacity and merit in terms of access and remuneration, although that does not mean there is no special institutionalized civil service. The diplomatic career model has some disadvantages in relation to foreign trade policymaking. For example, the diplomats' education is usually closer to the legal profession. Another problem is the regulated rotation of the civil servants' postings, which hinders specialization in foreign trade issues. This problem is heightened by remuneration policies, which encourage assignments at diplomatic missions abroad and discourage central managerial posts that are precisely where foreign trade policy is designed and coordinated.

However, some countries are starting to overcome these problems through two methods. The first is by widening the diplomatic selection process and favoring de facto specialization in foreign trade within a career (for example, the case of Brazil). The second is defining specific units within the foreign ministry. Examples of the latter are the establishment of a specialized foreign trade issues unit with expert staff of its own in the foreign ministry (the case of Chile), or absorbing a technical-commercial civil service group, within the diplomatic corps (the case of Argentina).

In general, in institutional models in which foreign trade policy is located in isolated trade ministries or linked to the ministry of economy or industry, no staff engaged in foreign trade is part of the career civil service. In terms of employment, subjective political-client criteria usually predominate, leading to high turnover. Nevertheless, the need for specialization in foreign trade forces those countries, to some extent, to recruit or maintain employees with more professional, though not formalized, criteria. But this alternative path does not guarantee professional stability either, since the low economic incentives also cause turnover: once public employees have sufficient technical capacity, they go on to provide their services in consultancies, private companies, or business interests.

In any event, some countries have managed to generate fairly stable groups of professional public employees (for example, Costa Rica and, more recently, Colombia), overcoming client pressure (without it disappearing altogether), but with considerable difficulties in eliminating the problem of low economic incentives. Other countries have received assistance from international organizations in order to create a more professional group of public employees specializing in foreign trade (for example, Peru and Ecuador). However, it is unclear whether these groups can withstand the pressures of deprofessionalization once the aid programs end.

In short, the lack of professionalism and a stable career path for public employees specializing in this field are the basic problems in relation to the deficit of institutional capacity in foreign trade in most Latin American countries. A client culture, lack of public values derived from a shaky administrative culture, and poor economic incentives are three major obstacles to the effective development of an institutionalized civil service in this area.

POLITICAL ECONOMY AND FOREIGN TRADE POLICY ORGANIZATIONS

Definition of Political Will: Government Decisionmaking

The tradition of government in Latin America is still conditioned by informal institutional elements, forged over many decades, which are difficult to transform, such as clientelism, old corporatism, or even leadership of the political boss variety. The new democratic regimes in the region find it difficult to overcome these historic rules of the game. Thus, when the public administration manages to partially modernize (basically through introduction of a civil service), it may well find a traditional economic and social structure in which key decisions are predetermined and overly influenced by big business groups. This is not favorable to the creation of the stable public welfare-oriented decisionmaking framework that is needed for handling trade policy today (Hommes 1999; Prats 2000).

To establish an effective foreign trade policy under such conditions is difficult. Thus, it is not surprising that, in Latin American countries, the difficulties encountered in formulating foreign trade policy are related, to a large extent, to the quality of politics, the institutions, and their capacity for dealing with collective action problems (North 1990). At the same time, the specific characteristics of trade policymaking in each country (in terms of high or low collective action, costs to players involved, and predominance of mobile or fixed factors, see Adserà and Boix, this volume) strongly influence the type of institutional design that could maximize policy performance (or, in negative terms, make certain configurations unfeasible).

In most cases, government decisionmaking in trade policy is channeled and conditioned by two factors. The first one is the role of political institutions. Here we have basically the character of the government and the role of the president, coupled with the degree of parliamentary control over foreign trade policy vis-à-vis the existing coordination structures within the government (Moe 1990). The second factor is the nature of the representation of interests. The basic components consist of the characteristics of collective action in the foreign trade policy network, including the concentration and structure of private and semi-public players, and the formal and informal formulas for participation of private players. The complex structuring of those dimensions leads to different government decisionmaking styles in foreign trade policy. Thus, the political options adopted depend, to a large extent, on the role played by each factor at the heart of the decisionmaking process.

In relation to the first point, the relatively passive role of the executive branch in most countries in the region is surprising; usually there is little participation in foreign trade policy. Nevertheless, there is growing participation in some countries, where it intervenes directly (Mexico, Colombia, Costa Rica, Brazil, and the Dominican Republic). In any case, the executive branch is strong in all countries and its usual scant participation in foreign trade policy may be attributed to priorities on the presidential agenda and subjective factors, such as the incumbent's knowledge of the subject. In any event, the lack of involvement of the presidents in foreign trade in the countries of Latin America is still surprising, especially compared with the growing involvement of the political leaders in industrial countries. This may indicate backwardness in Latin America, probably due to the fact that internal political, social, and economic tensions are still the priority areas on presidential agendas. The democratic institutions are weak and the presidents have to pay more attention to maintaining basic social balances than fostering foreign trade and, with it, the wealth of their countries.

As regards the parliament, in most countries in the region, its participation in foreign trade policy is scant or nonexistent, usually limited to ratifying treaties. The presidential model in Latin American countries is asymmetrical. Power is concentrated in the presidency, while the parliaments have a low level of political influence and technical capacity to control and guide the decisionmaking processes. In effect, the parliaments are not institutionalized, and usually play a secondary role in the framework of a presidential political system. One exception is Mexico, where the recent political change is redefining and boosting the role of the legislative branch, and focusing more attention on foreign trade issues.

With regard to the influence of the institutional models of foreign trade policy mentioned earlier, their effectiveness does not depend so much on which of the four predominates as much as its degree of institutionalization. If the level of institutionalization is low, the model does not respond in the expected theoretical way; if it is highly fragmented, the decisionmaking processes become extremely complicated. Moreover, when fragmentation exists, it is frequently combined with low institutionalization and low professionalism, since the lack of a civil service is predominant in the countries of the region. In those cases, the president becomes vital in terms of clarifying the situation, but usually stands back, except in major conflicts, and even then, at a terminal stage. Moreover, in situations of that type, the mechanisms of interministerial coordination—if any—will have a serious job to do to overcome internal incoherencies, such as the lack of definition of responsibilities.

Organization of Interests and Participation in Trade Policy

It seems that the lack of effective intervention by parliaments, presidents, and subnational governments, coupled with the weakness of institutional foreign trade models, encourages excessive intervention by semi-public and private players in decisionmaking processes. In most countries, private players are brought into the foreign trade decisionmaking processes and given a lead role in decisions concerned with international trade. The collective action of private players varies from one country to another in Latin America, although, to a large extent, the traditional business interests are well organized. Chambers of commerce and top business organizations are modern in most cases, although their capacity to influence government decisionmaking processes depends on the degree of political control wielded by the government.

To mention interest groups in foreign trade means talking fundamentally about private exporting interests and how they are structured. The two factors that create difficulties in the structuring of private players are economic diversity and territorial fragmentation. On the one hand, it is difficult to work with organizations that fully represent a productive sector, since, typically, many associations are in the same sector, all struggling to represent it. On the other hand, various associations linked to various territories in the country may represent a sector. The territorial dimension is important because many countries in Latin America have vast, poorly connected regions. Moreover, there is a need for associations representing various sectors. The chambers of commerce are broad representational institutions that are useful in this context, but they are fragmented across cities and regions. Traditionally, the economic elites of Latin America function as a network, so there is not a serious problem as regards lack of structure. What may be a problem, however, is the internal structure of those networks, since many of them tend to omit nontraditional productive sectors linked to emerging elites or the middle class.

The institutional weakness of the public organizations in charge of foreign trade aggravates the asymmetries of collective action in the representation of national interests. It is obvious that the stronger the public institutions are, the more likely they are to contribute to constructively channeling the opinions of the different interest groups into positions that support the public interest (Rajapatirana 1995). When weak public institutions predominate, if the ministry in charge of foreign trade does not have daily contact with national interest groups, it is easier to escape from particular pressures and thus be able to make foreign trade policy more oriented toward general interests. The closer the public foreign trade entities are to the interest groups, the higher the incidence of hijacking. In any event, the analysis need not always start from the viewpoint of extreme self-interest. Many business groups in the region are learning to make difficult decisions in order to ensure the survival of businesses nationwide in the context of globalization.

There are some interesting parallels between the participation of interests in decisionmaking in Latin America and the United States. The divisions within the U.S. political system are one distinguishing feature. The equilibrium between a powerful congress and the executive branch, coupled with the importance of lobbying, is a basic characteristic that is not shared by many Latin American countries (IDB 2000). Those characteristics mean that in the U.S. system the participation of private players takes on special importance and forces the executive to make pacts with them in the process of drafting trade policy. Otherwise, the executive branch will face opposition again in congress. If members of congress believe that the private sector's point of view has not been considered, they may block the ratification of treaties, particularly the members who represent the territories most affected (Lohmann and O'Halloran 1994). This is why negotiators know they must include the interests of the private players as much as possible, with the aim of making the policy effective and preventing it from being blocked by congress. Thus, as a formula for preparing positions for the international treaties, they have even brought in representatives of the private sector as advisors during the negotiating process, although without any formal status.

Occasionally, some countries in the region have imitated the participation model established in the United States without sharing the same political conditions. In these cases, the government was forced to give private interests a strong voice in the decisionmaking process, while fostering a countervailing strengthening of the public organizations. The results must be examined in depth, but the impression is that they have not been too successful. Given the difficulties of institutionalization in many countries, openly incorporating private interests in the negotiation process without significant counterweights in the public sector may have been a powerful element that distorted the government's responsibility and ability to defend the public interest.

In general terms, it can be argued that the lower the level of institutionalization and the greater the dispersion of the centers of power, the more susceptible the public entities are to a permissive environment. In this context, formal participation mechanisms cannot avoid the basic problems that arise from the mediation of interests, and, in certain circumstances, they can generate still more ambiguity and centrifugal tendencies.

To sum up, in Latin America, foreign trade policy decisionmaking processes—formal and informal—are complex and not very effective. The fundamental reason for the deficient decisionmaking processes is to be found in the low level of professionalism and lack of permanence of the different entities involved. These factors prevent the institutionalization of networks of players who could take part in decisionmaking processes.

TENTATIVE RECOMMENDATIONS

This chapter has discussed a wide range of organizational models for foreign trade policymaking in Latin America. It has also shown that there are no optimal and universal institutional designs, but different options that may or may not achieve the goals, according to whether they fit the political and administrative context of a country and whether the internal components are balanced.

It would be a mistake to limit proposals to exclusively technical improvements in institutions. Each state requires a unique set of responses, according to its political and administrative tradition, and the networks of public and private players linked to the management of foreign trade policy. With this in mind, it is possible to suggest various strategies for institutional improvement.

Can Institutional Changes Improve Foreign Trade Policy Management?

Institutional structures help to arrange the players and set the rules of the game among the leading ones. They also help to define the formulas for nongovernmental players to have access to the policy-drafting process. The government may try to alter these structures in order to modify the balance of power among the players, or even establish certain self-restraining mechanisms in relation to policymaking processes. However, for any country, deciding whether to create a new institution or to reform an existing one may be complicated. A subjective assessment of the future costs of each alternative has an effect, as well as expectations of the benefits it may eventually produce.

The difficulties in managing institutional transformation are of a different nature, and may arise simultaneously. On the one hand, the formal institutional and organizational structures may be improved, but the various players may continue to interact with the logic of the old institutions (decoupling). On the other hand, the new institutional designs may not be ideal for the political, social, and economic realities of the country. In this case, the phenomenon of mimetic isomorphism, in which there is a tendency to copy institutional models from industrial countries that have a very different context, or coercive isomorphism, when international institutions recommend introducing certain institutional models across the board without taking into account the specific features of each country, may be very negative. Another possibility is that the new institutional and organizational model may not be fully implemented because the transformation process is interrupted by a political change or a change in personal leadership. The final result might be a hybrid model, which retains elements of the old institutional order in its design combined with elements of the new one. Such an interrupted process is quite common in Latin America.

All these problems call for institutional and organizational changes to be shallow and swift, and to adapt to and optimize the traditional institutional designs of each country, taking advantage of the more positive elements of path dependency. In other words, in most cases, a reform with incremental modernization seems more advisable than an institutional revolution.

To What Extent Is Fragmentation Acceptable?

All the models of foreign trade policy management discussed in this chapter may be implemented successfully; they are, in fact, examples of situations in Latin American countries. However, the choice of organizational model is less important than the model's compatibility with the administrative tradition of the country (path dependency obligations) and the ability of the model to guarantee that the management of foreign trade policy is concentrated in a single government body.

Organizational fragmentation, with responsibilities shared among ministerial departments, does not usually provide any important advantages and is the source of many decisionmaking difficulties. It is vital to avoid internal bureaucratic struggles with their consequent fragmentation of strategic decisions. However, this does not eliminate the importance of intergovernmental coordination. If organizational unity in foreign trade cannot be achieved, it is crucial at least to clarify who is responsible for each policy area.

Where Should Staff Incentives Be Located?

Organizational culture and the standardization of the skills of public employees responsible for the management of foreign trade policy are the key factors related to human resources management. Client pressures in recruitment are an attack on the principles of capacity and merit, as well as permanence (since the renewal depends on the changes in political majorities in the government). Poor remuneration is another factor, as it generates precarious work conditions, low social esteem, and turnover of the best personnel.

The best option would be to adopt general civil service models to cover all the central spheres of the administrative systems or, as second best, to define a specific civil service model that would affect all staff responsible for foreign trade. However, it is difficult to make clear recommendations. For example, to introduce a highly flexible model directly in the Anglo-Saxon style in Latin America could involve risks of susceptibility to client and political pressures. A good initial option would be to choose more formalistic models, such as the continental ones, with a view to introducing new values and consolidating a renewed political and administrative culture, adapting them later to the needs for flexibility of each system.

There are two main stages in introducing a professional, stable human resources system for foreign trade policy management. First, it is possible to take advantage of the formal, or de facto, civil service models of the diplomatic corps, bringing experts in foreign trade into those bodies. It seems more difficult to create a new body of trade technicians in the framework of an informal, clientelist human resources management system, than to take advantage of the exceptional institutionalization of the diplomatic career system, which has taken place in many countries. Many diplomatic corps have been able to broaden their field of expertise to include foreign trade issues. Second, there is the possibility of taking advantage of aid from the international organizations for programs to strengthen institutions and civil service models. In any case, the international organizations must ensure that the systems introduced can stand on their own when the programs terminate. In addition, the countries receiving the aid will have to commit themselves as deeply as they can to the development of the new civil service model.

To What Extent Is the Participation of Private Interests Admissible for the Public Interest?

Frequently, private players are well structured, but their strength is distributed asymmetrically. That means that governments sometimes have to face strong interest groups that attempt to hijack the public institutions for their own benefit. This involves a danger of defining trade policies that are favorable to special interests, not the public interest. In this situation, retaining control and gaining information are the basic keys to promoting national interests in foreign trade and socially integrated, collective action.

As regards the first point, the hijacking of the public agenda in foreign trade negotiations by particular private interests must be avoided. The state can foster participation, but some care must be taken with more direct mechanisms, such as the "next room" phenomenon in trade negotiations, since it is difficult for those interactive, direct mechanisms to strike a balance in the representation of different sectors. As regards information, it is important for the public authorities to promote their own independent economic study and advisory units, which can analyze issues connected with the international and domestic economies. The objective is to avoid depending exclusively on the technical information provided by think tanks linked to certain interest groups. The fostering of independent research centers is one possible alternative strategy; another is using the resources of the leading universities.

Final Remarks

Since the early 1990s, a number of Latin American states have carried out processes to open up and liberalize trade, often during deep economic crises. This represented a change of direction in long-term development strategy, which took place in nearly every country in the region, and involved a new leading role for trade policy. That change brought about new imbalances in relation to previously existing organizational models. Objectives that previously had been complementary within the same ministry began to turn into substitutive ones. That produced a reduction in the efficiency of existing incentives—already weak in themselves due to difficulties of observation and control—and therefore led to the emergence of a growing need to introduce further changes into existing institutional models. Given this situation, the political leaders found themselves facing a major dilemma: whether to maintain the existing model, while reforming the institution in charge of trade policy (which also involved changing the other policies managed by the same department) so that it would be compatible with the new economic development strategy, or to change the model and establish another configuration more suited to that strategy.

There are few recent examples of successful institutional change in the region. In many cases, relatively important institutional reforms have been introduced, but the results have been uneven. The reforms have frequently stopped halfway on the road to the goals that they proposed. New civil service initiatives have not reached the critical point necessary to stabilize new organizations, and fragmentation problems have multiplied. Given the observed results, it might be more reasonable to be cautious regarding radical reforms of this type in Latin America, and consider how to promote incremental change based on reforming the existing institutional configurations.

Failure in institutional adaptation does not mean immediate failure in trade policy performance, analysis of which is beyond the scope of this chapter. However, there is no question that many countries have been active in recent years. They have developed a busy agenda in the international economic arena and have structured a network of treaties to cope with their new, long-term development strategy.

REFERENCES

Aucoin, P. 1990. Administrative Reform in Public Management: Paradigms, Principles, Paradoxes and Pendulums. *Governance: An International Journal of Policy and Administration* 3(2): 116–37.

Baldwin, Robert E. 1996. The Political Economy of Trade Policy: Integrating the Perspectives of Economists and Political Scientists. In R. C. Feenstra, G. M. Grossman, and D. A. Irwin (eds.), *The Political Economy of Trade Policy: Papers in Honor of Jagdish Bhagwati*. Cambridge, MA: MIT Press.

Barker, A., and G. K. Wilson. 1997. Whitehall's Disobedient Servants? Senior Officials' Potential Resistance to Ministers in British Government Departments. *British Journal of Political Science* 27(2): 223–26.

Boyne, G., G. Jenkins, and M. Poole. 1999. Human Resource Management in the Public and Private Sectors: An Empirical Comparison. *Public Administration* 77(2): 407–20.

Brock Group. 1992. The Formulation and Implementation of U.S. Trade Policy. Inter-American Development Bank, Washington, DC.

Carderera, L. 1997. La política comercial española: diez años de política comercial común. *Información Comercial Española* 766: 31–48.

Cortell, Andrew, and Susan Peterson. 1999. Altered States: Explaining Domestic Institutional Change. *British Journal of Political Science* 29: 177–203.

Dixit, Avinash K. 1998. *The Making of Economic Policy. A Transaction-Cost Politics Perspective.* Cambridge, MA: MIT Press.

———. 1999a. Incentives and Organizations in the Public Sector: An Interpretative Review. Paper presented at the National Academy of Sciences conference, "Devising Incentives to Promote Human Capital," December 17–18, Irvine, CA.

———. 1999b. Some Lessons from Transaction-Cost Politics for Less-Developed Countries. Paper presented at the XVII Latin American Meeting of the Econometric Society, August 2–6, Cancún, Mexico.

Durant, R. F. 1998. Agenda Setting, the "Third Wave," and the Administrative State. *Administration and Society* 30(3) July: 211–47.

Evans, Peter. 1997. The Eclipse of the State? Reflections on Stateness in an Era of Globalization. *World Politics* 50(1) October: 527–51.

Franco, Silvio, Alberto Eguren, and David Baughman. 1988. *Korea's Experience with the Development of Trade and Industry*. Policy Seminar Report no. 14, Economic Development Institute, The World Bank, Washington, DC.

Hall, Peter A., and Rosemary C. R. Taylor. 1996. Political Science and the Three New Institutionalisms. *Political Studies* 44: 952–73.

Hommes, Rudolf. 1999. Problemas de la administración pública. In R. Lüders and L. Rubio (eds.), *Estado y economía en América Latina*. Mexico City: CIDE-Porrúa.

Immergut, Ellen M. 1998. The Theoretical Core of the New Institutionalism. *Politics and Society* 26(1) March: 5–34.

Inter-American Development Bank (IDB). 2000. *Development beyond Economics. Economic and Social Progress in Latin America, 2000 Report.* Washington, DC: IDB.

Laffont, Jean-Jacques. 1999. Competition, Information and Development. In Boris Pleskovic and Joseph E. Stiglitz (eds.), *Annual World Bank Conference on Development Economics 1998.* Washington, DC: World Bank.

Lanzara, Giovan F. 1999. Por qué es tan difícil construir las instituciones? *Desarrollo Económico* 38(152).

Lohmann and O'Halloran. 1994. Divided Government and U.S. Trade Policy: Theory and Evidence. *International Organization* 48(4, Autumn).

Maor, M., and H. Stevens. 1997. Measuring the Impact of New Public Management and European Integration on Recruitment and Training in the UK Civil Service. *Public Administration* 75(3): 531–51.

March, J. G., and J. P. Olsen. 1989. *Rediscovering Institutions.* New York: Free Press.

Moe, Terry M. 1990. Political Institutions: The Neglected Side of the Story. *Journal of Law, Economics and Organization* 6(1): 213–54.

Moore, Mark H. 1998. *Creating Public Value. Strategic Management in Government.* Cambridge, MA: Harvard University Press.

Niskanen, W. A. 1971. *Bureaucracy and Representative Government.* Chicago, IL: Aldine.

North, Douglass C. 1990. *Institutions, Institutional Change and Economic Performance.* Cambridge: Cambridge University Press.

Organisation for Economic Co-operation and Development (OECD). 1996. *Ethics in the Public Service: Current Issues and Practice.* Public Management Occasional Papers no. 14, OECD, Paris, France.

Palmer, Matthew S. R. 1995. Toward an Economics of Comparative Political Organization: Examining Ministerial Responsibility. *Journal of Law, Economics and Organization* 11(1, Spring): 164–88.

Pearson, Paul. 2000. Increasing Returns, Path-Dependence and the Study of Politics. *American Political Science Review* 94(2).

Peters, B. G. 1999. *Institutional Theory in Political Science. The New Institutionalism.* London, UK: Pinter.

Peters, B. G., and J. Pierre. 2000. Citizens versus the New Public Management. The Problem of Mutual Empowerment. *Administration and Society* 32(1).

Pierre, J., and B. G. Peters. 2000. *Governance, Politics and the State.* New York: St. Martins Press.

Prats, J. 1996. Fundamentos conceptuales para la reforma del estado en América Latina: el redescubrimiento de las instituciones. *Revista Vasca de Administración Pública* 45(II).

———. 2000. Reforma del estado y desarrollo humano en América Latina. *Quórum. Revista de Pensamiento Iberoamericano* 1.

Rajapatirana, Sarath. 1995. *Post Trade Liberalization Policy and Institutional Challenges in Latin America and the Caribbean.* Policy Research Working Paper no. 1465, World Bank, Washington, DC.

Ramió, C. 2001. Los problemas de la implantación de la nueva gestión pública en las administraciones públicas latinas: modelo de estado y cultura institucional. *Revista del CLAD Reforma y Democracia* 21.

Rodrik, Dani. 2000. Institutions for High-Quality Growth: What They Are and How to Acquire Them. *Studies in Comparative International Development* 35(3).

Saint-Martin, D. 1998. The New Managerialism and the Policy Influence of Consultants in Government: An Historical-Institutionalist Analysis of Britain, Canada and France. *Governance: An International Journal of Policy and Administration* 11(3) 319–56.

Tolbert, P. S., and L. G. Zucker. 1983. Institutional Sources of Change in the Formal Structure of Organizations: The Diffusion of Civil Service Reform, 1880–1935. *Administrative Science Quarterly* 28: 22–39.

Viñas, Ángel. 1980. La administración de la política económica exterior de España (1939–1979). *Cuadernos Económicos del ICE* 13.

Weiss, Linda. 1998. *The Myth of the Powerless State*. Ithaca, NY: Cornell University Press.

World Bank. 1998. *Ecuador: International Trade and Integration Project*. Report no. 17882-EC, Washington, DC.

Yeatman, A. 1997. The Reform of Public Management: An Overview. In M. Considine and M. Painter (eds.), *Managerialism: The Great Debate*. Melbourne, Australia: Melbourne University Press.

Zysman, John. 1994. How Institutions Create Historically Rooted Trajectories of Growth. *Industrial and Corporate Change* 3(1): 243–83.

PART IV
THE PUBLIC-PRIVATE
SECTOR NEXUS

Chapter 10

Multinational Firms, Regional Integration and Globalizing Markets: Implications for Developing Countries

Rajneesh Narula

Policymakers in the developing world are once again enthralled by the concept of regional integration and its potential benefits. This has led to a revival of previously unsuccessful or dormant schemes and the establishment of a clutch of new agreements. Part of this renewed enthusiasm has to do with the benefits that have accrued to members associated with various European regional integration schemes and the North American Free Trade Agreement (NAFTA), in particular, the experience of Mexico in NAFTA.

It is not a coincidence that this renewed interest in regional integration has occurred while globalization has pervaded the world economy. The two are not unrelated, and some have argued that regional integration projects appear to represent an opportunity to redress the inequities of multilateral agreements (Baldwin 1997), and to increase their autonomy from outside forces (Vernon 1996). In other words, some observers see regional integration schemes as a response to globalization. There are several similarities between globalization and regional integration. Both are processes closely associated with cross-border economic activity, although globalization is more a consequence of increased cross-border activity, while regional integration is intended to cause it. The proliferation of cross-border activity is regarded as a primary symptom of globalization. Analysts believe that both globalization and regional integration provide opportunities for more rapid economic growth, associated in large part with the increased foreign direct investment (FDI) and trade that result from increased opportunities to exploit economies of scale.

This chapter seeks to examine the impact of regional integration on multinational enterprise (MNE) strategies. However, other developments have also significantly affected MNE strategies, and these need to be taken into account. Three powerful influences are highlighted. First, globalization has changed the capacity and the means of MNEs to organize and coordinate their spatially distributed affiliates. Second, a broad policy shift has occurred as most developing countries have shifted from import substitution toward export and FDI-driven outward orientation. Third, most countries are involved in multilateral liberalization within the framework of multilateral institutions.

The chapter examines MNE strategies in developing countries in four separate situations: (1) a pre-liberalization environment without regional integration; (2) a pre-liberalization environment with regional integration; (3) a post-liberalization scenario without regional integration; and (4) a post-liberalization scenario with regional integration. The chapter distinguishes between two groups of developing countries. Group I consists of least developed countries with little or no domestic industrial capacity. Group II countries possess an intermediate level of domestic capacity. The analysis contrasts these with industrial countries, that is, group III.

The chapter argues the following points. First, successful regional integration (such as the European Union and NAFTA) has been a consequence of globalization, a reinforcement of de facto integration (by globalization) with de jure integration (regional integration). Second, successful regional integration schemes and countries that have participated in globalization share a number of similarities. Both regional integration and globalization are ongoing processes rather than events. Successful regional integration projects have been marked by considerable efforts; the participating economies have developed institutions, through structural adjustment, and have created appropriate cross-border institutions over a long period of time. Third, FDI does not drive economic growth, although it may help enhance it. FDI is not a sine qua non for development. Fourth, the response of MNEs to regional integration schemes is profit-driven, and the net effect of regional integration schemes on the quality of their investments may well be negative, particularly for group I countries. Regional integration does not necessarily overcome the inequities of globalization, at least as far as the activities of MNEs are concerned. However, the structural adjustment necessary for de facto regional integration helps to position countries to participate more effectively in globalization.

THE CHALLENGES OF GLOBALIZATION AND REGIONAL INTEGRATION

Globalization as an Institution-Building Process

Although the term globalization is a much-abused one, it is generally accepted that it is an ongoing *process* rather than an *event*. "Economic globalization" as used here implies the growing interdependence of locations and economic units across countries and regions. Although a large literature has mushroomed describing the increasingly interwoven nature and cross-border dependence of locations and firms, it is by no means so for all locations, firms, or industrial sectors.

Perspectives on globalization vary considerably and depend on the unit of analysis. Nonetheless, it is manifest that cross-border interdependence between firms, institutions, and locations has increased dramatically over the past 50 years and is likely to continue in this vein. It is not simply the presence of MNEs and their level of trade that define a country's involvement in globalization, but the extent to which the economy at large is inextricably linked to the rest of the world.

I want to emphasize that dependency on nonnational actors is not the same as interdependence. Through much of modern history, economies have been dependent on others as customers or suppliers. But this has largely been an arms-length relationship. Termination of a relationship might have had adverse effects, but not disastrous ones. In an interdependent relationship, important components of production are co-located, such that the failure of one prevents the other from functioning. Interdependence includes both firm and nonfirm actors. Nonfirm actors are privately and publicly controlled organizations that determine the knowledge infrastructure that supplements and supports firm-specific economic activity.

"Knowledge infrastructure" is used in the sense proposed by Smith (1997) as being generic, multi-user, and indivisible, and consisting of public research institutes, universities, and organizations for standards and intellectual property protection that enable and promote science and technology development. These nonfirm actors are increasingly interwoven across borders and rely on nondomestic actors for crucial inputs, unlike in the past when every country's nonfirm sector was sovereign and independent.

Globalization cannot be credited as a primarily MNE-driven process; MNEs are simply the most visible of these processes. MNEs have sought to overcome cross-border market failures in their search for efficiencies, but there are numerous other concurrent and interrelated events, including technological developments (new technologies), political events (such as the Cold War), economic liberalization, and the associated development of supranational institutions and regulations.

It is not my intention to delve into the complexities of the causes and effects of globalization. Instead, the chapter highlights globalization's association with (among other things) changes in political economy. At the risk of oversimplification, the past half-century represents an about-face in terms of policy perspectives. Prior to World War II, nation-states were de facto inviolable, individual, and sovereign entities with clearly defined borders in both a political and economic sense. Well before import-substituting arguments were formalized, the centerpiece of economic growth was the concept of national self-sufficiency. Dating at least as far back as the first industrial revolution, every nation-state has considered it essential to possess national capacity in so-called essential industries. Inward FDI was largely controlled and limited in scope, unless it met stringent conditions that promoted the self-sufficiency view by enhancing the host country's domestic sector.

Today—whether voluntarily or through World Bank–sanctioned structural adjustment programs—the view is largely the opposite. Policies are oriented toward export-led growth and increased cross-border specialization and competition, and most countries try to promote economic growth through FDI and international trade—what has been referred to as the "New Economic Model" (Reinhardt and Peres 2000). This wave of liberalization is part of the new received wisdom that is focused on tackling the deep-rooted causes that underlie market distortions. Unfortunately, countries prefer to view their task as "getting the prices right" because this allows them to avoid root-and-branch restructuring.

Liberalization has happened gradually through the Triad countries (the European Union, Japan, and the United States) over the post–World War II era, but much more suddenly within developing countries. Policies among European countries, for instance, have gradually evolved over 50 years, while almost the entire developing world has attempted to restructure since the late 1980s (and the formerly centrally planned economies only during the 1990s).

Developing countries find themselves in a new multilateral milieu, one in which they have little experience. They have hitherto operated their economies on a national basis, and by looking inward they have been able to minimize exposure to external shocks. Institutions—the "sets of common habits, routines, established practices, rules, or laws that regulate the interaction between individuals and groups" (Edquist and Johnson 1997)—remain largely independent and national. They create the milieu within which economic activity is undertaken, establish the ground rules for interaction between the various economic actors, and represent a sort of culture. Institutions are both formal and informal, and have taken years—if not decades—to create and sustain. Modifying and developing institutions is a complex and slow process, particularly since they cannot be created simply by government fiat. Such change is even more complex where the new institutions require synchronization between countries. The Triad countries have taken 50 years to adjust and reform institutions, but even here there is inertia. The European Union, for instance, has failed to reform its agricultural sector. Norway remains largely mired in an import-substituting world, with a strong tendency toward central planning and state-owned economic actors (Narula 2002).

Liberalization is an important force in economic globalization because it requires a multilateral view on hitherto domestic issues and promotes interdependence of economies. It is implicit within this view that FDI and MNE activity can be undertaken with much greater ease than previously. This view is enforced because countries have explicitly sought to encourage MNE activity as a source of much-needed capital and technology. In addition to financial crises, the general warming of attitudes toward FDI emanates from an accelerating pace of technical change and the emergence of integrated production networks of MNEs (Lall 2000).

Comparing Globalization and Regional Integration

Despite numerous studies, there is no clear consensus on the universality of the welfare effects of regional integration (see, for example, Baldwin and Venables 1995). Much of the empirical work has been undertaken for various European integration schemes and NAFTA, which point to a positive impact for participants; few studies have been undertaken on the nearly 100 other "lesser" integration schemes. The continued proliferation of South-South integration schemes is a matter of some consternation (see Baldwin 1997). Indeed, Venables (2000) argues that under certain situations, regionalism promotes divergence (see also chapter 3 of this volume). It should be noted, however, that much of this (more economics-focused) work has concentrated on trade effects, neglecting the effects on FDI despite the anticipated benefits from regional integration's association with trade and investment.

From the perspective of economics, regional integration schemes result in both long and short-run static and dynamic gains. This is due, among other things, to improved economies of scale and scope, increased efficiency through the rationalization and reallocation of activities of firms, and improved interregional linkages (Eden 2001). The improved economic conditions are also expected to positively influence inflows of FDI. These positive externalities will, of course, vary by types of regional integration. At one extreme, there are *shallow integration schemes*, which essentially involve the reduction of tariff and nontariff barriers between member countries. A vast majority of regional integration schemes in developing countries falls into this category. Other agreements relax restrictions on government procurement and cross-border FDI, as is the case with NAFTA.

At the other extreme, *deep integration schemes* may include common industrial policies, elimination of all intraregional tariff and nontariff barriers, and the adoption of common external barriers, and may progress as far as monetary and political union. Most prominent among these is the European Union initiative, which has itself evolved over time from a rather limited free trade agreement to a political and economic union. The net benefits of accession to regional integration schemes vary by the depth of integration. It is axiomatic that the benefits from membership in shallow agreements that have been in place for a short period are unlikely to prove as beneficial as deep integration agreements that have been implemented for a long period.

A number of parallels and similarities between regional integration and globalization deserve attention, especially since the current regional integration schemes are being undertaken with globalization as a backdrop. The big difference is this: regional integration schemes are attempts at social and economic engineering, while globalization has been almost a virtuous intertwining of a variety of social, political, and technological developments and events. However, the most significant similarity is that both create larger de facto markets from several de jure smaller ones (Narula 1999). In addition to creating larger markets, regional integration, like liberalization, is expected to generate benefits from the rationalization of economic activity across borders by exploiting differences in comparative advantage.

Regional integration, like globalization, is an ongoing process. Countries cannot simply jump from nonintegration to deep integration. Regional integration also requires the modification of existing institutions and establishment of new ones. Despite being primarily a North-North scheme, the experience of European integration is instructive for several reasons. First, European political economy mirrors the policy shift typical of developing countries today, except that it has occurred gradually rather than suddenly. Second, it illustrates the effects of moving from a shallow agreement to an increasing level of intensity of integration, a professed aim of several regional integration schemes among developing countries. In addition, there exists a series of concentric agreements within European regional integration. Apart from the European Union, there are associated agreements within the framework of the European Economic Area linking the European Free Trade Area with the European Union, as well as numerous associate members among the Central and Eastern European countries. That is, there are (or have been) considerable differences in development levels between participants.

Third, European integration is instructive because it demonstrates development over a longer-term perspective (unlike NAFTA, arguably the only other regional integration scheme that has experienced some level of success, which has a much shorter history). Nonetheless, these schemes were initiated prior to the advent of global liberalized markets. Regional integration in the case of the European Union can be regarded as a preliminary experiment in multilateralism, a kind of mini-globalization.

Particular emphasis needs to be drawn to the European experience in building institutions. Even the most shallow regional integration scheme requires a considerable transition period. Institutions need to adjust if they are not to experience adverse shocks. Institutions need to align with economic structures among members, and this is the primary reason for multi-track membership trajectories for various applicant countries to join the European Union. Countries such as Sweden and Finland did not require a long transition period for full membership, while Poland and the Czech Republic seem to need considerably longer, and Bulgaria longer still. Not all sectors can evolve toward the common standard at the same rate; various transition periods and exceptions are marked out for particular sectors.

In other words, it seems that a certain congruence of economic systems and relevant institutions is a precondition for successful regional integration. It is for this reason that considerable investment has been made (through the structural and framework programs) to achieve such a convergence between member countries of the European Union. The level of convergence required for shallow agreements may be much less, but the point is the same.

In a sense, regional integration acts as a catalyst for convergence and hence globalization. Certainly, in the case of European Union integration, this has been an explicit objective. At its heart, there has been a belief that cooperation by (both firm and nonfirm) economic actors across the various European countries represents a means by which the technological and economic gap between the various participants (as well as relative to the United States) might be narrowed.

MULTINATIONALS AND ECONOMIC DEVELOPMENT

FDI is regarded as a primary and explicit means for promoting growth. Furthermore, it is axiomatic that the availability of foreign capital and technology is an important means for economic catch-up. However, although inward FDI does not represent the only option available to developing countries, given the urgency and limited resources, there are four reasons why it may represent the most efficient option (Narula and Dunning 2000). First, acquiring technological and organizational know-how through arms-length means is an expensive undertaking, and, given the shortage of capital, this option is not open to many developing country governments with limited resources. Second, liberalized markets mean that firms, other things being equal, are likely to be more eager to maintain control of their assets and internalize the market for themselves, either through wholly owned subsidiaries or joint ventures. Third, infant industry protection is de rigueur in creating a domestic sector from scratch, and protected markets are a limited option within the World Trade Organization (WTO) framework. Fourth, a viable and strong domestic sector requires capital and knowledge-intensive resources, complementary clusters, and assets. The role of competition in fostering viable domestic industry is an especially important point. This is best illustrated by the failure of the import-substituting program to achieve just this objective in a large number of countries.

However, in addition to FDI, three other conditions need to be satisfied to achieve economic development:

- The FDI must generate significant spillovers.
- The domestic sector needs the capacity to absorb these spillovers. In addition (especially in the case of least developed countries), the country must have a domestic sector.
- The FDI should complement domestic industry.

The determinants of economic development are similar to the determinants of FDI, but this does not mean that there is a simple cause and effect between them. Particular types of FDI tend to be attracted to countries with certain levels of economic development and appropriate economic structures (Narula and Dunning 2000). But FDI will not necessarily catapult a country to a higher stage of development.

Indeed, the presence and condition of the domestic sector are crucial. Without a domestic sector (say, in a least developed country), there can be no opportunity to absorb spillovers from FDI. In a perfectly liberalized world, MNEs would have no incentive to encourage the development of domestic firms to meet their needs because other MNEs would be able to do so, either through imports or FDI. In an extreme case, there may actually be no FDI inflow because MNEs would prefer to locate production in a regionally optimal location and simply import. Thus, FDI in a completely liberalized milieu would not necessarily lead to growth in the domestic sector. The benefits of FDI only occur when there is domestic investment, and where domestic investment has the ability to internalize the externalities from FDI.

Although such an ideal world does not exist, the point is that FDI does not guarantee growth. FDI and economic development are highly correlated phenomena, and both are strongly dependent on a country's specific resources, institutions, economic structure, political ideologies, and social and cultural fabric. Furthermore, countries at different stages of development attract (or wish to attract) different kinds of FDI activity (Dunning and Narula 1996; Narula 1996). Indeed, these two issues are closely related. Although every individual investment is a unique event, both the type of investment and the stage of economic development of the host country fundamentally differ in the catching-up and converging countries (Narula and Dunning 2000).

The availability of foreign-owned capital (either portfolio or direct) for developing countries is not at issue here. There have been capital flows of both kinds to viable projects in the least developed countries, particularly in extractive industries and through privatization programs. However, in general, these activities do not provide much opportunity for technological spillovers and beneficial externalities. In other words, it is not FDI activities that are hard to attract, but certain kinds of FDI. There are two (interrelated) perspectives that need to be considered from a micro level. First, there is considerable variation in the motivation for investment. Second, from the MNE perspective, there is considerable variation in the types of subsidiaries. The following subsections discuss these assertions in some detail.

Motives for Multinational Investment in Developing Countries

There are four main motives for investment: to seek natural resources; to seek new markets; to restructure existing foreign production through rationalization; and to seek strategically related assets. These motives fall into two broad categories. The first three motives are primarily *asset-exploiting* in nature; that is, the investing company's primary purpose is to generate economic rent through the use of its existing firm-specific assets. The fourth motive is an *asset-augmenting* activity, whereby the firm wishes to acquire additional assets that protect or augment the firm's existing created assets in some way.

In general, least developed countries are unlikely to attract much asset-augmenting FDI. Such investment is primarily an activity undertaken in intermediate industrializing and industrial economies. Although there has been an increase in the location of asset-augmenting activity in some developing countries during the past decade, this continues to be the exception rather than the rule. The human resources, technological capabilities, and organizational skills that these countries (or their firms) possess tend to be in relatively low-technology and natural resource-intensive sectors that have become "generic" over time (Dunning, van Hoesel, and Narula 1998).

Resource-Seeking Foreign Direct Investment

With resource-seeking FDI, existing national technological assets and knowledge infrastructure do not play a significant role in determining FDI inflows. Where a region or country possesses an absolute advantage in a given scarce resource, it is in a strong position to extract rent from the MNE, despite the absence of infrastructure or a domestic sector. Where the resource sought is a natural one, the marginal cost of its extraction to both parties is close to zero. As such, the location is able to generate economic rent depending on the resource's rarity and accessibility in other locations.

Resource-seeking investment generally (but not always) implies a low-value-added activity and low capital expenditure on plant and equipment (extractive industries being the exception). Such FDI is more footloose. A purely resource-seeking investment is not normally tightly integrated into the investing firm's organizational structure; indeed, MNEs rarely engage in complete internalization of raw material markets, preferring instead to conclude nonequity agreements with foreign firms or to purchase their inputs at arms-length prices.

In general, FDI in least developed countries is often almost entirely resource-seeking. Since there are few other advantages to offer MNEs, this is often the only kind of FDI present. Where vertical forward integration and further value adding does occur, either to exploit markets or to access other advantages, the "stickiness" of the investment increases.

Market-Seeking Foreign Direct Investment

Market-seeking FDI gains prominence only in situations where the local or adjacent markets provide access to significant opportunities to achieve economies of scale in production. This requires not only a sizeable population, but also the ability of the market to support (within a reasonable time frame) the expected demand on which the investment is based. In addition, there is often a "follow-the-leader" strategic response by other firms, whereby a market that might have supported two or three competitors is inundated with a larger number of new entrants than the market can efficiently support.

The Chinese and Indian automobile markets represent examples of such a scenario, where, despite the potential for high demand levels, few participants are actually able to make a profit. This is not the case with all sectors—investments in food and personal products, for instance, are much more likely to achieve economies of scale because these products have a relatively low income elasticity of demand. Indeed, the automobile industry may represent a special case in these countries because what is now described as aggressive market-seeking investment in developing countries, in many cases, began life as defensive import-substituting investments. These were only permitted under certain stringent conditions, but the MNE normally expected to have access to a captive, protected market in return.

Market-seeking FDI is largely based on a single, central location advantage. Its presence or absence is stage-dependent but is essentially an exogenous event, with one exception. Membership in a free trade area allows countries that have small domestic markets to expand their de facto market size. In such situations, however, several formerly sovereign markets become integrated, and the choice of location then rests on other advantages. This may have detrimental effects; for example, once sanctions against South Africa were lifted, a certain hollowing-out of market-seeking FDI in neighboring countries was observed as a result of their free trade agreements with South Africa.

Efficiency-Seeking and Strategic Asset-Seeking Foreign Direct Investment

Efficiency-seeking and strategic asset-seeking FDI are similar in that they both normally require a certain threshold level of created assets, and both are generally regarded as being associated with the process of globalization. They are generally associated with middle-income and industrializing countries; especially in the case of asset-seeking FDI, they are associated with industrial countries.

As such, efficiency-seeking investment in the least developed countries is an ambiguous concept, although for many years MNEs have engaged in export-oriented resource-seeking investment, which is de facto efficiency-seeking FDI. Moreover, efficiency investment—in the sense that different aspects of manufacturing activity are located in particular locations to exploit the economies of cross-border specialization and the uneven distribution of immobile created assets—is a relatively new phenomenon.

In both of these types of investments, the role of subnational clusters and the agglomeration of related activities are significant. Countries that are home to centers of agglomeration or that possess the necessary science and technology infrastructure to attract asset-augmenting FDI have externalities that are considerably different from those of countries that primarily attract asset-exploiting FDI. However, centers of excellence and agglomeration in a given industry do not imply that further knowledge-intensive investments will be attracted to the same location by virtue of a single cluster unless clear spillovers or externalities exist. Nonetheless, countries that have agglomerative economies—or the basis for them—are the ones likely to receive such FDI.

Typology of MNE Subsidiaries

Although there are several typologies of affiliates, they serve different purposes. In particular, analysts have primarily focused attention on industrial country MNEs located in industrial countries. Some of these typologies have tended to examine particular aspects of value-adding activity or particular industries. In this chapter, I use a modification of a typology based on Pearce (1989, 2001) and Doz (1986).

The nature of the activities undertaken by a subsidiary and its potential level of embeddedness in the host economy vary according to the level of competence of the subsidiary and the scope of its activities (Benito, Grogaard, and Narula 2001). Figure 10–1 illustrates the typology of subsidiaries according to these two scales. From a level-of-competence perspective, the typical value-adding chain consists of strategic and operational elements. Activities such as sales and manufacturing are operational in nature, while the functions of research and development (R&D) centers and headquarters are strategic in nature.

In general, strategic elements tend to be located close to areas that MNEs regard as important. Following Bartlett and Ghoshal (1989), there is a close link between the influence of the subsidiary and the strategic importance of its local environment. First, strategic elements perform a critical role in a network of units, adding value by contributing their own expertise as well as by coordinating the flow of knowledge within the network. Second, there is considerable variation between subsidiaries in the scope of their activities, with certain subsidiaries performing single and specialized activities, and others performing a larger variety that are of greater value (figure 10–1).

Truncated Miniature Replicas

As their name implies, truncated miniature replicas (TMRs) are essentially a duplication of the parent firm, although perhaps with a smaller scale of production and fewer components of value-adding activity. Typically, TMRs do not undertake basic research but may modify and adapt products originally developed by the parent. Although TMRs vary in the extent to which

Figure 10–1

Typology of Multinational Enterprise Subsidiaries

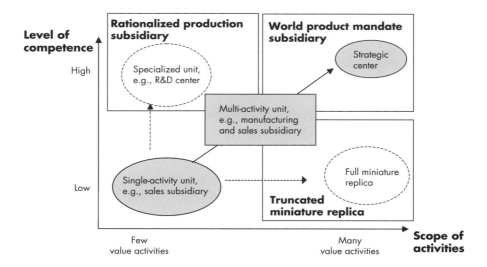

Source: Based on Benito, Grogaard, and Narula (2001).

they are truncated, generally speaking, they tend to have a low or medium level of competence (figure 10–1). TMRs tend to have an extensive market scope, in the sense that they have a large product range, but they supply a limited and isolated market (Pearce 2001). TMRs tend to have a considerable degree of autonomy in their activities, although the parent company exerts overall strategic control. This means, for instance, that the parent decides on new additions to the product range. TMRs are nationally responsive and, apart from a few advantages derived from being part of the MNE network—such as lower cost of capital and technology—they are similar to other indigenous firms. Their primary motive is market seeking, and they are most often associated with import-substituting programs. The parent-affiliate relationship is weakly developed, and the two are essentially independent of each other.

Rationalized Affiliates

Rationalized affiliates are much more closely integrated into the MNE network. Their operations are based on an efficiency-seeking motivation, aimed at optimizing costs over multiple locations, and they often produce a small range of products. There is a strategic interdependence between the MNE network and the affiliate. Pearce (1989, 2001) distinguishes between two types of rationalized affiliates: the rationalized production subsidiary and the world product mandate subsidiary. Pearce and Tavares (1998) propose a further subclassification of world product mandates into regional product mandate subsidiaries and subregional product mandate subsidiaries. Fundamentally, a rationalized production subsidiary is part of the MNE's global strategy and produces value added based on specific competitive advantages relative to other subsidiaries. Its products are often intermediate goods, or products or services complementary to other rationalized production subsidiaries. R&D is typically not associated with a rationalized production subsidiary, and the headquarters exerts control over its operations. The rationalized production subsidiary's activities are confined to operating activities, but not strategic ones.

World product mandate subsidiaries, by contrast, have a greater strategic role and more decisionmaking power, and are often engaged in higher value-adding activity. They are based on a strategic asset–seeking motivation, as well as an efficiency-seeking one. World product mandates maintain global or regional control over a particular product line or functional area, and are designated "centers of excellence." That is, the strategic affiliate's responsibilities include activities such as R&D and headquarters functions, and it exerts control over other affiliates in the same region or worldwide.

Rationalized production subsidiaries and subregional product mandate subsidiaries are truncated versions of world product mandates, in that they have a broader mandate toward a region (such as participants of a regional integration scheme) or a subregion (say, the Nordic countries or South Asia). In particular, these subsidiaries are designed to respond to a smaller catchment area. Both types of subsidiaries aim to meet particular market needs that may be unique to a given group of countries because the region or subregion requires services and products that need to be differentiated from other subsidiaries, or because local conditions require greater responsiveness (Pearce and Tavares 1998).

Single-Activity Affiliates

Single-activity affiliates are a cross between TMRs and rationalized production subsidiaries. On the one hand, they represent an extreme version of a TMR, in that they undertake a single aspect of value-adding activity. In other words, they are severely truncated. On the other hand, such affiliates may in fact be part of a company's rationalized strategy because the comparative advantage of the location is best suited for such activities. Nonetheless, a differentiation needs to be made particularly in the developing country scenario because such affiliates are often marginal to the firm, in terms of strategic importance, unlike rational production subsidiaries, which may also specialize in one form of activity. Single-activity affiliates are generic in the sense that there are often numerous such affiliates in various developing country locations. Although they may be dependents, they contribute nothing unique to the assets of the firm and are easily substituted. These affiliates are not involved in decisionmaking or strategic planning and are virtually at arms-length to the MNE.

Such affiliates typically tend to be engaged at the extremes of the value-adding chain. The first type is trading affiliates, which are engaged in trading activities and, in the limit, marketing and after-sales services. The second subcategory is resource-extractive affiliates, which are engaged solely in acquiring (primarily through extractive activity) scarce or otherwise valuable crude resources for the express purpose of exporting these raw materials for use in other locations, whether by another affiliate or by an unrelated firm.

There is considerable variation between industrial sectors, individual MNEs, and host and home country factors. For instance, in the food and beverages sectors, subsidiaries are organized primarily as TMRs. MNEs with greater international exposure and dependence on foreign markets are more inclined toward rationalized production subsidiaries or world product mandates.

It is axiomatic that subsidiary roles evolve over time, due both to internal, MNE-specific factors and to changing nonfirm, exogenous developments, including liberalization of markets and regional integration (Mariotti and Piscitello 2001; Birkinshaw and Hood 2000). The changing external environment will inevitably induce some changes in subsidiary roles. Once an MNE rationalizes the number of subsidiaries or reorganizes the activities across borders, the remaining and/or new units will likely experience changes in scope and areas of responsibility. Increases in scope can typically be found when a number of subsidiaries are rationalized or when local conditions encourage localization of activities (Birkinshaw 1996). Similarly, the scope may be narrowed to focus on specific activities and build expertise within the selected area (Surlemont 1998). Hence, changes in scope are often related to both organizational and spatial considerations.

MULTINATIONAL ENTERPRISE STRATEGIES, LIBERALIZATION, AND REGIONAL INTEGRATION

This section examines MNE strategies in response to liberalization and regional integration in four scenarios: (1) a pre-liberalized environment; (2) a regional integration scheme in a pre-liberalized environment; (3) a post-liberalization scenario; and (4) a regional integration scheme in a post-liberalization scenario. The analysis considers three groups of countries. Group I consists of least developed countries with little or no domestic capability, group II is developing countries with intermediate domestic capability, and group III is industrial countries with high domestic capability that are home countries of MNEs. Figure 10–2 illustrates the finite number of regional integration schemes possible among these three groups. The section examines each of the scenarios from every practical option for developing countries.

Figure 10–2

Combinations of Regional Integrations

	Group I	Group II	Group III
Group III	Group I–group III (e.g., Costa Rica–Canada FTA)	Group II–group III (Mexico in NAFTA; Spain, Portugal, and Greece in the EU)	Intra-group III (e.g., EFTA, Canada–US FTA)
Group II	Group I–group II (Uruguay and Paraguay in Mercosur)	Intra-group II (e.g., Brazil and Argentina in Mercosur)	
Group I	Intra-group I (e.g., Andean Community, Caricom, CACM)		

MNE Strategies in a World without Regional Integration and Liberalization

Prior to liberalization—that is, in a situation where import-substituting policies are in force—group I countries tend to host single-activity subsidiaries. In groups II and III, MNEs respond to investment opportunities primarily by establishing miniature replicas, although the extent to which they are truncated varies considerably between countries. The extent of truncation is determined by the following:

- The size of the local market in terms of potential and actual demand.
- The extent to which the MNE is afforded a monopoly.
- The stringency of the import-substituting regime. Different countries apply different local content requirements and barriers on the imports of intermediate goods.
- The capacity of domestic industry to supply local content.
- The stringency of foreign ownership restrictions and the risk of expropriation. Ownership is significant to the MNE because it determines its ability to control the activities of the subsidiary and the use of its technological assets. Where domestic industry is weak or nonexistent, ownership restrictions also influence whether foreign-based suppliers might be able to engage in FDI to manufacture local content.
- The cost of capital relative to that available on international markets (or at home), and restrictions on where capital must be borrowed.
- The potential to generate rent, and restrictions on repatriation of dividends and interest payments to the rest of the MNE in hard currency.

This list is partial and the factors are interrelated. Numerous trade-offs exist between the factors. For instance, where local demand is large and rent-generation opportunities high (such as in China), MNEs are willing to accept greater restrictions on ownership (than, say, in Peru). For example, increased local content requirements and a potential loss of majority ownership triggered IBM's decision to divest from India in the mid 1970s. The issue in this case was control rather than ownership. During the same period, IBM's Indonesia subsidiary was a shell company, and a domestically owned company undertook its local operations. However, IBM had full operational and strategic control of the Indonesian firm.

The most important determinants of truncation and thereby of the scope of activities and competence level of the subsidiary (since, broadly speaking, most countries maintained similar import-substituting regulations prior to the mid 1980s) are associated with market size and the capacity and capability of domestic industry. Group I countries, without a domestic sector and with low demand, were host to the most truncated subsidiaries, often to the point of being single-activity subsidiaries. Activities were primarily in sales and marketing and natural resource extraction. Larger group II and group III countries (much of Europe still maintained some form of import substitution into the 1970s, and non-European Union countries, such as Norway, did so well into the 1980s) with domestic technological capacity (such as Brazil and India) hosted the least-truncated subsidiaries, often with R&D departments. Nonetheless, products manufactured by these TMRs were either obsolete in the home country or designed domestically strictly for local competition or for a limited export market (Mortimore 1998). Group II had limited competition and low domestic productivity, and, in many cases, did not reach economies of scale. Production costs were therefore higher than equivalent imports, and tariff and nontariff barriers induced market imperfections, allowing for rent generation.

Shallow Regional Integration without Liberalization

A shallow regional integration scheme without liberalization proposes a common internal tariff and a (higher) common external tariff, such that this de facto enlarges the market while maintaining an import-substituting (pre-liberalization) stance.

Group I–Group II and Group II–Group III Regional Integration Schemes

In the case of regional integration between countries A and B at different levels of domestic capability, assume that country B is at a lower level (whether group I or II) than country A (group II or III). Country A's existing TMRs might see an increase in the scope of their activities. Country B might see an upgrading of its single-activity subsidiaries to TMRs as market size increases.

In addition, there may be a redistribution effect to take advantage of differences in comparative advantage. Broadly speaking, however, this will be relatively small with shallow integration, depending on the extent and sectors for which intraregional barriers decline. Redistribution will also be lower with a group I–group II regional integration scheme compared with a group II–III scheme. In either case, there will be a net increase in FDI to both countries, and an increase in competence and scope of subsidiary activity. There will be no crowding-out of domestic investment, and possibly a crowding-in in the case of country A, which has the technological capability to nurture the domestic sector. Intraregional FDI will occur, primarily from A to B, depending on the industry, but it will be relatively minor, particularly where country A is a group II country, and either in the form of single-activity subsidiaries to exploit resources in B or in the form of sales affiliates. With a group II–III regional integration scheme, intraregional FDI will be greater, but primarily downward to exploit differences in comparative advantage (such as the *maquiladoras* in Mexico).

Investments in shallow agreements will tend to be local, with the objective of accessing individual local markets separately, rather than combined markets. This is borne out by investments in the earlier stages of NAFTA and the European Union. Much of the earlier FDI in European regional integration in the 1970s defensively exploited local markets (Dunning 1997). Investments in each country were primarily associated with its domestic market and with overcoming barriers to imports.

The evidence points to potential for a greater scope of MNE activities in a non-liberalization regional integration scenario for group I and group II countries, regardless of whether the regional integration was South-South or North-South. In the case of group I countries, MNEs invested in response to regional integration where otherwise little or no FDI might be attracted. However, opportunities—due to import substitution and alternative possibilities in country A—are limited for sequential FDI and upgrading. However, the potential for a higher quality and quantity of FDI does not mean that spillovers and externalities are internalized. Where domestic firms are able to internalize spillovers and improve their capabilities—for instance, by becoming efficient suppliers to MNEs—this acts as a reinforcing mechanism for upgrading the MNEs' competence levels. If the efficiency of the TMR approaches international levels, it is possible that the subsidiary in country A is upgraded to a subregional product mandate subsidiary or a rationalized production subsidiary.

Intra-Group I Regional Integration Schemes

In this case of regional integration between group I countries with similar comparative advantages, neither A nor B on its own possesses sufficient location advantages to attract TMRs, but together their combined market size may justify TMRs in some sectors. TMRs will be in basic sectors, such as resource processing and food—in other words, in Hecksher-Ohlin industries. However, it is unlikely that affiliates will improve domestic capacity, mainly because the domestic sector is nonexistent.

MNE Strategies after Liberalization

Most South-South agreements established prior to the liberalization of the 1990s were de facto inoperative, as were most North-South agreements, with the exception of the Mexico–United States free trade area. Therefore, in a sense, liberalization was undertaken in a de facto unintegrated environment. Liberalization as undertaken by most developing countries has had the following consequences for MNE activity:

- Floating currencies, removal of exchange restrictions, and subsequent devaluation
- Reduction of tariff and nontariff barriers to manufactured imports
- Reduction of local content requirements for incumbent MNEs
- Removal of export requirements from MNEs
- Reduction of direct and indirect subsidies to domestic industry
- Privatization of some state-owned assets.

However, liberalization is a facet of globalization, and globalization has affected the ownership assets of MNEs in that it has changed the way in which they organize and undertake cross-border activities. This is not just a result of the global wave of economic liberalization and regional integration (particularly NAFTA and the European Union), but also a result of, among other things, the increasing enforceability of transactions across borders, increased competition, the growing need for competence in multiple technologies, and improved information and communications technologies.

Although the amount of total FDI stock directed toward developing countries may have increased, an increasing proportion of new investment requires the use of specialized created assets, and therefore tends to be directed to the more developed and wealthier developing countries with the necessary level of technological assets. On the one hand, MNEs seek more specialized inputs, and on the other, more countries offer generic inputs. Liberalization has meant that a much larger number of countries (possibly twice as many as two decades previously) offer generic location advantages, such as access to natural assets and basic infrastructure.

The problem of too many countries chasing a limited amount of FDI is exacerbated by the competition between provinces and regions within countries, which offer their own set of incentive schemes to funnel scarce investments to their locations (Mytelka 2002). Countries and provinces are therefore under pressure to give away bigger investment incentives in order to attract the FDI that is often central to their development strategies. There is a danger that, due to increased competition, countries may give away more than the potential benefits that accrue from MNE activity (Mytelka 2002; McIntyre, Narula, and Trevino 1996).

It is important to realize that the process of liberalization has increasingly become an exogenous event with a pervasive influence beyond any single country's control (Narula and Dunning 2000). Although opening up or liberalization is a country-specific (and therefore endogenous) event, the benefit that accrues to the country from this event is a function of the number of other countries that have also liberalized. Furthermore, membership in multilateral institutions such as the WTO (as well as free trade areas and other forms of economic integration), obliges the participating countries to conform their liberalization policies to a common standard. Membership in multilateral blocs can effect an involuntary change in policy because, with increasingly few countries still operating within a command economy or import-substituting regime, there are few opportunities for such countries to engage in economically sound nonmarket arrangements.

To sum up, globalization has affected the spatial distribution of MNE activity on a multi-country, international level as well as on an individual country basis. This is due not just to liberalization in an individual country, but also to liberalization as a multi-country phenomenon. Combined with the changing nature of MNEs' ownership-specific assets, this has led to a reorganization of MNE activities within countries and across countries.

The strategies of MNEs in any given developing country can be affected vis-à-vis their operations in three ways:

- *New and/or upgraded affiliates.* There are opportunities for new FDI inflows through new initial investment, resulting in new subsidiaries that did not exist previously, and through sequential investment as firms upgrade the scope and competence of existing subsidiaries. In a static and simplistic view, this leads to an increase in total capital (that is, domestic investment plus foreign investment).
- *Downgrading of subsidiaries.* MNEs may divest their operations in response to better location advantages elsewhere, or they may reduce the intensity of operations by low-

ering the level of competence and/or scope of their subsidiary. Total capital in this scenario may decrease.

- *Redistribution effect.* There is the possibility of a redistribution effect, with total capital staying constant. That is, sectors that were dominated by domestic capital may be transferred to foreign ownership.

Of course, in reality it is hard to separate these three effects, since these developments are hard to measure, not least because individual countries and MNEs are idiosyncratic and path-dependent. Firms may take particular strategic decisions because of long-term and noneconomic considerations, and countries may vary their policies between sectors and subsectors.

Nonetheless, there are certain broad trends that can be observed. It is clear, for instance, that the erosion of the kind of location advantages associated with protected trade and investment regimes has had far-reaching consequences. Although the benefits of liberalization in terms of encouraging inward FDI are notable, some MNEs have divested in response to liberalization where the initial MNE activity was to overcome tariff and nontariff barriers. Since the conclusion of NAFTA, for example, defensive import-substitution FDI in Canada has fallen sharply. Although information on divestment in developing countries has not been systematically collected, it is likely that, since proportionally more FDI prior to liberalization was defensive market seeking, this phenomenon might be a significant one.

Although the data suggest that there was a drastic decline in FDI stocks in group I countries in the late 1980s, this reflects in part the devaluation of domestic currencies relative to the dollar. Thus, while the property, plant and equipment, and scope and competence of an affiliate in, say, Argentina or Chile, may have remained identical before and after liberalization, its value on the books of the MNE may have declined in hard currency terms. Nonetheless, a wide variety of group I countries have seen a decline in the quality of TMR subsidiaries, particularly in sectors where the low productivity of affiliates' production was supported through market distortions induced by trade barriers.

MNEs have taken advantage of liberalization to exploit production capacity in a few locations to achieve economies of scale, especially where local consumption patterns are not radically different enough to justify local capacity, and where transportation costs are not prohibitive. This has meant that some TMRs have been downgraded to sales and marketing affiliates. Except for sectors where policy-induced distortions persist, FDI now largely reflects comparative advantages. Group I countries with abundant natural resources now receive much more resource-seeking FDI and less upstream FDI in manufacturing (ECLAC 2001).

Countries with superior nongeneric location assets—in other words, group II countries—tend to receive higher value-adding, knowledge-intensive FDI. Countries without this capacity—both in terms of physical infrastructure and necessary skilled human capital—are unlikely to be hosts to rationalized production subsidiaries, regional product mandates, or world product mandates. Deepening of affiliate activity is increasingly associated with the location's ability to be integrated with the rest of the MNE and its ability to provide unique knowledge-intensive inputs not available elsewhere. Data published by ECLAC (2001) suggest that FDI activity in Latin America—with the exception of Mexico and the Caribbean—continues to focus on serving local markets and traditional resource-seeking activities.

In other words, domestic capacity—whether in the form of knowledge infrastructure or an efficient domestic industrial sector—is a primary determinant of high-competence foreign affiliates. Some countries have succeeded in attracting such FDI, notably Mexico and the Caribbean Basin (ECLAC 2000, 2001; Mortimore 2000). In addition to providing domestic capabilities and a threshold level of physical infrastructure, some of these countries have invested in developing knowledge infrastructure (although to a lesser extent in the case of Mexico). More importantly, these countries have a long-term bilateral agreement with the United States in the Caribbean Basin Initiative. Like incentives, bilateral ties are not on their own sufficient conditions to attract FDI, but studies have shown that the longer they persist, the greater their effect (Mudambi 1998; Blonigen and Davies 2000).

An important avenue through which the redistribution effects of FDI can be seen is through privatization. Between 1988 and 1999, $107.3 billion worth of privatized firms had been acquired through cross-border mergers and acquisitions. Latin America and the Caribbean's share was roughly 79.8 percent (UNCTAD 2000). In other words, during this period, about 20 percent of the total inflows to this region were associated with privatization. Overall, liberalization has been beneficial to MNEs. Privatization, in particular, has allowed foreign investors to acquire fully operational (albeit often inefficient) firms in countries at relatively low cost, due to, among other things, depreciation of the exchange rates of the recipient economies.

From a national perspective, inflows from privatization represent a single, one-off phenomenon—MNE acquisitions through privatization schemes may initially generate a large initial infusion of capital, but subsequent inflows are by no means guaranteed. Indeed, in many cases, state-owned companies that have been most attractive for FDI have often been the more efficient ones, requiring relatively little in the way of upgrading. The majority of privatizations are in the services sector. Furthermore, because MNEs plan to generate rents from these investments, the net inflows can be expected to be significantly smaller in subsequent years. As such, the net effect on the economy is possibly neutral, and FDI represents simply a redistribution of assets from domestic to foreign capitalists or from the state to foreign firms.[1]

Regional Integration after Liberalization

Intra-Group I Regional Integration

Intragroup regional integration might occur, for example, when two countries in group I undertake shallow integration after liberalization. Assuming that this implies common external barriers, but relatively free (or at least lower) intraregional trade barriers, this gives MNEs (and domestic firms) an opportunity to exploit scale economies in market-seeking investment. Thus, an MNE may consider a TMR where two single-activity affiliates might previously have existed. Such an operation can be in either country A or country B. Assuming similar factor endowments and de facto freedom of movement of goods and services, the decision is often based on incentives and subsidies. Such contests can only erode the net benefits of FDI. In general, regional integration will have no influence on the spatial distribution of resource-seeking investments, since these are already based on comparative advantage.

Group I–Group II Regional Integration

Group I–group II regional integration has a clearer variation in endowments and location advantages. A regional integration–driven reorganization of MNE activity is certainly possible

---

[1] Much of the state-owned assets acquired by MNEs are in services and infrastructure. Such investments have an important welfare effect.

with the higher competence activities in the group II country (country A) and lower factor endowment–type activities in the group I country (country B). However, liberalization in neighboring countries means that—unless external barriers are very high—the MNE may yet prefer to locate higher competence in country C, which is located outside the boundaries of the regional integration. However, the determining factor in whether country A becomes host to a regional product mandate subsidiary is the efficiency of the country's existing operations relative to other countries; its participation in a regional integration scheme is only secondary.

North-South Regional Integration

Although redistribution of MNE activity follows along similar lines as group I–group II integration, there are two obvious advantages of participation in a North-South scheme that are not evident in group I–group II regional integration. First, the group III country (A) is home to a large group of MNEs that are more likely to invest in country B. The technological gap is much larger, and the pool of potential spillovers greater. Furthermore, such intraregional FDI is more likely to be efficiency–seeking. Second, country A provides a much larger market. Thus, in terms of linkages, and simply in terms of FDI, there is a greater order of magnitude in terms of benefits.

As an example, Mexico with NAFTA has enjoyed increased FDI flows, both from within NAFTA and from its agreement with the European Union. This has two advantages that (say) Mercosur does not have. First, NAFTA provides Mexico access to the United States. Certainly, many European Union firms would not have invested in Mexico if it provided ease of access to, say, Honduras or Brazil. Second, the European Union, the United States, and Canada are home countries for a majority of the largest MNEs. South-South regional integration schemes do not always have the managerial, technological, or capital capacity within the region to lead to an increase in intraregional FDI of the same order of magnitude. In addition, MNEs from the South are themselves interested in improving their global competitiveness because they must survive in global markets. Other things being equal, improved or cheaper access to another developing country is not in itself sufficient incentive, unless that location enjoys some considerable advantage over other developing countries.

Some Caveats

I have taken the example of two-country regional integration for illustrative purposes. It is self-evident that a larger group of participants acts as a more powerful magnet for investment, although coordinating policy across a larger group is fraught with complications. I have also had to assume that regional integration schemes have been implemented uniformly. Unfortunately, this is rarely the case. There are certain limitations that are associated with achieving even modest gains from regional integration. First, there is the lack of common institutions and the lack of political consensus for creating them. For instance, some of the members of the various and overlapping Latin American regional integration schemes have been in the throes of regional integration on a sporadic basis for more than two decades.

A recent study by the Inter-American Development Bank (2000) highlights the various problems in regulatory and institutional frameworks between Latin American countries. For instance, a truck carrying goods from Brazil to Chile requires 200 hours for a 3,500-kilometer journey, of which 50 percent is spent in the two border crossings. The development of common institutions is a slow and gradual process. It is here that the benefit of a history of regional integration attempts and a similarity of cultures helps the most. Previous cooperative institution building allows countries to continue in that vein, but political differences and lack of congruity in goals mean that regional integration schemes have remained largely incomplete.

A second limitation of actual regional integration schemes compared with the stylized one is that the actual schemes rarely conform to a common external barrier that is higher than the (common) internal barriers. A third limitation is the reluctance to agree among members about structural adjustment. Each country wishes to maintain its national champions and status projects, such that considerable duplication exists. Achieving consensus as to how to rationalize this is avoided by excluding such sensitive sectors from agreements. For instance, one industry in Latin America that might benefit from intraregional integration rationalization of production is the automobile sector. However, in the case of the Mercosur countries, which are hosts to a sizeable presence of MNEs producing automobiles for each domestic market dating back to the import-substituting era, there is some reluctance to allow intraregional free access (Mortimore 1998).

This was also the case initially with European integration. Until the early 1980s, much of FDI was defensive market seeking, and intra-European FDI was considerably low, as each country maintained its national champions. European firms are significant home countries for MNEs; indeed, many European countries are net outward investors, but not to other European countries. European MNEs possess significant ownership-specific assets (whether technological, managerial, or through privileged access to complementary assets) that are not available to developing country firms. This means that prior to regional integration, there was already a large, untapped potential for intra-European activity.

In addition, the presence of such large and competitive firms implies location-specific advantages in the form of institutions, infrastructure, and other economic actors that can serve as magnets for foreign (whether intra or extraregional) MNEs, quite apart from the attractions of a large market. However, intra-European Union FDI and rationalization of production within the European Union took place only after the European Commission made considerable efforts to push European Union firms to rationalize and create trans-European efficiency in their activities (Narula 1999). Member countries provided European Union firms a grace period of protection within which to improve their competitiveness, after which market forces would decide which players survived (in theory) regardless of national origin.

CONCLUSIONS

This chapter has tried to illustrate how the strategies of MNEs have responded to globalization, and to evaluate MNEs' response to regional integration before and after liberalization.

From the perspective of the MNEs, liberalization has had a greater effect on their strategies than has regional integration. Globalization of MNE activity and liberalization of countries has led to a downgrading of MNE activity in most least developed countries and in some more advanced developing countries. Many of the gains in FDI flows have been a result of redistribution, associated with the transfer of state and privately owned domestic firms to foreign ownership. Only a handful of countries have seen an improvement in the quality of FDI. These countries have a threshold level of domestic capability and physical infrastructure, as well as institutions that are more efficient. In general, regional integration schemes have reinforced these trends, benefiting those countries that have developed their domestic sector and worked toward creating the appropriate multilateral institutions to exploit cross-border efficiencies. Furthermore, these countries have been involved in North-South regional integration schemes.

The objective of development strategies in both pre- and post-liberalization phases has been to develop and sustain the competitiveness of domestic industry. Liberalization has brought with it more MNE-friendly policies, with the objective of leveraging FDI for capacity building. However, the quality of FDI and the potential for spillovers vary considerably, depending on the motivation for FDI and the kind of subsidiary. In general, there has been a downgrading of MNE activity in most group I countries and some group II countries. Much of the gains in FDI flows have been a result of redistribution, associated with the substitution of state and privately owned domestic firms to foreign ownership, and the gains have been dubious from a development perspective. The only countries that have attracted "the right kind" of FDI have been those that have the appropriate knowledge infrastructure; sound, stable economic policies; and the potential for a competitive domestic sector.

MNE subsidiaries do not develop in isolation from the domestic sector. In other words, participants of South-South agreements are unlikely to receive much FDI over and above that which they might have received in the first place in a post-liberalized world, based on their comparative advantage; indeed, they may suffer from negative redistribution effects. It is important to emphasize that the analysis here has focused solely on MNE strategies; there can be (and are) considerable other benefits from participation in regional integration schemes through other mechanisms.

For most developing countries, regional integration on the heels of liberalization has not improved matters, except possibly for group II countries in South-South regional integration schemes, and within North-South regional integration schemes. In other words, the situation has improved for the "haves" and not for the "have nots." Regional integration improves only one type of location advantage: regional integration is associated with increases in de facto market size, and thus logically the largest benefits from increased FDI are those that are motivated by efforts to acquire access to these markets. This is no different from the advantages that liberalization is purported to offer.

From the MNEs' perspective, liberalization is a bigger pull than a smaller, closed club of regional integration, unless that club offers some unique advantage not available elsewhere. In any case, most South-South regional integration schemes rarely achieve increases in market size because the schemes lack the regional and national institutions necessary to promote de facto cross-border efficiencies. Regional integration schemes have completely different outcomes before and after liberalization vis-à-vis MNE strategies; regional integration simply reinforces changes in MNE strategies in response to liberalization, rather than counteracting them. The analysis here finds the secondary evidence on regional integration to be broadly in line with the findings of Blomström and Kokko (1997), who conclude that the greater the liberalization associated with regional integration and the stronger the location advantages, the more likely it is that regional integration will lead to increased FDI inflows.

The sudden change from import-substituting to multilateral liberalization has taken most countries by surprise (Mortimore 2000). They need to respond to globalization, but this requires time and new institutions that are responsive to multilateral issues and an interdependent world. However, institution building is a slow and gradual process. This is where regional integration provides long-term benefits because it potentially allows countries to gradually respond to globalization in a controlled and stepwise manner.

Adjusting institutions and improving intraregional efficiencies should logically be easier within a small group of similar countries than among the entire membership of the WTO. Regional integration should be regarded as a stepping-stone to globalization. Regional integration offers developing countries a window of opportunity to dampen the shock of entry into a fully multilateral and globalizing world by practicing on a smaller version. Mexico is illustrative of the slow and gradual process of structural adjustment. Mexico has undertaken increasing regional integration within NAFTA while also deepening its integration with other partners, such as the European Union. This is acknowledged as part of a broader integration into the world economy (ECLAC 2000). The danger, of course, is that regional integration schemes can act as an excuse to return to a pre-liberalization world of excessive protection.

Development policies need to integrate a more sophisticated view of FDI. As Mortimore (2000) illustrates, although Latin American countries have succeeded in attracting a large *quantity* of FDI, they have thus far ignored the issue of the *quality* of FDI. Mortimore points out that there is a failure to fully integrate and coordinate domestic capacity improvement goals with FDI policies.

Regional integration can be seen to be a useful policy tool in promoting competitiveness if it is exploited carefully and within an integrated development policy agenda. Although regional integration per se may not have any great benefit for group I countries in terms of quality of FDI or direct spillovers to their domestic sectors, there are other reasons to participate. First, regional integration increases FDI flow (albeit of limited quality) and helps the least developed countries escape the vicious cycle of poverty. Increased resource-seeking investment and market-seeking investment are better than no investment at all. Second, regional integration allows least developed countries to prepare for greater liberalization, allowing for a gradual widening and deepening of cross-border interdependence.

The reasons that countries do not enjoy greater welfare benefits from regional integration are the same as those that limit the benefits from liberalization in general: lack of a threshold level of domestic capabilities (Borensztein, De Gregorio, and Lee 1998); lack of long-term political stability (Freeman and Lindauer 1999); and absence of efficient institutions, both domestic and regional. Participation in a regional integration scheme creates an imperative to improve at least some of these and, in many cases, acts as a catalyst to escape structural inertia and lock-in (Hannan and Freeman 1984). Furthermore, like liberalization, the costs of nonparticipation in a genuinely integrated regional integration scheme are high, particularly when most other countries are participating.

REFERENCES

Baldwin, R. E. 1997. The Causes of Regionalism. *The World Economy* 20(7): 865–88.

Baldwin, R. E., and A. J. Venables. 1995. Regional Economic Integration. In G. M. Grossman and K. Rogoff (eds.), *Handbook of International Economics*. Amsterdam, Netherlands: Elsevier.

Bartlett, C. A., and S. Ghoshal. 1989. *Managing across Borders: The Transnational Solution*. Boston, MA: Harvard Business School Press.

Benito, G., B. Grogaard, and R. Narula. 2001. The Effect of Regional Integration on Subsidiary Roles: The Heterogeneity of Subsidiaries in the Nordic Countries. Oslo, Norway. Mimeo.

Birkinshaw, J. 1996. How Multinational Subsidiary Mandates Are Gained and Lost. *Journal of International Business Studies* 27(3): 467–95.

Birkinshaw, J., and N. Hood. 2000. Characteristics of Foreign Subsidiaries in Industry Clusters. *Journal of International Business Studies* 31(1): 141–54.

Blomström, M., and A. Kokko. 1997. *Regional Integration and Foreign Direct Investment*. NBER Working Paper 6019, National Bureau of Economic Research, Cambridge, MA.

Blonigen, B., and R. Davies. 2000. *The Effects of Bilateral Tax Treaties on U.S. FDI Activity*. NBER Working Paper 7929, National Bureau of Economic Research, Cambridge, MA.

Borensztein, E., J. De Gregorio, and J. W. Lee. 1998. How Does Foreign Direct Investment Affect Economic Growth? *Journal of International Economics* 45: 115–35.

Doz, Yves L. 1986. *Strategic Management in Multinational Companies*. Oxford, UK: Pergamon Press.

Dunning, J. H. 1997. The European Internal Market Programme and Inbound Foreign Direct Investment (Part 2). *Journal of Common Market Studies* 35: 190–223.

Dunning, J. H., and R. Narula. 1996. The Investment Development Path Revisited: Some Emerging Issues. In J. Dunning and R. Narula (eds.), *Foreign Direct Investment and Governments: Catalysts for Economic Restructuring*. London, UK: Routledge.

Dunning, J. H., R. van Hoesel, and R. Narula. 1998. Third World Multinationals Revisited: New Developments and Theoretical Implications. In J. Dunning (ed.), *Globalization, Trade and Foreign Direct Investment*. UK: Elsevier Science.

ECLAC. 2000. *Foreign Investment in Latin America and the Caribbean: 1999 Report*. United Nations, Santiago, Chile.

———. 2001. *Foreign Investment in Latin America and the Caribbean: 2000 Report*. United Nations, Santiago, Chile.

Eden, L. 2001. Regional Integration and Foreign Direct Investment: Theory and Lessons from NAFTA. In M. Kotabe, P. Aulakh, and A. Phatak (eds.), *The Challenge of International Business Research*. London, UK: Edward Elgar.

Edquist, C., and B. Johnson. 1997. Institutions and Organisations in Systems of Innovation. In C. Edquist (ed.), *Systems of Innovation: Technologies, Institutions and Organisations*. London, UK, and Washington, DC: Pinter.

Freeman, Richard, and David L. Lindauer. 1999. *Why Not Africa?* NBER Working Paper 6942, National Bureau of Economic Research, Cambridge, MA.

Hannan, M., and J. Freeman. 1984. Structural Inertia and Organizational Change. *American Sociological Review* 49: 149–64.

Inter-American Development Bank (IDB). 2000. Periodic Note on Integration and Trade in the Americas. Department of Integration and Regional Programs. Washington, DC.

Lall, S. 2000. *Foreign Direct Investment and Development: Policy and Research Issues in the Emerging Context*. QEH Working Paper Series 43, Queen Elizabeth House, University of Oxford, Oxford, UK.

Mariotti, S., and L. Piscitello. 2001. Localized Capabilities and the Internationalization of Manufacturing Activities by SMEs. *Entrepreneurship and Regional Development* 13: 65–80.

McIntyre, J., R. Narula, and L. Trevino. 1996. The Role of Export Processing Zones for Host Countries and Multinationals: A Mutually Beneficial Relationship? *International Trade Journal* 10 (Winter): 435–66.

Mortimore, M. 1998. Getting a Lift: Modernizing Industry by Way of Latin American Integration Schemes. The Example of Automobiles. *Transnational Corporations* 7(2).

———. 2000. Corporate Strategies for FDI in the Context of Latin America's New Economic Model. *World Development* 28(9): 1611–26.

Mudambi, Ram. 1998. The Role of Duration in MNE Investment Attraction Strategies. *Journal of International Business Studies* 29(2): 239–62.

Mytelka, L. 2002. Locational Tournaments, Strategic Partnerships and the State. In Meric Gertler and David Wolfe (eds.), *Innovation and Social Learning: Institutional Adaptation in an Era of Technological Change*. Basingstoke: Palgrave.

Narula, R. 1996. *Multinational Investment and Economic Structure*. London, UK: Routledge.

———. 1999. Explaining Strategic R&D Alliances by European Firms. *Journal of Common Market Studies* 37(4): 711–23.

———. 2002. Innovation Systems and 'Inertia' in R&D Location: Norwegian Firms and the Role of Systemic Lock-in. *Research Policy* 31: 795–816.

Narula, R., and J. Dunning. 2000. Industrial Development, Globalisation and Multinational Enterprises: New Realities for Developing Countries. *Oxford Development Studies* 28(2): 141–67.

Pearce, Robert D. 1989. *The Internationalisation of Research and Development by Multinational Enterprises*. London, UK: Macmillan.

———. 2001. Multinationals and Industrialisation: The Bases of 'Inward Investment' Policy. *International Journal of Economics and Business* 8(1).

Pearce, R., and A. Tavares. 1998. *Strategies of Multinational Subsidiaries in a Context of Regional Trading Blocs*. Discussion Paper 257, University of Reading.

Reinhardt, N., and W. Peres. 2000. Latin America's New Economic Model: Micro Responses and Economic Restructuring. *World Development* 28(9): 1543–66.

Smith, K. 1997. Economic Infrastructures and Innovation Systems. In C. Edquist (ed.), *Systems of Innovation: Technologies, Institutions and Organisations*. London, UK, and Washington, DC: Pinter.

Surlemont, B. 1998. A Typology of Centres within Multinational Corporations: An Empirical Investigation. In J. Birkinshaw and N. Hood (eds.), *Multinational Corporate Evolution and Subsidiary Development*. Basingstoke, UK: Macmillan.

UNCTAD. 2000. *World Investment Report 2000.* Geneva, Switzerland, and New York, NY: United Nations.

Venables, A. 2000. Winners and Losers from Regional Integration Agreements. London School of Economics. Unpublished.

Vernon, R. 1996. Passing through Regionalism: The Transition to Global Markets. *Journal of World Trade* 19(6): 621–33.

Chapter 11

What Role for Regional Competition Policy in Latin America?

Simon J. Evenett

The last decade of the 20th century saw many industrial and developing nations, including those from Latin America, lower border measures—such as tariffs and quotas—as well as take steps to deregulate utilities and privatize state-owned industries. These reforms enhanced the role that prices played in allocating resources, and increased the potential for reducing inefficiencies, undermining entrenched market power, and stimulating productivity and innovation. Driven by the profit motive, firms responded to these liberalization measures in a number of ways—not all of which were benign.

Soon after the completion of the Uruguay Round, which, in turn, was reinforced by the signing of numerous bilateral and regional trading arrangements, came the largest wave of cross-border mergers and acquisitions that the world economy has ever seen. This has raised the disturbing possibility that international firms may be counteracting the beneficial effects of the policy reforms by consolidating and attempting to preserve—or even increase—their market power. This, in turn, has raised questions about the appropriate public policy response. In the case of competition policy, the issue that arises is whether national antitrust measures can improve resource allocation when the consequences of so many corporate decisions spill over national borders and affect other nations' economies.

In this chapter, I revisit the latter issue, drawing on economic first principles and selected aspects of international experience, to highlight the circumstances under which a supranational response might benefit a region such as Latin America. Given that most bilateral measures of interdependence—trade, foreign direct investment, and the like—taper off with distance, a related question is to what extent the gains from supranational reform could in fact be accomplished by regional measures.

Although I employ almost exclusively economic arguments in what follows, this does not imply that I regard as unimportant legal and institutional analyses of national competition laws and of cooperation on competition policy matters between nations.[1] Indeed, the eco-

---

The section on international cartels draws heavily on the author's prior joint work with Margaret C. Levenstein and Valerie Y. Suslow.

[1] See Tavares (2001) for an account of international cooperation in Latin America on these matters. For comparable European Union-United States experience with cooperation, see the chapters and case studies in Evenett, Lehmann, and Steil (2000) and Parisi (2000). Given this chapter's focus on regional competition policy, it is worth noting that European Union competition law is admirably discussed in Faull and Nikpay (1999); Goyder (1998); and, from a historical perspective, Gerber (2001). Graham and Richardson (1997) provide a stimulating overview of a number of nations' antitrust laws as well as an account of the principal economic questions relevant to the debate over international competition policy.

nomic arguments presented here argue for some type of supranational arrangements for dealing with competition policy cases with certain international dimensions. It would be churlish not to suppose that prior legal experience at the national and international levels has no bearing on the codification and implementation of such arrangements. Having said that, it is my hope that this attempt to clarify the critical economic issues at hand will be of value to legal scholars and those analysts whose primary training is not in economics.

This chapter distinguishes between competition policies and those trade and regulatory policies that may have some bearing on market outcomes. In an attempt to avoid the confusion that is apparent in some of the literature, I employ Tinbergen's (1952) distinction between the objectives of policymakers (the targets) and the means of accomplishing them (the instruments). The chapter then examines the often-heard claim that trade policy is an alternative to competition policy, an argument that—if true—calls into question why competition policy enforcement (at the national, regional, or multilateral level) is needed in a world undergoing continued trade liberalization. The section on cross-border mergers and acquisitions discusses how national merger reviews can distort regional or global resource allocation. The section on private international cartels explains why national anticartel measures often provide an inadequate deterrent to the formation of an international cartel, highlights deficiencies in recent enforcement experience, and describes some proposals to overcome them. The chapter concludes by reiterating the importance of identifying spillovers as the principal rationale for regional competition enforcement efforts, and offers the appropriate caveats.

COMPETITION POLICY: SOME PRELIMINARIES

To establish the parameters for the subsequent discussion, it is useful to state which set of government measures I take as constituting competition policy. For the purpose of this discussion, this set includes the following:

- Bans or constraints on the ability of firms to undertake predatory pricing; and the right to impose punishments on firms—and potentially their executives—for violating these limitations
- Limitations on the circumstances in which firms can exercise monopoly power (which is taken to be the ability to set prices above marginal or incremental cost); and the right to impose punishments on firms—and potentially their executives—for violating these limitations[2]
- The right to review and potentially prohibit or alter commercial transactions, such as mergers and acquisitions, that may result in the creation or enhancement of monopoly power
- The right to review and potentially prohibit or alter proposed and existing contracts between independent commercial entities that supply distinct markets (including so-called "vertical relationships," such as retail price maintenance, refusals to deal with other firms, and exclusive dealing arrangements)
- The right to investigate and prohibit or alter proposed or actual arrangements between competing firms in the same market (the so-called "horizontal" arrangements, which

---

[2] The terms market power and monopoly power are used interchangeably throughout this chapter.

include joint undertaking of research and development and marketing, and membership in trade associations)
- The right to ban and investigate allegations of actual or attempted price fixing, market
allocation, and bid rigging
- The right to grant exemptions to any of the practices outlined above.

This set of measures is collectively known as antitrust policy in the United States, and throughout the chapter, I use the terms antitrust policy and competition policy interchangeably.

Having defined which government measures constitute competition policy, a number of
comments are in order. First, the above definition leaves open the identity of the state agency
or agencies that implement, coordinate, and oversee competition policy. This differs markedly
across countries, with some granting a greater role to judicial oversight of antitrust enforcement, and others retaining more executive (or administrative) control. Furthermore, in some
federal constitutional structures, the central government need not be the only state actor that
undertakes antitrust enforcement—in which case there are undoubtedly conventions, laws, or
formats for dictating the circumstances under which state actors cooperate with, and potentially defer to, one another.

Second, the above set of government measures should be distinguished from the objectives (the targets) of state actors. I adopt the traditional distinction (traditional, that is, to
international trade economists) between economic and noneconomic targets. The former takes
as its policy objective the maximization of economic efficiency, which is equal to the sum of
the gains that consumers and producers obtain from economic exchange.[3] The latter refers to
any other objective (or combination of objectives)—such as maximizing employment or promoting exports. Admittedly, maximizing employment levels may sound "economic," but it is
typically termed "noneconomic" because it does not directly relate to economic efficiency.

In an analysis whose scope includes more than one nation, the concept of economic
efficiency must be further refined. The term "global economic efficiency" is said to occur when
the total gains from exchange in all nations' markets have been maximized.[4] By contrast,
"national economic efficiency" is said to occur when the economic actors in a given nation
have maximized the gains from exchange in all markets, both at home and abroad. This is
tantamount to maximizing the sum of a nation's consumer surpluses and the producer surplus
of that nation's firms, including those surpluses earned from exporting to foreign markets.
Hence, the notion of national economic efficiency implies that a country's policymakers would
be concerned about market outcomes in foreign nations in which their exporters sell goods
and services. Moreover, a nation's policy choices—such as whether to allow a merger between
two domestic firms that sell in export markets—are likely to influence the well-being of other
nations, and will be of interest to them as well.

The notion that the goal of competition policy is to attain national economic efficiency
is probably noncontroversial to international economists. However, there is little to suggest
that such a view is widely accepted by legal scholars or practitioners. Some of the latter believe
that antitrust policy should seek to maximize consumer surplus—and implicitly reject the
possibility of trading off losses to consumers for more than offsetting gains for producers. So,
for example, this viewpoint would object to any merger that resulted in a price increase for
domestic consumers—irrespective of its effects on domestic firms.

---

[3] In the language of microeconomics, this is the sum of the producer and consumer surpluses.
[4] In other words, it is where the global sum of the producer and consumer surpluses has been maximized.

Another viewpoint is that antitrust policymakers should consider only the effects within a nation's borders. As an example, consider the following scenario: Two U.S. firms propose merging and argue that the combined entity will be able to lower the cost of supplying goods abroad (attaining so-called efficiency in the export market), but no cost reduction is likely to occur in the U.S. market. This merger is likely to result in higher prices for domestic U.S. consumers and greater export opportunities for the merged firm. When faced with this hypothetical merger, Professor Robert Pitofsky, until recently Chairman of the United States Federal Trade Commission, could not be clearer about where he stood:

> If that argument were advanced, we would consider it but our approach would be skeptical. This is not a strictly chauvinistic interpretation of American merger law. First, it is inconsistent with the basic premise…that domestic firms are best able to succeed in international markets if required to compete vigorously at home…Second, balancing anti-competitive effects in a domestic market against efficiencies in a foreign export market is unusually difficult. Finally, it is an unattractive prospect to 'tax' United States consumers (as a result of the domestic anti-competitive effect) in order to confer benefits on U.S. exporters and non-U.S. consumers.[5]

Both the "consumer effects only" and "domestic effects only" views can be criticized because they ignore the gains from market exchange enjoyed by a nation's firms during their export activities. If a nation chooses either of these two views and conducts its antitrust policy accordingly, then it will almost certainly take actions that do not maximize national economic efficiency. (Of course, the more interesting question is whether two or more nations, each of which has adopted the national economic efficiency standard as its goal for antitrust policy, will make choices that also maximize global economic efficiency. The chapter returns to that question in the section on cross-border mergers and acquisitions.)

Third, competition policy instruments, as defined above, are distinguished from the large group of measures that fall under the umbrella of trade policies (for example, measures that discriminate against foreign commerce at the border, such as tariffs), industrial policies (subsidies, export credits, and tax credits), intellectual property rights laws (patents and copyrights), and regulatory policies (price setting, environmental restrictions, and conditions on entry of new firms). In any given market, competition policies and any of these other policies may operate, which has led scholars to ask if it is possible to rank these policies (or combinations of them) in terms of their likelihood of attaining some desired policy target, and whether any of these policies can substitute for one another (an important question because policies may differ considerably in their implementation costs). The scope of this chapter precludes discussion of the former question, but the latter question is addressed at some length in the next section.

Fourth, it is worth noting that more than 80 nations have some form of competition law on their statute books and that 60 percent of these laws have been introduced since the 1990s. No doubt, many developing economies are grappling with the domestic ramifications of their recently enacted antitrust laws, rather than the international considerations raised here. Worse still, enforcement capacities differ considerably across nations, calling into question whether policy choices are made in such a way as to maximize national economic welfare. These con-

---

[5] Pitofsky (1999).

cerns are important in forming an overall assessment of the deficiencies of a nation's enforcement system. However, my objective here is to show that even nations that have robust independent antitrust enforcers can still make choices that maximize national economic welfare at the expense of global welfare.

IS TRADE REFORM A SUBSTITUTE FOR COMPETITION POLICY?

Countries underwent extensive trade liberalization throughout the 1990s, particularly those developing economies that unilaterally lowered trade barriers. The greater ease with which imports can enter liberalized markets was thought to undermine the monopoly power of incumbent domestic firms, adding to the benefits of trade reform as prices were driven closer to marginal costs. In tradables industries, trade reform was helping accomplish the same goal as competition policy. Naturally, the question arose as to whether the former might be a perfect substitute for the latter.

Coupled with an open policy toward foreign direct investment that might inject competition into nontradables sectors, the view arose that erecting competition policy enforcement machinery could be superfluous in nations committed to international economic integration. This view has some respectable credentials of considerable vintage. For example, Bhagwati (1968) shows that, if a domestic monopoly in a small open economy were forced to face unimpeded competition from imports, then domestic prices would collapse to match world prices, and supply would be exactly enough so that output would ensure that the world price just covered the (marginal) cost of the last unit of production. Under these circumstances, import competition would not merely reduce, but would, in fact, eliminate the market power of the domestic monopolist. Indeed, if this theoretical result had widespread empirical validity, then perhaps much of the discussion of multilateral and regional competition policy would be rendered moot.

To assess the validity of this claim, there is a growing body of empirical evidence on exporter behavior and the response of import-competing firms. Some research examines the sensitivity of domestic firms' pricing decisions (specifically, the markup of price over marginal cost) to lower trade barriers.[6] The principal finding of this research is that, holding other factors constant, the larger the reduction in an industry's protection from imports, the greater the contraction in markups of prices over marginal costs. Furthermore, in response to trade reform, domestic firms have increased their productivity levels, reducing costs—some of which have been passed on to consumers in the form of lower prices. This evidence supports the view that integration into the market economy attenuates domestic market power. However, no one has demonstrated empirically that integration eliminates domestic market power, suggesting that trade reform is not yet a perfect substitute for national competition policy.

Although imports from existing overseas suppliers tend to rise in response to a rise in the prices of domestic firms, another tranche of empirical studies shows that such price increases are unlikely to induce new foreign firms to start supplying the domestic market immediately. Entering new markets requires considerable start-up costs (for establishing distribution net-

---

[6] Feenstra (1995) and Tybout (2000) survey this research program, drawing on the initial contributions of Levinsohn (1993) and Harrison (1994). Goldberg and Knetter (1997) review some of the latest techniques to estimate both the monopoly power of exporters and the extent of international market integration.

works, tailoring products to the new market, and marketing), and so the assertion of greater market power by domestic firms is unlikely to induce new foreign entrants unless the domestic price increases are large enough to enable those potential entrants to recover these costs over a plausible time horizon.[7] This implies that the short-term constraint on domestic market power is actual, rather than potential, foreign competition.

The same studies also show that, once a foreign firm enters the domestic market (perhaps owing to a favorable exchange rate movement or to falling impediments to trade), it takes especially unfavorable domestic market conditions for the firm to exit the market. The unwillingness of foreign firms to leave the market in anything other than severe downturns is related to the firms' desire to avoid having to reestablish their presence in the market once favorable conditions return. This finding implies that, as global integration unfolds, the extent of foreign competition faced by domestic firms ratchets up over time, posing an ever more serious threat to domestic market power. Taken together, these findings imply that, while existing foreign rivals provide the bulk of the restraint on domestic market power, there is a pronounced tendency for the number of these foreign rivals to increase over time. In sum, trade reform may threaten domestic market power—and that threat may grow over time—but the empirical evidence to date does not support the view that trade reform has entirely substituted for competition policy.

Another reason for doubting the case for placing all the weight on trade reform is that—unlike Bhagwati's theoretical model—firms can respond to the threat to their profits posed by trade reform by undertaking mergers, acquisitions, other forms of consolidation, and even forming a cartel. In doing so, firms may attenuate competitive pressures and erode the gains from trade liberalization. There is considerable case study and admittedly anecdotal evidence to support this point of view. In a series of insightful case studies, Levenstein and Suslow (2001) document how steel and graphite electrode producers used access to critical technological inputs and information to shut out rivals—especially new ones—from their markets and to strengthen their respective cartels. Furthermore, they show how firms in an oil country's tubular goods market recently used strategic alliances and joint ventures to limit, stall, and control entry by new firms, thereby sustaining their cartel. Perhaps most pertinent, Levenstein and Suslow's case studies show that the trigger for forming a cartel is typically a large price fall—which is exactly what a sizeable trade reform will generate.

A global wave of cross-border mergers and acquisitions has accompanied the recent bout of trade reform. Unlike the merger wave in the 1980s, which was concentrated in a small number of industrial countries—notably the United States and the United Kingdom—this latest wave is truly global in scale, with firms from many developing economies participating extensively. This is especially true for Latin America, where inward cross-border mergers and acquisitions grew to over US$40 billion in the late 1990s, at a rate of growth that outpaced that of developing economies in general (figures 11–1 and 11–2).

Furthermore, inward cross-border mergers and acquisitions in Latin America had a higher proportion of majority stakes changing hands than in other developing countries; by 1998, this proportion was as large as that of industrial countries (figures 11–3 and 11–4). Acquisition of majority stakes is more likely to result in consolidation in an industry, opening the possibility of growing market power and higher prices. This suggests that an exclusive focus on the

---

[7] For recent empirical evidence of the importance of sunk costs for exporter behavior, see Roberts and Tybout (1997); Clerides, Lach, and Tybout (1998); and Bernard and Jensen (1999).

Figure 11–1

Mergers and Acquisitions Boom in Latin America, 1991–98

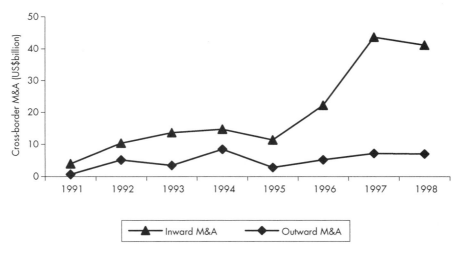

Source: UNCTAD (2000).

Figure 11–2

Latin America's Growing Share of Developing Economy Mergers and Acquisitions, 1991–98

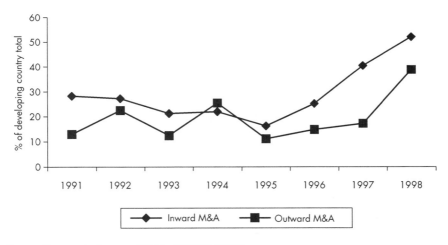

Source: Kang and Johannson (2000); UNCTAD (2000).

Figure 11–3

Inward and Outward Mergers and Acquisitions Involving Majority Stakes, Latin America, 1991–98

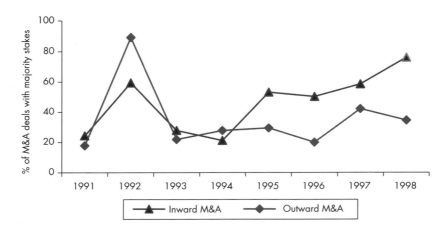

Source: Kang and Johannson (2000); UNCTAD (2000).

Figure 11–4

Mergers and Acquisitions Involving Majority Stakes, by Region, 1991–98

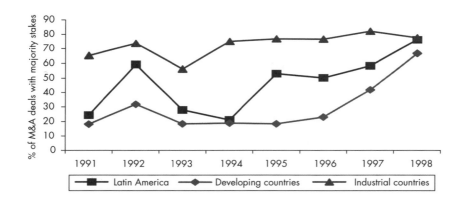

Source: Kang and Johannson (2000); UNCTAD (2000).

Figure 11-5

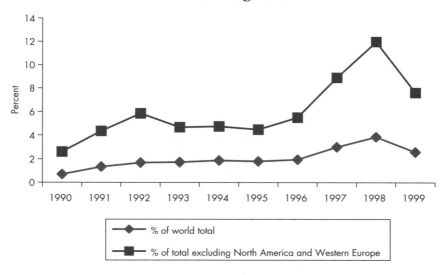

Growth of Strategic Alliances in Latin America Relative to Other Regions, 1990–99

Source: Kang and Johannson (2000).

monopoly power-reducing effects of trade reform may well be inappropriate, especially for Latin America in the mid-to-late 1990s.[8]

The final piece of evidence that is suggestive of a response to lower trade barriers is the growth of cross-border strategic alliances in the 1990s. Again, the number of such alliances among Latin American firms grew faster than the total for developing economies (figure 11–5).[9] Where classification was possible, most of Latin America's strategic alliances were in manufacturing activities (as opposed to marketing, research, and development) and, not surprisingly, with North American firms. These strategic alliances need not have anticompetitive effects; however, should these alliances be used as a mechanism for frustrating or tempering entry by new firms, then they might not have benign consequences.

The discussion in this section has drawn together econometric evidence on the effects of import competition; detailed case studies on international cartels; and the scale and scope of the recent wave of international mergers, acquisitions, and strategic alliances. The evidence implies that, first, the claim that trade reform has eliminated market power remains undemonstrated; and, second, firms can take steps that will help reassert their market power—which trade and investment reform has undoubtedly helped undermine. A role for competition policy remains, but can national antitrust enforcement alone ensure efficient market allocation in a globalizing world?

---

[8] Table 11A–1 (at the end of the chapter) provides more detailed information on the evolution of the latest wave of cross-border mergers and acquisitions.

[9] Tables 11A–2 and 11A–3 provide more information on the growth of these international strategic alliances throughout the 1990s, and specifically emphasize Latin America's participation therein.

CROSS-BORDER MERGERS AND ACQUISITIONS

The cross-border merger wave of the 1990s was associated with the rise (to more than 60) in the number of nations that require, under some circumstances, notification of mergers and acquisitions that exceed certain thresholds of economic activity in their jurisdictions or elsewhere. The last clause has become important as nations have increasingly demanded the right to review proposed transactions of firms whose activities are almost entirely located abroad. Table 11–1 provides an overview of the merger notification requirements of five Latin American economies. Argentina demands notification of transactions where there is a worldwide turnover of 2.5 billion pesos, although, in principle, not a single peso need be earned in that country. Brazil, by contrast, has a notification requirement that effectively exempts foreign transactions that have no corporate presence within the country's borders.

In addition to the diversity of notification requirements, the administrative procedures in the five nations differ considerably—no doubt adding to the costs of undertaking these types of international commercial transactions. These costs need not be trivial for medium-sized companies, especially given the costs of legal counsel and of complying with substantial information requests in a short time frame (often in more than one language, if many antitrust authorities are involved). These transaction costs have become a source of concern for the international bar and for national antitrust officials. There are sensible proposals for simplifying these procedures, with the goal of reducing compliance and filing costs, as well as the risk that inconsistent decisions by antitrust policymakers are made on the basis of different information supplies to these officials (see ICPAC [2000, ch. 4] for some thoughtful recommendations).

However, the central conceptual question for this section is whether simultaneous national merger reviews can result in decisions that might distort the allocation of resources away from the global optimum. In essence, this amounts to considering whether such reviews might result in one of the following two cases:

- Case 1. A proposed merger that improves the global allocation of resources is prevented from occurring by any one nation.
- Case 2. A proposed merger that distorts the global allocation of resources is granted permission by each nation to proceed.[10]

To fix ideas, consider a world with just two countries, A and B, both of which have a merger review statute. Assume also that both nations' antitrust officials must approve a proposed transaction before it can go forward. Under these circumstances, the following three factors can independently—or in combination—generate inefficient outcomes from the global perspective:

- Multiple vetoes. Each nation has the right to veto a proposed transaction and makes its evaluation based solely on the transaction's expected effects on its consumers' and producers' (including exporters') interests.

---

[10] I thank Edward M. Graham for encouraging me several years ago to start thinking about the international consequences of national merger review in these terms.

- Different standards. Each nation can attach different weights to consumer and producer surpluses.[11]
- No compensation scheme. Each nation decides whether to allow a given merger without reference to any other merger or policy matter of importance to both nations.

It is worth noting that the absence of a compensation mechanism in merger investigations is what differentiates merger policy, in large part, from international trade negotiations, where trade-offs across issues (usually reform of different sectors) are the norm. It is difficult to describe the depth of the opposition among antitrust officials and the international bar to what might be called "case linkage" or "issue linkage." The idea, say, of bundling cases in such a way as to make both nations better off is—despite its obvious theoretical appeal—steadfastly opposed by most practitioners.[12] Such opponents advance two arguments. First, they argue that such bundles would be subject (in some jurisdictions) to judicial review—and opponents to a proposed merger often have rights that bundling might effectively override. Second, they argue that practical difficulties would emerge in assembling bundles, especially if the magnitude of the gains and losses to each jurisdiction were difficult to ascertain or easy to miscalculate.

In the absence of such a compensation mechanism, it is not difficult to envisage a proposed merger that would involve considerable efficiencies—that is, cost reductions—that would increase world welfare but in which one nation would reject the merger because its combined consumer and producer surplus falls (case 1 above). Suppose the merger is in an industry in which both nations' firms supply the same homogenous goods to their own consumers, as well as to each other's consumers—that is, intraindustry trade exists. Suppose two of nation A's firms want to merge, and the primary motive is to rationalize their production facilities so as to lower marginal costs. If this merger goes through and the cost reductions are passed on, in part, to consumers, then there are plausible circumstances under which world welfare would improve.[13,14] However, the relative cost advantage enjoyed by the merged firm would shift producer surplus from nation B's firms to the merged firm (which is located in nation A). It is plausible that the gains from the merger's efficiencies to nation B's consumers are more than offset by the losses to its exporters, causing nation B to reject the merger.

Of course, this outcome could have been avoided if the two nations deferred to a single antitrust authority that considered the effect of the merger on both nations' welfare. Such a solution would involve pooling sovereignty and accepting that the losers from the merger are not going to be compensated by the winners (at least through the antitrust investigation). Another less radical alternative, which does not involve moving to a single decisionmaker and might be a potential intermediate step, would be for both nations to agree to allow any merger that was not expected to result in price increases in any market, and that was expected to generate a price decrease in at least one market. Such a rule would enable more efficiency-inducing mergers to go through.

---

[11] Recall that the national economic efficiency standard effectively gives $1 of consumer surplus the same weight as $1 of producer surplus. That is, each surplus could be traded off one-for-one.

[12] Given that international mergers tend to appear in waves, this suggests that there might be plenty of opportunities to put together such bundles.

[13] Essentially, the price reduction in nation B is large enough and, given current prices, the consumer surplus in nation B is much larger than that in nation A.

[14] Here I also make the assumption that a price fall in a given market leads to an increase in consumer surplus that is greater than the fall in the total surpluses of the firms supplying that market.

Table 11-1

Merger Notification Requirements in Argentina, Brazil, Colombia, Mexico, and Venezuela

Jurisdiction	Governing antitrust law	Antitrust agency responsible for merger enforcement	Filing deadlines	Filing threshold
Argentina	Competition Law 25616	National Commission for the Defense of Competition	Must notify within one week after the earliest of (a) execution of merger agreement, (b) tender offer, or (c) acquisition of a controlling interest.	Combined turnover of 200 million pesos in Argentina or 2.5 billion pesos worldwide.
Brazil[a]	Antitrust Law of 1994 (No. 8,884)	Administrative Council of Economic Defense (CADE) reviews notified transactions	Although the law specifies filing after closing, CADE practice requires filing within 15 days after entry of an agreement. The Economic Policy Secretariat of the Ministry of Finance (SEAE) has up to 30 days to prepare its technical report. The Economic Law of the Minister of Justice (SDE) has 30 days to conduct its fact-finding investigation, followed by 60 days for CADE's evaluation and ruling. The transaction may close while review is pending.	Notification is required if the combined entities have at least 20 percent of the product market share or if the worldwide gross revenue of one party exceeds R$400 million. A branch, agency, subsidiary, office, agent, or representative must reside in Brazil.
Colombia	Law 155 of 1959 (Antimonopoly Law)	Competition Division of the Superintendency of Industry and Commerce	File prior to closing.	Transactions involving parties with assets greater than 50,000 times the minimum monthly salary (approximately US$6 million) or combined market share of 25 percent must be notified.

Mexico	Federal Law on Economic Competition of 1992	Federal Competition Commission	Must notify the Commission before the transaction closes. Commission may request additional information within 20 days of filing. After compliance with request for additional information, the Commission has 45 days to issue a ruling.	Mergers must be reported if either (a) transaction value (defined as the higher of the combined entities' total revenues or assets) exceeds 12 million times the minimum salary in Mexico City (approximately $49 million); (b) the transaction involves the acquisition of 35 percent or more of the assets or shares of a business with assets or sales that exceed 12 million times the minimum salary in Mexico City; or (c) the combined entities' worldwide assets or sales exceed 48 million times the minimum salary in Mexico City and the merger involves the acquisition of assets in Mexico in excess of 4.8 million times the minimum salary in Mexico City. Transactions that do not involve the acquisition of Mexican assets are generally exempt.
Venezuela	Law to Promote and Protect the Exercise of Free Competition (1992); Regulation No. 2 (1996)	Superintendency for the Promotion and Protection of Free Competition (Procompetencia)	No deadlines, filing is voluntary.	No mandatory requirement. Parties may make voluntary filing. Authorities have jurisdiction to review any merger that exceeds certain relatively low thresholds.

[a] Note that proposed legislation is pending in Brazil that would overhaul the merger system.

Source: Cicerone (2001).

If a nation were to employ a welfare standard that placed more weight on producer surplus than consumer surplus, then it would not be difficult to see how a welfare-reducing merger—from a global perspective—could be approved by both nations. Consider the case where nation A has such a standard, while nation B trades off consumer and producer surplus dollar for dollar. Suppose two firms in nation A wish to merge, claiming that the transaction will enable them to lower their export marketing costs and neutralize the effects of increased market power in nation B's market—that is, the merger would have no effect on prices in nation B.

The effect in nation A's market—where there are no efficiencies—would be to raise prices, as the merged firms would enjoy greater market power. The higher price in nation A's market would hurt consumers in nation A, but would increase the profits of nation B's exporters. So long as the damage done to A's consumers was not too large (and recall their welfare receives less weight than that of producers), then nation A would approve the merger in the home market as its firms' surpluses in both the domestic and overseas markets would increase (the former due to price increases brought on by greater market power and the latter due to the efficiencies). The principal effect of the merger in nation B is that its producers would sell to A's consumers with greater profits, and so that nation's antitrust authority would approve the merger.

What is particularly distressing about this example is that a nation that has the national economic efficiency standard, once assured that its consumers will not be hurt by the merger, is prepared to accept a proposed merger that gouges consumers abroad. Its exporters would earn higher profits when the merged firm decides to exercise its strengthened market power to raise prices abroad. In sum, foreign nations cannot be counted on to point out when partners—even regional ones—are adopting suboptimal standards for evaluating mergers. The pressure for reform in a country with lax antitrust enforcement will not necessarily come from abroad.

The two examples highlight the inadequacies of national merger enforcement in a world where the consequences of a firm's decisionmaking spill over national borders. For those regional groups where international business transactions are primarily intraregional (as is likely when regional partners are geographically closer to each other than to other nations), one solution would be to adopt a system of regionwide merger review. Since 1989, the European Commission has had the power to review transactions over certain thresholds, and its experience may prove instructive.

It took many years for Brussels to acquire this power and events in 2001—notably the European Parliament's rejection of the proposed takeover code—suggest that member states are clawing back powers to national antitrust authorities and that this remains a highly contentious issue. Given the sensitivities to foreign takeovers of domestic firms, nations wishing to establish regional merger reviews may want to have modest goals at the beginning—for example, adopting high thresholds that result in a smaller number of transactions that have the potential for considerable regionwide ramifications. Credibility could be established over time by employing transparent procedures and offering full explanations for decisions, potentially backed by judicial review by a regional court (similar to, but hopefully more expeditious than, the European Union's Courts of First Instance and Justice). The drawback of this approach is that the largest commercial transactions—the ones with greatest potential regionwide impact— are likely to involve at least one large firm from the region with excellent political connections. Shielding regional antitrust officials from national political pressures is essential if credibility of the enforcement regime is to be established.

A final observation concerns many of the proposals for enhanced cooperation between antitrust authorities, whose purported benefit is to facilitate the convergence of substantive standards.[15] Although there may be circumstances under which such convergence improves resource allocation, the problems created by multiple vetoes and the absence of a compensation scheme remain. From the viewpoint of economic efficiency, convergence in standards is only one source of resource misallocation in a world of many national merger authorities.

PRIVATE INTERNATIONAL CARTELS

Unlike mergers, which can, under some circumstances, improve welfare, the formation of an international cartel is almost surely welfare reducing.[16] Price fixing, market allocation, and bid rigging all tend to raise the prices paid by consumers, with no obvious cost-reducing benefit that might offset the consumer surplus losses.[17] This section focuses on private international cartels or the so-called "hard-core" cartels, comprised of private producers from at least two countries, whose objectives are not solely to export. (Firms that form a cartel solely for export purposes are typically referred to as "export cartels.") Here I say little about state-run cartels, such as OPEC, which are arguably an important element of the international economic landscape—and are potentially ripe for banning in regional agreements on competition policy disciplines.[18]

The prevalence of hard-core cartels has been documented elsewhere (Evenett and Suslow 2000; Evenett, Levenstein, and Suslow 2001; Levenstein and Suslow 2001). To summarize the findings of one of these studies, of a sample of 40 cartels prosecuted by the United States and the European Commission in the 1990s, 24 (60 percent) lasted at least four years. Twenty of the 40 cartels had all together worldwide sales in the affected products of more than US$30 billion. Thus, it would seem that cartels are neither short-lived nor a trivial distortion to international markets.

The Deterrence Approach to International Cartel Enforcement

Before assessing the recent increase in international cartel investigations, it is useful to lay out—from a traditional "law and economics" perspective—the incentives supplied by national anticartel enforcement regimes and penalties.[19] This analysis motivates a discussion of the inadequacies of national anticartel enforcement in a world of many legal jurisdictions.

From the law and economics perspective, the objective of anticartel laws should be to deter and, where necessary, punish firms that engage in this undesirable act.[20] Three character-

---

[15] See, for example, ICPAC (2000).

[16] This section draws heavily on Evenett, Levenstein, and Suslow (2001).

[17] To the best of my knowledge, the only defense of forming a cartel is in export markets, where it is claimed that small firms cannot afford to individually bear the sunk costs of exporting to a new market, and that combining to form an export cartel helps spread these sunk costs across members. See Dick (1996).

[18] As indeed are provisions in national antitrust law exempting export cartels from antitrust disciplines.

[19] For a recent exhaustive survey of the law and economics literature, see Kaplow and Shavell (1999). The discussion here focuses on the incentives supplied by public enforcement practices. These incentives may be reinforced by private suits—brought for damages by cartel victims—that are permitted in some jurisdictions.

[20] As a testament to the influence of this perspective, it is worth noting that the Ministry of Commerce in New Zealand recently published a report on the effectiveness of the deterrence provided by that nation's enforcement practices and courts, which was explicitly built on the lines of reasoning discussed in this section (Government of New Zealand 1998).

istics of cartels are germane to understanding the incentives supplied by anticartel enforcement. First, cartels typically involve secret agreements between firms. Second, the objective of these agreements is to secure pecuniary gains for cartel members. Third, sustaining the cartel requires careful attention to designing incentive-compatible agreements between firms.

A group of firms is *collectively* deterred from forming a cartel in a nation's markets if that country's antitrust authority is expected to fine the firms more than the gains from participating in the cartel. Assuming that the firms are risk neutral, there are no costs to the firms in defending themselves before a fine is imposed; the pecuniary gain from forming a cartel equals G; and the probability of the antitrust authority detecting and punishing the cartel equals p, so that a fine f greater than or equal to (G/p) will provide the necessary collective deterrent. An important insight is that, although cartel agreements are typically secret—and so the probability of detection and punishment p is low—so long as p is positive, there exists a fine that will collectively deter the formation of a cartel. Secrecy may impede investigations, but deterrence is still feasible in principle. These arguments may also provide a rationale for why some nations, such as the United States, Germany, and Switzerland, have made the maximum fines of cartel members a function of the pecuniary gain from their illicit activity.

Antitrust officials have exploited the "incentive compatibility" problems faced by cartels through the introduction of corporate leniency programs. These programs—which offer reduced penalties to qualifying firms that come forward with evidence of cartel conduct—induce members to "defect" from cartel agreements. These programs have also been motivated by the observation that the successful prosecution of cartels typically requires evidence supplied by at least one co-conspirator. The U.S. corporate leniency program, last revised in 1993, can be rationalized in these terms. Currently, only the first firm to come forward with evidence about a currently uninvestigated cartel is automatically granted amnesty from all U.S. criminal penalties. This encourages a "winner-takes-all" dynamic, where each member of an otherwise successful cartel has an incentive to be the first to provide evidence to U.S. authorities.[21] A second feature is that even if a firm is not the first to approach the U.S. authorities, such a firm can gain a substantial reduction in penalties by admitting to cartel practices in other markets that are (at the time of the application for leniency) uninvestigated. This provision has set off a domino effect in which one cartel investigation can result in evidence for subsequent investigations. Since these and other changes were introduced, the United States has received, on average, one amnesty application per month, approximately 12 times the previous rate.

Jurisdictions differ considerably in whether they impose criminal penalties in cartel cases. In particular, few jurisdictions permit the incarceration of business executives responsible for forming a cartel.[22] U.S. officials strongly believe that criminal penalties, including the threat of incarceration, are essential deterrents to the formation of cartels.[23] How does the law and

---

[21] The German Bundeskartellamt (Federal Cartel Office) revised its corporate leniency program in April 2000 to include such a provision. Dr. Ulf Boge, President of the Bundeskartellamt, argues in explicitly economic terms: "By granting a total exemption from fines to the first firm that approaches us we want to induce the cartel members to compete with each other to defect from the cartel." See Bundeskartellamt (2000).

[22] Although the criminality of cartel behavior has considerable implications for international cooperation and evidence sharing, the role of these sanctions as a deterrent is the present concern.

[23] See, for example, Hammond (2000), who argues: "Based on our experience, there is no greater deterrent to the commission of cartel activity than the risk of imprisonment for corporate officials. Corporate fines are simply not sufficient to deter would-be offenders. For example, in some cartels, such as the graphic electrodes cartel, individuals personally pocketed millions of dollars as a result of their criminal activity. A corporate fine, no matter how punitive, is unlikely to deter such individuals." Hammond is the Director of Criminal Enforcement at the U.S. Department of

economics approach assess this claim? First, incarceration involves costly losses in and reallocation of output: managers' productivity is obviously less during their period of incarceration, and resources must be devoted to the construction and operation of prisons. If these were the sole considerations, incarceration would be a less desirable alternative to fines.

However, given the low probability of punishing a cartel and the sizeable gains from engaging in such behavior, the minimum fine that would deter a cartel may, in fact, bankrupt a firm or its senior executives. Bankrupting a firm that has engaged in cartel behavior could reduce the number of suppliers to a market, resulting in less competition and higher prices. Furthermore, personal bankruptcy laws bound from below what corporate executives can lose from anticartel enforcement. Incarceration may provide—through the loss of freedom, reputation, social standing, and earnings—the only remaining means to alter the incentives of corporate executives. This argument is particularly important because the use of stock options in executive compensation packages provides a strong incentive to senior executives to maximize firm earnings and stock market value.

The second law and economics argument is that incarceration is needed to reduce or eliminate the expected harm caused by repeat offenses. There may be legitimate concern that executives who have successfully arranged explicit agreements to carve up a market will, after the cartel is broken up, attempt more subtle forms of collusion (such as price leadership). The imposition of fines alone may not induce a firm's shareholders to replace the offending executives, especially if the latter can convince shareholders that the fine was a "cost of doing business" and that the benefits from implicit collusion (which they expect to secure in a market that they know well) will soon flow. Here, a clean break with the past may be needed, with incarceration simultaneously removing the relevant executives from their posts and acting as a threat to incoming senior executives not to attempt to re-form a cartel. Antitrust officials must also weigh the stronger deterrent effect of incarceration against the higher levels of evidence that are required to secure criminal convictions. Seeking incarceration exacerbates the difficulties that national antitrust officials face in securing enough evidence and testimony from cartel participants, which, in terms of the framework outlined above, effectively lowers the probability of detection and punishment p.

The law and economics perspective explains why national antitrust enforcement may be particularly ineffective in deterring international cartels. First, the ability of executives to organize cartels (including meeting and writing and storing agreements) in locations outside the direct jurisdiction of the national antitrust authority where the cartel's effects are felt can effectively reduce the probability of punishment p to zero. For example, in 1994, the U.S. case against General Electric, which, along with De Beers and several European firms, was thought to be forming a cartel in the market for industrial diamonds, collapsed with the trial judge citing the inability of U.S. enforcement authorities to secure the necessary evidence from abroad. Second, constraints on the ability to collect evidence and interview witnesses abroad reduce the probability of punishment p. Increasing the fines f imposed may not, given the substantial reduction in p and the limits imposed by bankruptcy, be sufficient to deter collusion. In sum, supplying the right deterrent is more difficult when conspirators can hatch their plans abroad.

Justice. In interpreting his remarks, it is worth bearing in mind that the maximum fine under U.S. law for individuals convicted of engaging in cartel behavior is $350,000, which, given recent trends in executive compensation, is likely to be much less than the potential stock option and other gains paid to an executive whose firm's profits have increased due to participating in a cartel.

Third, in a world of multiple markets, the gain from forming a cartel in a single additional market may well exceed the cartel profits from that market alone. As the number of markets in which a cartel operates increases, each cartel member can be more successfully deterred from cheating on the cartel agreement in any one market by the threat of retaliation by other members in all the markets in which the cartel operates. This "multi-market effect" implies that the extension of an international cartel into a new market can heighten collusion in all of the cartel's markets. Therefore, the fine that will deter collusion in the new market must include the increase in the cartel's total profits, not only the extra profits being earned in the cartel's new market. At present, even those antitrust authorities that base their fines on the illicit gains from forming a cartel do not consider the harm done outside their jurisdiction; thus, current practices are unlikely to deter multi-market cartels.

Finally, the effectiveness of national leniency programs is compromised by firms' participation in cartel activities in many nations. A firm may be reluctant (to say the least) to apply for leniency in a single jurisdiction if that leaves it potentially exposed to penalties in other jurisdictions. Furthermore, although a firm may be willing to offer evidence on cartel activities in many nations, a national antitrust authority will only value information on activities within its jurisdiction. Both factors reduce the benefits of seeking leniency.

Recent Trends in Private International Cartel Enforcement

The 1990s saw a sea change in official attitudes toward cartel enforcement. At the start of the decade, only one industrial nation—the United States—was taking aggressive action against international cartels, while other governments criticized these actions as an improper extraterritorial application of domestic antitrust law.[24] By the end of the decade, several high-profile enforcement actions had convinced policymakers in other industrial countries that stronger measures against international cartels ought to be taken. Consequently, several countries have revised or introduced corporate leniency programs, the OECD has proposed international norms for and reforms of cartel enforcement, and selected jurisdictions have developed bilateral cooperation mechanisms.

This subsection draws lessons for Latin America from recent industrial country experience in attacking international cartels. Much of this change had its origins in the events that followed the revision of the U.S. corporate leniency program in 1993. This revision led to a dramatic increase in international cartel prosecutions. Although U.S. enforcement actions were motivated by their effects within U.S. borders, the potential cross-border effects of these cartels and the substantial evidence proffered during leniency requests did not go unnoticed in other nations.[25] The European Commission introduced its own corporate leniency program—but its success has been less impressive than that of its U.S. counterpart, in part because automatic amnesty is not assured to the first firm that reports cartel behavior.[26]

---

[24] Concerns about extraterritorial applications of these U.S. laws reached a point where several industrial countries passed "blocking statutes," whose intent was to prevent their antitrust authorities, police, other national investigative agencies, and firms from cooperating with U.S. enforcement actions outside U.S. borders.

[25] U.S. officials have, through speeches, interviews, and written articles, extensively discussed their enforcement record in this area. In part, this effort is motivated by the view that the deterrent effect of the U.S. enforcement regime depends somewhat on its public profile. Many of these speeches can be downloaded from the website of the Antitrust Division of the U.S. Department of Justice (www.usdoj.gov/atr).

[26] It is noteworthy that German and British competition policy authorities have chosen to revise their corporate leniency programs along U.S., not European Community, lines.

Although cartel enforcement has increased in both the European Union and Japan, investigations remain hampered in both jurisdictions, albeit for different reasons. It has proved too difficult to reconcile the underlying tenets of the Japanese legal code with the introduction of a corporate leniency program. This restricts the flow of information on cartel behavior to the Japanese Fair Trade Commission, and is a source of considerable concern because the Commission appears to devote few resources to other means of uncovering cartels. That said, Japan and Korea have recently reduced the number of permitted exceptions to their anticartel laws.

The inability of European Commission officials to search the private homes of business executives who reside in Europe for evidence of cartel agreements has impeded more vigorous enforcement in the European Union. Worse still, European Community law only allows civil sanctions on undertakings (such as firms). Individuals cannot be sanctioned for antitrust offenses under community law, but can be subject to penalties under the appropriate national laws. Even so, since the late 1980s, the European Community has prosecuted more than 20 international cartels with fines rising to more than 100 million European Currency Units in recent years.

Recognition of the difficulties faced by national anticartel authorities in investigating international cartels has led to several initiatives between governments and within the OECD. Recent experience suggests that there are two circumstances where bilateral cooperation offers the most promise (by raising the probability of an international cartel being punished). First, if a nation's laws make forming a cartel or conspiring to form one a criminal offense, then that nation may be able to invoke the provisions of any mutual legal assistance treaties (MLATs) that it has signed with other nations. These treaties differ in scope (including coverage of antitrust offenses) and in the commitment to extend bilateral cooperation. The United States-Canada MLAT, signed in 1985, is perhaps the best example of an agreement that underpins bilateral cooperation that has been effective in prosecuting international cartels (Waller 2000). Of course, this mechanism is only available to those jurisdictions that have signed MLATs that cover antitrust matters, and Latin American nations may well consider signing such treaties among themselves.

The second route by which cooperation between national antitrust officials is effected is through explicit bilateral agreements on antitrust matters. This route, still in its infancy, is best characterized by the 1999 agreement between Australia and the United States, which provides for each party to request assistance from the other, irrespective of whether the alleged corporate actions in question are criminal acts under the requested nation's law. The bilateral assistance envisaged at the time of signing includes providing, disclosing, exchanging, and discussing evidence, as well as taking various steps to secure evidence from persons, undertakings, and other entities. Even more recently, a working group of officials from competition policy authorities in the Nordic countries proposed enacting legislation to enable them to exchange pertinent information in cartel cases (OECD 2000).

A critical stumbling block in most bilateral cooperative efforts is the exchange of business information or what many legal practitioners refer to as "confidential business information."[27] The fear is that corporate secrets and future planning will, if shared with a foreign antitrust authority, be used inappropriately or leaked to rival firms. This fear has long resulted in many bilateral cooperation agreements on antitrust matters containing restrictive provisions for the exchange of confidential business information and broad understandings of what information is considered confidential. But cartel investigations typically refer to prior (and occasionally cur-

---

[27] In the view of some, this stumbling block has seriously circumscribed cooperation between the European Community and the United States in cartel investigations (Stark 2000; Waller 2000).

rent) corporate practices; the evidence required is largely documentation of previous meetings and agreements between conspirators. Thus, prosecutions generally do not require reference to firms' forward-looking strategic plans. So the fear that future legal plans will be exposed appears to be exaggerated.[28] Finally, existing international cooperation on tax and financial securities permits far more exchange of business information than under bilateral antitrust agreements, especially when there is the suspicion that fraud or some other illegal act has taken place. The extension of cooperation to antitrust matters can easily build on these existing practices.

Many recent reforms in national anticartel enforcement and bilateral cooperation must be viewed against the backdrop of significant, ongoing discussions at the OECD. In 1998, these discussions culminated in the Council of the OECD adopting a "Recommendation ...Concerning the Effective Action Against Hard Core Cartels."[29] The essence of this recommendation is twofold: to call on member nations to enact anticartel laws that can effectively deter the formation of a cartel, and to lay out common principles to guide cooperation between antitrust authorities—cooperation that the Recommendation clearly endorses as being in OECD members' interests. In 2000, the OECD issued another report documenting the steps taken since the Recommendation was adopted. This report noted that, while some nations had eliminated exemptions to their cartel laws, revised corporate leniency programs, or allowed greater exchange of business information, less progress had been made on facilitating bilateral cooperation on cartel investigations than had been hoped. Nevertheless, these OECD initiatives demonstrate an emerging consensus on the undesirability of international cartels.

Taking together the conceptual concerns about the effectiveness of national enforcement measures against international cartels and the promising yet nascent bilateral cooperation, I conclude that even among the industrial economies at present, the cumulative effect of national enforcement systems is unlikely to provide sufficient deterrence to international cartels. And Latin America, without a well-established track record of attracting international cartels, is almost certainly providing insufficient deterrence to such centers.

Options for Reform in Latin America

Any proposed reform to international cartel enforcement should be assessed, in large part, on the deterrent it provides to firms to form a cartel in the first place. That deterrent's strength depends on the firms' perceptions of the probability of being punished and the size of any expected penalty. It is tempting to advocate creating a regional or even a global enforcement authority with powers to collect evidence, conduct interviews, compute the global gains from forming a cartel, and levy the appropriate fines. In principle, such a proposal could overcome the deficiencies of the current system of national enforcement and bilateral cooperation. However, at this juncture, no nation appears ready to pool sovereignty in such an aggressive manner, or to allow its citizens and firms to be punished by such a body. The European Community's relatively weak enforcement powers against cartels are a testament to the reluctance of European Union members, who have been pooling sovereignty in other areas for decades, to cede powers in cartel cases—although the distortions to the free flow of goods and services across European borders that cartels can engender are widely acknowledged. Without denying the intellectual appeal of such a far-reaching solution, I turn attention to more modest, and perhaps more likely, reform options.

---

[28] In a detailed analysis of the arguments advanced in support of restricting the exchange of business information in cartel investigation, the OECD (2000) came to a similar conclusion.

[29] This recommendation is reproduced in an appendix to OECD (2000).

The first and least ambitious reform option involves a region's members signing agreements similar to the United States-Canada or United States-Australia bilateral cooperation agreements on antitrust. Such a reform would promote evidence collection and information sharing, increasing the probability of cartel members being caught and punished. A slightly better alternative, which might ensure some degree of uniformity in the agreed forms of bilateral cooperation, would be to codify this bilateral cooperation through a regionwide agreement.

The second option builds on the first and addresses the deficiencies in the current system of national corporate leniency programs. The regional agreement would be amended in two ways. First, a provision should be introduced so that firms can simultaneously apply for leniency in multiple jurisdictions and have those applications evaluated based on the evidence of cartel formation. Second, to reduce the uncertainty faced by the first firm coming forward with evidence about a currently uninvestigated international cartel, corporate leniency programs should state minimum degrees of relief from penalties. Such a reform would further increase the incentive of any cartel member to defect, making the formation of a cartel harder to sustain.[30]

Although these two reform options can be thought of as improving the investigative technology, the pecuniary gains from forming a cartel would still be calculated on a nation-by-nation basis. The third option takes initial steps to remedying this deficiency. Once the investigation turns to the matter of calculating pecuniary gain, this inevitably controversial step could be turned over to a pre-selected panel of qualified, independent experts who reside in the signatories to the regional agreement. This panel would present estimates (with associated estimated standard deviations) of the cartel's gains across all affected nations that are parties to this agreement.[31] The panel would break down its estimate of the total gains to the cartel from each nation's markets, which enforcement authorities would take into account when penalizing cartel members. The panel itself need not hand down judgments or impose fines—this task could remain the preserve of the national antitrust and judicial authorities.

The obvious disadvantage of this latter reform option is that it does not take into account gains from forming a cartel in the markets of nonsignatories. Given the nontrivial amounts of information required to estimate a cartel's pecuniary gains, it is naive to insist that any supranational panel could estimate the global consequences of a cartel. Instead, this regional agreement should have open accession clauses to enable nonmembers with both developed national enforcement capabilities and a prespecified degree of international anticartel cooperation to join. Furthermore, thought could be given to informing nonsignatories that their interests are affected by a cartel in return for a commitment to treat leniently any firm that has volunteered information during the investigation.[32]

---

[30] The first two reform options do not rule out expanding the agreement to allow one antitrust agency to take the lead in a cartel investigation that might have ramifications for multiple jurisdictions, with other parties to the agreement providing whatever assistance is necessary. This might economize on enforcement resources, potentially enabling more actions to be taken within given budgets.

[31] The panel would have access only to the evidence required to compute these estimates and would be supported by qualified staff.

[32] Although calculation of the gain would take into account the cartel's effects in a number of signatories' markets, the fines and penalties in this third reform option would still be imposed by national authorities. This does not violate the apparent unwillingness of nations to penalize only cartel members for the harm done in their own jurisdictions. Requesting that signatories impose fines on the worldwide pecuniary gain—which includes the cartel's gains in the markets of nonsignatories—contradicts this established practice. Countries that allow private civil suits for damages could also expand their jurisdiction in international cartel cases to allow consumers in countries not party to such a regional agreement to seek redress in the home countries of the cartel members.

Furthermore, a reform process could unfold over time, in which nations move from their current arrangements to the first through third options. Strengthening national anticartel laws and commitments to enforcement are a necessary prerequisite. The enhanced cooperation will foster trust between antitrust agencies, which is essential if agencies are to have faith in the intent and capacity of others to use the ample discretion built into most anticartel laws to successfully conduct international cartel investigations. Admittedly, such a process would not lead to the creation of a supranational anticartel agency, but it does not prevent such an agency from being created eventually. Furthermore, the experience of mutual cooperation and assistance, combined with increasing harmonization of antitrust laws, would provide the basis for nations to create such an agency if they should choose to do so.

CONCLUDING REMARKS

This chapter has emphasized a number of themes that are pertinent to assessing whether Latin American nations might consider adopting a regional competition policy. First, international firms have adopted a number of important organizational and structural changes in light of the recent trend toward international economic integration. These changes need not be benign, and could well undermine some of the benefits of trade and investment reform. Keeping an open mind about the effects of these corporate changes appears to me to be the right advice to policymakers, and in the case of competition policy, officials need to be particularly vigilant. Second, in a globalizing world, there are good reasons to believe—based on economic first principles, as well as enforcement experience—that national antitrust enforcement could come at the expense of global welfare. International measures may well be warranted. Progress in the short term seems more likely in the area of mergers than in cartels, although the economics of the latter are more clear-cut than the former. However, mergers appear to receive greater attention from policymakers in such initiatives as the International Cooperation Network, at least for now.

Moving from the proposals considered here to implementation of reforms requires paying special attention to both the legal institutions and traditions of participating nations, as well as the lessons from European experience, where regional measures on competition policy have become firmly established. The economic arguments advanced here must be blended with careful legal and historical analyses of specific country circumstances, tailoring any reform to initial conditions and prior reform experience.

Central to any regional measure on competition policy is a clear identification of spillovers from corporate actions or national enforcement choices across borders. Given the growing trading and investment links within Latin America, the potential for both types of cross-border spillover in this region appears to be growing over time, calling for further analysis of regional cooperation mechanisms in this field. While European experience may provide some lessons, the nascent nature of competition law in Latin America is likely to imply that any regional initiatives should begin with modest objectives and be accompanied by national capacity-building efforts.

Table 11A-1

Cross-Border Mergers and Acquisitions in Latin America, 1991–98

(Billions of U.S. dollars)

Region, indicator	1991	1992	1993	1994	1995	1996	1997	1998	1991–98
Latin America									
Inward cross-border M&A	3.9	10.4	13.7	14.8	11.4	22.3	43.8	41.3	161.5
% with majority stakes	24.4	59.3	27.9	21.1	53.1	50.2	58.4	75.9	54.6
Outward cross-border M&A	0.7	5.1	3.4	8.5	2.8	5.2	7.2	7.0	40.0
% with majority stakes	17.7	89.2	21.8	27.8	29.4	19.9	42.1	34.5	32.6
Developing economies									
Inward FDI	41.7	51.1	72.5	95.6	105.5	129.8	148.9		645.2[a]
Inward cross-border M&A	13.8	38.2	64.5	67.2	70.3	88.3	108.1	79.3	529.8
% with majority stakes	18.2	31.8	18.4	18.9	18.4	23.1	41.8	66.7	31.9
% of inward FDI	33.2	74.7	88.9	70.4	66.6	68.0	72.6		69.8[a]
Outward FDI	8.3	22.7	34.9	42.5	45.6	49.2	61.1		262.4[a]
Outward cross-border M&A	5.4	22.7	27.4	33.4	25.1	35.1	41.7	18.0	208.9
% with majority stakes	31.8	65.8	27.4	27.4	34.1	29.4	42.0	49.2	37.6
% of outward FDI	64.6	100.0	78.6	78.5	55.0	71.5	68.3		72.7[a]
Industrial economies									
Inward FDI	114.8	120.3	138.9	141.5	211.5	195.4	233.1		1,155.4[a]
Inward cross-border M&A	71.4	83.7	97.8	129.1	167.0	186.2	232.9	478.6	1,446.8
% with majority stakes	65.2	73.6	56.2	74.9	76.6	76.4	82.0	77.3	75.4
% of inward FDI	62.2	69.6	70.4	91.3	79.0	95.3	99.9		83.8[a]
Outward FDI	189.8	180.0	205.8	241.5	306.5	283.5	359.2		1,766.2[a]
Outward cross-border M&A	79.9	99.2	134.9	163.0	212.2	239.3	299.3	540.0	1,767.7
% with majority stakes	59.3	59.3	44.0	61.5	62.4	63.6	72.6	76.6	66.8
% of outward FDI	42.1	55.1	65.5	67.5	69.2	84.4	83.3		69.5[a]

[a] Sum for 1991–97.

Source: Kang and Sakai (2000).

Table 11A-2

Regional Distribution of Strategic Alliances, 1990–99

Region	1990	1991	1992	1993	1994	1995	1996	1997	1998	1999
Latin America	39	123	141	170	223	230	118	221	267	245
Asia and Pacific	1,117	1,783	1,817	2,774	3,847	4,135	1,743	1,868	1,590	2,554
Western Europe	1,280	2,018	1,922	1,926	2,089	2,357	1,101	1,286	1,315	2,008
North America	2,777	4,271	4,046	4,289	5,149	5,388	2,852	3,604	3,391	4,355
Eastern Europe	289	807	319	459	402	443	164	189	187	216
Africa	51	103	135	226	218	313	115	197	178	197
World total	5,553	9,105	8,380	9,844	11,928	12,866	6,093	7,365	6,928	9,575
% in Latin America	0.7	1.4	1.7	1.7	1.9	1.8	1.9	3.0	3.9	2.6
All regions except Western Europe and North America	1,496	2,816	2,412	3,629	4,690	5,121	2,140	2,475	2,222	3,212
% in Latin America	2.6	4.4	5.8	4.7	4.8	4.5	5.5	8.9	12.0	7.6

Source: Kang and Sakai (2000).

Table 11A-3

Regional and Sectoral Breakdown of Latin America's Strategic Alliances, 1990–99

Type of alliance	Region of alliance partner						Total
	Latin America	Asia and Pacific	Western Europe	North America	Eastern Europe	Africa	
Total alliances	233	160	337	1,108	11	12	1,861
Manufacturing	65	61	124	271	3	1	525
Marketing	30	24	64	233	3	3	357
R&D	2	5	10	41	1	0	59

Source: Kang and Sakai (2000).

REFERENCES

Bernard, Andrew B., and J. Bradford Jensen. 1999. Exceptional Exporter Performance: Cause, Effect, or Both? Journal of International Economics 47: 1–26.

Bhagwati, Jagdish N. 1968. The Theory and Practice of Commercial Policy. International Finance Section, Department of Economics, Princeton University, Princeton, N.J.

Bundeskartellamt. 2000. Leniency Programme for Exposing Cartels. Berlin: Bundeskartellamt.

Cicerone, Michael J. 2001. Overview: International Merger Control. Antitrust 15(2): 15–23.

Clerides, Sofronis, Saul Lach, and James Tybout. 1998. Is Learning-by-Exporting Important? Micro-Dynamic Evidence from Colombia, Mexico, and Morocco. Quarterly Journal of Economics 113: 903–47.

Dick, Andrew. 1996. When Are Cartels Stable Contracts? Journal of Law and Economics 39(1): 241–83.

Evenett, Simon J., Alexander Lehmann, and Benn Steil (eds.). 2000. Antitrust Goes Global: What Future for Transatlantic Cooperation? Washington, DC: Brookings Institution Press.

Evenett, Simon J., Margaret C. Levenstein, and Valerie Y. Suslow. 2001. International Cartel Enforcement: Lessons from the 1990s. World Economy (September).

Evenett, Simon J., and Valerie Y. Suslow. 2000. Preconditions on Private Restraints on Market Access and International Cartels. Journal of International Economic Law 3(4): 593–631.

Faull, Jonathan, and Ali Nikpay (eds.). 1999. The EC Law of Competition. Oxford, UK: Oxford University Press.

Feenstra, Robert C. 1995. Estimating the Effects of Trade Policy. In Gene M. Grossman and Kenneth Rogoff (eds.), Handbook of International Economics, Vol. 3. Amsterdam: North-Holland.

Gerber, David J. 2001. Law and Competition in Twentieth Century Europe: Protecting Prometheus. Oxford, UK: Oxford University Press.

Goldberg, Pinelopi Koujianou, and Michael M. Knetter. 1997. Goods Prices and Exchange Rates: What Have We Learned? Journal of Economic Literature 35: 1243–72.

Government of New Zealand. 1998. Penalties, Remedies and Court Processes under The Commerce Act 1986. Wellington: Ministry of Commerce.

Goyder, D. G. 1998. EC Competition Law. 3rd Edition. Oxford, UK: Oxford University Press.

Graham, Edward M., and J. David Richardson (eds.). 1997. Global Competition Policy. Washington, D.C.: Institute for International Economics.

Hammond, S. 2000. Lessons Common to Detecting and Deterring Cartel Activity. Speech made to The 3rd Nordic Competition Policy Conference. 12 September, Stockholm.

Harrison, Ann. 1994. Productivity, Imperfect Competition, and Trade Reform: Theory and Evidence. Journal of International Economics 36: 53–73.

International Competition Policy Advisory Committee (ICPAC). 2000. Final Report. Washington, DC: Government Printing Office.

Kang, Nam-Hoon, and Kentaro Sakai. 2000. International Strategic Alliances: Their Role in Industrial Globalisation. STI Working Paper 2000/5. Organisation for Economic Cooperation and Development, Paris.

Kang, Nam-Hoon, and Sara Johannson. 2000. Cross Border Mergers and Acquisitions: Their Role in Industrial Globalisation. STI Working Paper 2000/1. Organisation for Economic Co-operation and Development, Paris.

Kaplow, L., and S. Shavell. 1999. Economic Analysis of Law. Harvard University, Boston, MA.

Levenstein, Margaret C., and Valerie Y. Suslow. 2001. Private International Cartels and Their Effect on Developing Economies. Background Paper for World Development Report 2001, commissioned by the World Bank, Washington, DC.

———. 2002. What Determines Cartel Success? In Peter Grossman (ed.), How Cartels Endure and How They Fail. Edward Elgar.

Levinsohn, James. 1993. Testing the Imports-as-Market Discipline Hypothesis. Journal of International Economics 35: 1–22.

Organization for Economic Co-operation and Development (OECD). 2000. Hard Core Cartels. Paris: OECD.

Parisi, John. 2000. Enforcement Co-operation among Antitrust Authorities. Updated version of paper presented at the Sixth Annual London Conference on EC Competition Law.

Pitofsky, Robert. 1999. The Effect of Global Trade on United States Competition Law and Enforcement Policies. Speech given at the Fordham Corporate Law Institute, October 15.

Roberts, Mark J., and James R. Tybout. 1997. The Decision to Export in Colombia: An Empirical Model of Entry with Sunk Costs. American Economic Review 87: 545–64.

Stark, Charles. 2000. Improving Bilateral Antitrust Cooperation. Speech made at Conference on Competition Policy in the Global Trading System: Perspectives from Japan, the United States, and the European Union. 23 June, Washington, DC.

Tavares, Jose De Araujo Jr. 2001. Competition Policy. In Jose Manuel Salazar-Xirinachs and Maryse Robert (eds.), Towards Free Trade in the Americas. Washington, DC: Brookings Institution Press.

Tinbergen, Jan. 1952. On the Theory of Economic Policy. Amsterdam: North-Holland.

Tybout, James R. 2000. Plant- and Firm-Level Evidence on 'New' Trade Theories." Penn State University. Mimeograph.

United Nations Conference on Trade and Investment (UNCTAD). 2000. World Investment Report 2000. Geneva.

Waller, Spencer Weber. 1996. A Comparative Look at Failing Firms and Failing Industries. Testimony presented to U.S. Federal Trade Commission hearings on The Changing Nature of Competition in a Global and Innovation-Driven Age. 20 August, Washington, DC.

———. 2000. Anticartel Cooperation. In Simon J. Evenett, Alexander Lehmann, and Benn Steil (eds.), Antitrust Goes Global: What Future for Transatlantic Cooperation? Washington, DC: The Brookings Institution Press.